**Life-Span Development
and Behavior**

VOLUME 1

Life-Span Development and Behavior

VOLUME 1

Edited by

Paul B. Baltes

College of Human Development
The Pennsylvania State University
University Park, Pennsylvania

Academic Press

New York   San Francisco   London   1978

A Subsidiary of Harcourt Brace Jovanovich, Publishers

ACADEMIC PRESS, INC.
111 Fifth Avenue, New York, New York 10003

United Kingdom Edition published by
ACADEMIC PRESS, INC. (LONDON) LTD.
24/28 Oval Road, London NW1 7DX

LIBRARY OF CONGRESS CATALOG CARD NUMBER: 77-0531

ISBN 0-12-431801-0

PRINTED IN THE UNITED STATES OF AMERICA

Contents

**Implementation of the Life-Span View of Human Development:
The Sample Case of Attachment**

Richard M. Lerner and Carol D. Ryff

The Concept of Development from a Systems Perspective

Hugh B. Urban

A Life-Span Approach to Perceptual Development

Robert H. Pollack and Beverly M. Atkeson

Brain Electrical Activity and Behavior Relationships over the Life Span

Diana S. Woodruff

Cognitive Development and Life-Span Developmental Theory: Idealistic versus Contextual Perspectives

Gisela Labouvie-Vief and Michael J. Chandler

List of Contributors

Numbers in parentheses indicate the pages on which the authors' contributions begin.

Beverly M. Atkeson (85), Department of Psychology, University of Georgia, Athens, Georgia

Michael J. Chandler (181), Department of Psychology, University of British Columbia, Vancouver, British Columbia

Lita Furby (297), Department of Psychology, University of Oregon, Eugene, Oregon

Ann Higgins-Trenk (257), School of Education, Harvard University, Cambridge, Massachusetts

John L. Horn (211), Department of Psychology, University of Denver, Denver, Colorado

Aletha Huston-Stein (257), Department of Human Development, University of Kansas, Lawrence, Kansas

Gisela Labouvie-Vief (181), Department of Psychology, Wayne State University, Detroit, Michigan

Richard M. Lerner (1), Division of Individual and Family Studies, The Pennsylvania State University, University Park, Pennsylvania

Robert H. Pollack (85), Department of Psychology, University of Georgia, Athens, Georgia

Carol D. Ryff (1), Division of Individual and Family Studies, The Pennsylvania State University, University Park, Pennsylvania

Hugh B. Urban (45), College of Human Development, The Pennsylvania State University, University Park, Pennsylvania

Diana S. Woodruff (111), Department of Psychology, Temple University, Philadelphia, Pennsylvania

Preface

The creation of a new annual series, *Life-Span Development and Behavior*, is a reflection of the notion that a life-span view of the study of behavior has arrived. The formulation of a life-span or life-course approach to the study of behavioral development has been in the making for quite some time. It appears that during the recent decade, however, we have seen a crystallization of this perspective. There is a growing amount of research and theoretical discussion aimed at clarifying and implementing a life-span approach, a rapidly growing number of life-span oriented textbooks and doctoral training programs, and evidence of a developing life-span interest across the entire spectrum of the sciences concerned with behavior and ontogenetic development. In fact, perhaps for the first time, there is a concerted effort in a variety of disciplines (biology, economics, psychology, sociology, etc.) to consider developmental phenomena in a life-span, life-cycle, or life-course framework. This recent confluence of trends, in particular, holds high promise for the years to come.

This new serial publication is intended to provide programmatic reviews and summaries of research and theory in the field of life-span development as it applies to the study of behavior broadly defined. In order to permit a multidisciplinary and pluralistic approach to the study of development and behavior, no specific theoretical view or paradigm of life-span work is emphasized. On the contrary, special efforts will be made (perhaps more than is true for this first volume) to involve scholars from the full spectrum of behavioral and social sciences as the series evolves. As a result, the conceptualizations of development, behavior, and associated explanatory principles are expected to vary widely and to mirror diverse theoretical and disciplinary orientations and concerns.

No attempt will be made to plan each volume around a particular topic or theme. The emphasis is on quality, programmatic scholarship, and advances in the field. Manuscripts typically are invited and will come from investigators involved in extensive research or concerned with opening up new avenues of research on behavior development with a life-span or life-course orientation. All chapters—whether invited or submitted—

will be carefully reviewed with the assistance of an editorial board (Glen H. Elder, Jr., Aletha C. Huston-Stein, Bernice L. Neugarten, Matilda W. Riley, and K. Warner Schaie) and ad hoc consultants.

It is my conviction that the advent of this new series is a legitimate indicator of an emerging vitality and maturity of a research emphasis, and that the spectrum of life-span oriented data, theories, and conclusions is enough—in terms of persuasion and fertility—to attract more researchers to the laborious process of conducting the type of long-term and dynamic work that is basic to a life-span developmental approach. In this sense, the nature of the life span of this new series will, in part, be a signal for what a life-span perspective has to offer to behavioral and social scientists interested in advancing our knowledge about behavior in the context of ontogenetic and biocultural change.

My home college and institution, The College of Human Development, The Pennsylvania State University, have generously provided time and facilities for the launching of this work and for the preparation of this first volume. I wish to thank Diane Bernd, Kathleen Droskinis, and Jackie Unch for their able secretarial assistance. Finally, a number of consulting reviewers (Orville G. Brim, Jr., Steven W. Cornelius, Nancy W. Denney, Glen H. Elder, Jr., Frank H. Hooper, Gisela Labouvie-Vief, Richard M. Lerner, Gail R. Marsh, Bernice L. Neugarten, Carol D. Ryff, Harry L. Sterns, and Alison Okada Wollitzer) deserve much credit for improving the quality of this volume.

I am also happy to announce that Orville G. Brim, Jr. will join me as regular co-editor of this series beginning with Volume 2.

PAUL B. BALTES

To Klaus F. Riegel
1925–1977

Implementation of the Life-Span View of Human Development: The Sample Case of Attachment

Richard M. Lerner and Carol D. Ryff

DIVISION OF INDIVIDUAL AND FAMILY STUDIES,
THE PENNSYLVANIA STATE UNIVERSITY,
UNIVERSITY PARK, PENNSYLVANIA

1

Abstract

The core attributes of the life-span view are reexamined in this chapter with the goals of further clarification, expansion, and illustration. Descriptively, the perspective that development occurs across the life span is reiterated, and issues regarding the nature, directionality, and extensiveness of change raised by this assertion are evaluated. The need for conceptual and methodological pluralism with regard to charting developmental change is presented. Additionally, the search for developmental sequences in behavior-change processes and onotogentic linkages between such sequences are discussed. Implications of these attributes for the design of descriptive developmental research are indicated. Issues pertinent to how variable relationships can account for change within and between individuals are examined. Thus, conceptual advances in developmental explanation provided by the life-span view such as the status of the age variable, continuity–discontinuity issues, origins of developmental change, and the dynamic nature of developmental explanations are raised. The relevance of pluralism for developmental explanations as well as for the design of explanatory research are also discussed. In turn, implications of the life-span view of human development for intervention strategies are presented, with emphasis on the behavioral targets of interventions and the timing and mechanisms of intervention. Finally, to provide a more broad and active implementation of the life-span view, the above issues are illustrated through the sample case of attachment behavior. Drawing on specific examples of empirical findings and/or theory, it is shown how the life-span view reorders, extends, and enriches the attachment literature.

I. Introduction

The aims and assumptions of the life-span view of human development have been extensively discussed in recent years (Baltes, 1973; Baltes & Schaie, 1973; Goulet & Baltes, 1970; Huston-Stein & Baltes, 1976; Nesselroade & Reese, 1973). The need remains, however, for providing additional information regarding implementation of the view's objectives. Clarification of the theoretical and empiricial attributes of a life-span orientation is necessary for those who, while attracted to the view, have not yet incorporated it into their existing research programs. Consequently, examples must be drawn which illustrate how adoption of the life-span perspective modifies and extends previous theoretical frameworks, and what the view implies regarding empirical and methodological strategies.

Accordingly, the intent of this chapter is to reexamine and further clarify the core attributes and issues of the life-span view, discuss the theoretical and empirical implications of these attributes, and make suggestions for expanding the view's usefulness. To facilitate integration of this presentation with that of previous discussions, we will examine the life-span approach from the perspectives of description, explanation, and modification of developmental change. We will then illustrate how our major points may be implemented through drawing examples from the theoretical and empirical literature on attachment. It is hoped that our discussion and illustration will demonstrate the broad and heuristic applicability of the life-span view of human development.

II. Description of Developmental Change

The descriptive component of the life-span approach involves the systematic empirical report of developmental changes (both within and between persons) as they occur during the life-span of an individual (Baltes & Schaie, 1973). The discussion of this component will proceed in four major sections. First, the basic premise—that development occurs at all ages—will be reiterated, and its subsequent advances regarding the nature, directionality, and extensiveness of change will be examined. Second, the theoretical and empirical necessity of a pluralistic approach to description will be discussed. The need for identification of developmental sequences focusing on behavior-change processes and ontogenetic linkages constitutes Section II, C. This will be followed by a look at the implications of the previous points for designs of descriptive developmental research.

A. DEVELOPMENT ACROSS THE LIFE SPAN

Drawing primarily on research in intellectual abilities (Baltes, Baltes, & Reinert, 1970; Baltes, Cornelius, & Nesselroade, 1977a; Baltes & Reinert, 1969; Baltes & Schaie, 1973, 1976; Schaie, Labouvie, & Buech, 1973; Schaie & Strother, 1968), the pervasiveness of change throughout the life span has been empirically demonstrated. While the evidence represented but one behavioral domain, it provides a significant antidote to prevailing theoretical views of development as being finalized in early life (Flavell, 1970; Freud, 1949; Kohlberg, 1969; Piaget, 1972) or those characterizing the latter half of life in terms of decrement and deterioration (see Baltes & Labouvie, 1973; Birren, 1964; Hall, 1922). More important for subsequent research, these preliminary works lead to conceptual refinement on a number of levels to assist in the description of developmental change.

1. Nature of Change

A primary issue clarified is that of theoretical and empirical *continuity* versus *discontinuity* in developmental change (Baltes & Schaie, 1973; Kagan, 1969; Neugarten, 1969; Overton & Reese, 1973). Life-span researchers are encouraged to examine whether the behavior under study can be described by quantitative increases of elements present at earlier stages (continuity) or if behavior in later stages of development is new and qualitatively different from that in an earlier period (discontinuity). Moreover, it was reemphasized that decisions about the existence of continuity or discontinuity were dependent on methodological and data analytic strategies, as well as one's theoretical orientation (Baltes & Nesselroade, 1973; Lerner, 1976). Furthermore, the utility of both continuity and discontinuity models is promoted as useful to the life-span perspective, with sensitivity being given to the time period and behavior classes studied (Baltes & Schaie, 1973; Huston-Stein & Baltes, 1976).

2. Directionality of Change

Many early theoretical perspectives (Flavell, 1970; Kohlberg, 1969; Piaget, 1972) viewed the major developmental dynamics to be unidirectional and closed-ended in character. Moreover, some of these views (e.g., Freud, 1949; Erikson, 1963) held that later developmental changes reflected continuations of processes whose directions and quality were determined in earlier childhood periods. Such views have been countered by preliminary empirical investigations on biological, perceptual, and information-processing realms in later life which revealed regressive, decremental developmental trends (see Baltes & Labouvie, 1973; Birren, 1964; Botwinick, 1973), and by theoretical frameworks which describe progressive later life changes, such as creative expansion and self-fulfillment (Buhler & Massarik, 1968) or ego generativity and ego integrity (Erikson, 1963).

More recently, research in the area of intellectual development of children (Baltes *et al.*, 1970; Baltes & Reinert, 1969) and adults (Baltes & Schaie, 1976; Nesselroade, Schaie, & Baltes, 1972; Schaie, 1970; Schaie *et al.*, 1973; Schaie & Strother, 1968) indicates that change occurs across the life span. The key findings have revealed increased interindividual differences in the latter parts of the life span and greater multidirectionality of change processes (e.g., increases or decreases in ability scores). Moreover, these changes have been linked to birth-cohort-related processes (Baltes *et al.*, 1977a). The role of such sociocultural/historical factors in accounting for both intraindividual change and interindividual differences in such change is further illustrated by the personality research of Nesselroade and Baltes (1974) done with adolescent samples. Their longitudinal sequential study found very large shares of the variance (contained in cross-sectional age differences) in scores for independence, achievement, and superego strength to be related to cohort rather than chronological age. Additionally, intercohort differences in longitudinal age changes were substantial and indicated the age development of adolescents in the personality domain was neither normative nor invariant. Taken together, the data from these life-span works indicate that change occurs across the life span and takes multidirectional forms. Hence, both progressive and regressive models are necessary to fully account for the directionality of developmental change across the life span.

3. Extensiveness of Change

The need to reveal the extendedness of a variable or process involves two issues. The first, extension over time, deals with whether the variable or process can be adequately described via short-term concurrent strategies, or if long-term historical perspectives must be employed to thoroughly describe the developmental process. The second issue involves the extent to which changes in the target variable covaries with one or more other variables. For example, the attainment of a particular level of development in one process (e.g., high perceptual constancy) may not imply similar levels of development in other processes (e.g., identification with a same-sexed figure). Thus, the coordination of change processes for different domains of functioning as well as their persistence over time poses many important questions for life-span researchers. Although the issue of interprocess relations within ontogenetic development has been minimally addressed, theoreticians have formulated ideas about the even more complex dynamics among ontogenetic processes and the sociocultural, historical change of the environment (Buss, 1974; Riegel, 1972, 1976; Riley, 1976). Such efforts have sensitized researchers to the need for simultaneous descriptive indicators of change in many spheres. The recognition of the *interdependence* of change processes within these varied realms constitutes a major conceptual advance with regard to the description of developmental change.

The *origins of developmental change* have also been amplified through applications of the life-span view. Such related advances will, however, be discussed in the explanatory section of the chapter (Section III).

B. PLURALISM AND DESCRIPTIVE RELATIVISM

The combined advances made regarding the nature, directionality, and extensiveness of developmental change have led to conclusions more far-reaching than was perhaps envisioned by early writers on the life-span view. Primary among these is the recognition that the multiplicity and interdependence of change patterns characterizing human ontogeny and cultural/historical development can be described only through *conceptual and empirical pluralism*. Because behavior change phenomena are found to be both empirically and theoretically interdependent (Lerner, 1978

Riegel, 1976), and therefore linked to a multiplicity of variables, they can be adequately evaluated only when pluralistically approached. That is, to fully account for ontogenetic development across the life span, pluralistic analysis which encompasses a wide range of theories and empirical strategies relative to both the individual and his sociocultural milieu, must be conducted.

To illustrate, specification of the relative contributions of age, birth cohort, and time of measurement factors to developmental change functions (Baltes, 1968; Schaie, 1965) reveals the importance of considering numerous sources of variation in a single descriptive effort. So doing makes clear that comprehensive documentation of change cannot occur in vacuum-like contexts wherein single variables are charted as if removed from time and place. While a particular procedure, mode of analysis, or theory may be useful or necessary in the initial investigation of certain aspects of ontogeny, the notion of pluralism indicates that an *eventual* integration must be made with studies employing various procedures, modes of analysis, or theories, superordinately joined together to complete knowledge of the target phenomenon or process. In sum, a complete understanding of the interdependent range of ontogenetic/evolutionary variables requires a systematic, long-term commitment to pluralistic analysis.

The embeddedness or interrelatedness of these processes in each other forces life-span researchers to confront the issue of *descriptive relativism*. Each descriptive work must be recognized as being relative to its particular personological, contextual, and epochal aspects. Such awareness does not limit the extent to which generalizations can be made to other settings as much as it *refines* the accuracy and precision in so doing. Theories can no longer be casually shifted from one population to another or from one time period to the next, for so doing ignores the dynamic variations within each and their resultant implications for the patterning of relatively plastic (Lerner, 1976) developmental processes. Similarly, empirical findings have to be understood in terms of their embeddedness in a multiplicity of changing variables such that absolute outcomes which invariantly hold true for other times and places are no longer likely. What becomes possible, however, is the ability to disentangle the complex contributions to any given developmental change. Researchers can therefore use all avenues (theoretical and empirical) open to them to provide indices of the many influences on developmental change. In short, descriptive relativism promotes the idea that multiple world views, and their related theories and methods, must be used to understand complex change phenomena. Identification of these many components of change as well as their interrelations brings the developmentalist much closer to capturing ontogenetic change in its true intricacy and complexity.

C. SEARCH FOR DEVELOPMENTAL SEQUENCES

Identification of the wide variation involved in ontogenetic and cultural/historical change elevates the importance of establishing developmental sequences. That is, the complexity of influences surrounding any given process is reduced if regularities in the change patterns of the various influences are theoretically and empirically established. As research in advanced ontogenetic periods (see Baltes & Willis, 1977) suggests, there is a need to identify the processes involved in promoting multidirectionality on the one hand, and consistent interindividual patterning on the other. Joint applications of idiographic (e.g., ipsative) and nomothetic (e.g., differential) measurement techniques (see Baltes & Nesselroade, 1973; Lerner, 1976) are required to establish sequence regularities. The awesome task of following how inordinate numbers of variables move in inordinate numbers of directions is therefore reduced to that of identifying the key change sequences within major idiographic and/or nomothetic domains. Moreover, the change process is conceptually refined in this enlarged emphasis on developmental sequences.

1. The Behavior Change Process

While preliminary efforts to validate the life-span perspective centered on age-related change, the more recent emphasis has been phrased in terms of the "behavior-change process" which has intrinsic life-span properties (Baltes & Willis, 1977; Huston-Stein & Baltes, 1976). Here the focus is on *time-related* change processes which reveal normatization, parsimony, and generalization (on either the nomothetic or idiographic level). These change processes can be pursued in two major ways, the first involving the usual documentation of age change patterns. The second and more novel approach involves age-irrelevant but sequence-relevant patterns of change. Such changes reveal little correlation with chronological age but may evidence parsimonious ties with life events or historical experiences (Baer, 1970; Baltes *et al.,* 1977a; Dohrenwend & Dohrenwend, 1974; Riegel & Riegel, 1972). Given the growing empirical evidence of age-irrelevant change in the latter half of life (Baltes & Willis, 1977; Bortner, 1967; Britton & Britton, 1972; Busse, 1969; Datan & Ginsberg, 1975; Huston-Stein & Baltes, 1976), the emphasis on event or historically relevant determinants of change stands as a major asset of the life-span view.

The primary significance of this transition from age-related behavior to behavior-change processes is that the usual developmental marker variables (e.g., infancy, childhood, adolescence, adulthood, and old age) become only one of *many* potential ontogentic "signposts" in developmental research. Life experiences and historical events become potentially compelling variables as well. The selective criteria which determine the ultimate utility of each of these marker variables is that they are correlated with time-related, normative, parsimonious regularities in behavioral processes. Attention to an expanded range of variables is perhaps even more significant from the perspective that it brightens the possibilities for identifying *new* developmental phenomena which are salient in a life-span framework but would be overlooked if age-specific views were taken.

2. *Establishing Developmental Linkages*

Thorough understanding of change over the ontogenetic span requires that time-related processes be examined both in short-term and long-term frameworks. This is accomplished by comprehensive mapping of the dynamics *within* age, life event, or historical change processes, followed by extensions to other age, event, or historical periods. So doing reveals the transformations that occur over time and thereby augments understanding of the nature, directionality, and extensiveness of the given change process. Furthermore, verification of the presence or absence of ontogenetic linkages will allow developmentalists to describe when continuous processes underlie specific developmental functions at disparate ontogenetic periods (i.e., when homology exists), and/or when discontinuous processes subserve these same functions during such ontogenetic periods (or when analogy exists; see Lerner, 1976).

Developmental linkages *between* the various change processes must also be examined if a holistic view of ontogenetic development is to be achieved. Thus, life-event processes (e.g., death of spouse) must be examined not only as they relate to other life events (e.g., retirement) but also as they relate to historical (e.g., economic depression), physical environmental (pollution level of air), or numerous other processes.

D. IMPLICATIONS FOR THE DESIGN OF DESCRIPTIVE RESEARCH

The pluralistic approach to the personological, sociocultural, and historical variations in developmental processes has implications for the design of research strategies. The complexity of these influences requires that *all* methodological and interpretive tools available to science be mobilized in order to describe the nature, directionality, and extensiveness of a behavior-change process and to reduce the extent to which accurate descriptive work is limited by a particular theoretical or methodological strategy (Lerner, 1976; Werner, 1957).

To illustrate, the utility of age-specific research within the life-span perspective has been uncertain. Some have raised the question of whether the life-span perspective should consist of simple additive combinations of age-specific psychologies or if an alternative, fresh conceptualization was necessary to integrate long-term ontogenetic change (Baltes & Goulet, 1970). The proliferation of sequential research strategies (Baltes, 1968; Schaie, 1965) indirectly answered the query and may have appeared to render age-specific work passé. From a life-span pluralistic orientation, however, one sees that age-specific research is, in fact, vital to the task of describing development across the life span, given that one understands the type of questions which may be answered by such designs. For example, age-specific research is useful in identifying what is unique and representative of different life periods—it facilitates a comparative approach to the study of age differences. Furthermore, such research may be employed to simulate ontogenetic change processes across the life span (Baltes & Goulet, 1971; Ryff & Baltes, 1976; Sjostrom & Pollack, 1971). In sum, age-specific research constitutes a necessary step in elucidating and clarifying one's constructs (Huston-Stein & Baltes, 1976). Subsequent research designs focusing on long-term linkages and interdependent influences may then build on these preliminary efforts.

The expansion of marker variables resulting from clarification of the behavior-change process, when generalized to the level of research design, provides another illustration of the multiple avenues open to life-span investigators. Thus, while the generic strategy incorporates age, birth cohort, and time of measurement variables, additional sequential research could be conducted with a focus on age, *event cohort,* and time of measurement. The potential utility of such a design will be illustrated in our presentation of the life-span view of the development of attachment.

III.   Explanation of Developmental Change

The explanatory aspects of the science of human development refer to the clarification of behavioral outcomes by showing their relationship to antecedent or current conditions. While the primary aim in description is that of unbiased, thorough observation, in explanation the emphasis is on how variable relationships can account for change within and between individuals. Our discussion of the explanatory component will first examine the conceptual advances achieved through the life-span orientation (Section III, A). This will be followed by consideration of pluralism as an approach to explanation (Section III, B), and a final section (Section III, C) will focus on the implications for design of explanatory research.

A. CONCEPTUAL CLARIFICATIONS AND ADVANCES

1. The Age Variable

One of the first benefits derived from the life-span attention to explanation is the clarification of the age variable as being *noncausal* and inevitably in need of further explanation (Baer, 1970; Baltes & Willis, 1977; Wohlwill, 1973). Developmentalists were warned of the dangers of overlooking behavioral determinants by attributing undue explanatory power to chronological age, which is little more than a marker variable along which other experiences occur. This advancement can be usefully extended to other major demographic variables (e.g., sex, ethnicity, socioeconomic status) which are also significant at initial stages of inquiry but must eventually be explicated by more specific underlying processes, such as the life events or historical experiences that they serve to only incompletely mark.

Results of a study by Wolf (in Bloom, 1964) illustrate this point. While many reports indicate the correlation between such gross demographic variables as socioeconomic status and IQ is about .4, they do not indicate the precise processes within social class moderating this relation. Wolf inferred such processes may include those relating to parent–child interactions and, as such, studied the impact of 13 variables pertaining to this social process on IQ. Variables related to categories such as presses for achievement motivation, provisions for general learning, and presses for language development. The multiple correlation of these 13 process variables with IQ was .76. Thus, this study shows that gross demographic variables are inevitably related to underlying processes of behavior change which may be more important in explicating significant proportions of variance in development.

2. Continuity/Discontinuity

The life-span view further amplifies explanatory work through reapplication of the continuity/discontinuity issue. Explanatory continuity refers to the situation wherein invariant causes operate at all levels of ontogeny, while explanatory discontinuity pertains to those instances where behavioral antecedents differ from one period to another. As illustrated by parts of Piagetian theory, which stress invariant mechanisms operating at all levels of ontogeny (e.g., the equilibration model), and components of theoretical views of attachment (see Ainsworth, 1973), which stress genetic factors as the underlying principle in early development while experience is the important principle in later development, both continuous and discontinuous perspectives are seen as necessary in a complete accounting of change processes.

3. Origins of Developmental Change

The explanatory search for the origins or causes of developmental change has been advanced by the descriptive clarification of age, birth conort, and time of measurement influences (Baltes, 1968; Schaie, 1965). Thus, the issue of whether the major share of the variance in developmental change functions could be attributed to processes related to the individual, the environment, or interactions of both become clarifiable (cf. Schaie & Baltes, 1976). These concerns have been empirically demonstrated by personality research on adolescents (Nesselroade & Baltes, 1974) and adults (Woodruff & Birren, 1973) which reveal age differences to be related more to birth cohort than age. So doing greatly expands the significance of cultural/historical processes in accounting for developmental change as well as leads to further clarification of the status of the birth-cohort variable (Baltes *et al.*, 1977a).

4. Dynamic Explanations

A final advancement is the recognition that time-ordered systems of explanatory determinants require dynamic, potentially changing conceptions. Thus, while concurrent explanatory paradigms can provide time-specific explanations, their utility for the life-span perspective depend on historical paradigms which examine the homology within and between variables across time. If continuous invariant processes can account for change across the life span, then historical paradigms are not especially useful for developmentalists. This is, however, an empirical question, and the evidence to date, revealing an increased prominence of multidirectiona!, truncated change sequences as development progresses (Huston-Stein & Baltes, 1976), strongly suggests that behavioral antecedents are likely to differ from one age period to another. Such findings further indicate the importance of dynamic, change-oriented explanations. In short, explanation is no longer likely to be a once-and-for-all affair, but becomes as potentially protean as description. The need for complex, dynamic behavior/environment systems of multiple causality is thus highlighted.

B. PLURALISM AND EXPLANATORY RELATIVISM

The life-span perspective encourages a complete metatheoretical reorientation to the pursuit of developmental explanations. Given that explanations are always relative to particular theories which in turn reflect one's world view, they cannot be evaluated on the criteria of truth or certainty. To do so would fail to recognize that causality itself has constructive and representational features derived from an underlying theory. While such propositions can be evaluated as good or bad, useful or irrelevant, a given developmental explanation cannot be held as unequivocally superior to others. The choice of analytic procedure to carry out the explanatory task is therefore not a matter of internal logic but an issue of metatheoretical assumptions (Baltes & Willis, 1977; Lerner, 1976; Schaie & Baltes, 1976; Werner, 1957), which in themselves are irresolvable. In other words, from a life-span perspective, all changes may be interpreted as developmental, depending on the interpretive framework selected. Such change may be linked to variables having any one or several interrelated foci of influence, including those which may covary with historical epoch, environmental context, and sociocultural milieu. Hence, developmental change may be quite plastic during any ontogenetic period, varying in respect to the domain, rate, sequence, and direction of progression being considered, the theoretical, model-based interpretations proferred about such change, and the theory-based methods and data-analytic devices used to index change (Lerner, 1976; Werner, 1957).

Additionally, the major findings from the descriptive realm (e.g., increased multidirectionality and interindividual differences in developmental change) discourages the search for monolithic paths of determinacy or single causative agents. Instead, multiple theoretical explanations appear necessary to account for the complexity and cultural/historical dependency of change processes and outcomes (Baltes *et al.,* 1977a). In sum, a pluralistic approach to explanation more accurately encompasses the multiplicity of variables influencing development as well as prevents the short-sightedness resulting from blind devotion to any particular set of theoretical assumptions. More important, however, the vast array of interpretive frameworks available heightens the need for developmentalists to become more refined in their selection and use of existing models, theories, and methods. The successful developmental effort, henceforth, will be judged on its persuasiveness and integrativeness *across* interpretive frameworks, not merely within the confines of a single strategy or orientation. In short, pluralistic developmental work should have an audience both within its specific theoretical context as well as throughout other theoretical and disciplinary contexts.

The realization that explanations are always relative to their underlying theoretical framework and that multiple explanations must be endorsed to encompass the complexity in accounting for all the variation in developmental phenomena need not, however, lead to the noncritical acceptance of infinite explanatory interpretations. Each of these must, of course, be able to withstand the rigors of scientific scrutiny. Weak eclecticism is therefore avoided in favor of coalescing the carefully critiqued resources of multiple explanatory paradigms. In other words, explanatory relativism specifies the need for well-executed specific works followed by systematic multidisciplinary integration of all empirical and conceptual approaches to the multiplicity of factors influencing development.

C. IMPLICATIONS FOR DESIGNS OF EXPLANATORY RESEARCH

Explanatory research has typically been conducted within manipulative, experimental contexts. As life-span research aims toward the explanation of long-term developmental change, alternatives to the previous concurrent paradigms must be found. One such approach is the simulation strategy (Baltes & Goulet, 1971) involving experimentally produced short-term change functions which would be observed naturalistically as long-term change phenomena. The knowledge generated is then used to construct explanatory accounts which may lead to more pertinent simulations or naturalistic data for further refinement and testing (Baltes *et al.,* 1977b).

A second general approach to developmental explanation is that of causal modeling techniques and strategies (see Baltes *et al.,* 1977b). Such techniques build and test causal representations of phenomena, which are not experimentally tractable, through explicit mathematical specification of a network of hypothesized causal relationships among concepts and variables. Statistical procedures are then employed to estimate the parameters of the causal system and to evaluate its fit to the data. The procedures also allow for the use of mulitple indicators of theoretical constructs and the representation of reciprocal causation. The utilization of multivariate strategies has also been endorsed by life-span researchers (Baltes & Nesselrode, 1973; Nesselroade & Reese, 1973). While not specifically tied to the explanatory process, such strategies provide empirical tools capable of dealing with the multiple determinants and consequents of developmental change.

The espousal of explanatory pluralism on the theoretical level can be implemented only by a corresponding pluralism on the methodological or design level. Thus, a major implication of the life-span approach to developmental explanation is the need for additional strategies which incorporate long-term change, multiple systems of causality, and can be utilized from a variety of theoretical perspectives.

IV.   Implications of the Life-Span View for Developmental Intervention

The life-span approach to behavioral development with its emphasis on long-term change processes covering a wide array of domains leads to a reformulation of the general format of human development intervention. This section will discuss these changes focusing first on the basic assumptions involved in life-span intervention strategies, followed by a more specific look at the targets, timing, and mechanisms for developmental intervention.

A.   BASIC ASSUMPTIONS OF LIFE-SPAN INTERVENTION

Two major issues distinguish the life-span approach to intervention from other more generic perspectives. First, recalling the multiplicity and relativisms of factors influencing developmental change, as discussed in the descriptive and explanatory sections, the life-span interventionist *starts* with the expectation that the effects of a given treatment procedure are not likely to be identical for all persons since the effectiveness is moderated by the entire range of personological, cultural, and historical differences manifest in each individual (Baltes, 1973; Baltes & Schaie, 1973). In other words, the pluralism within the life-span view of development leads to a reformulation of the type of question asked regarding intervention. Rather than debate which behaviors should be the targets for intervention, or which theories, definitions, or "facts" about a given process are most useful, we must address the more difficult issues of which behaviors, for which individuals, in which contexts, and what time periods are most likely to lead to optimal developmental outcomes. Second, then, once these complex issues are confronted, the interventionist must examine his vast array of theories, methods, and analytic tools so as to extract those elements which will be most responsive to the particular array of behaviors, individuals, contexts, and time periods constituting the intervention target. In sum, there is no single yellow brick road to developmental optimization, for there is no single best optimization per se, but rather relativisms dependent on the individual, societal, and historical contexts. Moreover, if we wait until an adequate knowledge base regarding the long-term impact of our intervention exists, we will fare no better than those awaiting Godot, for the individual, social, and historical contexts are in themselves constantly changing and transforming. Operating in contexts of restricted validity therefore becomes inherent in life-span intervention strategies.

Thus, the life-span approach dissuades the insouciant divorcing of people from their surrounding worlds or life histories and rather seeks to identify the many past, present, or future influences impinging on their developmental patterns. Moreover, the more distant these influences are from the present, the greater the salience of the long-term orientation intrinsic to life-span thinking. While attention to the vast expanse of time-related variables reduces the chances of demonstrating large-scale treatment effects, it does refine the quality and precision of the intervention effort and thereby enhances the likelihood of producing meaningful, lasting effects.

In the main, previous intervention strategies have addressed themselves to a posteriori treatment of developmental dysfunctions (Baltes, 1973; Baltes & Schaie, 1973). That is, interventionists have *waited* for the problem to appear before they used their skills to eliminate it. The life-span approach, again due to its concern with change across the life-cycle, encourages the interventionist to employ his capabilities a priori, to *prevent* the appearance of the problem. At the heart of this intent lies the successful achievement of theoretical and empirical charting of developmental sequences and behavior-change processes across the life span. Once the developmentalist has uncovered these regularities in change processes (associated with the individual and/or the environmental context), (s)he is equipped with the requisite predictive resources to intervene ahead of time so as to optimize and enrich the developmental progression. Illustrations of such preventive strategies can already be seen in the work on cognitive performance among the aged (see Baltes & Labouvie, 1973), where attention has been drawn to redesigning environmental contexts (e.g., providing adult and second-career educational programs; see Baltes & Schaie, 1973).

The life-span perspective directly confronts issues of ethics and value systems underlying any attempt at intervention. Such openness is promoted and facilitated through the recognition that a truly pluralistic approach also supports a multiplicity of value rationales. That is, rather than become inert in the face of inescapable value judgments, the life-span researcher is aware there exists no one optimal developmental course either within a given time period or across time periods (Riley, 1976). It is not only likely but inevitable that researchers will disagree as to the type and form of change to be implemented. Such differences, however, prevent the adoption of monolithic intervention strategies and thereby enhance the possibility of the acceptance by practitioners of a range of modification perspectives. The broad expanse of developmental needs characterizing human ontogeny are therefore more likely to be met in the promotion of interventive pluralism.

Finally, the life-span perspective may result in a reordering of the description, explanation, intervention sequence. That is, since the criteria for evaluating a given description or explanation are not truth but utility, theories and methodologies are selected on the basis of which strategies lead to socially relevant implementations and possess the potential for optimization of developmental processes. Optimization is no longer the final and typically ignored aspect of a given work but becomes instrumental at the outset in identifying important questions to be asked and in formulating meaningful research strategies. The concern for enhancing the lives of developing humans may therefore actively serve to *generate* the necessary descriptive and explanatory strategies rather than follow from them.

B. TARGETS, TIMING, AND MECHANISMS OF INTERVENTION

1. Targets

As already suggested, life-span pluralism indicates that the key question regarding intervention targets is not which theory or definition of a process is most useful to intervention, but which concepts and ideas from a multitude of theories, methods, and designs can be employed to produce a particular outcome. For example, while cognitive deficiencies of the aged have been widely identified as important targets of intervention (see Baltes & Labouvie, 1973), others have called for the need for greater concern with maintaining or redirecting affective–emotional patterns (Looft, 1973). The pluralism of life-span research would support emphasis on both such target behaviors as well as countless others. Hence, the choice of target behaviors becomes more a matter of personal predilection, albeit justifiable predilection, than rigorous scientific deduction.

One seemingly obvious means of insuring personal preferences do, in fact, possess elements of larger social utility would be to ask the target populations themselves. That is, rather than rely on the merits of their own intuitive frameworks, scientists could wisely benefit from listening to the developmental needs voiced by those they study.

Additionally, a comprehensive intervention approach requires a joint focus on the ontogenetic life course as well as its relations to the processes of sociocultural and historical change. The identification of target behaviors therefore requires a concomitant awareness of the target and its context as well as the dynamics between the two.

2. Timing

One view of the timing of life-span intervention strategies parallels the descriptive and explanatory distinction between short-term (concurrent) and long-term (historical) change paradigms. The former type of developmental change could be implemented through immediate reinforcement procedures as in the laboratory or classroom setting. The latter might involve intervention into the system of generational transmission of values—that is, the more long-term processes involved in how adults transmit value patterns to children.

In addition to the above perspective, another view of the timing of life-span intervention strategies is found in paradigms which stress the probabilistic patterning of variables involved in behavior-change processes (Lerner, 1978). Here it is stressed that in ecologically valid developmental milieus the variables influencing behavior-change processes show interindividual variation in their interactive time course, and as such lead to variations in developmental outcome. Again, such variation may involve both short- and longer term modifications, but in either case the specific timing patterns are potentially characterized by wide interindividual variation.

3. *Mechanisms*

Knowledge of the developmental outcomes associated with altering the time course of the variables involved in behavior-change processes constitutes one mechanism for producing desired changes open to the life-span interventionist. Other mechanisms for producing the desired behavioral change could potentially involve learning principles (Hoyer, 1973; Labouvie, 1973), environmental change (Gottesman, 1973), attitude change (Looft, 1973; Schaie, 1970), or health delivery or economic support systems (Jacobs, 1972).

An important issue is that the mechanisms selected must reveal ontogenetic as well as social change principles. Thus, the acquisition, maintenance, or extinction of any behavior must be seen within the social context which facilitates or deters such behaviors. For example, while late childhood or early adolescent periods of the life span might be appropriate times to maximize achievement-related strivings, these behaviors might later be extinguished due to circumscriptions imposed by social conventions (e.g., mandatory retirement). The social context encourages such behaviors in early life but supports their disappearance in the later years.

V. Concept of Attachment

We have to this point discussed the attributes of the life-span view of human development and indicated the theoretical and empirical implications of these characteristics. However, we have not illustrated in detail how this view could be implemented. To accomplish this we will apply the life-span view to the understanding of attachment development. Probably no concept better stresses the basic social relatedness of the organism than does attachment. Empirical and theoretical analyses of both the animal and human development literatures (Lerner, 1978 ; Tobach & Schneirla, 1968; Weinraub *et al.*, 1977) indicate that in ecologically valid developmental milieus development always involves organism–organism (social) relations. Accordingly, while attachment would seem to be a notion useful for evaluating the nature of such relations, the concept has been rarely empirically and only minimally theoretically extended in analysis beyond early childhood (Cohen, 1974).

Thus, we have chosen to focus on the concept of attachment in order to illustrate how the attributes of the life-span view of human development might integrate and extend knowledge about an actual substantive area which in the past has been primarily pursued from a developmental–psychological orientation. We have made this choice because at this time in the evolvement of the life-span view it is important to demonstrate the view's utility for topic areas other than those typically considered (as, e.g., the work on intellectual abilities). Moreover, while developmentalists have recently called for an analysis of attachment phenomena from a life-span perspective (see Antonucci, 1976; Hartup & Lempers, 1973), such calls have to a large extent involved analyses primarily focused on particular points of the life span. Additionally, long-term ontogenetic linkages have not been addressed, nor has the attachment literature been evaluated in a manner which indicates the usefulness of life-span pluralism. Finally, insufficient attention has been paid to issues of evolutionary/historical change and implications for the nature of attachment development.

Concern with the above issues will enable us to illustrate how the life-span view may impose order on a literature in which non-life-span developmentalists have shown extensive concern (see Ainsworth, 1973; Maccoby & Masters, 1970), as well as provide the basis for extending the attachment concept across the entire ontogenetic span. So doing will not only augment the substance and usefulness of the attachment concept but may also enhance the understanding of life-course change processes. It should be noted that we will *not* attempt to comprehensively review the attachment literature, a task which has recently been done elsewhere (Ainsworth, 1973; Cohen, 1974; Maccoby & Masters, 1970; Masters & Wellman, 1974; Weinraub *et al.*, 1977).

A. DEFINITIONS OF ATTACHMENT

The primary problem in showing how the life-span view is helpful in integrating the attachment literature is that the phenomenon has a history of definitional elusiveness. Cohen (1974) and Weinraub *et al.* (1977) have persuasively challenged most of the frequently proferred components of definitions of attachment, while Knudtson (1976) has aptly said, "Defining attachment is like trying to operationalize a platonic ideal" (p. 196). To illustrate some of these problems we may note that Ainsworth (1973, p. 3), for example, distinguishes, on the one hand, between attachment, dependency, and object relations, and between attachment and attachment behavior on the other (Ainsworth, 1973, p. 2). However, she stresses that the "hallmark of attachment is *behavior* that promotes proximity to or contact with the specific figure or figures to whom the person is attached" (Ainsworth, 1973, p. 2, italics added), and in so doing she offers a conceptualization of attachment which appears markedly similar to what others call dependency (see Maccoby & Masters, 1970, p. 75). In fact, Maccoby and Masters (1970) believe that the term dependency has a technical meaning which includes the same classes of behavior that other authors (e.g., Bowlby, 1969) would call attachment.

One immediate use of the life-span view would be to lead researchers to consider integration of related attachment definitions, thereby illustrating the merits of employing a multiplicity of theories and theory-derived concepts about a phenomenon. Second, such integration would facilitate extension of attachment processes beyond the early childhood years (e.g., in the study of "dependency" in the adult portion of ontogeny, as in Kagan & Moss, 1962) and lead to establishing developmental linkages.

Consequently, we have integrated diverse conceptions of attachment to form a definitional consensus, and in the remainder of our analysis we will use the term attachment to represent the behaviors and processes described in this definition. The definition has five components, with each successive component representing an aspect of attachment having somewhat less consensus in the literature. Attachment, therefore, refers to behavior of the following kind: (1) proximity and/or contact-seeking and/or maintaining behavior; (2) shown to one or a few specific others; (3) which elicits reciprocal behaviors in, or the presence of, these others; (4) which, if these reciprocal behaviors are not seen, represents an aversive state for the person emitting the attachment behavior (e.g., as indexed through distress behavior); and (5) may lead the attached person to seek alternative attachment opportunities from among his/her broader social network (Lamb, 1977; Weinraub *et al.*, 1977).

B. CURRENT STATE OF THE ATTACHMENT LITERATURE

Perhaps more disturbing than the array of definitions that have been offered for attachment are the contradictory and equivocal empirical trends in the literature. The lack of uniformity has led some reviewers (e.g., Ainsworth, 1973) to consider the literature from only one theoretical perspective, while it has led others (Maccoby & Masters, 1970) to essentially dichotomize the theoretical review from the empirical summary. Moreover, in both reviewing formats, methodological diversity among studies has been represented as a major aspect of the literature, although the precise linkages among methodological variations and resulting empirical outcomes have rarely been specified (cf. Cohen, 1974).

1. Contrasting Theories of Attachment

A diverse array of theories has been preferred to account for attachment phenomena. Bowlby (1969) and Ainsworth (1973) have been the leading exponents of a ethological–instinct theory of attachment, while the work of Freud (1949) and Erikson (1959, 1963) may be seen as representative of a psychoanalytic–instinct view of attachment or dependency. Alternatively, various forms of social learning theory for attachment have been articulated (Bijou & Baer, 1965; Gewirtz, 1972, 1976; Mischel, 1966; Sears, 1972), and some extensions of cognitive developmental theory (Kohlberg, 1966) may be viewed as a theoretical attempt to understand attachment phenomena. More recently, systems theory approaches to the integration of attachment behaviors have been put forth (Bischof, 1975; Knudtson, 1976).

Each of these theories differ in regard to their definitions of attachment and, as such, vary in the behaviors on which they focus. Consequently, there has been virtually no attempt to draw from all views those domains of behavior best accounted for by each theory's constructs. As indicated before, however, a life-span developmental view, due to its pluralism and joint focus on both ontogenetic and historical perspectives in description and explanation, would suggest that such an integration is conceptually essential.

2. Methodological Variations

Analogous to the existence of alternative perspectives on attachment phenomena, methodological variation among related studies has involved evaluating attachment behaviors in different situations (e.g., controlled laboratory manipulative studies, controlled observations in structured or unstructured play and/or separation situations, and *in vivo* naturalistic assessments). Moreover, such situational variation usually results in different types of data, ranging from qualitative, nominal data to quantitative, interval-type data, and including either one observation or an array of information about each subject. These variations obviously necessitate different modes of data analysis.

3. *Empirical Findings and Conclusions*

Given the theoretical and methodological heterogeneity, one need not be surprised to find that the conclusions about attachment are equally varied. Major empirical issues addressed have been whether the mother or father is the major attachment figure, whether sex differences exist in infant attachment, whether there are age-associated differences in attachment, and whether there are differing developmental courses for various indices of attachment (e.g., selective smiling, crying on separation). Conclusions derived from these inquiries have generally lent support on both sides of the issue. Some reported data have indicated, for instance, that mothers are the major attachment figure (e.g., Ban & Lewis, 1974; Fleener & Cairns, 1970), while other data suggests that fathers are the major figure (Ban & Lewis, 1974). Still further data indicate no attachment differences toward the parents (Cohen & Campos, 1974; Lamb, 1975; Willemsen, Flaherty, Heaton, & Ritchey, 1974). Similarly equivocal data trends exist in regard to the other major empirical issues that have been addressed.

While such discrepancies in theories, methods, and findings may lead some to infer that attachment phenomena are too elusive and variable for comprehensive study, such an inference is not justifiable from the life-span view. Rather than regarding them as deficits, the current attributes of the attachment literature are, in fact, viewed as assets if carefully and systematically integrated within a life-span orientation. We will attempt to substantiate these benefits by organizing our discussion around the general concepts of the description, explanation, and modification of developmental change, as outlined in Sections II, III, and IV.

VI.　Life-Span Analysis of the Development of Attachment

A.　DESCRIPTION OF ATTACHMENT ACROSS THE LIFE SPAN

As already indicated, the predominant theoretical and empirical foci in the study of attachment have involved infancy and early childhood periods. But, as discussed by Weinraub *et al.* (1977), one of the least debated components of the attachment concept is that an attachment endures over time. Consequently, although an assumption has been that attachments extend beyond infancy and early childhood, data have not been collected enabling a direct demonstration of such extension across long portions of the life course. Thus, because the attachment notion seems to have intrinsic life-span properties, i.e., attachment behaviors are not finalized early in life, this view of human development of which it is a part suggests then that the behavior-change processes comprising attachment phenomena need be described within *all* segments of the life course. One reason for this is that: "With age, the child moves increasingly farther from his mother in terms of physical distance and time. By the time the child is in adolescence, he may leave the mother for years at a time, separating himself from her by many miles. Since the relationship may span many years, the behaviors used to maintain contact or to express attachment may drastically change . . ." (Weinraub *et al.*, 1977, p. 36).

Accordingly, while one may apparently describe attachment behavior across the life span, the precise behaviors defining attachment may be different at various developmental periods. Thus, in orer to accurately describe such developmental change, it is necessary to refine our study of attachment in a number of ways.

1. Nature of Change

The life-span perspective necessitates consideration of possible transformations in the behaviors comprising attachment at succeeding ontogenetic periods (Cohen, 1974; Weinraub *et al.*, 1977) and, as such, the issue of descriptive continuity versus discontinuity is raised. Cohen (1974) argues that the proximity-promoting behaviors characteristic of attachment during infancy and early childhood begin to diminish in occurrence thereafter. Accordingly, use of such behaviors as the sole criteria for attachment in later life would lead to the erroneous conclusion that attachment diminishes across the life span. Cohen (1974) thus contends that although broadly serving the same function, of promoting proximity, the class of behavior selectively directed to an attachment figure may be different at succeeding periods across the life course. Evidence for such transformation is derived from a report by Lewis, Weinraub, and Ban (1972). Proximity-seeking behaviors decreased with age and were replaced with distal attachment behaviors such as looking and vocalizing.

Thus, while discontinuity in the specific behaviors representing attachments may be altered across the life span, there may be continuity in functions subserved by these different behavior classes. As such, attachment phenomena illustrate the utility of joining continuity and discontinuity conceptions together within a life-span perspective which is attentive to the interrelation of behavior classes and ontogenetic period (cf. Baltes & Schaie, 1973; Huston-Stein & Baltes, 1976).

Initial attempts to extend attachment concepts beyond infancy were most often conceptualized as modifications of prototypic social relations of childhood (Hartup & Lempers, 1973; Riley, Foner, Hess, & Toby; 1969). Such analyses were incomplete, however, because they ignored the massive circumstantial differences between the world of the infant and that of the adult, and that of the sociocultural change context. They seemed, in fact, to reinforce the contention that we would not understand the psychological realities of adulthood by projecting forward those issues salient in childhood, a position critically evaluated by Neugarten (1969). Nevertheless, those first works represent progress, for life-span thinking has to *commence* before it can be refined; the preliminary processes must involve extrapolating from one age period to another, followed by an examination of the appropriateness of so doing.

For example, the lack of persuasiveness in the initial attachment extrapolations made clear the need for replacing the existing personological models, which viewed attachment as an attribute of the individual, with more interactional frames wherein the concept was reformulated as a dimension of social interaction (Hartup & Lempers, 1973). This advancement, while assisting life-span extensions, was also of significant benefit to the infancy literature. More recently, applying attachment to the middle and later years has resulted in a broadening of the "social bond" concept to include not only people, but groups, ideas, things, and the ability for self-produced feedback (Kalish & Knudtson, 1976).

Thus, projecting issues of infancy to adulthood and vice versa is a useful place to *begin* the documentations of long-term ontogenetic change processes and interage networks, for the fit/nonfit highlights the differences between age groups and their social environments, thereby sharpening the underlying concept. In some domains the fit may be good enough to encourage theoretical and empirical homology, thus building the case for continuity. In other instances, the fit may be sufficiently poor to convince the investigator of extreme discontinuity or even the nonexistence of the given content area in other periods of the life span. In any event, a benefit of such life-span extensions is the heightened sensitivity to capturing the frame of reference and behavioral dimensions appropriate to each life period, the person/environment differences, and the widened horizons resulting from all these.

2. *Directionality of Change*

As stressed in life-span writings (Baltes & Schaie, 1973; Baltes & Willis, 1977), behavior-change processes may develop in multidirectional manners. Such a possibility helps to organize attachment data, since both temporal stabilities and instabilities of attachment behavior have been reported (cf. Masters & Wellman, 1974).

For example, Maccoby and Feldman (1972) found that among 2- and 3-year-olds proximity seeking to mother did not change with age, but if the concept of distal attachment was employed (as indexed, e.g., through speaking, smiling, and showing objects), then such attachment behavior did increase with age. However, in a study by Coates, Anderson, and Hartup (1972a), distal attachment was not assessed. Rather, children (age 10, 14, and 18 months) were evaluated for their attachment through assessement of touching, proximity seekings, and vocalization behaviors. While vocalization showed significant stability only from 10 to 14 months, touching and proximity seeking were significantly stable from both 10 to 14 months and from 14 to 18 months. Finally, decreases in some classes of attachment behaviors have also been found. Stayton, Ainsworth, and Main (1973) studied infants during their first year of life. It was found that smiles on greeting were more frequently reserved for mothers among the yougest infants studied (i.e., 3–6 month olds); such selective response decreased thereafter. In sum, it appears that depending on the behavior class being described, attachment behaviors vary in their developmental direction.

3. Extensiveness of Change

As indicated earlier in this chapter, attempts to ascertain the extendedness of a variable or process involves two issues. First is the issue of whether short-term (concurrent) strategies or long-term (historical) ones are necessary for description, and the second component of extendedness involves patterns of covariation among a target variable and presumably associated ones. Addressing both issues serves to clarify attachment data through describing the interdependence of attachment behaviors on intraindividual, ontogenetic variables, and socioculturally and historically changing processes.

To illustrate, patterns of covariation may exist among attachment behaviors and physical or physiological variables. Fraiberg (1975), for instance, studied the development of attachment in 10 blind but otherwise neurologically intact infants over the course of their first 2 years of life. Her results indicated that several attachment behaviors (e.g., a familiar voice irregularly elicited a smile in the range of from 1 to 3 months, and negative reactions to strangers emerged between 7 and 15 months) emerged within an age range comparable to normal, sighted children. Thus, visual processes appeared not to be necessary components or precursors of these attachment behaviors. On the other hand, separation anxiety among blind children was first seen between 11 and 12 months—a delay in comparison to sighted children, yet comparable to the former group's delay in attaining particular levels of object permanence. Leifer, Leiderman, Barnett, and Williams (1972) also provide data illustrating the utility of physical/organic status data for attachment research. Here, reciprocal mother–infant behaviors were studied with groups of premature and full-term infants. Mothers of full-term infants smile at them and hold them close to their bodies more than do mothers of premature infants. Accordingly, maturity status appears associated with differential processes of mother–infant interaction.

Socioeconomic status, as a marker for variables presumed to be exerting a more long-term effect, may also be useful in explicating attachment processes. Tulkin (1973), for example, studied the attachment behaviors of middle- and working-class female infants in a play situation and after separation from their mothers. The two social class groups did not differ in their play behaviors or in the separation condition (the working-class children cried as often as the middle-class children). Middle-class children did, however, cry sooner in the separation condition. In addition, working-class infants of working mothers cried less frequently and crawled less often to the mother on her return after separation than did working-class infants of nonworking mothers.

Other important, although infrequently used, ways of evaluating the extendedness of attachment processes may be noted. First, animal comparative data may be used to assess the impact of long- or short-term manipulations which are either infeasible (e.g., because of life-span length) or ethically unacceptable with humans. For example, Mason and Kenney (1974) sought to provide data relevant to both the critical period hypothesis and the notion of the irreversibility of filial bonds. Rhesus monkeys were raised from birth for 1–10 months in one of several conditions (with mothers, with age-mates, or with cloth surrogates), after which they were separated and placed with dogs. Contrary to the critical period and the irreversibility notions, the monkeys formed intense and specific attachments to their canine surrogates.

Finally, cross-cultural variables, as markers of sociocultural and historical processes, may be useful for evaluating the extensiveness of attachment change. First, despite cultural and methodological differences, Ainsworth's (1963, 1964) study of Uganda children and Schaffer and Emerson's (1964) study of Scottish children found evidence for intercultural consistency in some aspects of attachment behavior. Thus, such comparisons may be seen as capable of providing evidence of the convergent

validity of particular behavior-change processes. Cross-cultural comparative research can therefore show the robustness of a particular aspect of a
behavior-change phenomenon, despite presumed cultural differences in
such behaviors as child rearing. For instance, a comparison was made by
Maccoby and Feldman (1972) between American home-reared children,
age 2½ years, and similarly aged Israeli Kibbutzim-reared children. Results showed a high similarity in reactions to mothers in separation distress and, as such, illustrate intercultural congruity despite known differences in the rearing conditions with infants from the two cultural groups.
Additionally, intercultural differences provide an initial empirical basis on
which to establish future investigations about the nature of these dis-
parities. Thus, Uganda children develop specific attachments earlier than
Scottish children, but they get intense stranger fears later than do Scottish
children (Ainsworth, 1973; Maccoby & Masters, 1970). These differences
may suggest to future researchers that it would be profitable to explore
familial interaction and child rearing practice differences between the two
cultural groups.

B. PLURALISM AND DESCRIPTIVE RELATIVISM

Earlier, we have shown how the descriptive advances made regarding
the nature, directionality, and extensiveness of developmental change led
to the recognition that conceptual and empirical pluralism were necessary
to explicate such change; moreover, we argued that the presentation of
such descriptions were always relative to the plethora of interdependent
ontogenetic and cultural/historical variables involved in the given developmental change. The recognition of such pluralism and relativism aids
the attachment researcher in the formulation of appropriate research
questions.

Previously, we noted that much attachment research has been devoted
to assessing such things as whether or not there are sex differences in
infant attachment, or whether the mother or the father is the major
attachment figure. However, from a pluralistic and relativistic perspective
such research is based on inappropriate questions. The life-span perspective would ask, instead, under which individual, sociocultural, and historical conditions does a given process lead to a given outcome. When
described from a pluralistic, relativistic stance, attachment behaviors
become interdependent, multidirectional phenomena that can be usefully
explicated through careful integration of data derived from a range of
methods.

To illustrate, the studies by Schaffer and Emerson (1964), Ainsworth

(1963, 1964, 1967), and Yarrow (1963, 1964) used different methods and designs to study attachment and employed these procedures in different cultural milieus. Yet, when viewed as an example of pluralistic assessment, and with recognition of the fact that behaviors defining attachment could vary in relation to the diversity of methods, concepts, and settings employed, the integration of such studies has the potential of providing convergent and discriminant validation (Campbell & Fiske, 1959) of developmental trends in attachment processes. These studies did, in fact, while each employing a unique theory and measurement strategy, *all* find a phase of undifferentiated social responsiveness preceding a phase of differentiated and discriminating social responsiveness. Thus, they together provide compelling convergent validation of an attachment transition process precisely because of their utilization of pluralistic theories, methods, and contexts.

C. SEARCH FOR ATTACHMENT DEVELOPMENTAL SEQUENCES

Pluralism and descriptive relativism not only compel the attachment researcher to be open to conceptual and methodological diversity, but also enhance the identification of numerous sequences in attachment development. Thus, the above convergence among the data of Schaffer and Emerson (1964), Ainsworth (1963, 1964, 1967), and Yarrow (1963, 1964) provide evidence for one such attachment sequence. The previously described data reported by Lewis *et al.* (1972), indicating that proximity-seeking behaviors are replaced at succeeding developmental points with distal attachment behaviors, represents another.

While a general search for sequences in attachment development has not been a prime goal among most researchers, extrapolation of potential sequences from the existing attachment literature may be a catalyst for future investigators. Since we have provided evidence that attachment represents a life-span transformational phenomenon, involving both continuity and discontinuity, it appears useful to speculate about the sequences involved in such attachment transformations. In this respect the Weinraub *et al.* (1977) idea of attachment as a social network phenomenon may be appropriate. These authors contend that most existing conceptualizations of attachment are restrictive in limiting most attachment behavior to an infant–parent dyad. They contend that this dyad is inevitably embedded in a larger social network, with *both* members of the dyad showing attachment behaviors to many other members of the network. Consequently, transitions may be identified such that behaviors shown by a child to a parent no longer represent the major attachment behaviors shown to an attachment figure; rather other behaviors, shown to other social network members, may be more salient indices of attachment.

1. The Behavior-Change Process

The above findings and speculations converge in suggesting that not only may sequences in attachment development be identified, but that they may be related to variables embedded in social and cultural contexts. As such, the study of attachment development may profitably proceed through descriptions of behavior-change processes related to either ontogenetic or social/historical events. Although such research may proceed along several lines, we will focus here on the use of the birth-cohort variable in exploration of behavior-change attachment processes.

The birth-cohort variable, with its ties to sociocultural and historical variables, has been virtually ignored in all research and interpretations in the attachment literature (cf. Ainsworth, 1973; Maccoby & Masters, 1970). The attempts to discover genetically biased (Bowlby, 1969) *and/or* environmentally controlled (Gewirtz, 1972) "universals" of attachment phenomena have failed to systematically consider the historical relativism of these phenomena. For instance, Martin (1964), in a study of nursery school children of four different birth cohorts, found a significant increase in absolute frequencey of dependency responses for one group, while finding no such change for the other three groups. While this difference may have been due to many sources, one potential interpretation might have focused on variation in historically related variables between the change and no-change groups. Yet, a failure by Martin to recognize that the four age groups represented different birth cohorts resulted in an omission of consideration of the impact of historical change.

Even though the interface between social scientific and historical analyses may be difficult and often post hoc, the attachment literature abounds with largely unaccounted for differences among groups (both within and between studies), which may be due, in part, to cohort variation. Ainsworth (1963, 1964, 1967), in fact, provides data indicating that components of behavior-change processes involved in attachment do vary in relation to sociocultural as well as cohort variables, but systematic consideration of these apparent dependencies is omitted. Thus, among Uganda children studied longitudinally in the late 1950s/early 1960s, stranger anxiety was seen. Yet, in an American sample, studied in the late 1960s/early 1970s, Ainsworth (1973) reported that most infants did not show stranger anxiety. While the variation might have been attributed to cultural differences, cohort variation is also a potential explanation.

Although systematic assessment of processes linked to specific birth cohorts, as they exist in particular sociocultural settings, may clearly be useful in accounting for variation in attachment phenomena, consistent awareness of the birth-cohort variable may have other uses. Recognition that findings of particular studies may be embedded in cohort-specific relations allows us to prospect about future, historically linked process changes represented by the cohort variable. For example, Lamb's (1975) report that significant attachment behaviors are shown to both mothers and fathers (in a similar number of different attachment categories) by male and female infants may highlight the changing role of fathers in current and future historical epochs. Alternatively, Blehar's (1974) findings that among 2- and 3-year olds in full-time group day care centers there were qualitative disturbances in mother–child relations not seen in a comparatively aged sample of home-reared children, may represent a maternal- and child- birth-cohort-specific phenomenon embedded in a particular historical era possibly no longer relevant to women and children developing in today's historical setting (see Hoffman, 1974).

2. Establishing Developmental Linkages

Although few attempts have been made by attachment researchers to extend developmental change processes through succeeding age, event, or historical periods, the utility of such integration for a thorough understanding of ontogeny is obvious. Consequently, we may illustrate the utility of establishing developmental linkages by integrating the data from already existing studies of attachment.

Although employing somewhat different methodologies and measures, the studies by Maccoby and Feldman (1972) and by Coates *et al.* (1972b) provide convergent findings indicating the stability of a proximity-seeking component of attachment behavior in an interage linkage spanning from 10 months through 3 years. Similarly, the Coates *et al.* (1972a) study provides results which can be integrated with the data from the study by Gershaw and Schwartz (1971), despite the fact that the latter investigation used a quite different method and different indices of attachment. Both studies converge in indicating increases in distress in mother-absent conditions, and thereby allow for an ontogenetic linkage to be established for this component of attachment, here from 10 months to 2 years.

The above studies (Coates *et al.*, 1972a, 1972b; Gershaw & Schwartz, 1971; Maccoby & Feldman, 1972) did not use the same sort of variables and/or modes of data analysis. Yet, their data converged and, as such, were useful in establishing interage networks. However, even if the data as presented by these researchers did not serve to establish this, that same data, when analyzed by different means, could serve such a function. Emmerich (1964, 1966), for instance, showed the utility of employing contrasting data analytic techniques for data previously analyzed by other means. His reanalysis of Martin's (1964) longitudinal data through use of multivariate procedures (factor analysis) found stable individual differences enabling one to predict a 5-year-old's behavior from behavior seen at age 3, but not in the sense of predictability (continuity) of the "same" behavior, and again, as such, illustrates the transformational nature of attachment behavior-change processes.

Similarly, although failing to employ the appropriate control groups, the Martin (1964) study involved four short-term longitudinal sequences and provided a matrix of observations consistent with that derived from a longitudinal sequential study. Accordingly, Martin's data could be further analyzed to assess the relative contributions of age, birth cohort, and time of measurement to the findings reported by Emmerich (1964, 1966).

Thus, reanalysis and/or integration of data can not only be useful in assessing the relative contributions of the components of developmental change functions but, as illustrated by Emmerich's (1964, 1966) work, may be helpful in identifying when various combinations of continuity–discontinuity and stability–instability (Lerner, 1976) characterize development. These pluralistic "tools," in combination with the others we have described as representative of the life-span approach to human development, will enable identification of intraindividual transformations in behavior-change processes (as in the changing salience of dependency for males and females, respectively, from their first years of life to their young adulthood, as reported by Kagan & Moss, 1962), as well as allow for understanding of the differential impact of people's changing world on the long-term development of these processes.

In addition, the life-span view enriches understanding of the *ontogenetic* changes involved in attachment behavior. Interpersonal relationships beyond those involved in the early infant–caregiver dyad characteristically emerge in later childhood (e.g., involving, the same-sex "gang"), in adolescence (e.g., involving the heterosexual peer group), in young adulthood (where in-laws may be involved), in middle adulthood (e.g., involving colleagues and neighbors), and in the aged years (e.g., involving other retirees). Certainly, the behaviors used to initiate, maintain, and terminate relationships at such different ontogenetic points may differ. For example, dating relationships during adolescence are initiated with behaviors different from those used in initiating later marriage relationships (a ceremony is involved), and terminating the former type of relationship certainly involves behaviors different than those in the latter (wherein suing for divorce is involved). Nevertheless, ontogenetic linkages can be made on the basis of such behaviors which, while different in content, subserve functions which are descriptively similar; furthermore, linkages may be established in that affective reactions (e.g., distress) seen in regard to parameters of attachment (relationship termination) may remain similar despite ontogenetic variation in the basis of the parameter; for example, in childhood a best friend's moving from the neighborhood, while in middle adulthood, divorce or separation, and in aged years, death of a spouse or companion may result in distress.

D. IMPLICATIONS FOR DESIGNS OF DESCRIPTIVE ATTACHMENT RESEARCH

As indicated above, a life-span analysis of attachment not only involves a search for developmental sequences, an appraisal of behavior-change processes, and the establishment of ontogenetic linkages, but such objectives coalesce to indicate that these descriptions may best be understood by a dynamic utilization of the array of theories, methods, and analytic tools available. In fact, our application of the life-span view to the description of attachment phenomena has been based on an integration of data derived from such diverse, pluralistic sources.

However, in addition to using the integrative data derived from diverse methodologies and research designs, the descriptive identification of ontogenetic and evolutionary/historical events involved in attachment behavior-change processes has reciprocal import for the advancement of the methods and designs used to study these processes. The clearest instance of such import involves the inclusion of an event-cohort dimension, instead of a birth-cohort one, in the design of sequential research.

The birth-cohort variable has the same status as does the age variable in developmental research (see Baltes *et al.*, 1977a) and, as such, is a "to-be-replaced" variable. That is, when a birth-cohort effect is found it must be further related to the underlying processes or events affecting the differing cohorts and thereby producing diverse outcomes. Thus, the birth-cohort variable, as currently used in the sequential research strategies of life-span research (see Baltes *et al.*, 1977a), will eventually be replaced by "event"-cohort or "process"-cohort variables *if* this sequential research is to be successful and pluralistic in providing information regarding the dynamics of individual and social change.

Clarifications of developmental processes in attachment that may be made by substitution of the event-cohort concept for that of birth cohort may be illustrated in a study by Schaffer and Emerson (1964). They followed 60 Scottish infants longitudinally in an attempt to discover if infants who show the most intense attachments at one age remain more intense than other infants as they grow older. All relations were low in initial correlation of intensity scores for successive chronological ages (e.g., scores for children at age 6 months were correlated with their scores when they were age 7 months). However, when children were grouped by *an event*—onset of the first specific attachment—and correlations were then computed on the basis of the number of months that has passed since the onset of this event, moderate levels (e.g., significant *rho*s from .32–.61) of short-term consistency emerged. Similarly, Schaffer and Emerson found that month-to-month consistency in nonspecific attachments was higher than the correspondingly measured consistency for specific attachments, but again only when the children were grouped in terms of their event cohort (onset of specific attachment) and not in terms of their chronological time of birth. Thus, to encompass the full potential of life-span process-oriented research, attention must be given to expanding the cohort variable beyond the confines of age and birth.

However, the life-span view of attachment behavior has implications for the design of descriptive research which extend beyond those involved with the event-cohort variable. As indicated in the preceding section, linkages may be established across ontogeny among behaviors which differ in content but either subserve the same function and/or maintain the same emotional valence. Accordingly, research designed to describe the course of transformations in the behaviors used to represent attachments across the life span, and the relationships wherein emotional attachments are expressed, is necessary to enrich understanding of the range of dyadic and network relationships representative of attachment behavior within and between ontogenetic periods (cf. Weinraub *et al.*, 1977). For instance, such research may determine if a person who expresses a particular type of attachment at one ontogenetic period (e.g., high contact-maintaining behavior toward a caregiver in infancy) shows more or less of an analogous attachment behavior at a later ontogenetic period (e.g., high proximity maintenance toward a companion or a spouse in early adulthood; see Kagan & Moss, 1962), or if individual differences in the emotions shown in regard to attachment at one portion of the life span (e.g., high separation distress in early childhood) are maintained at later parts of the life course (e.g., when a spouse leaves or dies) or are attenuated due to a refocus of attachment behavior on alternative figures in the social network (e.g., grandchildren).

E. EXPLANATION OF ATTACHMENT DEVELOPMENTAL CHANGE

Application of life-span thinking to the explanation of developmental changes in attachment behavior may enrich and add precision to accounts of change both within and between individuals across time. However, contrary to the situation regarding the utility of the life-span view for the description of attachment changes, there are few examples in the existing attachment literature pertaining to life-span explanatory perspectives. While this situation will necessitate our being more speculative in regard to explanation than to description, the utility of the life-span view will be illustrated precisely in its ability to reorder attachment phenomena through advancing and altering existing explanatory accounts.

1. Conceptual Clarifications and Advances

Corresponding to portions of Section III of this chapter, we will indicate four conceptual clarifications in the explanation of attachment phenomena provided through application of the life-span view.

a. The Age Variable. As indicated earlier, life-span attention to explanation has clarified that age, as well as other major demographic variables, is a noncausal variable. Thus, while age is seen as a marker variable that must eventually be explicited by underlying behavioral processes, such thinking has not been generally applied to attachment research.

To illustrate, Cohen (1974) details the research controversy surrounding the issue of the age of onset of selective crying in infants. Based on the assumption that determination of this index will serve to explicate attachment development, numerous studies have been designed to discover the youngest age showing such selective responding and/or to confirm a previous discovery (e.g., see Cohen & Campos, 1974; Fleener & Cairns, 1970; Kotelchuck, 1973; Schaffer & Emerson, 1964; Stayton *et al.*, 1973). In so doing, such research has neglected to search for processes covarying with age which may more thoroughly account for the emergence of such selective responding. Consequently, reports (Wolff, 1963) indicating that the emergence of selective responding, such as smiling, may be associated with particular types of interactive behaviors, such as vocalization, with particular attachment figures, such as mothers, have been generally ignored in attempts to explain attachment development. Other independent data (Stayton *et al.*, 1973) also suggest the prominence of such interactions at early portions of infancy (Cohen, 1974). Thus, although little emphasis has been given to clarifying the processes underlying age-related attachment developments, the data do suggest rich possibilities.

b. Continuity/Discontinuity. The life-span view has emphasized that both continuous and discontinuous explanatory perspectives may be necessary to completely account for behavior-change processes across the entire life course. Such a combination appears equally necessary to explicate attachment processes as they occur during infancy. Ainsworth (1973), for instance, suggests that while the very initial emergence of attachment behaviors may be explained by genetically biased processes (Bowlby, 1969), subsequent attachment behavior can best be accounted for by nurture-based principles of social learning (e.g., Gewirtz, 1972, 1976). Similarly, Huston-Stein and Baltes (1976) point out that while the first appearance of attachment-related behaviors (e.g., smiling) may be a function of maturation, the succeeding development associated with the behavior may primarily involve environmental stimulation and reinforcement.

   c. Origins of Developmental Change. Although we have indicated that existing attachment research may be construed as consistent with attempts to descriptively clarify the roles of age, birth cohort, and time (see our above discussion of Martin, 1964), no attachment research has been conducted to date with the goal of ascribing the variance in attachment-change processes associated with historical/evolutionary variables. Explanatory research designed to ascertain the contributions of such historical processes may, however, be forthcoming, given recent theoretical accounts of attachment as a social network phenomenon (Lewis & Feiring, in press; Weinraub *et al.,* 1977). These accounts view humans as necessarily embedded from birth in more than an infant–caregiver dyad. Infants are embedded in a social network which, in turn, varies as a function of the larger historical and cultural context. Such views are currently leading to research (Lewis & Feiring, in press) which assesses attachment development in its dependence on historically changing social network patterns.

   d. Dynamic Explanations. With such current theoretical stress on the embeddedness of developmental change in sociocultural and historical processes, the dynamic interplay between ontogenetic and cultural/historical variables involved in attachment development are brought to the fore. In fact, a recent review of research pertaining to the social world of the infant (Lamb, 1977) has stressed the need to employ explanations which emphasize the dynamic, reciprocal interaction between the young child and its social milieu. Such dynamic explanations appear necessary to account for reciprocal shaping processes throughout the entire life span as well (Lamb, 1977; Lerner & Spanier, in press).

2. Pluralism and Explanatory Relativism

   As previously indicated, the life-span perspectives of pluralism and explanatory relativism lead to a recognition of the need for multiple accounts of behavior-change processes derived from diverse theoretical positions. In short, a multiplicity of explanatory paradigms may be both useful and necessary to understand developmental change.

   The attachment literature illustrates the potential of such an approach.

Yarrow (1963, 1964), for example, reports that the development of attachment is predicated on visual discrimination learning *and* on the development of the schema of object permanency. Accordingly, an integration of ideas associated with social learning (Gewirtz, 1972) and cognitive developmental theory (Kohlberg, 1966; Piaget, 1970) appears necessary. Another instance of the need to use multiple theoretical systems to completely account for attachment data may be drawn from the extensive work indicating that reciprocal appetitive system maintaining and aversive system reducing (Bell, 1974) interrelations must be established between infant and caregiver in order for appropriate infant (and in some cases, caregiver) development to proceed (Ainsworth, 1973; Bell, 1974). To adequately understand the initiation, maintenance, and termination of these reciprocal social relations, one may need to utilize concepts from both the psychoanalytic and ethological forms of instinct theory. In addition, it seems necessary to employ explanations derived from social exchange research on the rewarding characteristics of behavioral reciprocities (Homans, 1974), and from organismically derived research stressing infant-produced maternal hormones which maintain the mother's reciprocities (Rosenblatt, Turkewitz, & Schneirla, 1961). Thus, pluralism and relativism emerge, not only as contributions to explaining attachment behaviors, but as prerequisites to thoroughly so doing.

3. Implications for Design of Explanatory Research

As the conceptual clarifications and advances of the life-span view of developmental explanation contribute to the study of attachment development, a broadening of the strategies for and designs of explanatory research will necessarily ensue. Research will have to be planned to incorporate the design and explanatory traditions of diverse theoretical perspectives (e.g., see Hultsch, Nesselroade, & Plemons, 1976), and sequential and multivariate research will be necessary in order to evaluate the explanatory roles of the multiplicity of variables contributing to developmental change functions. Moreover, given that attachment is a transformational behavior, and as such its quality and extendedness is not finalized in early development, complete explanatory research programs will have to encompass the life course and should deal with issues relevant to accounting for attachment transformations.

For example, one such issue involves determination of the equivalence of attachment behaviors across the life span, despite the transformations in such behaviors across time. Rather than pursue "life-span fair tools" (Knudtson, 1976), which fail to capture the significance of life-span strategies, one must ask what would be gained if it could be determined that an attached child (measured by one instrument) was the same as an attached adult (measured by another form of the same measurement). Given that the two operate in completely different contexts, the finding would be essentially meaningless. If, however, one could substantiate that a successful mother/child attachment experience, while operationally different from a subsequent relationship, was conceptually related to and therefore predictive of a successful husband/wife relationship, progress would have been made. The most useful information gained would come not so much from measurement equivalence but from focusing on how and why multiple measures must be modified to be relevant from one age to the next. We, therefore, endorse the assessment of behavior-change processes through *systematic variation* rather then systematic equation (see Bitterman, 1960).

To illustrate, the attachment literature in infancy has drawn on bodily propinquity, gazing, mimicry, and touching measures, all primarily derived from observer frequency counts, while in adulthood the measures have changed to residential contiguity, frequency of face-to-face visiting, quality of relationships, and shared family rituals, values, and norms, primarily obtained from phenomenological inquiry (Hartup & Lempers, 1973; Troll & Smith, 1976). These measurement differences contain much more information than the sheer quantification of discrepant attachment behaviors. They suggest the sequential presence of important socialization processes in which one learns to discriminate the appropriate modes of attachment expressions from one age to the next, they reveal the transformational nature of the attachment concept, and they illustrate that a multiplicity of potential developmental patterns and sequences of attachment may exist. Research designed to understand these implications leaves one well on the way toward explaining the content and form of the transitional processes that constitute the basis of attachment across the life span.

F.   ATTACHMENT AND THE LIFE-SPAN VIEW FOR DEVELOPMENTAL INTERVENTION

1.   Attachment and Basic Assumptions of Life-Span Intervention

Attachment phenomena are exemplars of behavior-change processes amenable to the life-span view for developmental intervention. Given the plasticity as well as the sociocultural and historical dependency of attachment-change processes (Lamb, 1977; Weinraub *et al.,* 1977) and their transformational qualities across the life span, strategies may be designed for implementation at any one or all of these change levels. For example, proximity- or contact-producing behaviors may be maintained, extinguished, or replaced with alternative (e.g., distal, attachment-related) behaviors depending on the goals and values of the interventionist, the portion of the life cycle being studied, and the level of change process of concern. This general possibility may be illustrated through specification of the targets, timing, and mechanisms of intervention.

2. *Targets, Timing, and Mechanisms of Intervention*

a. Targets. Since attachment may not be expressed by a single behavior class either within or between developmental periods, but rather can be expected to show situational and life course transformations (Weinraub *et al.,* 1977), an almost infinite array of behaviors become potential targets. While the choice of a given behavior may essentially be dependent on the idiosyncratic predilection of the interventionist, a crucial component of the life-span view of intervention is that any target behavior is embedded in sociocultural and historical milieus. As such, target behaviors at any point in the ontogenetic span should be chosen in recognition of such embeddedness.

For example, American mothers are more likely than are Japanese mothers to use distal behaviors to interact with their 3-month-old infants (Caudill & Weinstein, 1969). Japanese mothers, on the other hand, tend to use proximal behaviors for interaction with their infants (Weinraub *et al.,* 1977). Similarly, at later portions of the life span it may be less likely to see a father of Anglo-Saxon descent expressing affection to a grown son through such proximal behaviors as kissing than is the case with a father of Mediterranean (e.g., Italian) descent (Weinraub *et al.,* 1977, p. 35). Thus, the interventionist must understand the expression of attachment behaviors across the life span as they are dynamically embedded in such sociocultural contexts.

b. Timing. Recognition of the cultural and historical embeddedness of ontogentic transformation in the expression of attachment leads to an illustration of the timing parameter for life-span intervention. Modifications of particular attachment behaviors (e.g., proximal behaviors such as kissing) may involve relatively long-term (historical) change paradigms; for example, interventions aimed at the sociocultural level, and designed to alter the sex role prescriptions involving adult male–adult male affectional interactions, may be instituted to increase the probability of such behavior. Alternatively, relatively shorter term or even concurrent change paradigms may be instituted—through reinforcement procedures derived from social learning views of attachment (e.g., see Gewirtz, 1972, 1976); these paradigms may also be designed to affect the dyadic or social network level of analysis in order to alter the probability of the target behavior.

c. Mechanisms. Our illustrations of the variation in the timing of intervention strategies also indicated that an array of techniques may be used to modify attachment behavior. Mechanisms for producing change may range from alterations of the schedules of reinforcement for attachment behavior in one individual to modification, redesign, or invention of new social institutions fostering attachment to numerous figures involved in a broad social network (e.g., day care centers for the young and retirement communities for the aged).

As implied above, however, such mechanisms must be selected in recognition of the cultural meaning attached to particular target behaviors at different ontogenetic times. Thus, attachment behaviors designed to be acquired or maintained at particular ontogenetic segments may have to be extinguished or redirected to alternative figures. In early infancy it may be appropriate, for example, to design intervention strategies to increase the probability of proximal attachment behaviors to one or a few specific others. However, as a transformation in attachment occurs during later infancy (cf. Weinraub *et al.,* 1977), and distal attachment behaviors supercede proximal ones, the goal of intervention might be to extinguish proximal behaviors while insuring acquisition of distal behaviors to the same figures. Still later, in childhood, it may be necessary to design strategies to maintain distal attachment behaviors, although to different attachment figures (e.g., day care workers). Finally, during the adult and aged years the interventionist might once again institute procedures to alter attachment figures, as well as to employ paradigms involving the extinction of particular types of distal attachment behaviors (e.g., direct vocalization, looking) and the acquisition of still other forms of such behaviors (e.g., letter writing, telephoning).

VII. Conclusions

The conceptual, theoretical, and methodological diversity of the attachment literature has allowed us to illustrate the essence of life-span thinking. Application and implementation of this view of human development does not insure tidy capsules tying life-span phases together. Rather, it provides a fuller recognition of the complexities involved in describing, explaining, or modifying behavior at any given ontogenetic point. The life-span framework does not provide superordinate tools to integrate the whole of ontogenetic change and development, but instead demands more broadened thinking and pluralistic research about the dynamics of change, and thus brings us closer to gazing through our social scientific lenses with accuracy and precision. Life-span applications enrich, they do not simplify.

Indeed, within any one single content area, the possibilities for, and potential parameters of, life-span research seem endless. Even more attractive than the wide array of opportunity, however, is the realization that each individual effort is a part of a larger, unifying perspective, and that findings will not drift into isolated disuse but will bring developmentalists one study nearer a holistic understanding of the ontogenetic and social change processes involved in human behavior across the life span.

References

Ainsworth, M. D. S. Patterns of attachment behavior shown by the infant in interaction B. M. Foss (Ed.), *Determinants of infant behavior* (Vol. 2). New York: Wiley, 1963.

Ainsworth, M. D. S. Patterns of attachment behavior shown by the infant in interaction with his mother. *Merrill-Palmer Quarterly,* 1964, **10,** 51–58.

Ainsworth, M. D. S. *Infancy in Uganda: Infant care and the growth of love.* Baltimore: Johns Hopkins University Press, 1967.

Ainsworth, M. D. S. The development of infant-mother attachment. In B. M. Caldwell & H. N. Ricciuti (Eds.), *Review of child development research* (Vol. 3). Chicago: University of Chicago Press, 1973.

Antonucci, T. Attachment: A life-span concept. *Human Development,* 1976, **19,** 135–142.

Baer, D. M. An age-irrelevant concept of development. *Merrill-Palmer Quarterly,* 1970, **16,** 238–246.

Baltes, P. B. Longitudinal and cross-sectional sequences in the study of age and generation effects. *Human Development,* 1968, **11,** 145–171.

Baltes, P. B. Prototypical paradigms and questions in life-span research on development and aging. *Gerontologist,* 1973, **13,** 458–467.

Baltes, P. B., Baltes, M. M., & Reinert, G. The relationship between time of measurement and age in cognitive development of children: An application of cross-sectional sequences. *Human Development,* 1970, **13,** 258–268.

Baltes, P. B., Cornelius, S. W., & Nesselroade, J. R. Cohort effects in developmental psychology: Theoretical and methodological perspectives. In W. A. Collins (Ed.), *Minnesota Symposium on Child Psychology* (Vol. II). Minneapolis: University of Minnesota, 1977. (a)

Baltes, P. B., & Goulet, L. R. Status and issues of a life-span developmental psychology. In L. R. Goulet & P. B. Baltes (Eds.), *Life-span developmental psychology: Research and theory.* New York: Academic Press, 1970.

Baltes, P. B., & Goulet, L. R. Exploration of developmental variables by manipulation and simulation of age differences in behavior. *Human Development,* 1971, **14,** 149–170.

Baltes, P. B., & Labouvie, G. V. Adult development of intellectual performance: Description, explanation, and modification. In C. Eisdorfer & M. P. Lawton (Eds.), *The psychology of adult development and aging.* Washington, D.C.: American Psychological Association, 1973.

Baltes, P. B., & Nesselroade, J. R. The developmental analysis of individual differences on multiple measures. In J. R. Nesselroade & H. W. Reese (Eds.), *Life-span developmental psychology: Methodological issues.* New York: Academic Press, 1973.

Baltes, P. B., Reese, H. W., & Nesselroade, J. R. *Life-span developmental psychology: Introduction to research methods.* Monterey, Calif: Brooks-Cole, 1977. (b)

Baltes, P. B., & Reinert, G. Cohort effects in cognitive development of children as revealed by cross-sectional sequences. *Developmental Psychology,* 1969, **1,** 169–177.

Baltes, P. B., & Schaie, K. W. On life-span developmental research paradigms: Retrospects and prospects. In P. B. Baltes & K. W. Schaie (Eds.), *Life-span developmental psychology: Personality and socialization.* New York: Academic Press, 1973.

Baltes, P. B., & Schaie, K. W. On the plasticity of intelligence in adulthood and old age: Where Horn and Donaldson fail. *American Psychologist,* 1976, **31,** 720–725

Baltes, P. B. & Willis, S. L. Toward psychological theories of aging and development. In J. E. Birren & K. W. Schaie (Eds.), *Handbook of the psychology of aging.* New York: Reinhold-Van Nostrand, 1977.

Ban, P., & Lewis, M. Mothers and fathers, girls and boys: Attachment behavior in the one-year-old. *Merrill-Palmer Quarterly,* 1974, **20,** 195–204.

Bell, R. Q. Contributions of human infants to caregiving and social interaction. In M. Lewis & L. A. Rosenblum (Eds.), *The effect of the infant on its caregiver.* New York: Wiley, 1974.

Bijou, S. W., & Baer, D. M. *Child development: Universal stage of infancy* (Vol. 2). Englewood Cliffs, N.J.: Prentice-Hall, 1965.

Birren, J. E. (Ed.). *Relations of development and aging.* Springfield, Ill.: Thomas, 1964.

Bischof, N. A systems approach toward the functional connections of attachment and fear. *Child Development,* 1975, **46,** 801–817.

Bitterman, M. E. Toward a comparative psychology of learning. *American Psychologist,* 1960, **15,** 704–712.

Blehar, M. C. Anxious attachment and defensive reactions associated with day care. *Child Development,* 1974, **45,** 683–692.

Bloom, B. B. *Stability and change in human characteristics.* New York: Wiley, 1964.

Bortner, R. W. Personality and social psychology in the study of aging. *Gerontologist,* 1967, **7,** 23–36.

Botwinick, J. *Aging and behavior.* New York: Springer, 1973.

Bowlby, J. *Attachment and loss* (Vol. 1). New York: Basic Books, 1969.

Britton, J. H., & Britton, J. O. *Personality changes in aging.* New York: Springer, 1972.

Buhler, C., & Massarik, F. (Eds.), *The course of human life.* New York: Springer, 1968.

Buss, A. R. Generational analysis: Description, explanation, and theory. *Journal of Social Issues,* 1974, **30,** 55–71.

Busse, E. W. Theories of aging. In E. W . Busse & E. Pfeiffer (Eds.), *Behavior and adaptation in late life.* Boston: Little, Brown, 1969.

Campbell, D. T., & Fiske, D. Convergent and discriminant validation by the multitrait-multimethod matrix. *Psychological Bulletin,* 1959, **56,** 81–105.

Caudill, W., & Weinstein, H. Maternal care and infant behavior in Japan and America. *Psychiatry,* 1969, **32,** 12–43.

Coates, B., Anderson, E . P., & Hartup, W. W. Interrelations in the attachment behavior of human infants. *Developmental Psychology,* 1972, **6,** 218–230. (a)

Coates, B., Anderson, E. P., & Hartup, W. W. The stability of attachment behaviors in the human infant. *Developmental Psychology,* 1972, **6,** 231–237. (b)

Cohen, L. J. The operational definition of human attachment. *Psychological Bulletin,* 1974, **81,** 207–217.

Cohen, L. J., & Campos, J. J. Father, mother, and stranger as elicitors of attachment behaviors in infancy. *Developmental Psychology,* 1974, **10,** 146–154.

Datan, N., & Ginsberg, L. H. (Eds.), *Life-span developmental psychology: Normative life crises.* New York: Academic Press, 1975.

Dohrenwend, B. S., & Dohrenwend, B. P. (Eds.), *Stressful life events.* New York: Wiley, 1974.

Emmerich, W. Continuity and stability in early social development. *Child Development,* 1964, **35,** 311-332.

Emmerich, W. Continuity and stability in early social development: II. Teacher's ratings. *Child Development,* 1966, **37,** 17-27.

Erikson, E. H. Identity and the life cycle. *Psychological Issues,* 1959, **1,** 18-164.

Erikson, E. H. *Childhood and society* (Rev. ed.). New York: Norton, 1963.

Flavell, J. H. Cognitive changes in adulthood. In L. R. Goulet & P. B. Baltes (Eds.), *Life-span developmental psychology: Research and theory.* New York: Academic Press, 1970.

Fleener, D. E., & Cairns, R. B. Attachment behaviors in human infants: Discriminative vocalization on maternal separation. *Developmental Psychology,* 1970, **2,** 215-223.

Fraiberg, S. The development of human attachments in infants blind from birth. *Merrill-Palmer Quarterly,* 1975, **21,** 315-334.

Freud, S. *Outline of psychoanalysis.* New York: Norton, 1949.

Gershaw, N. J., & Schwartz, C. The effects of a familiar toy and mother's presence on exploratory and attachment behaviors in young children. *Child Development,* 1971, **42,** 1662-1666.

Gewirtz, J. L. Attachment, dependence, and a distinction in terms of stimulus control. In J. L. Gewirtz (Ed.), *Attachment and dependency.* Washington, D.C. Winston, 1972.

Gewirtz, J. L. The attachment acquisition process as evidenced in the maternal conditioning of cued infant responding (particularly crying). *Human Development,* 1976, **19,** 143-155.

Gottesman, L. E. Milieu treatment of the aged in institutions. *Gerontologist,* 1973, **13,** 23-26.

Goulet, L. R., & Baltes, P. B. (Eds.), *Life-span developmental psychology: Research and theory.* New York: Academic Press, 1970.

Hall, G. S. *Senescence, the last half of life.* New York: Appleton, 1922.

Hartup, W. W., & Lempers, J. A problem in life-span development: The interactional analysis of family attachments. In P. B. Baltes & K. W. Schaie (Eds.), *Life-span developmental psychology: Personality and socialization.* New York: Academic Press, 1973.

Hoffman, L. W. Effects of maternal employment on the child—A review of the research. *Developmental Psychology,* 1974, **10,** 204-228.

Homans, G. C. *Social behavior: Its elementary forms* (Rev. ed.). New York: Harcourt, 1974.

Hoyer, W. J. Application of operant techniques to the modification of elderly behavior. In P. B. Baltes (Ed.), Strategies for psychological intervention in old age: A symposium. *Gerontologist,* 1973, **13,** 18-23.

Hultsch, D. F., Nesselroade, J. R., & Plemons, J. K. Learning-ability relations in adulthood. *Human Development,* 1976, **19,** 234-247.

Huston-Stein, A., & Baltes, P. B. Theory and method in life-span developmental psychology: Implications for child development. In H. W. Reese & L. P. Lipsitt (Eds.), *Advances in child development and behavior* (Vol.11). New York: Academic Press. 1976.

Jacobs, A. Strategies of social intervention. Past and future. In A. Jacobs & W. Spradlin (Eds.), *The group as agent of change.* Chicago: Aldine, 1972.

Kagan, J. The three faces of continuity in human development. In D. A. Goslin (Ed.), *Handbook of socialization theory and research.* Chicago: Rand McNally, 1969.

Kagan, J., & Moss, H. A. *Birth to maturity.* New York: Wiley, 1962.

Kalish, R. A. & Knudtson, F. W. Attachment versus disengagement: A life-span conceptualization. *Human Development,* 1976, **19,** 171-181.

Knudtson, F. W. Life-span attachment: Complexities, questions, considerations. *Human Development*, 1976, **19**, 182–196.

Kohlberg, L. A cognitive developmental analysis of children's sex-role concepts and attitudes. In E. E. Maccoby (Ed.), *The development of sex differences*. Stanford, Calif.: Stanford University Press, 1966.

Kohlberg, L. Stage and sequence: The cognitive-developmental approach to socialization. In D. A. Goslin (Ed.), *Handbook of socialization theory and research*. Chicago: Rand McNally, 1969.

Kotelchuck, M. The nature of the infant's tie to his father. Paper presented at the biennial meeting of the Society for Research in Child Development. Philadelphia, Pennsylvania. March 1973.

Labouvie, G. V. Implications of geropsychological theories for intervention: The challenge for the seventies. In P. B. Baltes (Ed.), Strategies for psychological intervention in old age: A symposium. *Gerontologist*, 1973, **13**, 10–15.

Lamb, M. E. The sociability of two-year-olds with their mothers and fathers. *Child Psychiatry and Human Development*, 1975, **5**, 182–188.

Lamb, M. E. A Re-examination of the infant social world. *Human Development*, 1977, **20**, 65–85.

Leifer, A. D., Leiderman, P. H., Barnett, C. R., & Williams, J. A. Effects of mother-infant separation on maternal attachment behavior. *Child Development*, 1972, **43**, 1203–1218

Lerner, R. M. *Concepts and theories of human development*. Reading, Mass.: Addison-Wesley, 1976.

Lerner, R. M. Nature, nurture, and dynamic interactionism. *Human Development*, 1978, **21**, 1–20.

Lerner, R. M., & Spanier, G. B. (Eds.), *Child influences on maritial and family interaction: A life-span perspective*. New York: Academic Press, in press.

Lewis, M., & Feiring, C. The child's social world. In R. M. Lerner & G. B. Spanier (Eds.), *Child influences on marital and family interaction: A life-span perspective*. New York: Academic Press, in press.

Lewis, M., Weinraub, M., & Ban, P. *Mothers and fathers, girls and boys: Attachment behavior in the first two years of life* (Res. Bull. RB-72-60). Princeton, N.J.: Educational Testing Service, 1972.

Looft, W. R. Reflections on intervention in old age: Motives, goals, and assumptions. *Gerontologist*, 1973, **13**, 6–10.

Maccoby, E. E., & Feldman, S. S. Mother-attachment and stranger-reactions in the third year of life. *Monographs of the Society for Research in Child Development*, 1972, **37**(1, Serial No. 146).

Maccoby, E. E., & Masters, J. C. Attachment and dependency. In P. H. Mussen (Ed.), *Carmichael's Manual of Child Psychology* (Vol. 2). New York: Wiley, 1970.

Martin, W. Singularity and stability of social behavior. In C. B. Stendler (Ed.), *Readings in child behavior and development*. New York: Harcourt, Brace, 1964.

Mason, W. A., & Kenney, M. D. Redirection of filial attachments in rhesus monkeys: Dogs as mother surrogates. *Science*, 1974, **183**, 1209–1211.

Masters, J. C., & Wellman, H. M. The study of human infant attachment: A procedural critique. *Psychological Bulletin*, 1974, **81**, 218–237.

Mischel, W. A. A social learning view of sex differences in behavior. In E. E. Maccoby (Ed.), *The development of sex differences*. Stanford, Calif: Stanford University Press, 1966.

Nesselroade, J. R., & Baltes, P. B. Adolescent personality development and historical change: 1970–1972. *Monographs of the Society for Research in Child Development*, 1974, **39**(1, Serial No. 154).

Nesselroade, J. R., & Reese, H. W. (Eds.), *Life-span developmental psychology: Methodological issues.* New York: Academic Press, 1973.

Nesselroade, J. R., Schaie, K. W., & Baltes, P. B. Ontogenetic and generational components of structural and quantitative change in adult behavior. *Journal of Gerontology,* 1972, **27**, 222–228.

Neugarten, B. L. Continuities and discontinuities of psychological issues in adult life. *Human Development,* 1969, **12**, 121–130.

Overton, W. F. & Reese, H. W. Models of development: Methodological implications. In J. R. Nesselroade & H. W. Reese (Eds.), *Life-span developmental psychology: Methodological issues.* New York: Academic Press, 1973.

Piaget, J. Piaget's theory. In P. H. Mussen (Ed.), *Carmichael's Manual of Child Psychology* (Vol. 1). New York: Wiley, 1970.

Piaget, J. Intellectual evolution from adolescence to adulthood. *Human Development,* 1972, **15**, 1–12.

Riegel, K. F. Time and change in the development of the individual and society. In H. W. Reese (Ed.), *Advances in child development and behavior* (Vol. 7). New York: Academic Press, 1972.

Riegel, K. F. The dialectics of human development. *American Psychologist,* 1976, **31**, 689–700.

Riegel, K. F., & Riegel, R. M. Development, drop, and death. *Developmental Psychology,* 1972, **6**, 306–319.

Riley, M. W. Age strata in social systems. In R. H. Binstock & E. Shanes (Eds.), *Handbook of aging and the social sciences.* New York: Van Nostrand, 1976.

Riley, M. W., Foner, A., Hess, B., & Toby, M. L. Socialization in the middle and later years. In D. A. Goslin (Ed.), *Handbook of socialization theory and research.* Chicago: Rand McNally, 1969.

Rosenblatt, J. S., Turkewitz, G., & Schneirla, T. C. Early socialization in the domestic cat as based on feeding and other relationships between female and young. In B. M. Foss (Ed.), *Determinants of infant behavior* (Vol. 1). New York: Wiley, 1961.

Ryff, C. D., & Baltes, P. B. Value transitions and adult development in women: The instrumentality-terminality sequence hypothesis. *Developmental Psychology,* 1976, **12**, 567–568.

Schaffer, H. R., & Emerson, P. E. The development of social attachments in infancy. *Monographs of the Society for Research in Child Development,* 1964, **29**(3, Serial No. 94).

Schaie, K. W. A general model for the study of developmental problems. *Psychological Bulletin,* 1965, **64**, 92–107.

Schaie, K. W. A reinterpretation of age-related changes in cognitive structure and functioning. In L. R. Goulet & P. B. Baltes (Eds.), *Life-span developmental psychology: Research and theory.* New York: Academic Press, 1970.

Schaie, K. W., & Baltes, P. B. On sequential strategies in developmental research: Description or explanation? *Human Development,* 1976, **18**, 384–390.

Schaie, K. W., Labouvie, G. V., & Buech, B. U. Generational and cohort-specific differences in adult cognitive functioning: A fourteen-year study of independent samples. *Developmental Psychology,* 1973, **9**, 151–166.

Schaie, K. W. & Strother, C. R. Across-sequential study of age-changes in cognitive behavior. *Psychological Bulletin,* 1968, **70**, 671–680.

Sears, R. R. Attachment, dependency, and frustration. In J. L. Gewirtz (Ed.), *Attachment and dependency.* Washington, D.C.: Winston, 1972.

Sjostrom, K. P., & Pollack, R. H. The effect of simulated receptor aging on two types of visual illusions. *Psychonomic Science,* 1971, **23**, 147–148.

Stayton, D. J., Ainsworth, M. D. S., & Main, M. B. Development of separation behavior in the first year of life: Protest, following, and greeting. *Developmental Psychology,* 1973, **9**, 213–225.

Tobach, E., & Schneirla, T. C. The biopsychology of social behavior of animals. In R. E. Cooke & S. Levin (Eds.), *Biologic basis of pediatric practice.* New York: McGraw-Hill, 1968.

Troll, L. E., & Smith, J. Attachment through the life-span: Some questions about dyadic bonds among adults. *Human Development,* 1976, **19**, 156–170.

Tulkin, S. R. Social class differences in attachment of ten-month-old infants. *Child Development,* 1973, **44**, 171–174.

Weinraub, M., Brooks, J., & Lewis, M. The social network: A reconsideration of the concept of attachment. *Human Development,* 1977, **20**, 31–47.

Werner, H. The concept of development from a comparative and organismic point of view. In D. B. Harris (Ed.), *The concept of development.* Minneapolis: University of Minnesota Press, 1957.

Willemsen, E., Flaherty, D., Heaton, C., & Ritchey, G. Attachment behavior of one-year-olds as a function of mother vs. father, sex of child, session, and toys. *Genetic Psychology Monographs*, 1974, **90**, 305–324.

Wohlwill, J. F. *The study of behavioral development.* New York: Academic Press, 1973.

Wolff, P. H. Observation on the early development of smiling. In B. M. Foss (Ed.), *Determinants of infant behavior* (Vol. 2). New York: Wiley, 1963.

Woodruff, D. S., & Birren, J. E. Training for professionals in the field of aging: Needs, goals, models, and means. In I. N. Mensh & A. N. Schwartz (Eds.), *New professional approaches to the old.* Springfield, Ill.: Thomas, 1973.

Yarrow, L. J. Research in dimensions of early maternal care. *Merrill-Palmer Quarterly,* 1963, **9**, 101–114.

Yarrow, L. J. Separation from parents during early childhood, In M. L. Hoffman & L. W. Hoffman (Eds.), *Reviews of child development research* (Vol. 1). New York: Russell Sage Foundation, 1964.

The Concept of Development from a Systems Perspective

Hugh B. Urban

COLLEGE OF HUMAN DEVELOPMENT,

THE PENNSYLVANIA STATE UNIVERSITY,

UNIVERSITY PARK, PENNSYLVANIA

Abstract

Efforts to explicate developmental processes which characterize the human person have faltered due to ambiguities in the conceptual models which have come to be employed. The use of a systems perspective is advocated as a means of remedy. Such a view permits useful distinctions to be drawn between the phenomena of change, and a subset of those changes defined as developmental. Development is represented in terms of systems transformation, and developmental processes as successive transitional states. An integrative view of the human is made possible by a model of generically distinct subsystems, interrelated by coupling mechanisms, both laterally and vertically organized, acting both concomitantly and sequentially in relation to the passage of time, The merits of such a perspective are described, with special emphasis placed upon its capabilities for serving a synthetic function at the metamodel level, and its long-term prospects of analytic rigor and precision. It is also argued that a systems perspective is particularly suited for dealing with a number of salient issues in theory and method identified by life-span researchers.

I. On Behavior and Human Development

Since his earliest beginnings man has known that he constitutes a complex of differing elements and processes which interrelate with one another in multiform fashion, and that by virtue of such interrelationships he is enabled to operate as an integrated whole. The organizational characteristics of the person which this recognition implies has been widely understood as a general principle; it has been equally understood that such a principle applies to human persons at large, whether one chooses to examine them as they operate on an individual basis, or within the collective patterns of activity which their social groups represent. An inspection of classical literature from Greco-Roman and biblical times, and a tracing of philosophical thought throughout the Western tradition, displays a sustained interest over the centuries in finding useful and satisfactory ways to understand how it is that man functions in complex and integrative fashion, and manages to do so in relation to the complex physical and social contexts under which he is called upon to operate. The search for a coherent knowledge framework which provides an integrative view of the human person as he grows and changes throughout the course of his life, and to characterize in similar fashion the complex and integrated social organizations which he forms to meet his requirements, is hardly an enterprise of recent origin.

The recognition of need, however, does not automatically carry with it an understanding of the means by which it can be accomplished. Despite a vast outpouring of effort, the goal of developing a comprehensive and integrative view of the human person has proven to be elusive. The intricacies of the task have been sufficient to defeat man's best efforts. And yet, extraordinary progress has nonetheless been made.

It has been learned, for example, that man participates in the world of things, and that he is composed of many elements which characterize the physical world, is governed by many established mechanical, electrical, and fluid processes, and is affected by physicochemical influences impinging upon him from his surroundings.

He has also been recognized to be a participant in the domain of living organisms, and to be composed of comparable cellular structures and organ networks, engaged in comparable anabolic and catabolic processes, maintaining membership within similar colonies, and his survival intertwined with other organisms of a nonhuman sort.

But man participates not only within a world of objects, or of organisms, but within a universe of symbols as well (Bertalanffy, 1966). Man's capabiltity for collecting and representing information in symbolic form, and then processing and utilizing that information in multiple ways, constitutes his most distinctive activity; it is therefore of great significance in comprehending man's characteristics, the manner in which he conducts his affairs, and the accomplishments of which he is capable.

Finally, the accomplishments of man are invariably associated with collaborative arrangements. The network of associations which humans form with one another, dictated by their inability to achieve their purposes and objectives in singular fashion, places man invariably within a universe of social structures of staggering variety. These social groupings are effected by man, but in turn come to govern to a great extent what he can and cannot do, or what he does or tends not to do.

Despite the accumulation of masses of information with regard to these various facets of the human person, and the domains in which he participates, it has still not proven possible to find a way to interrelate these findings effectively with one another, and to emerge with a conception of man as an integrated whole.

Part of the difficulty, of course, stems from the manner in which the information has been ordered and collected. Our segmentation of the human into facets of functioning, and our corresponding pursuit of disciplinary inquiries, have generated a collection of disparate frameworks, tools, methods, and conventions for the report of findings. The difficulties have stemmed from more than our disciplinary arrangements and practices, however; how to effect such interrelationships continues to remain unclear. The human sciences simply have not succeeded in representing how man's symbolic and cognitive activities (psyche) interact with his biological structures (soma) in any detailed and useful way. And yet, interrelate they appear to do, since what goes on in one sphere seems to have profound import on occurrences in the other, and the interplay appears to be consistently reciprocal. Efforts to find ways to interrelate the phenomena of the physical and biological domains have been no more successful, reflected in the persistent problem of specifying the

ingredients of life, and understanding the relationship of animate organisms to the inanimate ingredients which go to make them up (Weiss,
1970).

Responses to these dilemmas have, of course, taken many forms. There
are those who propose that the occurrence of events in one sphere is
interpretable in terms of the elements and principles of another; efforts
are made to account for social phenomena in psychological terms or
psychological phenomena in biological or physicochemical terms. Others
have argued that these occurrences constitute different levels of operation, and therefore require concepts and propositions peculiar to each.
Still others have continued with the segmented investigatory approach, in
the belief that in the millennium ways will have been found to effect their
integration.

A variety of efforts toward a synthesis continue to have been made
however. One such effort has been the emergence of "multidisciplinary
approaches." The rise of fields and associations, such as criminology or
gerontology, has been a reflection of such attempts. Too often, however,
these have represented differences which haven't made a difference,
since lapses into traditional formats of inquiry are frequent, due to the
continued absence of effective integrating frameworks.

A comparative newcomer to the province of the human sciences has
been a "field" which has come to designate itself formally as Human
Development. Characteristically espousing a multidisciplinary posture, it
has added a developmental perspective, presuming that more adequate
representations of the human person can be gained by a scrutiny of
"structural and behavioral growth and change from conception to death"
(Harris, 1971). Although the general outlines of the approach have been
pursued since the 1920s and 1930s (Looft, 1972), it remains at an initial
level of development. It is undoubtedly premature to attempt a judgment
as to the utility of such a perspective and its viability as a field despite its
optimistic prospects, outlined by Frank (1963). It has not, of course,
escaped the basic underlying dilemma, since one can hardly trace the
sequences of growth and change over time without first succeeding in
specifying the nature of the phenomenon with which one is concerned.
And thus, the field of human development has inherited all of the difficulties which have plagued the nondevelopmental human sciences with regard to the absence of a unifying comprehensive framework.

Of late, the realization has been developing that these difficulties are a
product of our own making; or, as Hamlet is said to have observed, the
fault lies less in the stars than in ourselves. Human science struggles with
these dilemmas precisely because of the ways in which it has concep-

tualized the phenomena with which it attempts to deal. To the extent that this is the case, a reconceptualization would be in order.

II. Models and Their Use

We have learned that our impressions of objects and events cannot be the same as those occurrences themselves, and that our notions concerning what is and what might be instead, are products of the mind of man himself. We deal not with reality itself, but with symbolic "guesstimates" concerning it (Wymore, 1976). In our efforts to develop understanding, prediction, and control over occurrences, we develop a series of "as-if" constructions as Vaihinger characterized them, parallels to "reality" which are therefore in the nature of analogs. These symbolic representations have come to be termed models.

We have also learned that there are an infinite number of such constructions which are in principle possible; all such constructions, however, will be found to be in error to a greater or lesser degree. At the point of action we operate ideally in terms of that manner of construing which appears to provide for the least expedient error; at times when we are freed from the necessity for practical action, we devote our energies to the refinement of our models in an effort to reduce such error (Popper, 1957). The process of inquiry is one of the abandonment of one model in exchange for another where it is demonstrated to show smaller error; a good model is one which holds together long enough to lead to a better one (Hebb, 1949).

With each individual construction which becomes developed, there are a number of implications peculiar to it. Out of the myriad events with which it is possible to deal, certain ones are specified by the model to be of significance. Conceptual representations for them are developed, conditions for their observation are designed, modes of measurement are constructed, and investigatory strategies evolve. As a result, events are not presented to investigators in the form of givens (data); they are extracted from the ongoing stream of occurrences and construed in a particular way (copta). Facts and theory are inextricably bound (Craik, 1943). Moreover, questions pertinent to one model construction are often simply irrelevant to another. And, each construction implies a methodological strategy, so that differing investigatory procedures will be found to have differential utility depending upon the model undergoing exploration and development.

As a consequence of this process, models of very different character have become formed in varying fields of inquiry. Models of some utility in the explanation, prediction, and control of events in the physical world are in many instances so much at variance with those undergoing development within the biological, psychological, or social domains, that a detailed comparison typically reveals them to be operating within different realms of discourse entirely. Although a certain amount of borrowing between these domains characteristically takes place, and thus some commonalities come to occur, the dominant models which characterize these domains remain so very different in language, structure, procedure, and method that their commonalities are exceedingly difficult to detect, and ways to interrelate them remain obscure.

To compound our difficulties there are hierarchical characteristics associated with our models. Thus, upon inspection, any particular model can be found to fall at some level along a continuum of models, ranging from a level of concreteness and specificity, up to a level of abstractness and generality. First-order models which endeavor to map the world of concrete experience both imply and can be shown to derive from a more general second-order model, which in turn is related to a more encompassing model at still a higher level—on up to the most general order— those epistemological and metaphysical models which speak to one's conceptions of reality in general, and to man's capabilities for apprehending it (Laszlo, 1972). These have been termed metamodels by Reese and Overton (1927), or paradigms and world views in the language of Kuhn (1962).

The extent to which models at lower levels of investigation are governed by such metamodel constructions has often remained unrecognized because of the preoccupation by science with model construction at lower levels of abstraction, and an unwarranted presumption by many that science as a whole was operating within the same paradigmatic frame. As a consequence, the fundamental propositions upon which the subsidiary models were based remained implicit and unstated until subjected to exposure. When this has been done, they have typically been found to be poorly defined and articulated, and to stand in fairly primitive condition.

The process of exposure, however, is a critical one to pursue, since it serves to reveal the variety of paradigms which have characterized the sciences, to highlight not only their differences, but also their underlying incompatibilities, and to elucidate the futility of persistent controversies between investigators when they are found to be working within essentially different paradigmatic frames.

It is possible for such metamodel discrepancies to persist and "peacefully coexist" indefinitely without the problems they generate rising to the fore. As long as they are pursued in comparative isolation from one another and utilized to explicate segmented sets of occurrences, inherent difficulties they may pose stand in abeyance. It is not until the same phenomena are addressed from the vantage point of discrepant paradigms on the one hand, or efforts are made to synthesize a variety of such paradigms into a larger coherent frame on the other, that the complications arising from the incongruities become apparent. Because the effort to frame an effective model for the study of the human and his development has entailed the necessity to try to do both, the field of human development has been forced to deal with the perplexing complications which result.

III. Models in Human Development

Some of the issues associated with the accomodation of models are encountered immediately in relation to the very two terms which identify the substantive realm of concern—the study of human development. Efforts to forge a satisfactory and integrative framework must deal successfully both with the concept of development itself, and with a useful way to conceptualize what can be encompassed under the general term human. The necessity for this has been earlier recognized, as for example Harris (1957a).

The occurrences or processes to which we apply the term development can be considered to be the more fundamental of the two, unless one chooses to suppose that conceptualizing things in developmental terms is of utility to the study of human phenomena alone. Presumably, a developmental approach is one which can be generic to the study of phenomena at large, and would be equally applicable to the study of crystallization in minerals, or the formation of complex molecules. Thus, the elaboration of a satisfactory model hinges first of all upon the way in which the presumed phenomena of development come to be conceptualized and rendered accessible to study, and second upon the issue of how best to conceptualize those human phenomena whose development is the focus of concern.

A. THE CONCEPT OF DEVELOPMENT

The field of human development has encountered a great deal of difficulty with the conceptualization of development itself. In its early stages, a signal effort was made in the form of a conference, comprised of representatives from many fields of investigation, to articulate what was meant by the use of such a term (Harris, 1957a). At the time it was characterized as a single unitary term of only crude descriptive power

(Scott, 1957) which carried no standardized definition (Olson, 1957). Its status appears not to have changed markedly in the intervening years. Inspection of the range of materials which have continued to appear makes it clear that a consensual definition has not yet emerged as to precisely what it is that the term is intended to represent.

It is supposed by virtually all to be related somehow to the phenomena of change, and change in turn is tied to the passage of time. However, by some it is used to refer to all changes which can be identified to occur, whereas others choose to refer to only some subset of changes designated as being of a developmental sort (Baltes, Reese, & Nesselroade, 1977). The problem of specifying development as inclusive of all discernible change over time is, of course, that events cannot be differentiated as such without some kind of detectable change, and time is our basic marker-variable in terms of which such changes are identified. Thus, everything to which we are capable of responding entails change of some sort, and constitutes the basis for the axiom that everything in the universe with which man is familiar undergoes constant change. A definition which encompasses the universe of phenomena is not one calculated to advance one's inquiry particularly well.

An avenue selected by others, to the effect that all development entails change, but not all change is developmental, presents one with the task of specifying the means by which to identify which is which. Unfortunately, this has not been adequately effected; it is apparently easier to identify by name those kinds of changes (such as oscillation or performance variation) conceived to fall outside the class of developmental change than it is to specify the kinds of phenomena which fall within. Definition by exclusion, however, is only partially satisfactory.

It has been equally unclear whether the term is most usefully applied in the form of a concept as opposed to a hypothetical construct. Ordinarily, a concept is considered to be a term used to stand for and to represent a class of occurrences (objects, persons, or events) which are accessible to observation and which can be specified in terms of those minimally necessary attributes which they are judged to hold in common, and which serve to differentiate them from another class. Successfully developed, such concepts permit unambiguous judgments to be made as to whether a particular occurrence does or does not earn membership in such a class. By contrast, a construct is considered to be a term used to refer to a set of events whose occurrence cannot be directly observed, but which is hypothesized as taking place, and thus remains a matter of inference. Such an inference is deemed necessary to account for phenomena which are observed to occur, and is made on the basis of a network of converging operations (MacCorquodale and Meehl, 1948).

The term development would appear to have been subject to both sorts of usage. A biologist, in a position to abort the stream of ongoing events, freeze them in time, and dissect the structural properties of an organism, might thereby detect, describe, and measure changes designated to be of a developmental sort. To suppose that comparable sorts of change (development) might and do take place with respect to other aspects of the human which remain inaccessible to direct observation, and to invoke them in order to account for changes which are observed, is to capitalize on observations in regard to change in one sphere, and to infer comparable sorts of change in another. The principal danger in the use of such constructs is, of course, the temptation to employ them in the form of negative hypotheses, and to formulate essentially useless "explanations." Whenever the term development is used to refer to change processes of an inferred and essentially unknown sort, then efforts to explain one set of events (observed changes) by the postulation of another set of events (development) antecedent to them reduces one merely to a process of substituting one unknown for another.

Surrounding the notion of process is another series of perplexities. Process is a word intimately tied to the phenomena of change, since the presumption is characteristically made that changes in nature take place within an orderly series of occurrences which emerge with a particular result or end. Development thus becomes cast in terms of a series of progressive changes (Hamburger, 1957; Schneirla, 1957; Timiras, 1972) or in terms of systematic and orderly sequences (Nagel, 1957; Werner, 1957). With the occurrence of change viewed in this fashion, the term development may be used to apply to the series of changes leading to each "end" or state, to the succession of states which appear to emerge as a consequence of such transitions, or to be inclusively employed to refer to both. According to Harris (1971), the Dedham Conference was split between those concerned with the transitions, and those who insisted that transitions were from one state of affairs to another.

It has been tempting to certain critics to advocate abandonment of the term entirely. It is noteworthy, for example, that a variety of models addressing the phenomena of change have had no recourse to such a notion, and have proceeded effectively to study complexities of changing phenomena without it. Chemistry, for example, is also interested in change and in the study of extended change sequences (process). Specific instances of change are referred to as reactions, and the study of the rate and conditions of such reactions is referred to as chemical kinetics. Change processes are conceptualized in terms of a succession of reactions of first-, second-, third-order, and so on, and in terms of extended processes, such as step and chain reactions. Such reaction series are recognized as being interspersed at intervals by chemical equilibria, quasi-stable states in which both reactants and products are simultaneously present in some ratio, and are maintained for a period of time by a set of particular conditions. Atomic physics conceptualizes changes series in a somewhat analogous fashion. Indeed, with the exception of the biological sciences and some aspects of the field of psychological studies, the term development has not been characteristically employed at all. Its use in the arena of application, such as in engineering, or in the areas of social, economic, or political action, is intended to refer to processes of a very differing sort.

Those familiar with efforts to construe the human circumstance within a life-span framework will recognize analogous issues to underlie efforts to distinguish between development and aging (Birren, 1959). Here one encounters what appear to be an additional set of change processes, leading to corresponding questions as to the merits of attempting to separate developmental changes from them (Baltes & Willis, 1977).

However difficult it may be to employ effectively, the term development persists because of its demonstrated utility in the study of biological phenomena and because of its intuitively perceived usefulness in the comprehension of the human. And, as Craik (1943) observes, a word with its everyday usage is a thing to be regarded with great respect, since it is a tool which has usually been found to fit some aspect of a complicated reality sufficiently well to enable practical results to be obtained. As a consequence, a continued search for a cross-model conceptualization of the phenomena of both change and development would appear to have merit.

B. REPRESENTATIONAL MODELS OF THE HUMAN

With the term development, the concern lay with common model structures cutting across differing domains of events. Turning to the human, our concern is directed toward differing model structures and their application to a common set of events, those which characterize the properties of the human person and the modification of those properties with the passage of time.

Anyone who enters upon such an arena and endeavors to address the array of alternate models which have been proposed as useful frameworks for the investigation of human events, searching for the similarities and differences which they represent, will be struck and initially overwhelmed by the virtually limitless variety which appears to be available. Taken collectively, the human mind is indeed ingenious, and no greater testimony to this ingenuity could be found than the multiplicity of possible representations of human process which have been suggested. One need merely recite to oneself the range of theological, political, economic, social, psychological, biological, and physical models available on the contemporary scene to be reminded of this heterogeneity; moreover, within each of these reside subsidiary models of even greater variety; psychology alone has available a fantastic array—the psychoanalytic models of Freud and his followers, the behavioristic models of Pavlov, Watson, Hull, and Skinner; the mathematical models of Estes and Bush and Mosteller; the information-processing models of Simon and Newell or of Neisser; the phenomenological models of Snygg and Combs and Rogers; the interpersonal models, such as that of Sullivan; or the humanistic models of a theorist such as Maslow. An exhaustive listing of the alternatives is probably not possible, and there is considerable doubt as to how fruitful such an undertaking would prove to be. As Simon (1968) has noted, science does not progress by the sheer accumulation of information, but rather by the organization and compressing of information; the same may be said concerning models. The proliferation of alternative models cannot be expected to advance one's inquiry; rather a reordering and an amalgamation of models is to be preferred.

One such reordering has been under way of late in the domain of developmental psychology, through an inspection of the metamodel structures which appear to undergird the more particularized model constructions concerned with human development. A consensus appears to have developed that developmental approaches tend to fall into one of two dominant metamodel frames, one being termed an organismic model, considered to have arisen within the European tradition, and the other referred to as a mechanistic model, thought to be more distinctively American (Riegel, 1976; Wohlwill, 1973). In a succession of conference papers, Reese and Overton (1970) and Overton and Reese (1973) developed the view that these two paradigms have proven to be the major base for the representations of developmental processes in the human person. By a careful explication of the epistemological and metaphysical propositions of these paradigms, it became possible to demonstrate the multiple ways in which the respective models remained incompatible with one another, and that because the differences related to such fundamental issues as the criteria for defining truth, the paradigms and the subordinate models developed in relation to them remained in different realms of discourse and were essentially irreconcilable.

In subsequent writings, Looft (1973) and Lerner (1976) have tended to agree. Although both of these latter commentators emphasized that lower-order models derived from these more general paradigms do not necessarily fit perfectly with the metamodels which each of them implies, it remains possible to categorize most developmental theories into one or the other of these two dominant views. It is in the metamodel structures, mechanistic and organismic, where it is possible to discern the principal ingredients of their alternative representations of the nature of man (Looft, 1973).

It is extremely unlikely that the entire array of models developed in order to represent man and his nature may be reduced to one or the other of these families—in fact, Riegel's (1976) concern with a dialectical model as a third more comprehensive metaparadigm is a reflection of this. It is, however, plausible that the majority developed within the scientific ethos of the current century could be so identified, and that these alternate paradigms have remained the dominant viewpoints. Certainly the characterization of models in mechanistic versus organismic terms has recurred throughout the human sciences, and is a differentiation familiar to even the lay public. Criteria serving to differentiate the two have been repeatedly developed; the criteria lists differ from one another only with respect to phraseology and detail.

It has been customary to attempt such differentiations in terms of a list of issues considered essential or fundamental, along which the paradigms appear to differ. In his exposition of such issues, Looft (1973) followed largely the suggestions made by Overton and Reese (1973), and enumerated a set of 12 questions which he considered to be basic to any paradigmatic model which attempted to represent the phenomena of human development. Lerner's (1976) representation of the essential differences speaks to many of the same fundamental issues which Looft had addressed, in his instance differentiating them along five to six dimensions. (Looft had noted that many in his list of questions were closely interrelated; the difference in the number of issues reflects alternative ways in which the questions can be classified and discussed.) At this juncture, relying upon Lerner's representation, the mechanistic paradigm is described as a natural science position, emphasizing quantitative change, continuity, reductionism, a preference for physicochemical representations of events, and concerned with additive effects, whereas the organismic paradigm is described as an epigenetic position, emphasizing qualitative change, discontinuity, emergence, and concerned with multiplicative and interactive effects (Lerner, 1976).

C. IN SEARCH OF A SYNTHESIS

Some observers of this circumstance have remained sanguine over the possibility of reconciling such paradigms (Reese & Overton, 1970. Indeed, if the metamodels remain cast in their current terms, it is possible that there is no foreseeable way in which their differences may be bridged.

The task of reconciling one with another typically entails the capitulation by one into the other's terms. This latter avenue has, of course, been often attempted. The human sciences have become accustomed to seeing the advocates of one model attempt to coopt the viewpoint of another by translating its representations and recasting them into its own terms. As Reese and Overton (1970) succeeded in demonstrating, this cannot be legitimately effected without violating many of the paradigmatic assumptions upon which the second is based.

Others have suggested an alternate route. Riegel (1975, 1976) has argued that the alternate paradigms can be conceptualized as thesis and antithesis, and that a synthesis is possible by architecting a larger and more encompassing paradigm within which the two may be subsumed. Riegel's position is in turn subsumed under a more general dialectical paradigm. It is not clear, however, whether this paradigm reflects primarily a different theoretic orientation, or differences in methodological and procedural (rather than metatheoretical) prescriptions as well.

Looft (1973) emerged with a comparable position, urging the development of a new metamodel, reflecting a different conception of reality and its representation, and accordingly a different set of developmental models with more powerful concepts, propositions, methods of inquiry, and generative information. Indeed, developmental researchers of a life-span orientation (e.g., Huston-Stein & Baltes, 1976; Labouvie & Chandler, this volume) are particularly concerned with the formulation of a new paradigm which would permit the representation of the kinds of multilevel and multidirectional change processes putatively salient in life-span research on development.

The search for synthetic viewpoints to incorporate those which have gone before is motivated by profit. Syntheses are designed to capitalize upon the capabilities of the respective elements upon which they become constructed, and to lead to more adequate representations of new data. Were it not for the extraordinary strength and accomplishments of these respective viewpoints, there would be a poor basis for architecting such syntheses; one would be discarded in preference for another, or both would be discarded to be replaced by a third. The capabilities of these respective paradigms to develop useful modes of description, prediction, and application have earned them a strong measure of respect and admiration; interest in taking advantage of these strengths persists.

As indicated earlier, however, the problem is not simply one of reconciliation between antithetic viewpoints. Not only is each incomplete without ingredients drawn from the other, but it also remains exceedingly difficult to identify how either one, in combination with the other, can prove adequate to the task of representing in scientific terms the complexities of human life, the intricacies of human organization and its continuous modification and change in relation to the multiplicity of influences which affect the person, the various ways in which the person in turn affects his environment, the person's goal-oriented and planful undertakings, or his complex participations in social groups in which he inevitably engages. The search for such overarching paradigmatic frames is, therefore, equally motivated by the effort to find ways to fill in the gaps left by the physicalistic, or biological, social, or psychodynamic accounts of human process, and to emerge with a framework for analysis of more adequate scope (White, 1952).

In the following materials an effort is made to articulate and illustrate another paradigmatic form which holds considerable promise for the representation of human development by effecting such a synthetic function. It has been developed under a number of labels, being variously referred to as: systems theory, "the" systems approach, systems analysis, or more generally, the systems view. This approach has "metamodel" characteristics, although in many ways of a different order than those of Reese, Overton, Riegel, and others which have been earlier cited.

IV   Evolution of a Systems View

A.   SOME HISTORY

The emergence of what we here refer to as the systems view has been the product of a confluence of factors; prominent among these has been that of general systems theory. A biologist by the name of Ludwig Von Bertalanffy is generally credited with the primary authorship for originating the orientation and providing the continued impetus for the development of what is now labeled in formal fashion General Systems Theory. The notion that phenomena could be usefully examined in terms of system organizations and properties was, of course, not original with him. Physics had sometime earlier conceptualized the universe in terms of a thermodynamic system; chemistry had used a systems framework in its study of equilibrated states; and physiology had long been accustomed to representing structural and functional networks of occurrences in system and subsystem terms. Indeed, it is not possible to enter upon any field of inquiry without encountering models developed around the concept of system and system processes, or at least finding those in which ingredients of a systems perspective are readily detectable. Thus, precursors to systems thinking are encountered in psychology in the work of

Angyal (1941), Goldstein (1939), Köhler (1947), or Lewin (1935), and frank characterizations of the person in systems terms appear in the writings of Allport (1955) or White (1952). Bertalanffy's early work was of such an order, dealing initially with organismic biology, and subsequently with the characteristics and properties of open systems.

However, beginning in 1945 and continuing thereafter, Bertalanffy (1945, 1950, 1955, 1962, 1967, 1968) proceeded to enunciate the ingredients of a bold new framework in human thought. His innovative stroke was the hypothesis of a set of principles which cut across the range of system organizations, principles which were applicable to systems in general, irrespective of their components, or of the relations or "forces" between them. Over a period of time, he began to enunciate a number of such principles, held to be descriptive of systems at large, whether they be mechanical, biological, symbolic, or social in form and operation. It was a framework focused as much upon the ingredients of model-building and abstract generalization as upon the particularities of system functioning, and proved to be an idea "whose time had come." It was not long before writers such as Ashby (1958), Boulding (1956), and others began to elaborate upon the framework and render an increasingly sophisticated point of view.

B. RELATED DEVELOPMENTS

The appearance of general systems theory in the domain of thought was paralleled by a number of additional frameworks which, with the passage of time, inevitably became intermeshed. On the one hand was operations research, primarily a creature of the exigencies of World War II. Ackoff (1963), a leading figure in the development of this approach, acknowledges its intimate dependence upon systems concepts, and characterizes it primarily as a methodology by which to analyze the functioning operation of systems as a whole, rather than in terms of their conglomerate parts. With the development of cybernetics, the science of communication and control (Wiener, 1948), still an additional dimension to the representation of systems and their analysis was made possible and led to the detailed analysis and design of control systems, with both cybernetic and servomechanistic properties. Similar convergences have occurred with the development of set theory, game theory, decision theory, organization theory, computer science, programming, modeling, and simulation. A final development has been that of mathematical systems theory with its efforts to architect mathematical models to serve as representations of system function (Rapoport, 1956).

As Ruesch (1967) has remarked, the speed with which these

frameworks, methods, and procedures have undergone adoption and development was not anticipated, particularly since the general posture entails such a profound shift in manner of thinking. Nonetheless, the power and capabilities of these frameworks have been tried and tested in virtually every domain of application imaginable. An indication of its generic character is shown by a partial listing of such domains—the nature of models and model construction (Laszlo, 1972; Sutherland, 1973); characteristics of systems models (Ackoff & Emery, 1972; Emery, 1969); neurological system functions (Arbib, 1972); biological control systems (Milsum, 1966); behavioral patterns and sequences (Bischof, 1975; Mayr, 1974; Miller, 1955, 1965 a,b,c,d; Royce & Buss, 1976); human cognition (Arbib & Kahn, 1969; Craik, 1966; Hunt, 1971; Neisser, 1967; Newell & Simon, 1972); psychopathological behavior (Gray, Duhl, & Rizzo, 1969; Grinker, 1975; Menninger, Mayman, & Pruyser, 1963); psychotherapeutic processes (Phillips & Wiener, 1966); social organizations (Berrien, 1968; Buckley, 1967, 1969; Katz & Kahn, 1966; Miller, 1971, 1972; Seiler, 1967); political and economic institutions (Boulding, 1961); and formal managerial organizations (Beer, 1959; Carzo & Yanouzas, 1967).

The foregoing investigators have had a common interest in the analysis and explication of extant systems, and the architecture of suitable models and procedures for that purpose. It is important to emphasize that an even greater thrust has taken place in association with the general field of engineering and its concern with systems design. In the former, the preferred posture has been one of descriptive and analytic study of variations in phenomena as they can be observed to occur, either under open field conditions, or under arrangements established for controlled observation. Persons in the applied fields of engineering (broadly defined), on the other hand, are ordinarily directed toward the examination of an extant system which is intended to accomplish defined objectives, and to seek ways in which that system might be improved so as to accomplish its objectives more effectively. One may also design innovative and novel arrangements with which to achieve definable purposes, and successively refine and upgrade those arrangements through a process of error reduction. The engineering approach is one which eschews the study of the virtually limitless variations in occurrence which can take place with respect to a set of phenomena, and elects instead to restrict its mode of inquiry to the generation of effects which are deemed desirable. It is thus an alternative, and in many ways an equally powerful avenue to the study of phenomena and their explication.

It has been primarily in connection with such engineering efforts that specific technologies have been developed—strategies, procedures, devices, methods—with which to accomplish practical ends. Within the engineering disciplines concrete means for describing, analyzing, measuring, and evaluating the properties and capabilities of system functions have appeared. With the development of such tools as path analyses and function notation, the systems analyst no longer needs to content himself with conceptual representations of systems in abstract form, but is equipped with concrete tools with which he can proceed.

C. PRESENT STATUS

At this juncture in time it is possible to represent the systems perspective as an integrate of these many elements. First, as Grinker (1967) has emphasized, and persons such as Laszlo (1972) and Sutherland (1973) have developed, system models imply more general model structures, and thus the systems perspective encompasses an alternative paradigm or world view (the systems view).

Second, at more particularized levels, it constitutes a set of models by which the functioning and operation of organized occurences can be conceptualized, and descriptively represented, so as to lead to orderly prediction and control (systems theory).

It is, third, a family of strategies for investigation and analysis of extant systems (systems analysis) and for the modification and design of artificial systems (systems design); the strategies as a group are referred to as the systems approach.

Finally, it is a family of methods by which the purposes of systems analysis and systems design can be effected (systems technology).

One can become speculative only as to the bases for the enthusiasm which this set of developments has engendered. For some, like Bertalanffy, its attraction lies in its potentiality for overcoming the inadequacies of mechanistic models as a framework for science; for Rapoport (1966), for counteracting the fragmentation of science into isolated specialties; for Ashby (1958), for addressing problems of complexity; for Boulding (1956), for the construction of new and more useful metatheoretic frameworks; for Grinker (1967), for serving as a unifying framework for the study of human activity; for many others it represents a family of procedures with which to increase the likelihood that concrete products and services considered of utility to humans can be developed (systems engineering).

In the present context, it is with its potentialities for serving as a more general paradigmatic frame about which we are concerned. In the materials which follow, an effort will be made to accomplish two things. Initially, an attempt will be made to explicate some of the more significant features of such a systems view, with particular attention to those aspects of relevance to the concept of development in general and the conceptualization of human development in particular. This will be followed by an effort to derive from this view a specification of human development from a systems perspective. It is hoped that in the course of doing these two sets of things, the capabilities of a systems view as an integrative and synthesizing framework for studies in human development will become apparent.

V.   The Systems Perspective—An Overview

It is exceedingly difficult to characterize a systems view in a concise and informative fashion, and to do so in a convincing manner. It is first of all a framework intended to reflect the complexity of the phenomenal world and, therefore, the framework itself has inevitably become correspondingly complex. The extensive writings of persons such as Bertalanffy and Miller are testimony to the degree of intricacy with which one becomes involved in one's efforts to become usefully specific and detailed in its explication.

It is equally difficult to liberate oneself from the modes of representation derived from other metatheoretic views. In one's efforts to operate within a systems viewpoint, one recurrently discovers oneself reverting to mechanistic or organismic or other metamodels; demonstrating to others that it is more than a simple translation of tired principles into new language is a corresponding problem.

Finally, the language of a systems view is to some its greatest asset, while to others it is an unwanted and unnecessary liability. Designed to be generic to the study of systems at large, it is in a real sense content-free. Mathematics has been characterized as a means of representing the relational aspects of the world with our perceptions subtracted out; in similar fashion, the language of the systems view casts phenomena into a symbolic form, abstracted from day-to-day experience, and therefore devoid of phenomenal content; in its general form it does not display an obvious isomorphism with the characteristics of our phenomenal world. The intent of such a language is not only to express the generalities which apply across the particularities of events, but also to permit one to operate disencumbered by the heterogeneous meanings attached to our concepts arising from our everyday language, our prior technical attempts, and our personal, private, and idiosyncratic experience (Harris, 1971). The relevance of systems models and the language symbols which carry them can be identified only when they become applied to concrete sets of events.

Despite such difficulties, an attempt will nonetheless be made to extract from the systems view in general those aspects and characteristics which appear especially pertinent to the questions at hand.

A. SOME MAJOR CHARACTERISTICS OF A SYSTEMS VIEW

1. Systems as Models

The first and foremost answer to the question: "What is a system?" is to identify it as a *model*. A system is a man-made construction designed as a tool to facilitate the analysis of extant phenomena encountered in the world of events, or to engineer and to arrange events so as to accomplish particular effects. All systems are abstract representations of what the events of concern are construed to be; they are characteristically expressed in the form of symbols (verbal and numeric), in the form of graphics and schematics, or in three-dimensional representational form.

A system is, therefore, a model of reality; the properties of such models are not presumed to be immanent within the objects, persons, or events they are intended to characterize. Attention is focused upon the elaboration of the model in such a way as to progressively reduce the apparent discrepancy between the representation of the system (the model) and happenings as they are collectively experienced and observed.

The design of such systems reflects the use of a viewpoint—a template through which the world of events is viewed. Everything with which man is familiar and to which he can respond is construable in terms of change. The existential form of reality for the human characterizes phenomena into structures on the one hand (objects, persons, and things) and processes on the other (activity, events, behavior); the first are regarded as comparatively stationary and fixed, and the second to be active and changing. However, such differentiations are possible only because of differential rates of change—reality itself is conceived of as activity, which is constant, continuous, and never-ceasing. Structural versus functional representations of phenomena are products of man's approach to variations in perceived change. In the architecting of an abstract model with which to represent change, one is endeavoring to formulate a representation which demonstrates greater power and utility than the phenomenal models with which people proceed and employ on a day-to-day basis.

2. System and Organization

The heart of the systems view derives from the concept of *organization*, and reflects the proposition that events can be most usefully represented in terms of their participation within a network of interdependent and interrelated events; a system is usually defined as an organized arrangement of elements which comprise a network of interdependent and coordinated parts, and which functions as a unit, especially for the purpose of harmonious and concerted action. It is recognized that these same organizations of occurrences may be viewed as aggregates of bits and pieces, but it is proposed that they can only begin to be understood when the elements *and* their interrelationships are made the objects of study.

Such a view has applicability across the entire spectrum of phenomena. From such a perspective, systems would appear to be everywhere. Anything which consists of parts connected together can be construed as if it were a system: a car, a pair of scissors, an economy, an ear, a response or response pattern, or a set of ideas. However, not just anything would be legitimately characterized as a system; it is possible to encounter aggregates of elements in which the units which go to make them up do not display the *kinds* of interrelationships which characterize a system. Relationships displaying merely spatial or temporal contiguity among elements would not qualify such an arrangement as a system. Systems are composed of elements interconnected in some form of regularized interdependence which makes possible the functioning or performance of the unit as a whole.

3. System Diversity

The definition suggests the possibility of many different kinds of systems—as, for example, systems encountered in nature, man-made systems, or hybrid systems composed of both natural and constructed elements. Inspection of the variety of systems with which man is already familiar reveals, to paraphrase a statement by Kluckhohn and Murray (1949) in relation to the human: that every system is in some respects (a) like all other systems; (b) like some other systems; and (c) like no other system.

General systems theory endeavors to identify those principles which cut across and serve to characterize the operation of systems at large (regardless of whether they are construed to be physical, biological, social, or symbolic systems). At the same time, it is useful to recognize system subtypes, with characteristics specific to them and serving to differentiate their modes of operation from one another. Finally, it is recognized that in the strict sense no two systems, even of the same general sort, are ever precisely alike. Thus every system is in some respects unique. One may elect to focus upon a particular system for detailed scrutiny, to inspect the operating properties of a class of systems which have captured one's interest, or one may address the question of the properties which systems in general appear to share and the principles according to which they appear to respond. The *system of reference* is designated as that particular system, or set of systems, upon which one's attention is focused for the purpose of study and analysis.

4. System Structures and Functions

The detailed representation of a system and its functioning moves along several fronts. One may first of all be interested in the manner of its organization and operation; a summary representation of all of its characteristics at a specific point in time and under a given set of conditions is referred to as the *state* of the system. A state description may concern itself with a description of the apparent structural elements which go to make up the system; such structural elements are referred to as *components,* and thus a structural analysis of a system yields a representation in terms of components and their relationships. The same system can also be represented in terms of the functions or processes which appear to take place; functional elements of a system are referred to as *subsystems;* analysis of a system in terms of the functions (or performances) which apparently occur will yield a characterization of subsystem processes and their interdependent relationships. The distinction is a useful one to maintain, since in many complex systems the same structural components appear to participate in a variety of subsystem functions.

The interrelationships among the components or subsystems constitute the connectiveness of the system and make possible its organized and integrated operation. The general nature of such relationships are recognized to be *transactional.* Recurrent inspection of the operation of many systems has demonstrated that they cannot be adequately represented in terms of active, reactive, or even interactive elements. The essential characteristic of a transactional relationship is the exchange of influence which occurs; with two elements involved each is affected by its interrelationship with the other. All relationships both within and between systems are construed as reciprocal exchanges. The implications of this principle are exceedingly numerous. For example, the behavior of an element is recognized to be a function of the network of related elements of which it is a part; the same element will be found to function somewhat differently if it is extracted from its context and allowed to "run free." Correspondingly, if that same element were to become embedded within still a different configuration, changes in its mode of operation can be expected. Verification of this principle has been effected so often that it has assumed the characteristics of a "truism."

5. System Operation and Control

Whenever events (or elements) are interrelated in such a way that the operation of one serves to regulate and govern the occurrence of another, the latter may be considered to be operating under the control of the other. *System control* (system regulation) is, therefore, another name for the connectiveness within and between systems.

By virtue of their organization (the network of interrelationships), control is an attribute of a system. Because there are multiple patterns of interrelationships, there are multiple types of control mechanisms, ranging all the way from the simplest type of control which operates to convert signals from one signal form to another (a transducer) all the way up to intricate system organizations which have become highly specialized and whose principal role is that of exercising a governing and regulatory control over a complex of subsidiary performance units. The latter would be referred to as a *control system,* in contradistinction to the more generalized properties of system control (DiStefano, Stubberud, & Williams, 1967). Of particular interest to systems analysts have been those system arrangements which demonstrate the capabilities for self-regulation on the one hand, and which operate in command relationship to other system units on the other; particular organizations are required for systems to be capable of such cybernetic (governing) properties.

6. *System Change*

All systems undergo constant and persistent change. There is a variety of ways in which one can endeavor to represent such change. One can, for example, graphically represent a system by drawing a circle containing an array of dots. The connectiveness of the system can be represented by drawing lines between the dots—some dots may be connected to all other dots, but in some cases a dot may be connected to only one of its fellows. In this way, one comes to look at a system as a kind of network of elements and the pattern of their interrelationships.

The pattern changes from moment to moment as the system operates within itself to function in the way in which the particular system behaves. The changes with respect to such a system can be quite rapid, and accounting for this behavior in detailed fashion would obviously require a vast investigation; correspondingly the rate of change can be comparatively slow. The detection of such changes can only be effected in relation to the passage of time; or, to put the matter differently, from the human perspective, the occurrence of activity requires the passage of time. Therefore, the representation of system change is invariably accomplished in relation to a *time line,* which is conceptualized as being unidirectional—that is, one functions under the constriction that one can never move backward in time.

Since in principle all systems are in a constant process of change in relation to the ongoing passage of time, the representation of system change can be given by an account of the successive states of the system in relation to some specified temporal frame. It is analogous to taking a succession of Polaroid camera shots of an object in the process of change, and by lining them up along a time line, thereby gaining a representation of change without the change simultaneously taking place. The succession of states of a system from one time to another is referred to as the *transitions* of a system, and the changes within the system by which such transitions are effected are referred to as the *transformations* of the system. The term transformation is one of deliberate choice; it serves to emphasize that the nature of the change is in terms of the form, or configuration, which the system progressively assumes as time proceeds.

7. *Closed versus Open Systems*

Where the transforms obtained from a transformation include no fresh items, but are concerned entirely with the rearrangement of items which are already present with respect to the system, one speaks of a closed system. It is a moot point whether such a system can be identified in nature; although theorists differ as to what constitutes a closed system, the definition employed here would suggest that only a perpetual motion machine would qualify. In such an instance, the concept of a closed system becomes an aid to thinking about phenomena analogous to the concept of infinity, and not such as to lead one to expect to encounter such a system in the world of concrete events.

Systems which require the infusion of energy, matter, or information from outside the system to accomplish their operations, to perform their functions, and to maintain themselves for these purposes, are referred to as open systems. Stated another way, all system processes occur as a result of the transmission of energy in the form of matter or information within or between systems. Open systems are systems wherein the transmission of energy resources from other systems is essential to the maintenance and continued functioning of the system. As such open systems continuously carry on active exchanges of energy with system organizations with which they are interrelated. All systems are conceptualized as energy-processing organizations.

8. *System Processes*

With all change sequences reducible to a transmission of energy within and between systems, the convention has been to represent such transmission into three major subsets: *input, transformations,* and *output.* It will be recognized that such a three-unit categorization of system processes is in *functional* as opposed to structural terms. It is a way of representing process, and intended as a framework for analysis which is generic to system arrangements at large.

The input refers collectively to the transmission of energy/matter/ information across a boundary into a system; systems are characteristically selective, and thus inputs are selectively withdrawn. The term transformation refers to all the internal processes within the system by which the energy becomes transformed, aggregated, stored, and utilized in a coordinated way—in simple terms, work gets done. By output is meant the transmission of energy by the system across system boundaries into other systems with which it is interrelated; outputs represent the "response" of the system, and characteristically are divisible into two major categories—those which are associated with what are conceived to be the essential performances of the system, and those which are characterized as by-products or waste. Living systems, then, are represented as energy/matter/information-processing systems, geared to generate certain categories of output, but requiring certain energy inputs, and having to transform those energies in particular ways in order to accomplish those performances.

9. System Coupling

Systems are said to be *coupled* when they are arranged in such a way that the output of one system provides the input of another, so that the operation of the first governs the operation of the second. This governance is subject to the earlier observations concerning transactions. Systems which remain coupled are enabled to do so by a pattern of *matched specificities*. In a fashion analogous to the interdigitation of a lock and key, the energy outputs of one system occur in a form capable of being utilized as input by the next. It is this kind of specificity which enables subsidiary systems to be bound dynamically into units of higher order, and thus constitutes the basis for organization. It is also such matched specificities which permit systems to "interface" and to engage in transactional exchanges with other systems of a very different order.

B. DETERMINANTS OF SYSTEM PERFORMANCE

The operation of systems is thus usefully studied from multiple perspectives—of what they seem to be composed, the manner in which they appear to be organized, the resources required, and the ways in which such resources are utilized and transformed so as to generate an output effect. The interrelationship of these several aspects can be understood by looking at the performance characteristics of systems.

The performances of a system are those activities which the system is characteristically geared to generate. What the system can and cannot do defines the system's performance capabilities at any particular place and time, and is a product of a variety of factors.

1. Performance as a Function of Organization

A system's performance is first of all governed by the organization of the system. For any particular performance, the requisite performance elements must be available, in place, arrayed in a particular order, interrelated in appropriate fashion, and functionally operable. It will prove insufficient if some elements are available, but not others; if all elements are available, but not appropriately organized; if elements are appropriately arranged, but functionally segmented and hence not operationally interrelated. It is in this fashion that the way a system is organized will determine the performances of which it is capable; the organization both defines and delimits what a system can do.

Thus, system performance is viewed as an "all-or-none" affair. If a system performance occurs at all, it is indicative of the fact that the system has become so arranged as to make that performance possible. If it entailed a reorganization of the system, then a single occurrence of the performance is sufficient to indicate that the necessary modifications in the system have taken place. Whether or not the performance capabilities have achieved certain levels of reliability, however, is another issue.

2. Performance as a Function of Resource Input

A second factor governing the performance capability of a system is related to the kind and extent of the inputs which are available. All systems must be fed, since the exercise of activity entails the utilization of energy resources, whether these be in the form of matter or of information. Different systems call for different inputs, and input deficiencies will inevitably be reflected in a systems performance; deprivation of necessary inputs will result in a cessation of system function, and if these inputs are critical to the maintenance of the system, such deprivation will result in the degradation of the system to the point where it ceases to function and "dies." Variations in input to a system, therefore, can be expected to produce variations in system performance. If a system constitutes a cybernetic organization, then the feedback it generates is an essential element in its input, and deficiencies in feedback will likewise lead to performance deficiencies.

3. Performance as a Function of System Context

A third factor affecting performance and generative of variability stems from the environmental surround; few systems are so admirably insulated that they are invulnerable to the influences which emanate from the systems in which they are embedded; variations in effects produced by systems which constitute the environment of a system will modify the performance of the system to the extent that the system is susceptible to such effects. When such environmental system influences operate so as to detract from the systems capability for generating its performance effects in maximal fashion, they are viewed as "perturbations from the environment" and ordinarily considered undesirable. In artificial systems, the effort is usually directed toward insulation of a system from such disturbances, or developing system properties which can serve to compensate for them. Those systems which have tended to survive under naturalistic conditions would appear to be those with compensatory performances which have adaptive characteristics.

Thus, a certain amount of variation (error) is associated with the performance of any component, subsystem, or system which one chooses to examine. The variables of systems are constantly fluctuating. Since inputs constantly change, systems correspondingly remain in a condition of constant change; moreover, all systems recurrently undergo a variety of perturbations fron the system surround to which accommodations and adjustments must be continuously effected; and a moderate change in one variable may produce greater or lesser alterations in all other aspects of the system with which it is interrelated. These alterations may or may not subsequently be modifiable.

C. SYSTEM TRANSFORMATION

In general, however, systems are capable of undergoing modification. Systems are modified by the occurrence of conditions external to them. It should be noted, however, that changes in external conditions do not "cause" a process in an otherwise inert system; they can only participate in the alteration of processes which are already going on. System modification is effected by a reorganization of the components, or functions, or the pattern of their interrelationships. Such modifications are referred to as *transformations of a system* (as distinct from the energy transformations of the resources which the system utilizes). Such modifications in the form, configuration, or ordering of parts which characterize the system would necessarily generate changes in output (performance).

These system transformations can occur as a consequence of a number of factors, depending upon the makeup of the system. Certain systems, for example, are capable of accumulating more matter/energy in the form of input than is required for the maintenance of the system on the one hand, and the energy which the system is called upon to output in the form of system performance on the other. With an excess of matter/energy available within the system beyond that required to carry out its work, the opportunity exists for that energy to be used for other purposes—for example, *growth*. Other systems, geared for the processing of information as opposed to matter, function in such a way as to collect and store informational elements in an organized form, such organizations becoming subject to transformation in relation to additional and novel inputs. Information-processing systems with these capabilities are considered susceptible to "learning."

System transformations, however, are not restricted to those types of reorganizations which coincide with people's value systems as to what constitutes the "good." Depending upon the perspective of the observer, transformations may be characterized as "positive" or "negative," beneficial or disadvantageous. Thus, systems can undergo a variety of transformations in directions conceived to be degenerative or deteriorative as a consequence of depletions in requisite resources entering into the system, intrusion into the system of incompatible elements emanating from other systems, or damages to the integrity of the system from influences external to it. The study of system transformation for any particular class of systems entails an analysis of the entire range of conditions whose transaction with a system leads to its transformation.

D. ANALYTIC REPRESENTATIONS OF EXTANT SYSTEMS

1. Plurality of Models

The study of a system, or a class of systems, can be pursued in a great variety of ways. There are multiple forms in which the representation of systems can occur; alternative models of the same type of system will demonstrate differential utility, depending upon the purposes for which they are designed.

Thus, for example, systems analysis has its elementary conceptual–arithmetic, as well as its elaborate computerized–algebraic forms. It is true that systems thinking is permeated with the belief that the properties of events (physical, biological, psychological, or social) are as Galileo said, "written in the language of mathematics" (Pylyshyn, 1972). This does not mean, however, that they are capable of being represented only in mathematic symbolic form. Even less does it mean that the only occurrences of significance are those which can be measured and subjected to calculation. Systems analysis does not have to await mathematicians and computers, even though in the long run one is working toward more sophisticated forms of modeling (Ramo, 1973).

The analysis and representation of systems of interest can begin, if need be, with their characterization in nominal and narrative form. These may be aided by schematic representations intended to parallel their apparent organization, or with initial attempts to specify component or subsystem interrelationships in simple additive or multiplicative terms. A variety of tools are available for such purposes. The definition of many intricate system organizations originally began at precisely such elementary levels.

2. General Steps in System Definition

The sophisticated analysis of a system, or a system subset, can be recognized to be an intricate and time-consuming process, although when pursued collectively it can and has been effectively accomplished. The details of such analyses vary as a function of the properties of the system(s) under investigation, and can employ pluralistic modes of representation. However, a generic strategy has tended to evolve, described by Wymore (1976) as well as others.

The overall strategy entails the execution of a succession of steps, beginning with a specification of the system of reference. The intent here is to generate a set of statements intended to provide unambiguous information as to the organization of occurrences which constitute the system of concern. Characteristically, the system model is assigned a name.

The second step calls for a specification of the time scale over which the operation of the system is to be studied. The selection of the time scale within which observations are to be made is arbitrary and depends upon the system to be modeled. Time frames may be as brief as a fraction of a second, or extend for comparatively lengthy periods of time. The passage of time is marked by temporal indices; calendar years may be the units chosen, and chronological age can be a marker variable. Time scales may also be conceptualized as continuous or discrete, and for certain purposes may be specified as continuing indefinitely along the time line.

Once the time frame has been determined, it is necessary to define, describe, or enumerate the state (or alternate possible states) of the system. The specification of these internal configurations may be effected in terms of components, subsystem functions, signal flows, programmatic sequences, or a variety of other modes of representation depending upon the nature of the system with which one deals. A *static* representation of the status of such systems represents an effort to characterize its condition at the moment of time in question; it is understood that such a representation is possible only as a result of the artificial "freezing" of action. A *dynamic* representation of change permits the definition of the succession of states, once the initial state is know (Rapoport, 1970). For the latter purpose, additional information is needed.

It is necessary to define, describe, or enumerate all possible inputs to the system. This can be as simple as a short list, but where systems have a variety of input ports, such a list must include the several different kinds of inputs to which the system is responsive.

With information concerning the system state at *t*, plus a knowledge of the inputs which constitute additive elements with respect to that state, it becomes possible to characterize the state transition functions, and to demonstrate how the state of the system at a future time t + 1 is determined by the present state of the system and the inputs to the system from the present to that future time. The representation of the behavior of the system lies in these state transition functions. One will know if the selection of descriptors of the states and inputs are useful and appropriate means by which to model the phenomena when it becomes apparent that, knowing one input to the system at time *t* and the state of the system at time *t*, the state of the system at time t + 1 is completely determined.

Finally, one becomes concerned with a specification of the output that is observed or received from the system when the system is in a particular state. For any given system, there is rarely simply one output that may be considered intrinsic to the representation of the system. In large-scale, complex systems, the outputs of significance depend upon the observer. However, logically the performance output of any system is a function of the state of that system; therefore, an additional criterion concerning the merits of any suggested model is available. That model is to be preferred which provides all the necessary information concerning each state of the system so as to permit the computation of the desired output at any given time. System testing is characteristically required, and may be accomplished through experimental or simulated means; this is necessary in order to establish the input–output pairs, and to expose the systems states which mediate between them.

No system beyond a certain level of complexity can be completely "known" (modeled) in all of its detail. With intricate and complex systems, one's intent lies in singling out certain salient properties which can adequately represent the behavior of a system in those respects in which one is interested (Rapoport, 1970). Further, transitional states which are proximal in time can ordinarily be represented in greater detail than those more distal.

VI. Applications of the Systems View to the Study of Human Development

A. APPLICABILITY OF THE SYSTEMS PERSPECTIVE

It would appear from the foregoing that the systems perspective has a number of properties which argue for its utility in the study of developmental processes which characterize the human. A number of these can be enumerated.

1. It provides a basis for the cross-disciplinary conceptualization of change and development earlier advocated. From such a view it is possible to conceive and endeavor to model organizations of occurrence as varied as an electrical signal, a chemical compound, a crystal, a virus, an organism, a person, or a group; to address networks of ideas, conceiving of them as symbolic organizations responsive to variations in input; indeed, in systems engineering, methods are under development whereby system-processing systems may be studied—inputs to a system undergoing design may themselves be systems, and one's interest may be in designing the system so as to drive the inputted systems to some desirable state (Wymore, 1976). It has the capabilities for serving a synthetic function at the metamodel level.

2. It provides a means with which to differentiate usefully between change on the one hand, and developmental change on the other. The study of development from a systems perspective would entail a representation of the rate and mechanisms by which modifications occur in the form, configuration, or ordering of parts which characterize the system, under varying sets of conditions, in relation to specified intervals of time. The representation of such developmental changes could only be accomplished by a specification of the succession of transformed states through which the system proceeds. Such state sequences could be construed as developmental processes. One suspects that this posture with respect to the study of development is in principle highly congruent with many earlier characterizations of the key features of a developmental approach as enunciated by Harris (1957b), as well as others.

3. The systems perspective provides a framework within which to order and interrelate the multiple elements of which the human appears to be composed. The integrate which the human constitutes can be represented in terms of interrelated subordinate systems—systems which are relatively comparable to one another and transact at comparable levels of organization (e.g., cell–cell interconnections); systems which are arranged in quasi-echelon formations with heirarchical interrelationships (e.g., tissue–organ organizations); and systems which are of differing genera (e.g., electrical transmission systems, communications systems, physical fluid systems, respiratory systems, motor performance systems, information-processing systems, or cognitive control systems). Differing analytic units will be found necessary at different levels of analysis; different types of systems can be legitimately represented with differing descriptive/quantitative terms. Thus, segments of the human integrate may be separately modeled, but it will not serve one's purpose to model

one system component in the language of one model, and another in symbolic structures of a very different sort. They wiil need to be represented in compatible terms, so that when they become independently understood, it will prove possible to discover their interrelationships. It is for this purpose that a generic system language can and needs to be employed, so that all systems, regardless of type, can be symbolically represented in comparable terms.

4. The systems perspective provides a vehicle with which to interrelate not only the characteristics of the person, but also the conditions in the person's surround which exercise a governing effect upon what the person comes to be and do. A systems perspective not only permits a representation of the network of environmental system arrangements within which human activity takes place, it makes such a representation mandatory. It is the environmental surround which permits the transactional relationships for the inputs required for system performance as well as exchanges necessary for the performances themselves. The person and environment items in Lewin's equation, $B = f(P)(E)$, are capable of being modeled in comparable terms.

5. The systems perspective also permits the maintenance of the distinction between competence and performance, a distinction recurrently advocated in the literature concerning development and learning, but over which so much controversy has developed (Pylyshyn, 1972). From a systems view the organizational properties of a system define what it is organized (competent) to do, whereas resource inputs and situational conditions in transactional relationship with that organization govern what it comes to do (performance).

The merits of the perspective can be amplified at greater length; one may cite, for example, the essentially mathematic structure to its language, the congruence of models at multiple levels, or its utility for integrating sciences across disparate disciplines. But perhaps enough has been said to indicate its potential for addressing the study of human development and to serve a synthetic function at a metamodel level which has been sought.

B. THE SYSTEMS PERSPECTIVE AND LIFE-SPAN DEVELOPMENT

The systems view also holds immediate implications for the advancement of theory and research in life-span development, the focus of the present volume. A systems perspective may help to clarify a number of "novel" issues in research and theory which have come to be identified and accentuated by investigators within the domain of life-span research.

A number of such investigators have argued, for example, that their findings call into question established conceptions concerning developmental processes, and correspondingly that different modes of inquiry are required. Thus, Huston-Stein and Baltes (1976) and Lerner and Ryff (this volume, Chapter 1) have taken the position that traditional concepts of development (insofar as they rely upon unidirectional change sequences) are inappropriate when applied within the study of life-span development, since the latter appears to entail diverse and multidirectional change to a much larger degree than appears true for the development of children. They further argue that life-span research is suggestive of discontinuity in model appropriateness for differing life stages or different levels. Memory research in children and the elderly would appear to be more usefully conceptualized in "mechanistic" model terms, whereas adult memory development suggests the use of "organismic" types of representation (Reese, 1976). Others have raised questions concerning the changing validity of measures in relation to development, and have pressed for models which differentiate contexts for development (ontogenetic vs. social change) as well as models to permit the representation of conjoint causality.

Systems frameworks in general would have no difficulty in incorporating such complications in analysis. As human system states undergo transformation in relation to time, changes in performance parameters are expected, and both qualitative and quantitative indicants of performance must be correspondingly modified.

Systems tools are available with which to model multilinearity in transitional processes, since these constitute characteristics of change which are not restricted to the human experience. Provision also exists for the development of discontinuous as well as continuous models, and for models of differing levels of complexity and reflective of differing manners of systems processing. A confluence of antecedent conditions which serve to generate a system effect (conjoint causality) is the norm in systems modeling; and the representation of components of the complex system surround which serves as the context for human behavior and development and exerts a governing effect upon what comes to take place can be part and parcel of a systems analytic process.

VII.   Some Future Indications

The capabilities of the systems perspective for elucidating the phenomena of human development impress this writer as truly enormous, and sufficient to warrant a serious commitment on the part of human development specialists to its elaboration and use. For any particular investigator, however, this should occur only as a consequence of a deliberative decision, since the ramifications of such a commitment are extensive.

Considerable labor is invariably required to become familiar with the perspective, since it entails an alteration (transformation) of the modes of thought to which many are accustomed and upon which they rely in order to model phenomena in which they are interested. To effect such transformations, a modification in the nature of one's input is necessary, and an immersion in the systems literature becomes a necessity. Among other things, this carries one into the domain of systems engineering as well as systems science, because the areas of analysis and design continue to be essential handmaidens of one another. Often it is the discovery of what one must introduce into artificial systems to make them work which permits the discovery of system analogs in nature; correspondingly the elucidation of natural systems and their operation often suggests the design of artificial systems along similar lines. One must also develop proficiency in the concepts and symbol notations with which system models are formed and described, and which permit their functioning and modification to become quantitatively expressed. It requires a willingness to engage in the time-consuming, and in many ways tedious, procedures of detailed specification which a systems approach demands; of course, systems specialists contend that it is precisely such commitment to detail that enables man to develop valid explanatory models, and to gain sufficient control over phenomena to ensure that our artificially designed systems will perform as we wish them to.

Finally, it requires a commitment to an interdisciplinary posture, since the explication of the human processes which undergo developmental change are as diverse as the situational contexts which so govern them. Interdisciplinary teams of investigators are desirable, possible, and—with respect to such a task as this—indispensable. Experience in managing such interdisciplinary teams, however, has demonstrated the absolute requirement that project members and project teams work within a common systems perspective so as to make possible the interdigitation of their independent efforts. Considerable knowledge has accumulated concerning the necessary conditions for the effective orchestration of multidisciplinary and multiprofessional organizations; this knowledge has been painstakingly acquired in the course of implementing large-scale research and development organizations directed toward the architecting of complex systems. Effective membership in such an organization requires an appreciation by each participant of the functioning of the system as a whole, and the integration of the subsystems needed (including themselves) to render the undertaking effective (Chase, 1974).

Although the "end item" which a systems approach to the human and his development—a comprehensive and detailed modeling of human developmental processes in all of their complexity—inevitably lies in the distant future, steady progress can nonetheless be made. One may have recourse to an African adage: "How does one eat an elephant? One little bite at a time."

VIII. Summary

This chapter has endeavored to outline the rationale of a systems perspective for the study of human behavior, and to disclose its potential utility in promoting theory and research in human development. The argument developed can be briefly summarized.

Our success in comprehending the nature of man and his existence hinges upon our capabilities for developing and refining effective models with which to proceed. A simple proliferation of multiple alternatives will prove insufficient for such a task; a reordering and an amalgamation of models are to be preferred. Efforts to represent human processes so as to permit their explication, prediction, and control will continue to falter until a model structure has become formed which has certain requisite characteristics.

What is needed is a framework for thinking which will serve an integrative and synthetic function. We need ways to examine human activities and events which will be ordered and consistent with metaphysical constructions of both higher and lower orders of abstraction; compatibilities are needed throughout the vertical heirarchies of our models. Similar compatibilities are required across differing domains of inquiry in general, and those which encompass the human sciences in particular (the horizontal dimension). Finally, the compatibilities must be evident along the temporal dimension, where the models which represent event circumstances at a fixed moment in time are comparable to models which endeavor to trace event sequences (change) and particular kinds of change (development).

The use of a systems perspective is advocated as a means for effecting such an integration. With such a view one has the possibility of congruence of models at multiple levels of analysis; one also has the prospects of integrating sciences across disparate disciplines. And, one has the capabilities of drawing useful distinctions between the phenomena of change and a subset of those changes defined as developmental. In order to effect this, development must be represented in terms of systems transformation, and developmental processes characterized in terms of the succession of transitional states throughout which such transformations proceed. In addition, the perspective mandates a representation of situational and contextual factors involved in such developments, with their modeling taking place in compatible systems terms. An integrative view of the human is made possible by a model of generically distinct subsystems both laterally and vertically organized, acting both concomitantly and sequentially in relation to the passage of time.

Finally, the systems perspective operates from an essentially mathematic posture. It seeks a mathematic structure underlying the observed behavior of the human person, permitting one to operate disencumbered by the heterogeneous meanings attached to our everyday language, and our personal and phenomenal experience. Both the analysis of complex human organizations as they unfold and develop within naturalistic settings, and the design of deliberate procedures in order to beneficially modify those developmental processes in directions which people seek, thereby become susceptible to analytic precision and detailed rigor.

The perspective shows sufficient promise as to commend itself to serious pursuit by specialists in the human sciences and in human development as well. Collective and coordinate inquiry over a sustained period of time will be required to effect its elaboration and to employ it usefully in the world of human affairs. Initial applications of the approach are already underway, and contributions to theory and research in the field of human development as well. Finally, the perspective would appear able to manage a number of issues raised within life-span research; rather than delegating such issues to the level of error or uncertainty, a systems perspective is sufficiently comprehensive to permit their use as key ingredients in systematic theory construction.

References

Ackoff, R. L. General system theory and systems research: Contrasting conceptions of systems science. *General Systems,* 1963, **8,** 117–122.

Ackoff, R. L. & Emery, F. E. *On purposeful systems.* Chicago: Aldine Press, 1972.

Allport, G. W. *Becoming: Basic considerations for a psychology of personality.* New Haven, Conn.: Yale University Press, 1955.

Angyal, A. *Foundations for a science of personality.* New York: Commonwealth Fund, 1941.

Arbib, M. A. *The metaphorical brain: An introduction to cybernetics as artificial intelligence and brain theory.* New York: Wiley, 1972.

Arbib, M. A., & Kahn, R. M. A developmental model of information processing in the child. *Perspectives in Biology and Medicine,* 1969, **12,** 397–415.

Ashby, W. R. General systems theory as a new discipline. *General Systems,* 1958, **3,** 1–8.
Baltes, P. B., Reese, H. W., & Nesselroade, J. R. *Life-span developmental psychology: Introduction to research methods.* Monterey, Calif.: Brooks/Cole, 1977.
Baltes, P. B., & Willis, S. L. Toward psychological theories of aging and development. In J. E. Birren & K. W. Schaie (Eds.), *Handbook on psychology of aging.* New York: Reinhold-Van Nostrand, 1977.
Beer, S. *Cybernetics and management.* New York: Wiley, 1959.
Berrien, F. K. *General social systems.* New Brunswick, N.J.: Rutgers University Press, 1968.
Bertalanffy, L. V. Zu einer algemeinen systemlehre. *Blätter für Deutsche Philosophie,* 1945, **18,** 3–4.
Bertalanffy, L. V. An outline of General Systems Theory. *British Journal for the Philosophy of Science,* 1950, **1,** 134–165.
Bertalanffy, L. V. General System Theory. *Main Currents in Modern Thought,* 1955, **11,** 75–83.
Bertalanffy, L. V. General System Theory—A critical review. *General Systems,* 1962, **7,** 1–20.
Bertalanffy, L. V. General System Theory and psychiatry. In S. Arieti (Ed.), *American Handbook of Psychiatry.* New York: Basic Books, 1966.
Bertalanffy, L. V. *Robots, men, and minds.* New York: Braziller, 1967.
Bertalanffy, L. V. *General System Theory: Foundation, development, applications.* New York: Braziller, 1968.
Birren, J. E. Principles of research on aging. In J. E. Birren (Ed.), *Handbook of aging and the individual.* Chicago: University of Chicago Press, 1959.
Bischof, N. A systems approach toward the functional connections of attachment and fear. *Child Development,* 1975, **46,** 801–817.
Boulding, K. E. General systems theory: The skeleton of science. *Management Science,* 1956, **2,** 197–208.
Boulding, K. E. Political implications of general systems research. *General Systems,* 1961, **6,** 1–8.
Buckley, W. (Ed.). *Sociology and modern systems theory.* Englewood Cliffs, N.J.: Prentice-Hall, 1967.
Buckley, W. (Ed.). *Modern systems research for the behavioral scientist.* Chicago: Aldine, 1969.
Carzo, R., Jr., & Yanouzas, J. N. *Formal organization: A systems approach.* Homewood, Ill.: Richard D. Irwin, 1967.
Chase, W. P. *Management of system engineering.* New York: Wiley, 1974.
Craik, K. J. W. *The nature of explanation.* London and New York: Cambridge University Press, 1943.
Craik, K. J. W. The nature of psychology. In S. L. Sherwood (Ed.), *A selection of papers, essays, and other writings by the late Kenneth J. W. Craik.* London and New York: Cambridge University Press, 1966.
DiStefano, J. J., Stubberud, A. R., & Williams, I. J. *Feedback and control systems.* New York: McGraw-Hill, 1967.
Emery, F. E. (Ed.). *Systems thinking.* Baltimore: Penguin Books, 1969.
Frank, L. K. Human development: An emerging scientific discipline. In A. J. Solnit & S. A. Provence (Eds.), *Modern perspectives in child development.* New York: International Universities Press, 1963.
Goldstein, K. *The organism.* New York: American Book, 1939.
Gray, W., Duhl, F. J., & Rizzo, N. D. (Eds.). *General systems theory and psychiatry.* Boston: Little, Brown, 1969.

Grinker, R. R., Sr. (Ed.). *Toward a unified theory of human behavior* (2nd ed.). New York: Basic Books, 1967.

Grinker, R. R., Sr. *Psychiatry in broad perspective.* New York: Behavioral Publications, 1975.

Hamburger, V. The concept of "development" in biology. In D. Harris (Ed.), *The concept of development.* Minneapolis: University of Minnesota Press, 1957.

Harris, D. B. (Ed.). *The concept of development.* Minneapolis: University of Minnesota Press, 1957. (a)

Harris, D. B. Problems in formulating a scientific concept of development. In D. B. Harris (Ed.), *The concept of development.* Minneapolis: University of Minnesota Press, 1957. (b).

Harris, D. B. The development of human behavior: Theoretical considerations for future research. In E. Tobach, L. R. Aronson, & E. Shaw (Eds.), *The biopsychology of development.* New York: Academic Press, 1971.

Hebb, D. O. *Organization of behavior.* New York: Wiley, 1949.

Hunt, E. B. What kind of computer is man? *Cognitive Psychology,* 1971, **2**, 57–98.

Huston-Stein, A., & Baltes, P. B. Theory and method in life-span developmental psychology: Implications for child development. In H. W. Reese & L. P. Lipsitt (Eds.), *Advances in child development and behavior* (Vol. 11). New York: Academic Press, 1976.

Katz, D., & Kahn, R. L. *The social psychology of organizations.* New York: Wiley, 1966.

Kluckhohn, C., & Murray, H. A. (Eds.). *Personality in nature, society and culture.* New York: Knopf, 1949.

Köhler, W. *Gestalt psychology: An introduction to the new concepts in modern psychology.* New York: Liveright, 1947.

Kuhn, T. S. *The structure of scientific revolutions.* Chicago: University of Chicago Press, 1962.

Laszlo, E. *Introduction to systems philosophy.* New York: Harper Torchbooks, 1972.

Lerner, R. *Theories and concepts of human development.* Reading, Mass.: Addison-Wesley, 1976.

Lewin, K. *A dynamic theory of personality.* New York: McGraw-Hill, 1935.

Looft, W. R. The evolution of developmental psychology: A comparison of handbooks. *Human Development,* 1972, **15**, 187–201.

Looft, W. R. Socialization and personality throughout the life span: An examination of contemporary psychological approaches. In P. B. Baltes & K. W. Schaie (Eds.), *Life-span developmental psychology: Personality and socialization.* New York: Academic Press, 1973.

MacCorquodale, K. B. F., & Meehl, P. E. On a distinction between hypothetical constructs and intervening variables. *Psychological Review,* 1948, **55**, 95–107.

Mayr, E. Behavior programs and evolutionary strategies. *American Scientist,* 1974, **62**, 650–659.

Menninger, K., Mayman, M., & Pruyser, P. *The vital balance: The life process in mental health and illness.* New York: Viking Press, 1963.

Miller, J. G. Toward a general theory for the behavioral sciences. *American Psychologist,* 1955, **10**, 513–531.

Miller, J. G. Living systems: Basic concepts. *Behavioral Science,* 1965, **10**, 193–237. (a)

Miller, J. G. Living systems: Cross-level hypotheses. *Behavioral Science,* 1965, **10**, 380–411. (b)

Miller, J. G. Living systems: Structure and process. *Behavioral Science,* 1965, **10**, 337–379. (c)

Miller, J. G. The organization of life. *Perspectives in Biology and Medicine,* 1965, **9,** 107–125. (d)

Miller, J. G. Living systems: The group. *Behavioral Science,* 1971, **16,** 302–398.

Miller, J. G. Living systems: The organization. *Behavioral Science,* 1972, **17,** 1–182.

Milsum, J. H. *Biological control systems analysis.* New York: McGraw-Hill, 1966.

Nagel, E. Determinism and development. In D. B. Harris (Ed.). *The concept of development.* Minneapolis: University of Minnesota Press, 1957.

Neisser, U. *Cognitive psychology.* New York: Appleton, 1967.

Newell, A., & Simon, H. A. *Human problem solving.* Englewood Cliffs, N.J.: Prentice-Hall, 1972.

Olson, W. C. *Development theory in education.* In D. B. Harris (Ed.), *The concept of development.* Minneapolis: University of Minnesota Press, 1957.

Overton, W. R., & Reese, H. W. Models of development: Methodological implications. In J. R. Nesselroade & H. W. Reese (Eds.), *Life-span developmental psychology: Methodological issues.* New York: Academic Press, 1973.

Phillips, E. L., & Wiener, D. N. *Short-term psychotherapy and structured behavior change.* New York: McGraw-Hill, 1966.

Popper, K. R. *The poverty of historicism.* Boston: Beacon Press, 1957.

Pylyshyn, Z. W. Competence and psychological reality. *American Psychologist,* 1972, **27,** 546–552.

Ramo, S. The systems approach. In R. F. Miles, Jr. (Ed.), *Systems concepts: Lectures on contemporary approaches to systems.* New York: Wiley, 1973.

Rapoport, A. The diffusion problem in mass behavior. *General Systems,* 1956, **1,** 48.

Rapoport, A. Mathematical aspects of general systems analysis. *General Systems,* 1966, **11,** 3–12.

Rapoport, A. Modern systems theory: An outlook for coping with change. *General Systems,* 1970, **15,** 15–25.

Reese, H. W. The development of memory: Life-span perspectives. In H. W. Reese & L. P. Lipsitt (Eds.), *Advances in child development and behavior* (Vol. 11). New York: Academic Press, 1976.

Reese, H. W., & Overton, W. F. Models of development and theories of development. In L. R. Goulet & P. B. Baltes (Eds.), *Life-span developmental psychology: Research and theory.* New York: Academic Press, 1970.

Riegel, K. F. Toward a dialectical theory of development. *Human Development,* 1975, **18,** 50–64.

Riegel, K. The dialectics of human development. *American Psychologist,* 1976, **31,** 689–700.

Royce, J. R., & Buss, A. R. The role of general systems and information theory in multi-factor individuality theory. *Canadian Psychological Review,* 1976, **17,** 1–21.

Ruesch, J. The old world and the new. *American Journal of Psychiatry,* 1967, **124,** Editorial.

Schneirla, T. C. The concept of development in comparative psychology. In D. B. Harris (Ed.), *The concept of development.* Minneapolis: University of Minnesota Press, 1957.

Scott, J. P. The genetic and environmental differentiation of behavior. In D. B. Harris (Ed.) *The concept of development.* Minneapolis: University of Minnesota Press, 1957.

Seiler, J. A. *Systems analysis in organizational behavior.* Homewood, Ill.: Irwin-Dorsey, 1967

Simon, H. A. The future of information processing technology. *Management Science,* 1968, **14,** 619–624.

Sutherland, J. W. *A general systems philosophy for the social and behavioral sciences.* New York: Braziller, 1973.

Timiras, P. S. *Developmental physiology and aging.* New York: Macmillan, 1972.

Weiss, P. A. Whither life science? *American Scientist,* 1970, **58,** 158–163.

Werner, H. The concept of development from a comparative and organismic point of view. In D. B. Harris (Ed.), *The concept of development.* Minneapolis: University of Minnesota Press, 1957.

White, R. W. *Lives in progress.* New York: Dryden Press, 1952.

Wiener, N. *Cybernetics.* New York: Wiley, 1948.

Wohlwill, J. F. *The study of behavioral development.* New York: Academic Press, 1973.

Wymore, A. W. *Systems engineering methodology for interdisciplinary teams.* New York: Wiley, 1976.

A Life-Span Approach to Perceptual Development

Robert H. Pollack and Beverly M. Atkeson

DEPARTMENT OF PSYCHOLOGY,

UNIVERSITY OF GEORGIA,

ATHENS, GEORGIA

Abstract

An attempt is made to adapt Werner's organismic developmental viewpoint as a theory of perceptual development applicable to the total life span. Previous theoretical conceptions, such as that of Piaget, have dealt with segments only (e.g., childhood) with no concern for either middle life or old age. Some of these conceptions and a part of the existing empirical literature are reviewed. Particular note is taken of theoretical statements put forward by Botwinick and Eisdorfer concerning the aging process. Elements of these positions are combined with the perceptual development theory constructed by Pollack in his work with children. This extended theory is applied to that part of the life span beyond age 20. Some preliminary studies are summarized and discussed within this theoretical framework. An outline of plans for future experimentation concludes the chapter.

I. Introduction

Perception is a psychological process which exhibits age-related changes from birth to death. Despite this all too obvious fact, there have been very few attempts to integrate ontogenetic data across the life span within a single theoretical framework. Most theorizing is carried out within the artificial but quite distinct compartments of infancy, child development, classical perception, and a tiny cubbyhole devoted to aging. We ourselves have been guilty of confining our research and theoretical efforts to child development and classical perception until recently when we began to expand our efforts to include the adult part of the life span.

The present chapter will begin with a brief review of the experimental and theoretical literature on changes in adult sensory and perceptual processes. This review will be limited to topics which, when coupled with Pollack's previous work, form the basis of our own theoretical and empirical efforts toward understanding life-span processes. More extensive reviews of sensory and perceptual changes in both children and adults are already available (Botwinick, 1973; Corso, 1971; Reese & Lipsitt, 1970; Weiss, 1959). We will then present the research conducted by Pollack and his colleagues on perceptual aging and development during childhood, and our initial efforts and plans to extend this theoretical framework to examine sensory and perceptual changes across the entire life span.

It is important to state at the outset that we will be dealing with age changes, some of which are developmental in nature and some of which are not. For us, development implies either a differentiation of function accompanied by hierarchic integration or a reversal of this process: dedifferentiation accompanied by disintegration. Quantitatively continuous aging functions across the life span are treated, but we do not consider them developmental in nature. Our viewpoint is an adaptation of Heinz Werner's orthogenetic principle (Werner, 1957). We have sought to separate the notion of development from mere age despite the coincidence of age and developmental level which occurs from time to time. We do discuss both types of change, but we have tried to keep them conceptually distinct insofar as we are able.

II. Previous Research on Visual Processes in the Aged

Although research on visual perception is extensive, there has been relatively little experimentation on changes in sensory and perceptual processes as a function of age. Of these studies, few have examined changes occurring in later life. The following is a brief review of those studies which are relevant to our own research program.

A. STRUCTURAL MODIFICATIONS

With increasing age there are at least two critical changes which occur in the eye and affect visual functioning. One is that the diameter of the pupil diminishes as a function of age (Birren, Casperson, & Botwinick, 1950; Kadlecova, Peleska, & Vasko, 1958; Leinhos, 1959). If the data from the studies on senile miosis (pupillary constriction) are compared, it appears that the decrease in pupillary area with age is more striking at low and intermediate levels than at high levels of illumination (Weale, 1963).

A second structural change in the eye concerns the crystalline lens. With increasing age, the nuclei and cell membranes of the old fibers become compressed, lose water, and shrink (Leopold, 1965). This progressive accumulation of inert tissue at the center of the lens reduces its transparency. Also contributing to the lens' decrease in ability to transmit light is its increase in thickness and yellowing with age (Weale, 1963).

The major effect of these changes in the pupil and crystalline lens of the eye is a general reduction in the amount of light reaching the retina. The constriction of the pupil directly reduces the amount of light which enters the eye, whereas the changes in the lens of the eye act as a filter to further reduce the intensity of the light transmitted to the retina. In addition to this quantitative change with increasing age, there is a change in the spectral quality of the light reaching the retina because of the yellowing of the lens. This senile yellowing results in an increased reduction in the blue part of the spectrum (Said & Weale, 1959).

B. ABSOLUTE THRESHOLD

A general rise in absolute threshold with increasing age has been shown in numerous studies (e.g., Birren, Bick, & Fox, 1948; Luria, 1960; Robertson & Yudkin, 1944; Steven, 1946). Using a white light as a stimulus, Robertson and Yudkin (1944) measured the absolute threshold of over 1000 individuals aged 10–70 years. Comparing their obtained thresholds with those expected as a result of the diminution of pupil size with age, they conclude that, "the deterioration of dark adaptation with age can be explained entirely by the increase in the size of the pupil with age" (p. 7).

However, other threshold studies (Birren *et al.*, 1948; Steven, 1946) controlled for changes in pupil diameter through the use of an artificial pupil and still obtained a general rise in threshold with age. This finding, which is unexpected if Robertson and Yudkin's conclusion is correct, is due to the use of a blue test stimulus to obtain the threshold measures. Robertson and Yudkin's use of a white light minimized the possible effects of senile yellowing of the lens; however, a blue test stimulus would be more sensitive to threshold changes resulting from this progressive yellowing. Reviewing these studies, Weale (1963) concludes that the observed threshold changes with increasing age can be accounted for "largely in terms of senile miosis and alteration of the light trans- mitting properties of the crystalline lens" (p. 135).

C. VISUAL ACUITY

Once into adulthood, visual acuity declines with increasing age (Chapanis, 1950; Donders, 1864; Hirsch, 1960; Slataper, 1950). Although there is disagreement as to when this decline begins, generally there appears to be a slight decline in visual acuity from the mid-20s to the 50s. After age 50, the rate of decline accelerates.

Because visual acuity is directly related to the level of ambient illumi- nation, one would expect the resolving power of the eye to decrease with age because of the reduction in the amount of light reaching the retina. However, the decline in visual acuity is much greater than that which one would predict to result from senile miosis and lenticular yellowing alone (Weale, 1963). In fact, as Weale (1963) notes, senile yellowing of the lens can serve to reduce distortions due to chromatic aberrations and thus, in some instances, improve visual acuity. Retinal degeneration cannot be employed to explain this excessive decline, since the retina has been shown to be relatively free from age changes (Leopold, 1965). Thus, we are currently without a complete explanation for the decrease in visual acuity with age.

D. CRITICAL FLICKER FREQUENCY

Critical flicker frequency (CFF) is a measure of the temporal resolving power of the visual system. As might be expected, several studies have examined changes in the fusion threshold for a flickering light as a func- tion of age (Brozek & Keys, 1945; McFarland, Warren, & Karis, 1958; Misiak, 1947, 1951). Combining the results of five studies, Weale (1965) estimated that between the ages of 20 and 60 years the average decline in fusion frequency is about 7 cycles per sec. Senile miosis is able to account for about 70% of this decline and lenticular yellowing for another 10% (Weale, 1965). Thus, it appears that the decrease in CFF with age can be attributed primarily to peripheral factors and, more specifically, to structural modifications within the eye.

Central factors may also be involved in changes in CFF with age. Some studies report a positive, although low, correlation between CFF and intelligence (Misiak, 1961). Additional implications for the influence of central factors in determining CFF are found when the task is made more difficult; if fusion frequency is measured in extrafoveal regions, the decline in CFF as a function of age is much larger. Weale (1963) suggests that a general decline in perceptual skills with age may be responsible.

E. FIGURAL AFTEREFFECTS

There are few studies on changes in figural aftereffects as a function of age. In general, it appears that with increasing age, susceptibility to the aftereffect decreases (Rich, 1957). Once the aftereffect is established, changes in its duration as a function of age are less clear. Several studies report that the duration of the aftereffect in the aged is the same as that of younger adults (Axelrod & Eisdorfer, 1962b; Thurner & Seyfried, 1962). However, Eisdorfer and Axelrod (1964) reanalyzed their earlier data (because of an error in data collection) and found that the duration of the aftereffect was longer for the older subjects than the younger.

F. ILLUSIONS

As is true with younger samples, changes in illusion magnitude during later life are dependent upon the illusion tested. Several studies have examined variations in illusion magnitude as a function of age using the Mueller-Lyer illusion and the Titchener Circles illusion (Comalli, 1965; Eisner & Schaie, 1971; Gajo, 1966; Wapner, Werner, & Comalli, 1960). These studies consistently report an increase in the magnitude of the Mueller-Lyer illusion in later adulthood. The results using the Titchener Circles illusion are somewhat contradictory. Most of the above studies report a decrease in illusion magnitude with increasing age; however, Gajo (1966) found an increase in the magnitude of the Titchener Circles illusion in his oldest group (60–77 years).

Two other illusions have been used in studying adult age changes. Leibowitz (Farguhar & Leibowitz, 1971; Leibowitz & Gwozdecki, 1967; Leibowitz & Judisch, 1967) reports that the magnitude of the Ponzo illusion decreases between middle and old age and that the magnitude of the Poggendorff illusion remains stable throughout adulthood.

As is evident from the above review, performance on sensory and perceptual tasks declines with increasing age. It appears that older people simply don't receive and process sensory information as well as younger adults. Research on the performance decrements observed with simple sensory tasks, for example, threshold and acuity tasks, has been quite fruitful. There is no doubt that the structural modifications in the eye contribute to the performance changes on these tasks.

The underlying causes of performance decrements on tasks using more complex stimuli are not yet understood. Most of the explanations proposed have been largely descriptive and post hoc. More research with specific hypotheses and predictions is needed if we are to understand perceptual changes which occur with age. The next section will examine a model which has been proposed specifically to explain changes in the processing of sequential information with age.

III.   Stimulus Persistence Model

One of the few theories or models concerning the processing of sensory information in the aged is the stimulus persistence model. Its possibility was first suggested by Axelrod (1963; Axelrod & Eisdorfer, 1962a) and is succinctly stated in the following:

> . . . in the senescent nervous system, there may be increased persistence of the activity evoked by a stimulus, i.e., . . . the rate of recovery from short term effects of stimulation may be slowed. On the assumption that the perception of the second stimulus as a discrete event depends on the degree to which the neural effects of the first have subsided, the poorer temporal resolution in senescence would then follow. (Axelrod, Thompson, & Cohen, 1968, p. 193)

Support for this model is found in both physiological and behavioral studies. At the physiological level, electroencephalograph records made by Mundy-Castle (1953, 1962) indicate that older subjects have longer-lasting aftereffects of cerebral activity in response to visual stimuli. This provides rather direct evidence for the persistence of neural activity in the senescent brain.

At the behavioral level, Botwinick (1973) has recently reviewed the results from aging studies which used tasks requiring the processing of successive information. Although his application of the stimulus persistence model to behavioral findings is entirely post hoc, the data seem to fit within this framework fairly well. For example, the stimulus persistence model can explain the fact that discrete, simple stimuli presented in rapid succession fuse more rapidly for the old than for young. This occurs not only with visual stimuli (CFF), but also with auditory clicks (Weiss & Birren, reported by Weiss, 1959, 1963) and shocks to the hand (Axelrod *et al.*, 1968). Although Botwinick is well aware of the contribution of peripheral, preretinal factors CFF, he postulates that stimulus persistence may account for the changes in CFF attributed to central factors.

Stimulus persistence may have either positive or negative effects in more complex perceptual processing:

> If the two stimuli are similar and do not come too rapidly together, and the two must be compared, the trace of the first can aid in judgments of the second. (Botwinick, 1973, pp. 135–136)

An example of this is found in an experiment by Landahl and Birren (1959). As part of their study, they compared the performance of young (18–32 years) and old (58–85 years) subjects on simultaneous and successive weight judgments. If each group's performance on the simultaneous task is taken as a baseline (because the old perceive weights less well than the young) for further age comparisons, the two age groups perform very similarly in the successive condition. On the basis of short-term memory studies with the aged, one might predict that the older subjects would not perform as well as the younger subjects in the successive task. Thus, the persistence of the first stimulus may have aided the older subjects in comparing the successive weights (Botwinick, 1973).

When dissimilar stimuli are presented in rapid succession, persistence of a stimulus will interfere with the processing of any subsequent stimuli. In support of this prediction, Botwinick (1973) cites the results from studies on speech perception in the elderly. Calero and Lazzaroni (1957) have shown that meaningful speech becomes less intelligible for older people when the speech is rapid.

The stimulus persistence model can also be used to explain the performance of older subjects with respect to ambiguous figures. If the trace of the initial percept persists in the older nervous system, it will fuse with subsequent incoming information, thus making the perception of new aspects of the stimulus configuration more difficult (Botwinick, 1973).

Kline is one of the few researchers who has attempted to directly test the stimulus persistence model. In his first two studies (Kline & Birren, 1975; Kline & Szafran, 1975) he employed a backward masking paradigm to measure changes in the speed of perceptual processing from young to old age. His results supported the stimulus persistence model: Older adults had longer interstimulus interval thresholds for both monoptic and dichoptic masking. Using a similar design, Walsh (1976) recently confirmed these findings.

In a subsequent study, Kline and Baffa (1975) presented young and old subjects with successive word halves at varying interstimulus intervals. With this design, the persistence of the first word half should aid in the recognition of the total word; thus, the stimulus persistence model would predict that older adults would do better than younger adults in this task. The results were just the opposite; the older adults were less able to identify the stimulus words.

A possible cause for stimulus persistence was inadvertently suggested by Welford (1965) in attempting to explain slowing in reaction time experiments with increasing age. Measurements of the conduction rate of peripheral motor nerves show only a slight slowing with age (Birren & Botwinick, 1955). When applied to reaction time experiments, this slowing can account for only 4% of the increased time needed by older adults to complete a simple perceptual–motor task. Reviewing this, Welford (1965) suggests that because these measurements were made of the spike discharges in large fibers, a similar percentage slowing would have more effect in smaller fibers; that is:

> . . . the absolute increase with age of time required for an impulse to travel a given distance in small fibers would be much greater than in large so that impulses which started together at one end of the trunk containing fibers of different sizes would arrive at the other end spread over a longer time in old than in young subjects. (p. 9)

Although Welford's suggestion was directed toward conduction rates in peripheral efferent fibers, it could also easily apply to neural processes in the visual system. This change in the relative speeds of conduction in different sized nerve fibers would extend both the time required to process a discrete stimulus event and the time over which the processing of sequential stimuli would overlap.

A second physiological change which might apply to the stimulus persistence model was suggested by Eisdorfer (1972). Based on the fact that with advancing age there is a loss in the number of functional neurons, Eisdorfer has hypothesized that the damping neurons in the visual system may deteriorate at a faster rate than other neurons. A reduction in this type of neuron could increase the duration of the neural activity generated by a stimulus.

IV. Pollack's Approach to Perceptual Development: Research and Theory

Pollack (1960) published a study on figural aftereffects designed to test the notion of permanent satiation proposed by Köhler and Wallach (1944). He hypothesized that the operation of this process should result in smaller and smaller aftereffects with increasing age. His results, however, showed that the frequency of both displacement and size aftereffects declines until middle childhood (10 years, 11 months), after which there is an increase in the occurrence of aftereffects into early adulthood. Besides failing to confirm the operation of permanent satiation, the U-shaped function suggested to Pollack that two separate processes might be responsible for the results. The decline in the frequency of aftereffects during early childhood was hypothesized to reflect a decline in receptor sensitivity as a result of the aging of the ocular structure. The subsequent increase in the frequency of aftereffects after age 11 was postulated to be the appearance of a higher level mechanism which integrates information through time (Pollack, 1976)

Pollack then suggested the applicability of these two mechanisms to findings from previous work with opticogeometric illusions. Prior studies of changes in illusion magnitude as a function of age had resulted in the delineation of illusions into two groups (Piaget & Lambercier, 1944; Piaget, Lambercier, Boesch, & Albertini, 1942). Proposed by Piaget, this typology divides illusions into primary or Type I illusions, those which decrease in magnitude with age, and secondary or Type II illusions, those with increase in magnitude with age. Piaget (1969) attempted to subsume all developmental changes in illusion magnitude, whether decremental or incremental, under a single explanatory principle, the Law of Relative Centrations. In Piaget's theory, Type I illusions result from an interaction between the stimulus configuration and the mode of viewing adopted by the observer (centration vs. decentration). Early in life, the child tends to view the whole figure and its dominant features with relatively few glances (centration); thus, he is unable to make the number of perceptual comparisons necessary to reduce or eliminate the distortion produced by the stimulus configuration. As the child grows older, decentration or integration of successive looks becomes the dominant mode of viewing. Consequently the magnitude of the Type I illusion decreases as the child is better able to analyze and compare the various parts of the figure. Type II illusions, however, depend upon successive comparisons for their effect. Thus, as the ability to integrate successive comparisons increases with increasing age, the magnitude of Type II illusions also increases.

Pollack rejected the single-mechanism explanation proposed by Piaget and suggested, instead, that the age changes observed in Type I and Type II illusions reflected the operation of two different mechanisms. More specifically, he hypothesized that the decline in Type I illusions was due to changes in the receptor process with age and thus reflected a non-developmental age change dependent upon factors of physiological aging. The mechanism underlying changes in Type II illusions was similar to that proposed by Piaget and involved the temporal integration of successive stimuli.

Corroborative evidence that changes in the visual receptor were in fact the primary determinants of illusion magnitude in Type I illusions came from a subsequent study. Pollack (1963) presented the Mueller-Lyer illusion tachistoscopically so as to minimize the conditions (successive glances) necessary to produce the ontogenetic trend in Piaget's theory and at the same time measured the threshold for the detection of a tachistoscopically presented contour. The threshold for the detection of a contour increased through childhood, whereas the magnitude of the Mueller-Lyer illusion declined with age. The correlation between the two functions was −.49. In addition, the correlation between IQ and magnitude of the Mueller-Lyer illusion was small, nonsignificant, and in the direction opposite to that expected by Piaget. Besides demonstrating that Piaget's explanation was not necessary, Pollack had shown that the decline in the Mueller-Lyer illusion was independent of higher cognitive factors and significantly related to the threshold for detecting a contour—a process largely determined by the efficiency of the receptor system.

In a second study, Pollack (1964) transformed the Mueller-Lyer illusion into a Type II illusion by temporally separating the presentation of the oblique inducing lines and the test line. When presented tachistoscopically to subjects aged 8–11, the age trend of the illusion magnitude reversed—increasing with increasing age and thus exhibiting a typical Type II function. Furthermore, correlation of illusion magnitude with mental age was significant and higher than that with chronological age. Thus, performance on Type II tasks appeared to involve a higher level perceptual process which integrates successive stimuli and is related to cognitive functioning.

Since these early studies, Pollack's research has been directed toward the examination of these two processes and their interaction. Experimentation has been extended to include other illusions—the Delboeuf illusion (Sjostrum & Pollack, 1971a), the Usnadze effect (Sjostrum & Pollack, 1971a), the Ponzo illusion (Quina & Pollack, 1971, 1972), and the Poggendorff illusion (Quina & Pollack, 1973)—and other perceptual phenomena—backward figural masking (Pollack, 1965a, 1965b; Streicher & Pollack, 1967), apparent movement (Pollack, 1966a, 1966b, 1966c), and the dark-interval threshold (Pollack, Ptashe, & Carter, 1968, 1969). The following is a recent summary of these research efforts:

The Type I process, which depends upon the interaction of the variables of relative intensity, duration, and contour orientation within the proximal stimulus, gradually declines with age as a function of decreasing receptor sensitivity. The effects of this loss of sensitivity are twofold. First, the strength of the interaction among these variables is reduced, thus decreasing the magnitude of Type I phenomena; second stimulus persistence in the receptor system is also reduced, thereby diminishing the magnitude of phenomena that depend upon the perceived simultaneity of stimuli presented in rapid succession. As the Type I process is declining the Type II process is progressively developing. The process, which involves the registration of stimulus traces and their integration with later stimuli in the series, becomes more manifest as the child grows older. Essentially, the child learns to compare the registered traces with new stimulation and begins to view the world in terms of sequences of stimulus events. (Pollack, 1969, p. 385)

V. Extension of Pollack's Work to Examine Perceptual Changes in Adulthood

A. TYPE I PHENOMENA

Our theoretical viewpoint leads to certain expectations during the adult portion of the life span with respect to Type I and Type II phenomena. Surprisingly, the theoretically simpler nondevelopmental notion of visual system aging used to account for the age course of Type I phenomena presents more of a problem in its extension to middle life and old age than the more complex developmental notion previously used to account for youthful changes in Type II phenomena. If the visual system merely continued to age all through the life span the way it apparently does through childhood to young adulthood, a continued decline in the magnitude of Type I phenomena would be expected. Except for the data on absolute sensory thresholds (Weale, 1963), virtually all the Type I phenomena studied thus far show an inflection in the age change curve somewhere in adulthood, with a definite increase in old age. Some of these increases exhibit magnitudes characteristic of those found in children. It should be noted, however, that none of these data were obtained under the experimental conditions which produced the findings on which we based our theory. All of them involved large figures under viewing conditions which permitted free head and eye movements through uncontrolled exposure durations.

The data collected thus far lead to a number of different but not necessarily conflicting possibilities. A Wernerian regression model could be tacked directly onto Piagetian theory which would state that senescence produces sufficient brain tissue deterioration to produce a regression from perceptual operations to reliance on field factors accompanied by a relative shift in mode of viewing from decentration to centration. Such a regression from perceptual operations fits the data but it would not apply to our more restricted experimental conditions where, in essence, the subject is forced to centrate because of the small central visual field, the instruction to fixate, and the brief exposure duration. In other words, if we were to find under our experimental conditions, age trends parallel to those found by Comalli (1965), Piagetian theory either could not account for them or would have to be bent considerably out of shape.

Some empirical evidence for an increase in the magnitude of a Mueller-Lyer illusion produced by a low-contrast figure as a function of increased exposure duration is found in an experiment by Ebert and Pollack (1972). They showed that if exposure time is increased from 500 to 1500 msec for high-, middle-, and low-contrast figures, the magnitude of the illusion for the first two declines somewhat, but that of the third increases significantly. The postulated stimulus persistence which occurs in the aged could well produce the equivalent of increasing the duration of a relatively low-contrast figure.

The naive stimulus persistence model put forth by Botwinick has its own difficulties in light of our data from childhood. We too have espoused a stimulus persistence notion to explain large Type I effects in childhood, but these persistence effects appear to be directly related to the sensitivity and efficiency of the visual system. None of the data on sensory thresholds suggest any improvement in such sensitivity in old age. Any increase in stimulus persistence starting in middle life must be brought about by a mechanism other than receptor sensitivity. Eisdorfer's hypothesis ceoncerning more rapid aging of thinner neural fibers offers a convenient way out of the persistence dilemma. There appear to be thin feedback fibers in the visual system whose action may be that of damping the duration of receptor fiber output. This system would have had to be wired in before birth and is probably functional shortly thereafter. It would gain strength through early life as receptor sensitivity declines, but at some point in middle life senescence would catch up with these fibers which then become nonfunctional over a period of time shorter than that required for relatively complete receptor deterioration. The result of such an aging process could well have no effect on absolute sensory thresholds but it would allow for increased persistence of suprathreshold stimuli. Such a mechanism could account for an increase in Type I phenomena found in previous experiments and provides a prediction for our proposed experiments as well.

At any rate, a planned future experiment employing red and blue illusory figures on gray backgrounds of equal lightness with young and old adults is expected to support the findings obtained earlier (Pollack, 1970) with younger subjects. This study showed the Type I age trend only with figures produced by lightness contrast and no age trend with figures produced by hue contrast. Such a finding rules out a cognitive explanation for age trends obtained under our conditions. If we could employ old enough subjects, however, we would expect a second inflection point and subsequent decline again in Type I magnitudes. Unfortunately, we have no idea as yet of the magnitude of individual differences to be expected in the aging of these hypothetical damping mechanisms. A broad spread could well mask a second inflection point in a population curve. Longitudinal data on a few subjects would be extremely useful provided that the population data fit reasonably well with the general hypothesis put forth.

In sum, our experiments can be expected to produce one of two results. Either the Type I age curve will continue falling or perhaps level out as would be expected from a straightforward application of our theory, or our data will parallel those already collected under less restricted conditions, in which case the Eisdorfer formulation tacked on to our theory offers a plausible explanation. Both of these findings do not require a psychological principle of development for their explanation. If the first possibility occurred, however, Comalli's data would require such a principle and the facile combination of Piaget and Werner proposed above would accomplish that task.

B. TYPE II PHENOMENA

Let us turn now to Type II phenomena where our task appears to be easier. These phenomena are produced by the integration of stimulus information across time and/or space. They require the registration and at least short-term storage of a trace of part of a total even configuration, the comparison of that trace with subsequent stimulation, and a general set to treat stimulus input in sequential terms. Given normal, nonretarded, nonbrain-damaged individuals, the capacities underlying trace registration and comparison are probably wired into the brain. The realization of the capacity to integrate information in sequence requires time and the firm establishment of the third component, the sequential set. The operation of this set represents a qualitative change in psychological organization that is, therefore, developmental in nature. It requires the differentiation of informational elements in a sequence perceived as such and the integration of these elements within a new higher level organizational framework. The rate of development will vary within individuals depending upon the level of complexity of the elements involved. The perception of sequential geometric illusions will proceed more rapidly than the integration of abstract mathematical concepts, but the underlying principle remains the same. This type of phenomenon should increase through childhood into adulthood, although the rate depends upon the content of the stimulation.

It is necessary at this point to discuss the trigger mechanism for the Type II integration process. The visual system seems to operate on a principle of least effort. Peripheral stimulation appears to pass up through the various levels of the visual nervous system from retinae, through lateral geniculate bodies, to the occipital cortex more or less isomorphically unless there are gaps in the information being transmitted. Such gaps are produced by the large size of the configuration being viewed so that it must be taken in multiple rather than single glances, actual large spatial gaps in the contours of the configuration, or a temporal sequence of presentation of parts of the configuration. Once the more central process is triggered, it takes control in true hierarchical fashion so that the variables which affect the more peripheral mechanisms are less important. The central process will operate as long as the peripheral stimuli are suprathreshold. In two experiments with the Delboeuf illusion and the Usnadze effect, Sjostrom and Pollack (1971a) simulated the aging of the lens of the eye by placing a yellow filter between the eye and the illusion configuration. The magnitude of the simultaneous Type I illusion (Delboeuf) decreased significantly, but that of the successive Type II effect (Usnadze) was virtually unchanged. The effect of simulated aging did not interact with real chronological age (Sjostrom & Pollack, 1971b). Thus both the principle of least effort and the assumption of control by the developmentally higher level control mechanism have found empirical support.

At first glance, the application of our theoretical conception to Type II phenomena in older adults is quite straightforward. The age curve through adulthood should be fairly flat until senescence weakens the central integrative mechanism which should in turn lessen the magnitude of Type II phenomena. Such a result follows from the notion of negative development or regression stated above. In other words, senescence should bring about a disintegration of hierarchic organization accompanied by dedifferentiation of function which would result in the impairment of integration of sequential perceptual information. At the same time there should be a resurgence of a concrete rather than an abstract attitude toward incoming stimulation if Goldstein (1939) is correct about the effects of brain tissue loss. Such an occurrence could be expected to weaken the general set toward viewing the world in terms of sequential events in favor of a here-and-now set of immediacy.

Stimulus persistence, however, could add a complicating factor to the comfortable straightforward position outlined above. If experimental situations are used in which temporal gaps in stimulation can be bridged by the persistence of relatively weak but suprathreshold stimuli, there could be a return to Type I conditions. In young children where persistence is mediated by an extremely sensitive, nonadapted receptor system in which stimuli change and weaken during exposure, such persistence can simulate Type II effects in that new strong stimulation is compared with the persistence of a stimulus which has changed during its exposure. For example, the inducing circles in the Usnadze effect diminish in size during their exposure duration as they lose figure ground contrast. Such shrinkage even with short-exposure duration has been demonstrated by Sjostrom and Pollack (1973). The subsequent high-contrast stimulation produced by the test circles is thus simultaneously contrasted with the persistent stimulus trace of the now shrunken inducing circles which produces the same effect as a true successive comparison. If the exposure times are properly manipulated one can produce a U-shaped age curve through childhood (Pollack, 1960) with a decline in illusion effect up to age 9 followed by an increase. In old age, however, the receptor system is not so sensitive and therefore will not adapt as fast to produce changes in the inducing figure of a successive illusion. The stimulus produced by this figure may persist in line with Eisdorfer's formulation, however, which could interact directly with the test figure, thus simulating the typical Type I situation. The result would be that the higher level Type II process, deteriorated or not, is not triggered. The subject would therefore report a reversed illusion (Type I) at some point in the later life span with -that illusion once again declining with further aging of the receptor system. In summary, our expectations are that Type II phenomena will begin declining in middle adulthood and may even reverse, at least temporarily, at some point in old age.

VI. First Study: Changes in the Magnitude of the Simultaneous and Successive Mueller-Lyer Illusion throughout Adulthood.

For our first study on sensory and perceptual changes in adulthood we selected two illusions—the simultaneous Mueller-Lyer illusion, a Type I phenomenon (Fig. 1), and the successive Mueller-Lyer illusion, a Type II phenomenon (Fig. 2). With the simultaneous illusion two predictions can be made. If there is a continuing decline in receptor sensitivity as a result of the physiological aging of the eye—as Pollack found for ages 6–20 years (Pollack, 1964; Ebert, 1974)—the magnitude of this illusion should also

Fig. 1. Stimulus figure for the simultaneous Mueller-Lyer illusion.

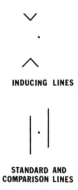

INDUCING LINES

STANDARD AND
COMPARISON LINES

Fig. 2.   Stimulus figures for the successive Mueller-Lyer illusion.

continue to decrease. If the physiological changes proposed by Eisdorfer are viable, the deterioration of the damping neurons should result in increased illusion magnitude in later adulthood.

Two predictions are also possible for the successive illusion. If the ability to integrate temporally separated stimuli decreases with senescence, the magnitude of the Type II illusion should decline in later adulthood. If the neural activity evoked by a stimulus persists in the senescent visual system, the illusion may reverse and become a positive illusion.

Both illusions were presented to 48 female adults divided into four age groups: 20–29 years, 40–49 years, 60–69 years, and 70–79 years. The stimulus figures used and the procedure followed replicated that of an earlier study with younger subjects (Ebert, 1974). The results of this study and that of two previous studies are presented in Fig. 3.

Because the variability for each illusion was different, separate one-way analyses of variance (ANOVA) were computed for each illusion. The one-way analysis for the simultaneous illusion was not significant. Two interpretations are possible. One, there is no change in illusion magnitude throughout adulthood, or two, the large variance with this condition masked the changes as a function of age. If this second interpretation is correct, then the data would support Eisdorfer's proposal. Deterioration of the damping fibers produces an enhancement of the illusion. This appears to begin in middle adulthood and peak in the 60s. After this, the illusion decreases again—perhaps as a result of the deterioration of other fibers within the visual system.

The one-way analysis for the successive illusion was significant at the .001 level ($F = 13.371$, $df = 3,44$). A trend analysis indicated a significant linear component accounting for approximately 85% of the variance ($F = 26.431$, $df = 1, 44$, $p < .01$). The quadratic component was not significant.

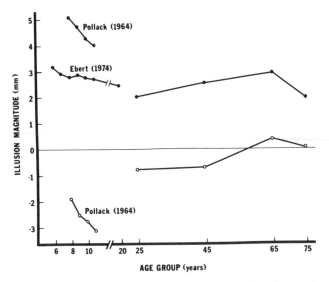

Fig. 3. Changes in the magnitude of the simultaneous (●——●) and successive (○——○) Mueller-Lyer illusions from age 6 to 75 years.

However, *t*-tests comparing the illusion magnitude at each age level to zero or no illusion revealed something quite interesting. For the 20- and 40-year-olds the illusion magnitude was significantly smaller than zero; thus these two age groups exhibited the expected negative illusion. But at age 60 the successive illusion reversed directions and became a positive illusion—significantly greater than zero. This finding can also be interpreted as support for Eisdorfer's proposal. Deterioration of the damping fibers results in the persistence of the inducing lines so that the successive presentation is processed as if it were a simultaneous illusion. For the 70-year-old group, the *t*-test was nonsignificant. The relative absence of an illusion at this age indicates that there was little integration between the successive presentation of the oblique inducing lines and the standard and comparison lines. This supports other studies which have found a decrement in temporal integration in later adulthood.

VII. Second Study: Changes in the Magnitude of the Delboeuf Illusion and the Usnadze Effect from Young to Old Age

For our second study, we selected two different illusions—the Delboeuf illusion, a Type I phenomenon (Fig. 4), and the successive Delboeuf or Usnadze effect, a Type II phenomenon (Fig. 5). These particular illusions

Fig. 4. Stimulus figure for the Delboeuf illusion.

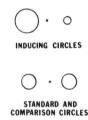

Fig. 5. Stimulus figures for the Usnadze effect.

were chosen for several reasons. One, there appear to be no experimental investigations using these illusions with older populations. Two, these two illusions had been used in a previous study by Pollack (Sjostrom & Pollack, 1971a); therefore, the data for magnitude changes in childhood were available for combination with adult data, once they were collected. Three, the magnitude of the Delboeuf illusion shows less variability between subjects than the simultaneous Mueller-Lyer illusion; therefore, it was hoped that age trends found with this illusion would be both significant and also replicate those found with the Mueller-Lyer illusion. The predictions were the same as those in the first study.

Although the data have not yet been collected for our middle-aged subjects, we have completed a young age group (20–29 years) and two older groups (60–69 years and 70–79 years). As with the first study, the stimulus figures and procedure replicated that of a previous investigation with children (Sjostrom & Pollack, 1971a). Figure 6 presents the data from our current study combined with the earlier one.

The results of a two-way ANOVA indicated that both the main effects of age and illusion were significant ($F = 5.51$, $df = 2,33$, $p < .001$). The interaction between age and illusion was not significant. Multiple comparisons between age groups indicated that only the 20- and 70-year-old groups were significantly different.

Although we have not yet collected the data for our middle-aged group, it appears that there is little, if any, change in the magnitude of the Delboeuf illusion when the 20- and 60-year-old groups are compared. After age 60, however, the illusion increases significantly. This age trend is similar to that obtained with the simultaneous Mueller-Lyer illusion except for the decrease in the last decade. It may be that the Delboeuf illusion, although belonging to the same illusion class as the Mueller-Lyer,

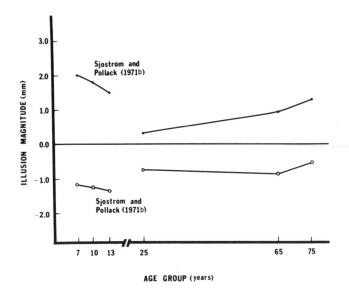

Fig. 6. Changes in the magnitude of the Delboeuf illusion (●——●) and Usnadze effect (○——○) from age 7 to 75 years.

exhibits a slightly retarded age function. If this is true, inclusion of an 80-year-old group might produce a decrement in illusion magnitude.

The magnitude of the Usnadze effect also remains constant between 20 and 60 years of age and then decreases in the 70-year-old group—showing the same retardation with respect to the successive Mueller-Lyer illusion. The results of this study resemble those obtained by others under conditions of free head and eye movement, large figures, and uncontrolled exposure times. However, our conditions—fixation, visual angle extent under 2°, and 500-msec exposure times—require explanations different from those permitted to these other investigators, explanations which are concerned more with the operation of the visual system itself rather than cognitive operations.

VIII. Summary and Conclusions

We have attempted to apply Werner's organismic developmental theory to a sampling of perceptual phenomena through the life span. The emphasis has been a bit more on the sensory half of the sensation–cognition continuum which characterizes the full range of perceptual phenomena. This choice has been deliberate in the service of what we believed was sound experimentation and theory construction. We have tried to deal with stimulus variables which we could control with reasonable certainty in settings which required the least equivocal of human responses without destroying the phenomenal experience we were trying to investigate.

The theoretical position we have developed from our previous work with children and adolescents is not bound to those age groups but, we believe, is applicable to any and all portions of the life span provided we take into account the special structural features of each portion. Furthermore, we agree with Werner that the theory transcends the ontogenetic and therefore can be applied with equal effect to phylogenetic and microgenetic sequences. Age, or better time, is not considered a determining variable, nor do its peculiar man-made units have any particular theoretical significance. It is merely the case that developmental sequences require time, whether this time is the eons of evolution or the milliseconds required for the emergence of a single percept. Thus the Wernerian orthogenetic and regression principles are timeless and are life span by nature if it is ontogenetic change which is to be our empirical focus.

We have defined two life-span sequences, one dependent on the nondevelopmental irreversible deterioration of neural tissue in the visual system which is called aging, and the other a higher level developmental sequence involving both orthogenesis and regression in the central activity which governs the integration of sensory experience.

The first or Type I sequence manifests itself by a reduction in the magnitude of certain phenomena as a function of lessened contrast of those contours producing the phenomena. This contrast loss is thought to be mediated by lenticular yellowing, deepening fundus pigmentation, permanent retinal adaptation, reduced density of primary corticol projection cells, or some combination of all of these factors. In middle adulthood, this continuous loss of sensitivity to patterned light stimulation appears to be complicated by the rapid aging of fibers which may serve to damp the duration of incoming stimulation. This secondary aging process described by Eisdorfer (1972) produces an apparent persistence of relatively low-level suprathreshold stimulation, which in turn produces at least a temporary increase in the magnitude of Type I phenomena. The result is a U-shaped life-span curve which may or may not have a second inflection point in advanced old age.

The second or Type II sequence is manifested in an increase in the magnitude of certain phenomena such as geometric illusions whose parts are presented sequentially with the inducing portions presented first (e.g., Usnadze effect, successive Mueller-Lyer, etc.). Because the appearance of such phenomena depends on the integration of percepts through time and are then mediated by more central cognitive processes, the expectation is that there would be some diminution in the magnitide of these phenomena at more advanced age levels. The Eisdorfer aging process mentioned above, however, could complicate the age trend. If the persistence of low-intensity inducing stimuli were to bridge the gap between their presentation and the test stimuli, Type II illusions could reverse and become Type I illusions at some point in the latter portion of the life span.

Thus far our data are fragmentary. We need the findings for the intervening decades for both sets of illusions in order to determine the actual shapes of the age curves. We know now, as well, that the findings for the illusions will not be identical despite their obvious class membership which means that we shall have to search for the determinants of the differences. Our program of research is set, however. A study on the dark interval threshold designed to get at the effects of stimulus persistence directly is under way. The next items on the agenda are figural aftereffects and a study of the Mueller-Lyer illusion using colored figures. Each of the studies has its own problems and each should contribute information which will either encourage or change our theoretical direction.

The aftereffect study will involve both lateral displacement and tilted line effects. We could get the same results as we have obtained with the Type II illusions or we could run into difficulty producing aftereffects at all as a result of increased eye tremors in old age despite the instruction to fixate. The tilted line situation should obviate the difficulty since that effect has been produced in the past without strict fixation. As stated above, the study with the colored illusion figures should determine the presence or absence of some central cognitive overlay in Type I phenomena in our experimental situation. We have other studies planned, designed to generalize our findings to other visual phenomena and to attack underlying perceptual mechanisms, but their exact nature cannot be stated until the present round of experimentation is completed and the data are analyzed.

Acknowledgments

The research on adults carried out by the authors and reported in this chapter was supported, in part, by a grant from the National Institute of Aging, Department of Health, Education and Welfare, Grant No. ROI AG 00297.

References

Axelrod, S. Cognitive tasks in several modalities. In R. H. Williams, C. Tibbitts, & W. Donahue (Eds.), *Processes of aging* (Vol. 1). New York: Atherton Press, 1963.

Axelrod, S., & Eisdorfer, C. Auditory time-error and context effects in the aged. In C. Tibbitts & W. Donahue (Eds.), *Social and psychological aspects of aging.* New York: Columbia University Press, 1962. (a)

Axelrod, S., & Eisdorfer, C. Senescence and figural aftereffects in two modalities. *Journal of Genetic Psychology,* 1962, **100,** 85–91. (b)

Axelrod, S., Thompson, L. W., & Cohen, L. D. Effects of senescence on the temporal resolution of somesthetic stimuli presented to one hand or both. *Journal of Gerontology,* 1968, **23,** 191–195.

Birren, J. E., Bick, M. W., & Fox, C. Age changes in the light threshold of the dark adapted eye. *Journal of Gerontology,* 1948, **3,** 267–271.

Birren, J. E., Casperson, R. C., & Botwinick, J. Age changes in pupil size. *Journal of Gerontology,* 1950, **5,** 216–221.

Birren, J. E., & Botwinick, J. Age differences in finger, jaw and foot reaction time to auditory stimuli. *Journal of Gerontology,* 1955, **10,** 429–432.

Botwinick, J. *Aging and behavior.* New York: Springer, 1973.

Brozek, J., & Keys, A. Changes in flicker-fusion frequency with age. *Journal of Consulting Psychology,* 1945, **9,** 87–90.

Calero, C., & Lazzaroni, A. Speech intelligibility in relation to the speed of the message. *Laryngoscope,* 1957, **67,** 410–419.

Chapanis, A. Relationships between age, visual acuity, and color vision. *Human Biology,* 1950, **22,** 1–33.

Comalli, P. E. Cognitive functioning in a group of 80–90 year-old men. *Journal of Gerontology,* 1965, **20,** 14–17.

Corso, J. F. Sensory processes and age effects in normal adults. *Journal of Gerontology,* 1971, **26,** 90–105.

Donders, F. C. *On the anomalies of accommodation and refraction of the eye.* London: New Sydenham Society, 1864.

Ebert, P. *Ontogenetic changes in the magnitude of the Mueller-Lyer illusion as a function of lightness contrast.* Unpublished doctoral dissertation, University of Georgia, 1974.

Ebert, P., & Pollack, R. H. Magnitude of the Mueller-Lyer illusion as a function of lightness contrast, viewing time, and fundus pigmentation. *Psychonomic Science,* 1972, **26,** 347–348.

Eisdorfer, C. Personal communication, Spring, 1972.

Eisdorfer, C., & Axelrod, S. Senescence and figural aftereffects in two modalities: A correction. *Journal of Genetic Psychology,* 1964, **104,** 193–197.

Eisner, D. A., & Schaie, K. W. Age changes in response to visual illusions from middle to old age. *Journal of Gerontology,* 1971, **26,** 146–150.

Farquhar, M., & Leibowitz, H. W. The magnitude of the Ponzo illusion as a function of age for large and for small stimulus configurations. *Psychonomic Science,* 1971, **25,** 97–99.

Gajo, F. D. Adult age differences in the perception of visual illusions. (Doctoral dissertation, Washington University, 1966). *Dissertation Abstracts,* 1967, 27(12), 4573B (University Microfilms No. 67–7036).

Goldstein, K. *The organism.* New York: American Book, 1939.

Hirsch, M. J. Effect of age on visual acuity. In M. J. Hirsch & R. F. Wick (Eds.), *Vision in the aging patient.* Philadelphia: Chilton, 1960.

Kadlecova, V., Peleska, M., & Vasko, A. Dependence on age of the diameter of the pupil in the dark. *Nature (London),* 1958, **182,** 1520–1521.

Kline, D. W., & Baffa, G. *Age and the sequential integration of form.* Paper presented at the annual meeting of the Gerontological Society, Louisville, October, 1975.

Kline, D. W., & Birren, J. E. Age differences in backward dichoptic masking. *Experimental Aging Research*, 1975, **1**, 17–25.

Kline, D. W., & Szafran, J. Age differences in backward monoptic visual noise masking. *Journal of Gerontology*, 1975, **30**, 307–311.

Köhler, W., & Wallach, H. Figural aftereffects: An investigation of visual processes. *Proceedings of the American Philosophical Society*, 1944, **88**, 269–357.

Landahl, H. D., & Birren, J. E. Effects of age on the discrimination of lifted weights. *Journal of Gerontology*, 1959, **14**, 48–55.

Leibowitz, H. W., & Gwozdecki, J. The magnitude of the Poggendorff illusion as a function of age. *Child Development*, 1967, **38**, 573–580.

Leibowitz, H. W., & Judisch, J. M. The relation between age and the magnitude of the Ponzo illusion. *American Journal of Psychology*, 1967, **80**, 105–109.

Leinhos, R. Die Altersabhangigkeit des Augenpupillendurchmessers. *Optik*, 1959, **16**, 669–671.

Leopold, I. H. The eye. In J. T. Freeman (Ed.), *Clinical features of the older patient*. Springfield, Ill.: Thomas, 1965.

Luria, S. M. Absolute visual threshold and age. *Journal of the Optical Society of America*, 1960, **50**, 86–87.

McFarland, R. A., Warren, A. B., & Karis, C. Alterations in critical flicker frequency as a function of age and light:dark ratio. *Journal of Experimental Psychology*, 1958, **56**, 529–538.

Misiak, H. Age and sex differences in critical flicker frequency. *Journal of Experimental Psychology*, 1947, **37**, 318–332.

Misiak, H. The decrease of critical flicker frequency with age. *Science*, 1951, **113**, 551–552.

Misiak, H. Recent studies on the effect of aging on the fusion of intermittent light. *Acta Psychologica*, 1961, **19**, 159–160.

Mundy-Castle, A. C. An analysis of central responses to photic stimulation in normal adults. *Electroencephalography and Clinical Neurophysiology*, 1953, **5**, 1–22.

Mundy-Castle, A. C. Central excitability in the aged. In H. T. Blumenthal (Ed.), *Aging around the world: Medical and clinical aspects of aging*. New York: Columbia University Press, 1962.

Piaget, J. *The mechanisms of perception*. New York: Basic Books, 1969.

Piaget, J., & Lambercier, M. Recherches sur le développement des perceptions: V. Essai sur un effet d' "Eistellung" survenant au cours de perceptions visuelles, successives (effet Usnadze). *Archives de Psychologie*, 1944, **30**, 139–196.

Piaget, J., Lambercier, M., Boesch, E., & Albertini, B. V. Recherches sur le développement des perceptions: I. Introduction à l'étude des perceptions chez l'enfant et analyse d'une illusion relative à la perception visuelle de cercles concentriques (Delboeuf). *Archives de Psychologie*, 1942, **29**, 1–107.

Pollack, R. H. Figural aftereffects as a function of age. *Acta Psychologica*, 1960, **17**, 417–423.

Pollack, R. H. Contour detectability thresholds as a function of chronological age. *Perceptual and Motor Skills*, 1963, **17**, 411–417.

Pollack, R. H. Simultaneous and successive presentation of elements of the Mueller-Lyer figure and chronological age. *Perceptual and Motor Skills*, 1964, **19**, 303–310.

Pollack, R. H. Backward figural masking as a function of chronological age and intelligence. *Psychonomic Science*, 1965, **3**, 65–66. (a)

Pollack, R. H. Effects of figure-ground contrast and contour orientation on figural masking. *Psychonomic Science*, 1965, **2**, 369–370. (b)

Pollack, R. H. Effect of figure-ground contrast and contour orientation on the temporal range of apparent movement. *Psychonomic Science,* 1966, **4,** 401–402. (a)

Pollack, R. H. Initial stimulus duration and the temporal range of apparent movement. *Psychonomic Science,* 1966, **5,** 165–166. (b)

Pollack, R. H. Temporal range of apparent movement as a function of age and intelligence. *Psychonomic Science,* 1966, **5,** 243–244. (c)

Pollack, R. H. Some implications of ontogenetic changes in perception. In D. Elkind & J. H. Flavell (Eds.), *Studies in cognitive development: Essays in honor of Jean Piaget.* London and New York: Oxford University Press, 1969.

Pollack, R. H. Magnitude of the Mueller-Lyer illusion as a function of hue in the absence of lightness contrast. *Proceedings, 78th Annual Convention, American Psychological Association,* 1970, 53–54.

Pollack, R. H. Illusions and perceptual development: A tachistoscopic approach. In K. F. Riegel & J. A. Mescham (Eds.), *The developing individual in a changing world.* Chicago: Aldine, 1976.

Pollack, R. H., Ptashne, R. I., & Carter, D. J. The dark-interval threshold as a function of age. *Psychonomic Science,* 1968, **12,** 237–238.

Pollack, R. H., Ptashne, R. I., & Carter, D. J. The effects of age and intelligence on the dark-interval threshold. *Perception & Psychophysics,* 1969, **6,** 50–52.

Quina, M. K., & Pollack, R. H. A parametric investigation of the Ponzo illusion under conditions of tachistoscopic exposure. *Proceedings, 79th Annual Convention, American Psychological Association,* 1971, **6,** 77–78.

Quina, M. K., & Pollack, R. H. Effects of test line position and age on the magnitude of the Ponzo illusion. *Perception & Psychophysics,* 1972, **12,** 253–256.

Quina, M. K., & Pollack, R. H. Attraction of parallels as a function of intercontour distance. *Perceptual and Motor Skills,* 1973, **36,** 934.

Reese, H. W., & Lipsitt, L. P. *Experimental child psychology.* New York: Academic Press, 1970.

Rich, T. A. Perceptual after-effects, learning and memory in an aged group. (Doctoral dissertation, University of Florida, 1957). *Dissertation Abstracts,* 1958, **18**(1), 311–312 (University Microfilms No. 58–457).

Robertson, G. W., & Yudkin, J. Effect of age upon dark adaptation. *Journal of Physiology (London),* 1944, **103,** 1–8.

Said, F. S., & Weale, R. A. The variation with age of the spectral transmissivity of the living human crystalline lens. *Gerontologia,* 1959, **3,** 213–231.

Sjostrom, K. P., & Pollack, R. H. The effect of simulated receptor aging on two types of visual illusions. *Psychonomic Science,* 1971, **23,** 147–148. (a)

Sjostrom, K. P., & Pollack, R. H. Simulated receptor aging in the study of ontogenetic trends of visual illusions. *Proceedings, 79th Annual Convention, American Psychological Association,* 1971, **6,** 173–174. (b)

Sjostrom, K. P., & Pollack, R. H. Effect of short-term fixation on perceived size of a circle. *Perceptual and Motor Skills,* 1973, **36,** 1217–1218.

Slataper, F. J. Age norms of refraction and vision. *Archives of Ophthalmology,* 1950, **43,** 466–481.

Steven, D. M. Relation between dark adaptation and age. *Nature (London),* 1946, **157,** 376–377.

Streicher, H. W., & Pollack, R. H. Backward figural masking as a function of inter-contour distance. *Psychonomic Science,* 1967, **7,** 69–70.

Thurner, F. K., & Seyfried, H. Are figural after-effects dependent upon age? *Acta Psychologica,* 1962, **20,** 58–67.

Walsh, D. A. Age differences in central perceptual processing: A dichoptic backward masking investigation. *Journal of Gerontology,* 1976, **31,** 178–185.

Wapner, S., Werner, H., & Comalli, P. E. Perception of part-whole relationships in middle and old age. *Journal of Gerontology,* 1960, **15,** 412–416.

Weale, R. A. *The aging eye.* New York: Harper, 1963.

Weale, R. A. On the eye. In A. T. Welford & J. E. Birren (Eds.), *Behavior, aging, and the nervous system.* Springfield, Ill.: Thomas, 1965.

Weiss, A. D. Sensory functions. In J. E. Birren (Ed.), *Handbook of aging and the individual.* Chicago: University of Chicago Press, 1959.

Weiss, A. D. Auditory perception in aging. In J. E. Birren, R. N. Butler, S. W. Greenhouse, L. Sokoloff, & M. R. Yarrow (Eds.), *Human aging: A biological and behavioral study* (P.H.S. Publ. No. 986). Washington, D.C.: U.S. Government Printing Office, 1963.

Welford, A. T. Performance, biological mechanisms and age: A theoretical sketch. In A. T. Welford & J. E. Birren (Eds.), *Behavior, aging, and the nervous system.* Springfield, Ill.: Thomas, 1965.

Werner, H. The concept of development from a comparative and organismic point of view. In D. B. Harris (Ed.), *The concept of development.* Minneapolis: University of Minnesota Press, 1957.

Brain Electrical Activity and Behavior Relationships over the Life Span

Diana S. Woodruff

DEPARTMENT OF PSYCHOLOGY,
TEMPLE UNIVERSITY,
PHILADELPHIA, PENNSYLVANIA

Abstract

Brain electrical activity and behavior relationships are viewed from a developmental perspective to highlight critical points in physiological and behavioral development and to examine brain mechanisms in behavioral development and aging. Consideration is given to age changes in occipital electroencephalogram frequency and its significance in visual perception, attention, and the timing of behavior at various points of the life span. Developmental data on event-related potentials are described, along with implications for sensation, attention, and information processing. Asymmetries in the ongoing electroencephalogram and in event-related potentials are discussed as measures of the development of brain lateralization. Investigation of these asymmetries have provided insights to the development of receptive and expressive language and may also extend knowledge about the development and aging of verbal and spatial abilities and sex differences in these abilities.

I. Introduction

The purpose of this review is to highlight the usefulness of the life-span approach in the study of brain electrical activity and behavior, to demonstrate the number of behaviors and many points of the life span which can be better understood through analysis of electrophysiology and behavior relationships, and to stimulate developmentalists to consider electrophysiological data when they investigate behavioral development. While certain generalizations will be made on the basis of the data available, it will become apparent that complete integration of this large body of literature is impossible. The aim is to highlight profitable areas of research using the life-span perspective and to focus on critical periods of development at various points throughout the life span. Since the goal is to weave together and stimulate interest in this broad body of literature, critical review with close examination of each reported fact has been precluded.

The research reviewed here involves human subjects, and normal rather than abnormal development is discussed. The electrophysiological data include the scalp-recorded electroencephalogram (EEG) and computer-averaged signals called event-related potentials (ERPs) derived from scalp-recorded EEG. Behavioral relationships with ongoing EEG activity are discussed first, as this literature has the longest history and the greatest number of developmental studies. Consideration is given to points in the life span at which EEG changes may correlate with brain changes significant in behavioral development, and EEG is also discussed with regard to its functional significance in behavior and behavioral change over the life span. The ERP literature is discussed next to point out the potential of this approach to leading to insights about behavior over the life span. EEG and ERP research on the development of brain lateralization and its behavioral consequences is the final general topic of this chapter, and while developmental literature in this area is not extensive, its significance may cause this area to be in the forefront of developmental research in the coming decade.

A number of additional topics such as EEG and ERP relationships to intelligence and malnutrition as well as hormone, EEG, and behavior relationships are promising areas for developmental research, but these areas will have to be reviewed at a future time when more developmental data become available. Limiting the discussion to normal development also precludes treatment of a promising application of ERP research: the assessment of neural abnormalities involved in learning disorders and mental retardation. In a number of laboratories across the country ERPs are being used as diagnostic tools. John and his colleagues call this technique "neurometrics" (John & Thatcher, 1976). A recent volume provides evidence for the extent to which this approach is being tested (Karrer, 1976). The number of developmental issues just beginning to be investigated with EEG and ERP techniques suggests that many developmentalists and EEG researchers are sensing the rich prospects for combining these approaches.

II. Behavioral Relationships with Ongoing Electroencephalographic Activity

Electrical activity generated in the brain can be recorded from electrodes attached to the surface of the scalp, and this activity, the (EEG), has been useful in the identification of brain abnormalities as well as in the identification of brain–behavior relationships. Human scalp-recorded EEG consists of continuous rhythmic activity ranging in frequency from approximately 1–50 Hz. The amplitude of this spontaneously generated activity is measured in millionths of a volt and ranges from 2–400 μV. The most characteristic types of EEG waves and rhythms recorded in young adults are summarized in Table I.

The precise origin and mechanism for the generation of rhythmic brain activity is still unknown, but it is generally agreed that the EEG generators reside in the cortex. The maintenance and regulation of all of the rhythmic activity is probably not cortical, however, but rather originates in subcortical pacemakers most likely located in nonspecific nuclei of the thalamus (Andersen & Andersson, 1968). The observation that EEG activity in monozygotic twins is much more similar than activity in dizygotic twins (Lykken, Tellegen, & Thorkelson, 1974) and in unrelated individuals (Surwillo, 1977) suggests that the pattern of rhythmic electrical activity in individuals is an hereditary trait.

Since the human EEG was first reported by Berger in 1929 (Gloor, 1969), it has been associated with behavioral states, and in 1952 Lindsley summarized EEG data suggesting the frequency-related behavioral continuum presented in Table II. Lower frequencies in the delta and theta range appear prominently during sleep and lowered states of consciousness, while alpha activity is apparent during waking relaxation, and beta is evident in alert, attentive states. These general observations have continued to be supported empirically, and in addition to its clinical applications as an index of brain pathology, EEG frequency serves as a useful measure of the state of the organism (Lindsley & Wicke, 1974).

Attempts to find relationships between spontaneous EEG activity and more specific aspects of behavior in mature adults have met with mixed

TABLE I

Type of Waves and Rhythms in the Human Electroencephalogram and Their Approximate and Relative Specifications and Distributions, Including Condition When Present and Whether Normal[a]

Type of wave or rhythm	Frequency per second (range)	Amplitude or voltage (μV)	Percent of time present	Regional or diffuse	Region of prominence or maximum	Condition when present	Normal or abnormal
Alpha	8–12[b]	5–100	5–100	Diffuse	Occipital and parietal	Awake, relaxed eyes closed	Normal
Beta	18–30	2–20	5–100	Diffuse	Precentral and frontal	Awake, no movement	Normal
Gamma	30–50	2–10	5–100	Diffuse	Precentral and frontal	Awake	Normal—sleep deprived
Delta	.5–4	20–200	Variable	Diffuse	Variable	Asleep	Normal
	.5–4	20–400	Variable	Both	Variable	Awake	Abnormal
Theta	5–7	5–100	Variable	Regional	Frontal and temporal	Awake, affective or stress	Normal (?) / Abnormal
Kappa	8–12	5–40	Variable	Regional	Anterior and temporal	Awake, problem solving?	Normal
Lambda	Pos.–neg. spike or sharp waves	5–100	Variable	Regional	Parieto-occipital	Vis. stim. or eye opening	Normal(?)
K-Complex	Pos. sharp wave + other slow pos.–neg. + other	20–50	Variable	Diffuse	Vertex	Awake–aud. stim.	Normal(?)
		50–100	Variable	Diffuse	Vertex	Asleep–var. stim.	Normal
Sleep spindles	12–14	5–100	Variable	Regional	Precentral	Sleep onset	Normal

[a] From Lindsley and Wicke (1974).
[b] Lower for infants and young children.

TABLE II

Psychological States and Their EEG, Conscious, and Behavioral Correlates[a]

Behavioral continuum	Electroencephalogram	State of awareness	Behavioral efficiency
Strong, excited emotion (fear) (rage) (anxiety)	Desynchronized: low to moderate amplitude; fast, mixed frequencies	Restricted awareness; divided attention; diffuse, hazy; "confusion"	Poor (lack of control, freezing-up, disorganized)
Alert attentiveness	Partially synchronized: mainly fast, low amplitude waves	Selective attention, but may vary or shift, "concentration" anticipation, "set"	Good (efficient, selective, quick, reactions). Organized for serial responses
Relaxed wakefulness	Synchronized: optimal alpha rhythm	Attention wanders—not forced. Favors free association	Good (routine reactions and creative thought)
Drowsiness	Reduced alpha and occasional low amplitude slow waves	Borderline, partial awareness. Imagery and reverie. "Dreamlike states"	Poor (uncoordinated, sporadic, lacking sequential timing)
Light sleep	Spindle bursts and slow waves (larger). Loss of alpha	Markedly reduced consciousness (loss of consciousness). Dream state	Absent
Deep sleep	Large and very slow waves (synchrony but on slow time base). Random, irregular pattern	Complete loss of awareness (no memory for stimulation or for dreams)	Absent
Coma	Isoelectric to irregular large slow waves	Complete loss of consciousness, little or no response to stimulation; amnesia	Absent
Death	Isoelectric: gradual and permanent disappearance of all electrical activity	Complete loss of awareness as death ensues	Absent

[a] From Lindsley (1952).

115

success, leading many investigators to abandon simple EEG frequency measures for more complex computer-generated measures combining amplitude and frequency into spectral power analyses of background EEG. Another index, computer-averaged measures of EEG activity related to stimulus events (called event-related potentials, ERPs), has the advantage of reflecting brain responses to known external stimuli and has been favored over ongoing activity for this reason and because ERPs are more easily quantified and easier to relate to underlying brain structures. ERPs will be discussed with regard to development and aging in Section III.

There have been changes in background EEG activity reported at many points in the life span. Ellingson (1958, 1967) summarized the large body of literature on EEG development from conception to the first postnatal year. In brief, he reported that observations of nonviable fetuses and prematures indicated that spontaneous electrical activity is present in the human brain before the end of the first trimester of pregnancy. EEG records relatively free from artifact have been recorded in prematures at a conceptual age of 5 months. The EEG at this point includes occasional bursts of slow rhythmic activity against a predominant background of little voltage variation. By 8 months after conception the EEG has changed to the pattern observed at birth. This is the semirhythmic and irregular pattern presented in Fig. 1. The first EEG correlate of behavior is observed at this point when EEG changes associated with the transition from wakefulness to sleep become detectable. This can be seen in Fig. 1 which shows that higher amplitude, diffuse slow activity occurs in the record of the sleeping infant while faster, semirhythmic activity predomi-

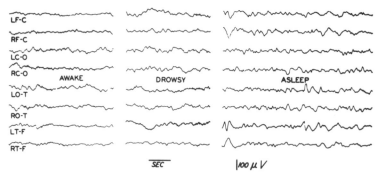

Fig. 1. EEG of premature infant of a conceptional age of 36 weeks (weight, 1660 gm) showing wakefulness–sleep transition. This is the earliest point in the life span when waking and sleeping EEG can be differentiated. In this figure an 8-electrode array was used. The electrode letter code at the left of the tracings is as follows: L = left, R = right, F = frontal, C = central, O = occipital, T = midtemporal. (From Ellingson, 1964.)

nates in the waking record. After this point in development, EEG activity during sleeping and during waking states becomes increasingly differentiated.

Dramatic developmental changes occur in sleep EEG patterns over the life span, the two major changes being a decreased proportion of sleep time spent in rapid eye movement (REM) and decreased time in the slow wave stage of sleep (Stage IV) (Kahn, 1970; Roffwarg, Munzio, & Dement, 1966). However, discussion of these changes and their implications is considered beyond the scope of this chapter. Feinberg (1969, 1974) and Feinberg and Carlson (1968) have documented these changes and presented convincing arguments for their significance in behavioral change. This work highlights the importance of the life-span perspective in assessing EEG changes during sleep. The present chapter will deal with the behavioral significance of life-span EEG changes in the waking state.

The EEG in the premature infant (conceptual age of 8 months) presented in Fig. 1 is similar to patterns recorded in neonates. Few changes occur in the neonatal EEG until 3 to 4 months postterm. Some rhythmic activity in the 6–7 Hz range can be recorded in rolandic areas in the first 3 months after birth, but the EEG is generally of low voltage (under 50 μV) and is not well organized rhythmically in any other brain area at this point. Around the end of the third month of life this picture changes rather dramatically when a predominantly occipital rhythm of 50 μV or more appears at a frequency of about 3–4 Hz. A number of those studying neonatal EEG (Dreyfus-Brisac, Samson, Blanc, & Monod, 1958; Ellingson, 1967; Lindsley, 1939) consider the beginning of organized, prominent rhythmic activity in occipital areas to be one of the most significant changes in the ontogeny of the EEG.

After the critical 3- to 4-month period, EEG changes occur rather rapidly with an increase in the occipital rhythm to 6–7 Hz by the end of the first year. The EEG begins to look more similar to adult patterns during this period (see Fig. 2). Activity becomes more synchronous between the two hemispheres, most likely reflecting the beginning of innervation of the cerebral commissures, particularly the corpus callosum. High voltage activity (100 μV) begins to appear after the first 6 months postterm. Some fast activity (13–30 Hz) appears in the record during the first year, but most activity is slower.

In the first year of life neuroanatomical development is rapid and is reflected in rapid changes in rhythmic EEG activity. Neuroanatomical changes such as dendritic branching and myelinization which occur earlier in sensory and motor than in association areas of the brain (Timiras, 1972) are paralleled by EEG changes appearing first in sensory and motor areas. While infancy involves the most rapid phase of brain maturation,

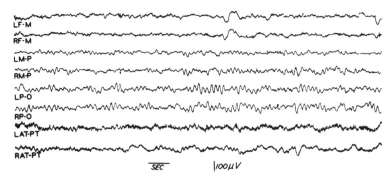

Fig. 2. EEG of a normal full-term infant during wakefulness at 7 months of age, showing the dominant occipital (alpha) rhythm at 5 Hz. This pattern is much more like the adult pattern (Fig. 3) than is the pattern apparent around birth (Fig. 1). Some continuous muscle potential activity is present in the two bottom tracings; eye-blink artifact is apparent in the top two tracings just right of center. In this recording a 12-electrode array was used. The electrode letter code at the left of the tracings is as follows: L = left, R = right, F = frontal, M = precentral, P = parietal, O = occipital, AT = anterior-temporal, PT = posterior-temporal. (From Ellingson, 1967.)

significant developmental changes in the brain continue throughout childhood, stabilizing only after adolescence. It is in the "silent" or association areas of the cortex which continue to develop slowly throughout childhood. Related to this is the growth and myelinization of collaterals to the brain stem reticular formation and the growth of pathways to diffuse thalamic nuclei (Yakovlev, 1962; Yakovlev & Lecours, 1967).

Paralleling the slower neuroanatomical development between the years of 1 and 12, EEG changes during this period are not as dramatic as changes in the first year. The occipital frequency gradually speeds to between 10 and 11 Hz (Bernhard & Skoglund, 1939; Eeg-Olofsson, 1971; Henry, 1944; Lindsley, 1936, 1938, 1939; J. R. Smith, 1937, 1938a; Weinbach, 1938), and activity in the delta and theta range apparent at various recording sites in the brains of awake children become infrequent in the waking records of adolescents and adults. With development EEG frequency becomes less variable, and the variability of the dominant frequency appears to be even more closely related to chronological age in childhood than is frequency itself (Surwillo, 1975a). The stable patterns in adulthood show characteristic amplitudes and frequencies at various brain locations with alpha activity more prominent in posterior than anterior areas. Figure 3 depicts EEG in the normal adult.

Gradual changes begin to occur in adult EEG patterns which are not readily detectable in raw EEG records until the sixth decade, and even at that point some individuals have EEG patterns impossible to distinguish

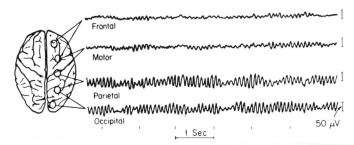

Fig. 3. EEG of a normal human adult. Alpha waves at about 10 Hz predominate in all regions but are largest posteriorly. Only a few smaller and faster beta waves are visible in the anterior regions. (From Lindsley, 1948.)

from the patterns of young adults. Nevertheless, investigators have reported four major changes in the brain wave activity of older adults. These include changes in frequency and abundance of the alpha rhythm, changes in the incidence of fast activity, diffuse slowing (especially noted in institutionalized elderly), and focal slowing and abnormal activity in the temporal lobes (Marsh & Thompson, 1976; Obrist & Busse, 1965; Thompson & Marsh, 1973). While the three latter changes have been reported in a number of laboratories, they do not occur as generally as do age changes in the alpha rhythm. The most reliable age change in EEG activity is the slowing of the dominant frequency, the alpha rhythm.

This brief overview of developmental changes in EEG rhythms indicates that a number of changes occur over the life span. Changes particularly apparent in posterior regions of the cortex are shifts in frequency of the alpha rhythm. These changes in the dominant frequency may have behavioral significance at several points in the life span.

A. AGE CHANGES IN MODAL EEG FREQUENCY

The alpha rhythm has been defined as "Rhythm usually with frequency of 8–13/sec, of almost sinusoidal form, in the posterior areas, present during relaxation when the eyes are closed, attenuated during attention, particularly visual" (Storm van Leeuwen, Bickford, Brazier, Cobb, Dondey, Gastaut, Gloor, Henry, Hess, Knott, Kugler, Lairy, Loeb, Magnus, Oller Daurella, Petsche, Schwab, Walter, & Widen, 1966, p. 306). Some investigators refuse to call occipital rhythm recorded in infants "alpha" because it is not within the 8–13 Hz frequency range. It has been demonstrated, however, that this activity has all of the other characteristics of the alpha rhythm. The generators for this activity are most likely the same at all ages, and its frequency increases gradually with development until it reaches the alpha range of 8–13 Hz. For these reasons, and because it is the modal rhythm at most points in development, the occipital rhythmic activity apparent during an awake, relaxed state will be called "alpha" regardless of frequency.

Obrist and Busse (1965) remarked upon this issue with regard to the aged. They noted that while alpha is usually considered to be activity between 8 and 13 Hz, because of the tendency for such rhythms to become slower in old age, investigators have often used a more liberal frequency classification, including waves of 7 Hz or less. This convention will be adopted for EEG recorded in old age.

The first year of life is when the alpha rhythm shows its most dramatic changes: the onset between 3 and 4 months and the rapid frequency increase to 6–7 Hz by the end of the first year (e.g., Dreyfus-Brisac, 1964; Ellingson, 1958, 1967; Hagne, 1968; Lindsley, 1936; Samson-Dolfus, Forthomme, & Capron, 1964; J. R. Smith, 1938b, 1939). This is followed by a period of no frequency change between the end of the first and the end of the second year. The increase in EEG alpha frequency during childhood (46–140 months) has been shown to be linear (Surwillo, 1971c), but if the infancy data are added, the best-fitting curve is described as a logarithmic function (Bernhard & Skoglund, 1939; Weinbach, 1938) since more rapid frequency increases occur during the first year of life. The period from puberty to adulthood is another time when no change of alpha frequency occurs. Figure 4 shows occipital EEG in one individual recorded at various intervals from birth to the age of 21.

As early as 1931 Berger noticed that patients with senile dementia had slower alpha rhythm than normal young adults, but he assumed that the slowing was related to the patients' illness. Berger did not associate the slowing with aging. Davis (1941), however, demonstrated that the alpha rhythm slowed with age, and her work has been upheld in later research (Brazier & Finesinger, 1944; Busse & Obrist, 1963; Friedlander, 1958; Harvald, 1958; Matousek, Volavka, Roubicek, & Roth, 1967; Mundy-Castle, Hurst, Beerstecher, & Prinsloo, 1954; Obrist, 1954, 1963; Otomo, 1966; Silverman, Busse, & Barnes, 1955). Most of these studies have also reported a decrease in the percentage of time older subjects produce alpha rhythm which is reported as a decrease in alpha abundance. The frequency of the alpha rhythm reaches its maximum between 10 and 11 Hz after puberty, and after the age of 25–30 the alpha frequency gradually slows (Matousek *et al.*, 1967). The average frequency for healthy adults in the 60s is around 9 Hz, and for adults beyond 80, it is further decreased to 8–8.5 Hz (Obrist, 1954, 1963, 1965; Obrist & Busse, 1965). Alpha recordings from healthy community volunteers between the ages of 28 and 99 years showed that the alpha period (reciprocal of alpha frequency) increased at a rate of 4 msec per decade (Surwillo, 1963). Similar results

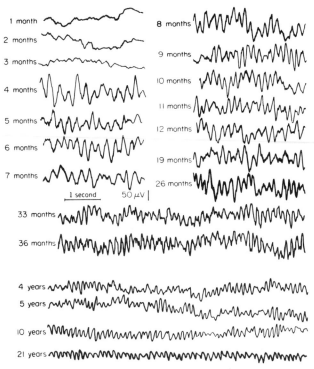

Fig. 4. Development of the occipital alpha rhythm. Serial recordings are from the same subject. Persistent alpha rhythm first appears at 4 months of age at 3 or 4 waves per sec, increases to 5 to 6 per sec at 1 year, and to an adult frequency of 10 per sec by 10 years of age. No further increase in frequency occurs at 21 years. All records are scaled to same size and time dimensions. (From Lindsley, 1960.)

have been reported in longitudinal studies of EEG (Obrist, Henry, & Justiss, 1961; Wang & Busse, 1969; Wang, Obrist, & Busse, 1970). The alpha slowing phenomenon in an old subject is shown in longitudinal data presented in Fig. 5.

The mechanisms underlying life-span changes in EEG alpha frequency remain unclear at the present time. In early life Conel (1939, 1941, 1947) has reported on the neurological development of the infant cortex and has demonstrated that cortical cell myelination and dendritic branching show little progress during the first month of life, but undergo marked maturational changes during the second and third months. This burst of neurological development immediately precedes the onset of occipital alpha activity. For this reason, the EEG of premature infants and neonates has been considered to be largely of subcortical origin (e.g., Dreyfus-Brisac, 1964). The absence of organized rhythms in the sensory zones of the cortex until 3–4 months of age indicates that either the generators in the cortex are not

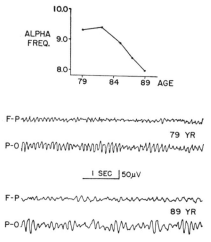

Fig. 5. Alpha frequency plotted as a function of age for a mentally "normal" old man over a 10-year period. The top tracing was recorded at age 79, the bottom tracing at age 89. The latter EEG was associated with mild signs of intellectual impairment. F-P = frontoparietal; P-O = parietooccipital. (From Obrist & Busse, 1965.)

sufficiently mature or that the subcortical structures, the thalamocortical pacemakers, are not functionally operative, or both (Lindsley & Wicke, 1974). Even after these structures become operative, they are still functioning to generate brain rhythms slower than in the adult. Increments in alpha frequency during childhood may also be primarily related to myelinization of brain structures which increases the efficiency and speed of neural transmission (Conel, 1947). The myelinization process continues to adolesence and proceeds most quickly in areas showing the first signs of organized EEG patterns (sensory and motor areas in the rolandic and then the occipital areas). That structures such as the diffusely projecting reticular-activating system and diffuse thalamic system are among the last structures to develop collaterals and to become myelinated correlates with functional changes in alpha activity. Prevailing neurophysiological theory contends that ascending pathways of the brain stem reticular formation, diffuse thalamic nuclei, and association cortices are extensively and reciprocally interrelated (Jasper, 1960). One of the consequences of this linkage is that nonspecific sensory activation results in desynchronization of the alpha rhythm—a phenomenon which Bernhard and Skoglund (1943) and Lindsley (1938) have shown to be slower in children up to the age of 6. Surwillo (1972) found no alpha-blocking latency relations to age in children aged 7–17, but he did find that alpha-blocking latency increases in old age (Surwillo, 1966). This change may involve the same systems as those which change during maturation. Yakovlev and Lecours (1967) noted that the brain stem and reticular core of senescent individuals were smaller and contained fewer fibers. Thus, changes in the reticulothalamic system might account for both maturational and aging changes in alpha-blocking latency.

Mechanisms underlying adult changes in the EEG alpha frequency are not understood. The association between measures of vascular function and EEG slowing in patient groups has raised the question of whether alpha slowing reflects cerebral metabolic changes. The fact that even the most healthy of aged subjects who have no detectable signs of cerebrovascular impairment have slowing of the alpha frequency (Obrist, 1963) suggests that other changes in the aging brain, such as neural changes reported above, may also operate in the slowing of the alpha rhythm.

B. BEHAVIORAL SIGNIFICANCE OF ALPHA FREQUENCY CHANGES OVER THE LIFE SPAN

Alpha frequency may serve as an index of brain maturation and functional integration and therefore may be a correlate of anatomical and neurochemical substrates of behavior. This seems likely in the early phases of the life span when the brain is becoming organized. Since there are currently few means of measuring neurochemical and anatomical changes in intact human brains, alpha activity can serve as one of the few measures available to relate underlying maturational changes in the brain to behavior development. Surprisingly, although Lindsley (1938) pointed out the significance of the onset of the occipital rhythm for behavior, and although investigators since that time have continued to call for developmental EEG-behavior studies (Ellingson, 1958, 1967; Melin, 1953), few such studies exist.

In addition to being an index of brain structure during maturation, alpha activity may reflect a basic property of the brain. Lindsley (1952) made a distinction between alpha rhythm, the high amplitude rhythmic activity recorded in humans from scalp electrodes, and most apparent in posterior leads, and alpha activity, the periodic waxing and waning in excitability of cortical cells which would not be recorded with scalp electrodes when large numbers of cells were not synchronized. In this model alpha rhythm is observable while alpha activity is inferred. Lindsley speculated that alpha activity was always present in the brain even when alpha rhythm could not be recorded, and he suggested that a cycle of approximately 10 Hz, as reflected in the alpha rhythm, is the basic metabolic rhythm of brain cells. A large body of research literature has accumulated to support

Lindsley's contention that the alpha frequency may mark a basic property of the brain. It may reflect functional integration of neurochemical and anatomical mechanisms which cannot be indexed in another fashion. This proposition treats the alpha rhythm as an important phenomenon in its own right—a phenomenon causally affecting behavior rather than serving as an index or correlate of phenomena affecting behavior. Several developmental studies suggest this role for the alpha rhythm (e.g., Karmel, Lester, McCarvill, Brown, and Hofmann, 1977; Surwillo, 1963, 1964a).

In the following sections data will be presented first to show that the alpha rhythm as a correlate of brain maturation can serve as a marker of points potentially crucial for behavioral change. In addition to considering the alpha frequency as an index of brain maturation, the alpha rhythm will be discussed as a timing mechanism in behavior throughout the life span.

1. Neonatal Behavioral Development: Hallmark of the Onset of Cortical Control

Since the onset of organized rhythmic activity in occipital areas was noted in 3- to 4-month old infants, investigators have speculated that this phenomenon had important behavioral implications. It was assumed that visual behavior would be particularly affected as the occipital lobes are the primary cortical projection area of the visual system. Thus, in 1938 Smith stated, "It would appear reasonable to assume that the emergence of the alpha waves at 3 or 4 months over the occipital lobes is correlated with the onset of function in the cortical visual mechanism" (J. R. Smith, 1938b, p. 466). In subsequent decades investigators have continued to highlight the importance of occipital rhythmic activity around the end of the third month in signifying functional capacity (Dreyfus-Brisac *et al.,* 1958; Ellingson, 1967; Lindsley, 1964; Lindsley & Wicke, 1974). Ellingson (1958) pointed out that researchers from Smith on emphasized the concordance among anatomical, EEG, and behavioral developmental patterns. This general concordance continues to be documented as more precise behavioral and EEG observations are made. Lindsley and Wicke (1974) recently argued that the onset of organized rhythmic occipital activity reflects a significant change in cortical organization, marking the period when the infant progresses from a subcortical to a cortical level of functioning.

Studies of the alpha frequency in monkeys (Caveness, 1962) indicate that alpha rhythm over visual areas appears as a 3–4 Hz rhythm around 15–20 days after birth and accelerates thereafter. Equating the monkey and human life span, this corresponds to a human age of 3–4 months. Age changes in alpha frequency follow a similar curve in both species, and behavioral development also coincides with EEG changes in monkeys

(Lindsley & Wicke, 1974). The onset of the occipital rhythmic activity corresponds in monkey and man with the time of change in reflex patterns such as the Babinski, Moro, and grasp reflexes. At approximately 3 or 4 months many reflexes drop out of the infant's behavioral repertoire (De-kaban, 1970; Fiorentino, 1972; Taft & Cohen, 1967), presumably due to increasing cortical inhibition of lower centers. Reflex arcs exist below the cortical level, and before integration occurs between subcortical and cortical structures, stimulation of the infant elicits an involuntary, subcor-tically mediated reflex response. As maturing cortical centers become integrated with subcortical areas, however, primitive reflex behavior inhibited. The infant thus progresses to a neurologically more mature, integrated state. The disappearance of primitive reflexes is a clear behavioral sign of central nervous system (CNS) development.

The parallels between human and monkey development and the similar concordance between EEG alpha onset and the disappearance of primitive reflexes in both species provide evidence that normal infants are functionally subcortical organisms (Lindsley & Wicke, 1974). These authors find additional evidence for subcortical dominance in neonates in the developmental parallels between normal infants and anencephalic monsters in the first 2 months of life. Born without a cerebral cortex, anencephalic monsters do not survive more than 2 months, but while they live they show reflex development similar to the patterns of normal human infants of the same age.

The onset of rhythmic occipital EEG activity has been thought to signal a critical period in neonatal development, and it has been inferred (though not directly demonstrated) that behavioral changes are associated with the EEG changes. Behavioral research has revealed that the neonate can perform a number of visual responses, and such reports led some reviewers to suggest that the entire visual system is functionally effective, though inefficient, almost from birth (e.g., Bond, 1972; Hershenson, 1967). In a recent review of the literature on neonatal visual behavior, Bronson (1974) argued that newborns rely on a phylogenetically older (subcortical) "second visual system" in the first months of life, and it is only in the third month that the newer (cortical) "primary visual system" dominates. Bronson (1974) contended that rather than conceiving a post-natal change in visual behavior as indicative of general improvement in the efficiency of the total system, changes in visual behavior in infancy can be interpreted in terms of underlying neural changes corresponding to the progressive development of increasingly sophisticated neural networks. Specifically, the progression involves first a subcortical system located in the superior colliculus and pulvinar, which is involved in processing stimulation falling on the more peripheral areas of the retina.

This system functions to transmit information about direction of salient peripherally located stimuli and is not capable of analyzing patterns. As development progresses, another system takes precedence. This is the primary visual system, the geniculostriate system involving foveal vision and pattern detection.

Behavioral evidence (e.g., Fantz & Fagan, 1975; Hershenson, Munsinger, & Kessen, 1965; Ruff & Turkewitz, 1975) suggests strongly that infants younger than 9–10 weeks attend to visual stimuli on a different basis than older infants. The differential response of the younger infants appears to be based on differences such as size or number of elements of the stimulus which have been considered to be quantitative aspects of stimulation (Schneirla, 1965). Infants older than 10 weeks, on the other hand, appear to respond differentially on the basis of qualitative differences in form or pattern rather than differences in quantity. Other more complex, and presumably cortically mediated visual responses, also fail to be performed before the age of 3 months. For example, infants 3 months or older will demonstrate a preference for novelty and habituation to familiar stimuli, while infants younger than 3 months will not (Jeffrey & Cohen, 1971; Martin, 1975; Wetherford & Cohen, 1973). Bronson (1974) argues that behaviors exhibited after 3 months of age require cortical mediation, while behaviors exhibited before that time do not.

Recent behavioral data on infants along with Bronson's (1974) elegant model involving cortical and subcortical visual systems continue to highlight the third month as a critical period. Perhaps it is the difficulty of measuring visual behavior in infancy which has kept EEG researchers from attempting EEG-behavior studies at this age. Recently published volumes on perceptual capacity in infancy (L. B. Cohen & Salapatek, 1975a, 1975b) attest to the availability of sophisticated behavioral techniques, and some of them are being used in our laboratory to assess behavioral development as it relates to EEG changes in a longitudinal study of neonates from the second week of life to the age of 4 months. It is predicted that the onset of the occipital rhythm will mark the time in individual infants when they will progress from visual responses such as fixation, and following which could be mediated subcortically to responses requiring cortical integration such as preference for form and for novelty and habituation to visual stimuli (Woodruff & Gerrity, 1976).

2. Behavioral Correlates from Infancy to Puberty

After the onset of the occipital rhythm during the third month, changes in the alpha frequency are of a quantitative nature, and attempts to relate such quantitative changes to qualitative changes in cognitive abilities as postulated by Piaget have met with limited success (Stevens, 1974). This is not surprising given that the alpha rhythm reflects aspects of brain function related primarily to states of the organism in adults. Additionally, Piaget's interactionist approach places equal emphasis on the significance of the environment in shaping cognitive development. Piaget argues that brain maturation presents only a partial impetus for cognitive growth. Nevertheless, it is interesting to note that the period between 1 and 2 years appears to be a period of little change in the frequency of the alpha rhythm. The rhythm has reached a frequency of 6–7 Hz somewhere between 9 and 12 months and appears to stabilize at that frequency until the age of 2 with some modifications in amplitude appearing around 18 months (Pampiglione, 1972). This critical period is the point at which Piaget feels the child becomes capable of symbolic thought, a capacity not apparent up to that point. The major changes in the alpha frequency at that point may signify functional integration in brain structures which serve as precursors for this development of ability.

While increases in alpha frequency with development after the first 1–2 years of life are not directly related to growth of complex cognitive abilities, frequency changes may be related to temporal characteristics of certain sensory response processes. These temporal response capacities which change as the dominant occipital frequency changes may place certain limitations on the ability of the young to respond beyond a certain rate.

One cortical response to repetitive photic stimulation or flickering light characteristic of the adult EEG has been called the "following response" or "driving response." As the names imply, the EEG "follows" or is "driven" by the photic stimulation, and this cortical response is maximal in occipital areas. The following response is different from sensory-evoked responses described in Section III, A as evoked responses can be observed while the rhythmic response is also present. Following responses have not been studied as completely as evoked responses, but data on them at most points in the life span indicate that the optimum frequency of following tends to be closely related to the frequency of the dominant occipital rhythm during wakefulness.

The following response is difficult to elicit in infants, and depending on technique, investigators have reported that it does not occur before 3 months postterm (Dreyfus-Brisac & Blanc, 1956), or that less than 50% of newborns showed the response (Ellingston, 1960; Glaser & Levy, 1965), or that the response was present in a majority of newborns (Eichorn, 1951; Ellingson, 1967; Hrbek & Mares, 1964). Regardless of technique, the response is clearly more difficult to elicit in neonates, and when it occurs it will only involve following over a frequency range of 1–5 Hz, with the optimal frequency following close to 3 Hz. Vitova and Hrbek

(1972) collected following response data cross-sectionally in 156 subjects between 32 weeks' gestation and 14 years and compared the data to records of eight adults of a mean age of 25 years. These results indicated that the frequency of optimal following increases with age. The responsiveness of the brain which is sluggish and slow in infancy increases throughout childhood, stabilizing about the time that the alpha frequency stabilizes, variously found to be between the ages of 10 and 14 and hence coincident with puberty.

In adults a behavioral correlate of the frequency following response is subjective brightness enhancement. Photic stimuli flashed at the rate producing optimal following are perceived as brighter and thus elicit more attention than stimuli flashed at slower or faster rates. Karmel *et al.* (1977) have shown that the rate at which stimuli are presented also affects attention and brain responses in infants. Using evoked responses instead of the frequency following response as a measure of cortical reactivity, Karmel and his associates concluded that visual attention in infants is closely related to the frequency of the occipital brain response. Thirty-two 13-week-old infants were shown identical checkerboard patterns modulated at various temporal rates (1.0, 1.4, 2.0, 2.8, 4.0, 5.7, 8.0 and 20 Hz), and durations of orienting responses were measured. Another 14 infants of the same age were shown a series of checkerboard patterns modulated at rates of 1.0, 2.0, 4.0, 6.0, 8.0, 10.0, and 12.0 Hz while EEG was recorded at a midline occipital lead (O_z). Behavioral attention in the first group and amplitude of the computer-averaged EEG response to the stimuli modulated at the various frequencies in the second group were significantly related to temporal frequency of stimulation. When Karmel and his associates plotted the behavioral and EEG data as a function of temporal rate, both functions were best described by an inverted U-shaped curve with similar maxima falling between stimulation rates of 4 and 6 Hz. Attention and evoked potential amplitude were maximal when stimuli were flashed at a rate close to the dominant occipital frequency. Unfortunately, no stimulation rate between 4 and 5.7 Hz was tested. The optimal range for the frequency stimulation leading to maximal behavioral and EEG responses might have been narrower and even closer to the 4-Hz dominant frequency at that age if more stimulation rates close to the dominant frequency had been tested.

The data indicated to Karmel and his associates that a common neurophysiological mechanism might be involved in infants' visual attention and occipital brain response to temporal frequency. Karmel speculated that stimuli particularly tuned to intrinsic timing relationships in the CNS at particular points in development would optimally drive the system and thus have their signal strength maximized in the CNS and would be the stimuli most likely to elicit attention. Such a position emphasizes the significance of EEG measures as indices of behavioral capacity in infancy. Karmel and his associates stated, "If these preference changes are related to the systematic organizational (structural and functional) changes of CNS development, then general indices of state of neurological organization such as the 'resting EEG' may be directly related to the ontogeny of attention" (Karmel *et al.*, 1977).

Attention mechanisms in infancy may well be linked to prominent features of the EEG, and Karmel has provided a new means to investigate attention in infants as well as presented an intriguing hypothesis about attention mechanisms in infancy. As development proceeds, however, it becomes more difficult to find clear relationships between EEG frequency and behavior. For example, attention is a more complex behavior in children because learning and experience as well as temporal and spatial characteristics of stimuli play a role. Nevertheless, it would be interesting to carry out the task of Karmel *et al.* (1977) in children to see if attention continues to be maximal to stimuli modulated at the dominant frequency.

The investigator who has given the most attention to alpha frequency and behavior relationships in childhood is Surwillo. After demonstrating impressively high correlations between reaction time and EEG alpha frequency in adults (Surwillo, 1963, 1968), Surwillo attempted to extend his results to early development where the most dramatic changes in alpha frequency occur. Although statistically significant, correlations between simple and choice reaction time and alpha frequency in children were much smaller than in adults (Surwillo, 1971c). He was also unable to show impressive alpha frequency relationships to behaviors such as digit span (Surwillo, 1971a), backward digit span (Surwillo, 1971b), or word-association latency (Surwillo, 1973).

Measuring alpha activity between the onset of an imperative signal and the initiation of the subject's response in 110 boys ranging in age from 4 to 17 years, Surwillo (1971c) found a correlation of $-.874$ between simple reaction time and age, but age changes in EEG alpha period could account for only a small fraction of these high correlations. Surwillo noted, however, that in his sample there was a rather abrupt stabilization of the average number of half-waves recorded in the interval between stimulus and response between the ages of 11 and 12, which is within the period many investigators had reported that EEG frequency reaches its adult values. Surwillo analyzed data from subjects of 140 months and beyond, and for this group of 39 cases the correlation between simple reaction time and age was smaller $(-.272)$, and declined to $-.043$ when EEG period was partialed out of the correlation. These data suggest that an important transition takes place around puberty, and brain and behavior relationships not apparent in the immature brain become similar to brain and behavior relationships observed in adults. Surwillo (1971c) remarked:

> We cannot say whether this means that by 140 months the information processing operations associated with reaction tasks are already functioning at the adult level. Nevertheless, the fact that 140 months, or approximately 11.5 years, represents a critical stage is of special interest when viewed in the context of Piaget's representation of intellectual development. Thus, in Piaget's scheme, the transition to "formally operational intelligence," which is the last of his four chronologically successive stages in the development of intelligence, occurs at or beyond the 11th year. (Surwillo, 1971c, pp. 479–480)

As noted previously, the stabilization of EEG activity between the first and second year of life coincides with the progression from dealing with the environment purely in sensory and motor responses to dealing with mental representations of the environment. Another period of stabilization occurs after the eleventh year and coincides with the onset of abstract logical capacity. These parallels between no change in the dominant brain rhythm and qualitative changes in cognitive abilities may be coincidental, or alpha frequency changes early and late in childhood may serve as an index of underlying brain changes making possible qualitative changes in cognitive ability. Even if changes in alpha activity signal neurophysiological changes important for cognitive development, such a relationship is far less direct, accounting for much less of the behavioral variance than the relationships between temporal qualities of stimuli and attention, perception, and the timing of behavior. In the instance of the EEG and cognitive stage relationships, the alpha rhythm may serve as a correlate of underlying brain maturation which interacts with experience leading to a qualitative change in thinking. In the case of alpha frequency relations with attention, perception, and reaction time, the alpha rhythm may code a functional property of the CNS.

Although he subsequently reported greater variability of the dominant frequency in early development than in adulthood, Surwillo (1975a) tended not to interpret his failure to find alpha frequency and reaction time relationships in children simply as a measurement problem. He was led, instead, on the basis of the variability data to augment his model of EEG and the timing of behavior. He added to the original model in which speed of information processing was governed by the time characteristics of the cortical gating signal (the alpha rhythm), the notion that there is a recovery cycle of the information-processing operations which are activated by the gating signals. Several studies suggested that the recovery cycle notion was useful in predicting reaction time on the basis of alpha activity in childhood (Surwillo & Titus, 1976) and adolescence (Surwillo, 1975b). However, additional evidence including studies in which individual subject's EEG frequency and refractory period are used to predict their reaction time are needed to confirm the model more directly.

Investigation of alpha frequency and reaction time relationships in the early part of the life span is relatively new and has just recently led to the formulation of models of brain-behavior relationships during development (Karmel *et al.*, 1977; Surwillo, 1975a, 1975b). Alpha frequency and reaction time relationships in adulthood have been examined more extensively and have generated a large body of literature and several competing models.

3. Adult Brain Organization and the Alpha Rhythm: The Timing of Behavior

Consideration of the alpha rhythm as a timing mechanism for behavior in adulthood began almost with the discovery of the human EEG. At least two general hypotheses have been developed to account for EEG frequency and reaction time relationships.

The more general hypothesis involving the concept of arousal suggests that brain wave frequency is associated with different states of consciousness and excitability in the cortex. This approach relegates the alpha rhythm to the position of a correlate of underlying brain states affecting behavior. Proponents of the arousal hypothesis would expect to see a general relationship between brain wave frequency and performance because brain wave frequency is roughly correlated with the qualitative states associated with delta, theta, alpha, and beta waves (see Table II). Within specific frequency bandwidths of theta or alpha, however, no specific one-to-one correlation between EEG frequency and reaction time is necessary to support this position.

The excitability hypothesis postulates that the waxing and waning of excitability in the CNS is marked by the alpha rhythm, and signals input at points in the cycle close to the point of maximal excitability will be processed and responded to more quickly than signals input at less optimal points. The most specific form of this hypothesis, the perceptual moment notion, is that stimuli are sampled at discrete intervals of time, and the longest reaction times will occur if a stimulus is presented when a new sample is just beginning, while the shortest reactions should occur when a sample is just about to end. Since the alpha cycle (lasting 100 msec for a 10-Hz alpha rhythm) is thought to be related to the points where the sample opens and closes, there should be a strong relation beween the alpha phase at which a stimulus is presented and the time it takes for the subject to recognize that it has been presented. The subject cannot react to the stimulus until the stimulus is perceived, so reaction time is a function of alpha phase and the maximum difference between reaction times obtained in this way should be equal to the duration of one "moment" or "scan" (predicted to be around 100 msec for a full alpha cycle or 50 msec if the alpha half wave represents the "scan") (Kristofferson, 1967).

While imputing various levels of significance to the role of the alpha rhythm itself in affecting the timing of behavior, the arousal hypothesis and the excitability cycle hypothesis predict that slower brain wave frequencies (which occur in childhood and late adulthood) lead to slower perception and reaction.

Space limitations preclude a discussion of the large number of non-developmental studies relating EEG activity to CNS excitability and the timing of behavior. Interested readers are referred to reviews by Harter (1967b) and Sanford (1971). Both reviewers find scant evidence for the perceptual moment hypothesis, and Harter concluded that the notion was not solidly based on empirical evidence. Sanford argued that the phenomenon would be difficult to identify on technical grounds even if it did exist. Nevertheless, both reviewers present evidence that EEG frequency is related to behavioral timing. Life-span developmental studies suggest similar conclusions.

A proponent of the excitability cycle hypothesis who has addressed himself to the developmental implications of alpha frequency changes is Walter Surwillo. For the past 18 years Surwillo has reported a large number of studies testing individuals over the life span which led him to devise a model in which frequency of the EEG alpha rhythm determined the frequency of a cortical gating signal (Surwillo, 1963, 1968).

Because alpha waves seemed to be related to reaction time, and because older individuals had slower alpha waves and slower reaction times, Surwillo (1960, 1961) attempted to determine if reaction time and duration of alpha rhythm cycle were related. Measuring the duration of waves occurring between the onset of an auditory signal and the initiation of the subject's response, Surwillo found a statistically significant rank-order correlation of .81 between reaction time and alpha period in a group of 13 subjects between the ages of 18–72 years, and he replicated these results in a larger sample ($N = 100$) ranging in age from 28–99 years (Surwillo, 1963). In this study a correlation of .72 was obtained between average reaction time and average EEG period. Disjunctive reaction time as related to age and duration of alpha cycle was also studied by Surwillo (1964a), and the correlation coefficient for brain wave period and disjunctive reaction time was .76. In both experiments there was a low but statistically significant correlation between reaction time and age which disappeared when brain wave period was partialed out. The presence of slow brain potentials appeared to be necessary for the occurrence of slow reaction time in old age, and this fact suggested to Surwillo that EEG frequency is the factor behind age-associated drops in processing capacity of the brain. He further speculated that the frequency of the EEG may reflect the operation of a "biological clock" within the CNS which is a determining factor in how rapidly and effectively information can be processed (Surwillo, 1968).

Surwillo (1975a) claimed that his work summarized in 1968 led to a model which could account for the prolonged reaction time in senescence. Surwillo has been praised for providing one of the few testable models about age changes in performance in the gerontology literature (Marsh & Thompson, 1976; Obrist, 1965; Thompson & Marsh, 1973), but gerontologists have not been as willing as Surwillo to accept the proposition that alpha slowing can account for the slowing of reaction time in senescence. Data collected by Birren (1965), Boddy (1971), and Woodruff (1972) in attempts to replicate Surwillo's work did not provide consistent support for the model. Variations in EEG recording and analysis as well as the use of smaller and more homogeneous age groups of subjects. thus limiting the range over which alpha frequency could vary, could account for Birren's and Boddy's failures to replicate. Surwillo (personal communication) maintained that Woodruff's failure to replicate resulted from the way she analyzed frequency in her data. She used a spectral measure, averaging EEG filtered at several frequency bandwidths, and Surwillo felt that this method of analysis confounded amplitude and frequency. Additionally, Surwillo analyzed only trials in which alpha rhythm was clearly defined, while Woodruff included trials in which alpha was present and in which alpha was absent. These considerations led Woodruff (1975) to conclude that her data did not refute Surwillo (1963), and Surwillo (1975b) claimed that Woodruff's data were consistent with, if not in support of, his model.

Another criticism of Surwillo (1963, 1968) is that he based a model predicting causal relationships on correlational data. He was aware of this issue and stated, "It is worth noting here that our hypothesis also demands that experimental alterations of brain wave frequency should be accompanied by corresponding changes in speed of response. This interesting proposition also deserves investigation" (Surwillo, 1963, p. 113). Conditions which produce changes in the EEG alpha frequency are accompanied by changes in reaction time (Creutzfelt, Arnold, Becker, Langenstein, Tinsch, Wilhelm, & Wuttke, 1976; Harter, 1967a; O'Hanlon, McGrath, & McCauley, 1974), but these studies could all be explained in terms of metabolism changes which affected both reaction time and EEG frequency, causing them to covary.

Direct means for affecting alpha frequency were attempted by Surwillo (1964b) who used a photic driving technique. He applied flickering visual stimulation at frequencies above and below the modal alpha frequency in an attempt to drive subjects' brain activity at faster and slower rates. Only 5 of the 40 subjects tested manifested adequate synchronization of alpha with flash rate, and there was some evidence of correlation between alpha period and reaction time in those subjects. These limited results did not provide conclusive support for Surwillo's model. Additionally, since EEG does not appear to be directly related to neuronal firing, the activity resulting from photic driving is probably generated by mechanisms different from those involved in the generation of the alpha rhythm.

Another attempt to manipulate alpha frequency to test Surwillo's model was undertaken by Woodruff (1975). Using the operant conditioning technique called biofeedback, Woodruff trained 10 young and 10 old subjects to increase the abundance of alpha activity at modal alpha frequencies and at frequencies 2 Hz faster and 2 Hz slower than the mode. Reaction time was tested when subjects reached criteria of two-thirds time in modal alpha and one-third time above baseline abundance in the faster and slower frequencies. Comparison with control groups of 5 young and 5 old subjects indicated that biofeedback itself did not affect reaction time performance, and all 10 of the old and 7 of the young subjects had faster reaction times when they produced fast brain waves than when they produced slow brain waves. The reaction time differences between the fast and slow brain wave conditions were statistically significant. In an attempt to directly replicate Surwillo (1963), Woodruff correlated reaction time and EEG data collected in a baseline condition before feedback began. While between subject correlations were statistically significant ($r = .40, p < .05$), they were only about half of the magnitude of Surwillo's correlations. Within subject correlations ranged from $-.31$ to $+.35$ and in no way approximated Surwillo's results.

Woodruff (1975) felt that the arousal hypothesis rather than an excitability cycle hypothesis was the most parsimonious interpretation of her results, since in a given subject brain wave frequency was not correlated with reaction time. To produce faster brain wave frequencies, subjects may have been more aroused and hence produced faster reaction times.

With the discovery of the midline reticular system and its association with various states of consciousness came the notion of arousal and the evidence that EEG desynchronization and fast activity was related to cortical "activation" (Moruzzi & Magoun, 1949), while slowing of the EEG frequency is an index of low arousal (Lindsley, 1960). Such fluctuations in arousal are attributed to activity of the brain stem and thalamic reticular systems (e.g., Gastaut, 1958; Jasper, 1958), and simultaneous recordings from thalamic structures tend to support this view (e.g., Fuster, 1957; F. Morrell, 1960; Yoshii, 1957).

The early human work attempting to relate EEG indices of arousal to performance attempted to find associations between alpha-blocking latency (the well-known phenomenon in which ongoing alpha rhythm is attenuated into faster, desynchronized activity at the onset of stimulation) and beta (13–40 Hz) activity and reaction time. Attempts to relate alpha-blocking latency directly to reaction time have not been successful. While Fedio, Mirsky, Smith, and Perry (1961) and Lansing, Schwartz, and Lindsley (1959) reported faster reaction times when alpha was "blocked" by a warning signal than when there was no warning signal to block alpha, and also faster reaction time when intervals between warning and imperative signals were long enough to lead to alpha blocking, Botwinick and Thompson (1966) and Leavitt (1968) demonstrated that the results of Fedio *et al.* and Lansing *et al.* were a function of the testing paradigm they used rather than a direct function of the frequency of brain waves. Stamm (1952) observed that blocking latency and reaction time were essentially independent, and Surwillo (1972) extended this finding in a developmental study of boys between the ages of 7 and 17.

Fast brain frequencies above the alpha bandwidth have not been associated with faster reaction time, but beta activity has been observed as a correlate of learning lists of nonsense syllables (Thompson & Obrist, 1966) and paired associates (Freedman, Hafer, & Daniel, 1966). Thompson and Wilson (1966) also demonstrated in a group of 15 elderly subjects that "good learners" had significantly more beta activity and tended to have less slow wave activity than "poor learners." In this study EEG was not measured during learning but during the course of photic stimulation, and Thompson and Wilson argued that the brain waves of poorer learners were less reactive (more sluggish alpha blocking as well as less beta activity) than the EEG of good learners.

Thompson and Wilson's poor learners were old subjects who had more

EEG activity in the frequency range below 8 Hz, and recent data suggest that it is when EEG slows into the borderline theta range and below that the most consistent relationships between EEG frequency and performance are observed. This body of research literature was recently summarized and extended by Kornfeld (1974).

Among the studies which Kornfeld (1974) reviewed was the work of Davies and Krkovic (1965) who found decreases in detection rate in an auditory vigilance task when the amount of alpha rhythm decreased. Visual inspection of the polygraphic data indicated that increases in theta activity (4–7 Hz) appeared during the periods of increased errors. Kornfeld (1974) followed up the Davies and Krkovic work with careful analysis of the EEG data generated by subjects during a visual tracking task and observed low frequency EEG activity to correlate significantly with increased performance decrement. Reaction time studies corroborate these results. L. K. Morrell (1966) reported that slower reaction times reliably occurred on trials which were preceded by slow alpha or EEG activity shading into theta bandwidths, and Groll (1966) found a consistent rise in slow frequency activity paralleling slower reaction times of subjects instructed to respond to a light flash with a button press. In sleep-deprived subjects Williams, Granda, Jones, Lubin, and Armington (1962) also found a relation between brain wave activity bordering in the theta range and slow reaction time.

Further support for the relationship between poor performance and slow brain wave frequencies comes from studies in which direct attempts have been made to manipulate brain wave frequency. Beatty, Greenberg, Deibler, and O'Hanlon (1974) used biofeedback of theta activity over the right occipital hemisphere during a long radar watch and successfully affected changes in the efficiency of detection. Operantly produced increases in theta activity increased the amount of decrement, whereas controlled decreases in theta activity removed the decrement. These results were replicated in a group of experienced radar operators (Beatty, 1977).

The fact that older individuals have slower modal brain wave frequencies and the fact that slow brain wave activity is associated with lowered states of arousal has been used as one of the rationales for suggesting that compared with young individuals, the aged are in a state of underarousal (Thompson & Marsh, 1973). In addition to the EEG and ERP data which suggest underarousal in the older CNS, psychophysiological studies of aging using a number of bioelectric measures of the autonomic nervous system (ANS) suggest underarousal in the aged (Thompson & Marsh, 1973). While some studies using biochemical measures in the aging nervous system have suggested that older individuals may be overstressed or overaroused in some situations (Eisdorfer, 1968), recent evidence suggests that this may be a transitory phenomenon (Froehling, 1974).

At this point in time neither the excitability cycle nor the arousal hypothesis has been conclusively supported or refuted. Surwillo (1975b) recently noted that while some data in support of the EEG gating signal hypothesis have been reported, the presently available evidence is only suggestive rather than conclusive. A number of studies interpreted in terms of the arousal model suggest a relationship between low arousal, poor performance, and EEG in the theta frequency range, but these data do not conclusively rule out an excitability cycle interpretation. Thus, while a large number of studies suggest that age changes in the EEG alpha frequency have significance with regard to the timing of behavior, it is not clear whether alpha slowing is functionally involved in behavioral slowing or whether slowing of the alpha frequency serves as an index of CNS or metabolic changes and hence merely a correlate of behavioral slowing.

III.   Age Changes in Event-Related Potentials and Implications for Behavior

Brain electrical responses to specific stimuli are usually not apparent in recordings of ongoing EEG, but by taking a number of epochs in which the same stimulus event has occurred and summing or averaging across these epochs, the activity related to the stimulus becomes apparent. The assumption is that random activity not associated with the stimulus cancels to a flat voltage pattern, while activity time-locked to the stimulus cumulates and emerges from the random background "noise" of the ongoing EEG. A number of different bioelectric signals exhibit stable temporal relationships to a definable external event, and these can be elicited in any of the sense modalities. It has been proposed that these signals be named "event related potentials" (ERP), and five classes of signals have been distinguished (Vaughan, 1969). These include: (1) sensory-evoked potentials; (2) motor potentials; (3) long latency potentials related to complex psychological variables; (4) steady-potential shifts; and (5) potentials of extracerebral origin. The distinction between these classes can pose problems as more than one class of potential may be recorded simultaneously, but since the classes are usually treated separately in the ERP literature, we will follow that convention. For the most part, developmental and aging studies have involved Vaughan's Class 1, sensory-evoked potentials, but some data at scattered points in the life span are available on Class 4, steady-potential shifts, and a few recent studies of aging have measured Class 3, long latency potentials. These three categories of ERPs will be discussed, while motor potentials and extracerebral potentials will be considered as artifacts in the measurement of cortically generated potentials related to psychological constructs. While Classes 2 and 5 potentials will not be discussed, they cannot be ignored in ERP recording. Motor potentials contaminate the CNV and peripheral factors such as pupil size, eye blinks, and eye movement potentials can contaminate ERP data when they are not controlled. This issue is of special concern in developmental studies since the effects of eye artifacts appear to be more severe in children (Eisengart and Symmes, 1971) and in some groups of older adults (J. P. Schaie, Syndulko, & Maltzman, 1976).

A. SENSORY-EVOKED POTENTIALS

Since Dawson (1947, 1951, 1954) developed averaging techniques, it has been possible to record brain potentials resulting from passive stimulation to the various sensory modalities. Though differences of opinion exist concerning the precise origin and significance of the sensory-evoked potential, it is generally unquestioned that its origin is cerebral. Genetically similar individuals have strikingly similar ERPs which are much more closely correlated than the ERPs of dizygotic twins or age-matched unrelated individuals (Dustman & Beck, 1965). Thus, like ongoing EEG patterns, individual differences in ERPs reflect hereditary influences. Another widely accepted generalization about sensory-evoked potentials is the association of the early components of the waveforms (the first 80–100 msec after stimulation) as reflecting activity in the primary sensory systems and processing of the physical parameters of the stimulus. The later components are associated with more diffusely projecting pathways and are considered to be more involved in complex information processing.

Sensory-evoked potentials have been measured at all points of the life span from prematurity to senescence. Of the investigators working on developmental aspects of evoked potentials, however, few consider development beyond a relatively narrow span of years. Since techniques vary in different laboratories, absolute comparisons between different age groups can be difficult. Additionally, apart from longitudinal studies of a few individuals for intervals usually not exceeding 10 years, the data are cross-sectional and hence open to biases inherent in this developmental design (Baltes, 1968; K. W. Schaie, 1965). On the other hand, since the major results continue to be replicated on various cohorts of individuals, and since some laboratories have collected data over wide periods of the life span, there has emerged a fairly consistent picture of age changes in sensory-evoked potentials. Detailed reviews of this literature are available for infancy (Ellingson, 1964, 1967; Hecox, 1975) and for aging (Marsh & Thompson, 1976), and Beck, Dustman, and Schenkenberg have collected in one laboratory data from subjects ranging in age from 1 month to 86 years (Beck & Dustman, 1975; Beck, Dustman, & Schenkenberg, 1975; Dustman & Beck, 1966, 1969; Schenkenberg, 1970; Schenkenberg, Dustman, & Beck, 1971). Since these data have been published and summarized elsewhere, they will be presented only briefly here.

It has been estimated that evoked responses to visual stimuli (VER) probably appear prior to the end of the second trimester of pregnancy (Ellingson, 1967). The VER is present in all normal full-term human newborns, but the waveforms at this point are less complex, having fewer positive and negative deflections than the waveforms of children and adults. By the end of the first year many subjects show the polyphasic response characteristic of adult patterns, but this response may not completely appear in some children before the ages of 2–3 years. The changes in the VER from prematurity to the first year postterm are shown in Fig. 6. The most rapid changes in the VER occur in the first months of life, and developmental changes in the VER again highlight the significance of the period around the end of the third month of life. It is around this time that the latencies of the various VER components which are prolonged at birth begin to approach adult values. Another marked difference in the immature VER is its greater fatigability. There is a relative inability of the system to respond to stimuli presented even as slowly as 1 flash per sec, but the ability to respond at higher rates of stimulation improves rapidly after birth. The other difference in the neonatal VER is its topographical distribution. When diffuse flashes are used as stimuli, both short and long latency components can only become dispersed over a wider topographical area by 3 months postterm.

The first several months of life also involve marked changes in the auditory-evoked response (AER) (Hecox, 1975; Ohlrich & Barnet, 1972). Like the VER, the latency of the AER components is great at birth and decreases with increasing age. The AER waveform also increases in complexity during infancy. Variability of sensory-evoked potentials has been shown to be much greater in infancy than in adulthood, and neonates showed slightly greater variability than 12- to 13-week-old infants (Ellingson, Lathrop, Danahy, & Nelson, 1973). If variability rather than

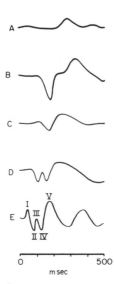

Fig. 6. Tracings of summated responses to brief light flashes, recorded by means of an analog summating computer, in 5 subjects. Each tracing represents the algebraic sum of 60 responses derived from a midoccipital left ear lobe lead. Downward deflections signify relative positivity at the occipital lead. (A) Long-latency negative response commonly seen in the early premature (rare at term). (B and C) Positive–negative responses commonly seen at term. (D) Double positive–negative response often seen at term. (E) Complex response very rarely seen at term but common by the end of the first year. The roman numeral designations are those of Ciganek (1961). (From Ellingson, 1967.)

prolonged latency is used as a criterion for maturity of the VER, Ellingson *et al.* (1973) demonstrated that the VER of 3-month-old infants is very immature. Decreasing variability with increasing age from childhood to adulthood has been demonstrated for both AERs and VERs (Callaway & Halliday, 1973). The data on variability of sensory-evoked potentials coupled with Surwillo's (1975a) data on variability of the dominant EEG frequency indicate that the young nervous system is much less stable and that variability may be one of the most sensitive indices of development in the nervous system.

The most extensive collection of life-span data on sensory-evoked potentials has been carried out in the Salt Lake City, Utah laboratories of Edward Beck, Robert Dustman, and their associates. They have provided normative data on visual-, auditory-, and somatosensory-evoked potentials collected cross-sectionally in large samples of males and females. A portion of this work is presented in Fig. 7. Schenkenberg, Dustman, Beck, Cannon, and Callner (1976) briefly summarized this research in the

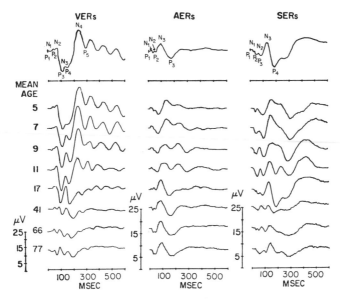

Fig. 7. Composite VERs, AERs, and SERs of subjects in eight age groups. Each plot is a composite of 20 subjects: 10 males and 10 females in each age group. VERs are from left occipital scalp; AERs and SERs are from left central scalp. P = positive peak; N = negative peak. (From Dustman, Beck, & Schenkenberg, 1977.)

following manner:

A variety of measures were employed to compare evoked responses across age groups. Peak delays and component amplitudes were perhaps the most meaningful of these measures and reflected clear age-related differences. Peak delays during early (up to 100 msec) portions of the responses tended to remain stable throughout the age range tested (4 to 86 years). Peak delays during the 100–200 msec interval of VERs and SERs decreased to adolescence and then increased again through senescence. AER peak delays decreased to adolescence and remained stable through senescence.

In regard to amplitude, early portions of the responses remained stable until senescence, when some increases in amplitude were noted. Amplitudes of VER and SER components in the 100–200 msec interval increased to adolescence and then decreased to old age. The AER amplitudes reached a peak during adolescence and remained stable through senescence. Amplitude of late VER components during the period of alpha after-discharge decreased dramatically from about age 9 through age 77.

Clear hemispheric differences were seen in VER amplitude in responses recorded from central scalp (R>L) throughout the age range investigated. Responses of males were generally larger than those of females in childhood while the reverse was true after the teenage years. (pp. 1–2)

These results are representative of data collected in the Salt Lake City laboratories and in other laboratories at various points of the life span.

However, this work is only an initial step toward collecting life-span ERP data. For example, it is difficult to determine from these data the causes of age changes in evoked potentials, as simple mechanisms such as pupil diameter which changes over the life span can influence VER latency and amplitude. The stimuli have been presented rapidly, and age differences in habituation may affect the results. Also, in addition to being sensitive to various attributes of the stimulus, sensory-evoked potentials are very responsive to psychological parameters such as motivation, attention, and arousal which may not have been constant in a passive stimulation situation in different age groups of subjects. Thus, while the life-span data on sensory-evoked potentials represent an important contribution to the life-span literature, these data highlight the extensive task which remains to determine ERP and behavior relationships over the life span.

A major criticism of the VER literature as it applied to development in infancy was that the data were poorly anchored to specific behaviors other than state (Karmel & Maisel, 1975). This criticism applies to developmental literature on VERs at all points of the life span. For example, most developmental VER research has involved the use of diffuse flashes for visual stimuli. Karmel has argued that patterned stimuli are important to investigate as the primary visual system is most likely organized around contour detection involved in the detection of pattern.

Karmel, Hoffmann, and Fegy (1974) presented checkerboard patterns tachistoscopically to infants 8–15 weeks old and recorded VERs in the primary visual projection area (O_z). Four reliable components of the VER appeared in the subjects' records. One of these components, a positive peak (P_2) appearing around 130–150 msec after the stimulus in these subjects was strongly affected by contour density. The relationship was best described as an inverted U-shaped curve, and the maxima of the function varied with the age of the infants. Younger infants (mean age = 2 months) had greatest P_2 amplitudes for large check sizes. The maximum P_2 amplitude was elicited by greater contour density in older infants (mean age = 3½ months). Ellingson (1967) had identified P_2 as a component which decreased in latency as a function of visual system maturation. This component also appears to reflect maturation in response to patterned stimulation.

Infants' preference for stimuli as evidenced by length of fixation on various pattern sizes changes with age, with patterns of greater contour density being fixated longer with increasing age. Relating behavioral data collected in previous studies to the VER data, Karmel and Maisel (1975) concluded that maximum P_2 amplitude was a good predictor of behavioral preference in subjects over the age of 8 weeks. They suggested that common underlying mechanisms are probably involved between the neural and behavioral responses, and argued that contour-dependent neuronal activity in the primary visual system could account for the results. There is a tremendous span between infant visual behavior, infant VERs, and the response of single neurons in the lateral geniculate nucleus and occipital cortex of cats, but Karmel and Maisel (1975) presented cogent arguments for relating their data on human infants to the work of Hubel and Wiesel (1962, 1963) on visual receptive fields in kittens and cats. Space limitations preclude a fair treatment of those arguments here. While much work is needed before such a span can be bridged with certainty, Karmel and Maisel's (1975) position merits careful empirical scrutiny as an engaging new hypothesis in developmental biopsychology.

The Karmel and Maisel (1975) position fits rather well with Bronson's (1974) primary and secondary visual system hypothesis. The former authors report on data collected in Hoffmann's 1973 doctoral dissertation in which 5- and 12-week-old infants' VERs to checkerboard stimuli were recorded at cortical sites outside the primary visual area (P_z, C_z, and T_3) as well as over that area (O_z). The P_2 component appeared only in recordings at O_z, while a long-latency negative component occurred in records at all sites. In the older infants the P_2 component at O_z was the only component showing an inverted U-shaped curve as a function of contour density and relating to preference behavior. In the infants below 6 weeks of age the long-latency negative component was related to contour density and behavioral preference, but P_2 showed no such relationship. In young kittens Rose (1971) and Rose and Lindsley (1968) identified two major sources of VER components which changed with development; a short-latency, positive–negative complex attributed to the primary visual system and recorded only directly over the primary visual cortex, and a long-latency negative component attributed to nonprimary subcortical sources including the midbrain reticular formation and perhaps the superior colliculus. The nonprimary system is comprised of more diffuse projections and responses from this system can be recorded in kittens over a wide scalp area in addition to the primary visual cortex. That the presumably subcortical component is related to visual responding in young infants while the component recorded over primary visual cortex corresponds to behavioral preference in older infants suggests that there may be a major change in the functioning of the visual cortex in infancy. While P_2 can be recorded from birth, indicating an intact geniculostriate system, P_2 amplitudes do not reflect differences in contour density until at least 2 months of age. Such data suggest that the primary visual system is not functionally related to behavior in early infancy.

Other uses of the infant VER have been to establish that an infant's visual acuity changes rapidly in infancy (Harter & Suitt, 1970) and attains the level of adult acuity—20/20—around the age of 6 months (Sokol & Dobson, 1976). Spectral sensitivity of the 2-month infant has also been estimated with VERs to colored stimuli (Dobson, 1976). These data suggested that at this point in development the infant visual system is similar to the adult system in sensitivity to wavelengths above 550 nm, but it may be more sensitive than the adult system to wavelengths below 550 nm. This may be due to differences in the density of the macular pigment and thus reflects retinal rather than central differences in the nervous system.

The use of AERs in infancy to more accurately describe behavioral phenomena and to explore nervous system correlates of auditory behavior has received less attention than the use of VERs. In a recent review of this literature, Hecox (1975) pointed out that information about brain stem-evoked potentials (very short latency potentials of 1–10 msec to auditory stimuli) as well as cortical-evoked potentials may lead to an understanding of mechanisms involved in infants' higher thresholds to auditory stimuli. Hecox presented evidence that both peripheral and central mechanisms are responsible for higher thresholds to auditory stimuli in infancy. The neurophysiological data indicated that the human infant is more sensitive to auditory stimuli at a brain stem level than had been indicated by the behavioral data. The more rostral the response is processed in the auditory system, the higher the threshold. Thus, Hecox presented new electrophysiological evidence that in the auditory system, brain stem or subcortical mechanisms mature earlier than cortical mechanisms. This provides evidence for parallel developmental patterns in auditory and visual systems and suggests that neonates operate at subcortical levels early in life.

Apart from data on young adults, developmental data relating sensory-evoked potentials to sensation and perception at other periods over the life span have not been collected. It has been suggested that application of Karmel's techniques in old subjects to determine if acuity and VER relationships change could provide information about receptive field size in old age (Caskey, 1976). Measuring brain stem-evoked potentials in late adulthood might have important clinical applications such as the early detection of hearing loss and the diagnosis of the cause of the hearing loss (Woodruff, 1976).

B. ACTIVE PROCESSING AND EVOKED POTENTIALS

Evoked potentials are sensitive to stimulus attributes such as intensity and pattern, and passive stimulation procedures can provide information about maturation and aging of evoked potentials with regard to sensation and perception. Evoked potentials are also influenced by the meaning of stimuli, and thus they can provide information about complex behavior development. Regrettably, evoked-potential studies of subjects during active information-processing states have only seldom been carried out with regard to development. Examination of a few developmental studies, limited to various points in the life span, are presented to highlight the insights to be gained from knowledge of such behavior and ERP relationships over the life span.

1. Contingent Negative Variation

The term contingent negative variation (CNV) denotes a class of negative slow potential shifts lasting in the order of seconds, and developing on the scalp in conjunction with certain sensory, motor, and cognitive activities. Walter, Cooper, Aldridge, McCallum, and Winter (1964) initiated recent interest in the phenomenon when they demonstrated the development of a negative slow wave occurring when two stimuli are presented as a pair, the first serving as a warning signal and the second requiring a motor response. In the interval between the first and second stimulus the negative wave develops, and it shifts rapidly in the positive direction after the onset of the second stimulus. It is a negative shift which appears dependent on the contingency that the second stimulus always follows the first, and this led to the name contingent negative variation.

One of the developmental questions to be asked about the CNV is when can it first be initiated. This question was recently considered by Karmel and his colleagues (Hofmann, Karmel, & Lester, 1977) who have programmatically investigated attention in infancy with ERP methods. Karmel and Maisel (1975) in reviewing this research argued that their work provided evidence for mechanisms in the infant CNS for sustained attention to external stimuli. These mechanisms involved tuning of the nervous system to temporal and spatial features of stimuli. Using these salient stimuli in visual and auditory modalities and presenting them at various fixed interstimulus intervals, the investigators were able to record CNVs in 14-week-old infants. However, they emphasized the preliminary nature of the results. The CNV in infants could only be recorded from occipital sites, although it is more apparent in adults anteriorly in parietal regions and at the vertex. Additionally, the stimulus conditions were created specifically to elicit maximal attention in this young group and were different from most CNV procedures as visual and auditory stimuli were used simultaneously and were modulated. This led Hofmann and his associates to consider that the results might not be replicated if stimulus conditions were changed. Nevertheless, this procedure did elicit a CNV in one adult subject who was tested.

If the signals recorded by Hofmann *et al.* (1977) can be considered to be the precursors of the adult CNV, then there appear to be developmental changes in the anatomical distribution of the CNV. Although auditory as well as visual stimuli were used with the infants, no CNV could be recorded in parietal regions. Gullickson (1973) obtained large CNVs in children age 2–3 years using visual and auditory stimuli and not requiring a motor response, but the potentials were maximal even more anteriorly, with the adult pattern emerging around 12 years of age (J. Cohen, 1973). The degree to which these differences reflect anatomical maturation is unknown, but Hofmann and associates suggested that the entire cortex may not need to be mature for the CNV to be apparent in one region and to affect behavior. By discovering a means to elicit a CNV-like phenomenon early in infancy, Hofmann and associates provided a new means to investigate attention and arousal mechanisms in infancy.

J. Cohen (1973) reviewed developmental changes in the CNV in children. In addition to the topographical differences discussed above, amplitude differences have been reported in children's CNVs with lower amplitudes being typical of younger subjects. This result may be more related to motivational properties of the stimuli, however, as Gullickson (1973) found CNVs of higher amplitude than the CNVs of adults when he used highly attractive stimuli. Characteristic of the sluggish nature of the immature nervous system, the CNVs of children do not change in the positive direction after the second stimulus as rapidly as the CNVs of adults but show a gradual termination.

Developmental data over the adult age range are not available, but studies have been undertaken comparing young and old adults. These studies were reviewed by Marsh and Thompson (1976). Since attention and arousal have been behaviors thought to change in old age, and since age changes in the late components of sensory-evoked potentials were thought to reflect age changes in brain mechanisms associated with such processes, investigators initially believed that the CNV might show large age differences. For the most part, however, studies involving active as opposed to passive responding on the part of old subjects show fewer age differences (Thompson & Marsh, 1973). For example, Thompson and Nowlin (1973) found no age differences in CNV amplitude between young and old subjects. Since CNV was related to reaction time performance in young but not old subjects in this sample, while heart rate deceleration and reaction time were related to performance in both groups, it was suggested that coordination of CNS and ANS responses may deteriorate with age. In a recent extension of this study in healthy elderly subjects, CNV and reaction time measures were related. The differences between these results and the results of Thompson and Nowlin (1973) were explained in terms of health factors and practice effects (Harkins, Froehling-Moss, Thompson, & Nowlin, 1976). Loveless and Sanford (1974) found no age differences in CNV amplitude, and the only age differences in these bioelectric signals in their study was in the shape of the CNV waveform in long preparatory intervals. A study by Marsh and Thompson (1973b) suggested that CNV amplitude and performance was similar in young females and old subjects and different from young male subjects who performed the best of all the subject groups. The cause of these differences could not be determined.

It is apparent from this work that there are sufficient gaps in the developmental literature on CNV to make comparisons across the life span impossible. While inferences about developmental changes in physiological and behavioral responses during active processing could expand our understanding of cognition over the life span, the studies presently available in the literature are not comparable. There is some suggestion that the topography of the CNV changes with age in early development, but due to differences in stimulus, response, and recording characteristics of the various studies, even this generalization requires further testing. CNV topography should also be explored in late life. On the other hand, since the CNV is so easily contaminated by eye movement artifacts, and since other ERPs such as the late positive component (LPC) appears to be generating more interest and research, developmentalists might find it more profitable to focus attention on life-span work on these potentials.

2. Late Positive Component

Late components in evoked potentials, especially in evoked potentials to stimuli requiring active processing, are effected by the significance and meaning of the stimulus. Prominent in the late components under certain conditions is a large positive wave called the late positive component (LPC) or the P_3 or P_{300} (because it is the third positive component and often appears around 300 msec after a meaningful stimulus). Research interest has been high in this evoked potential component as evidenced by the approximately 150 studies published over the 10 years following its discovery by Sutton, Braren, and Zubin (1965). These studies were collected in a bibliography by Price and Smith (1974). Stimulation has been provided by the great sensitivity of the LPC to a variety of task and stimulus conditions and by its clear association with processing functions in the CNS.

Given this bioelectric measure which clearly is related to complex information processing and decision-making, it is surprising that there is so little developmental information on it. No studies of the LPC in childhood appear in the Price and Smith bibliography, and the only developmental studies found in the present literature search have been undertaken by gerontologists. Marsh and Thompson (1976) reviewed most of the recently completed LPC studies investigating age-related changes, and their data are similar to those presented in Fig. 8, which shows the LPC elicited in the classic Sutton *et al.* (1965) paradigm (D. B. D. Smith, Tom, Brent, & Ohta, 1976). The main difference between LPCs

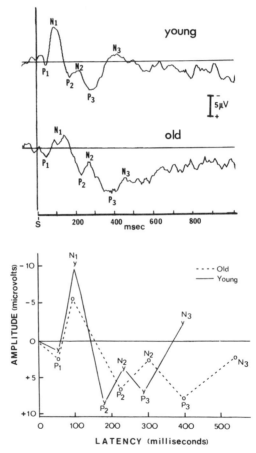

Fig. 8. In the top part of the figure are the AERs of a young and an elderly subject recorded at the vertex (C_z). These potentials illustrate the general form of the response observed in the Sutton, Braren, and Zubin (1965) paradigm. The components are quantified and show longer latencies in old age. In the bottom part of the figure is a composite graph of the mean amplitude and latency of AER components as observed in young and elderly subjects in the experiment above. P = positive peak; N = negative peak. (From Smith, Tom, Brent, & Ohta, 1976.)

in young and old subjects is that the latency is longer in old subjects. This has also been demonstrated in a memory scanning task in which LPCs in young and old subjects were of longer latency for tasks resulting in longer reaction time. While LPC latency was longer in aged subjects in this paradigm, it did not reflect the magnitude of the age differences in reaction time on the task (Marsh, 1975). There is also a tendency for the amplitude of the LPC evoked to visual stimuli to be greater in old subjects (Marsh, 1974), but Marsh (personal communication) suggested that the larger LPC in older subjects may not be a general phenomenon and may occur only under certain circumstances. The LPC provides direct evidence for what geropsychologists have inferred for years, that the slowing observed in old people is a CNS phenomenon (e.g., Birren, 1965, 1970, 1974). The fact that the LPC may not reflect the magnitude of slowing observed in the performance of the elderly may be related to the fact that peripheral as well as CNS phenomena are involved in the slowing.

Given the potential of the LPC to illuminate developmental changes over the life span in decision-making and cognition, it is with regret that a review of the life-span literature must be postponed until a future time when the data have been collected.

IV.　Electroencephalogram and Event-Related Potential Asymmetries, Brain Lateralization, and Behavior Development

Research described in previous sections has been discussed in terms of the examination of relationships between EEG and behavior over the life span using measurements of brain electrical activity recorded at one electrode site. Another strategy is the investigation of interactions among various brain areas and of similarities and differences in ongoing and evoked activity at various sites during different types of behavior. Of particular interest to neuroscientists has been the discovery of lateralization in the brain such that the right and left hemispheres appear to be specialized for different kinds of information processing.

EEG studies of brain asymmetries and especially developmental EEG studies of brain lateralization have been initiated only recently, and there are relatively few developmental studies of lateralization to report. Nevertheless, this is a rich area for research on brain and behavior relationships and an area in which EEG and ERP studies can make important contributions to an understanding of development and aging. The EEG data collected at various points of the life span on lateral specialization and behavior suggest that this will be an exciting, productive area for developmental research in the next decade.

The notion that the brain is lateralized is not new. In 1836 Dax ascribed language to the left hemisphere, and since that time the issue of localization of function has been debated and investigated by a number of prominent neuroscientists (Benton & Joynt, 1960; Penfield & Roberts, 1959). Clinical research involving brain-injured or brain surgery patients established that loss of the dominant hemisphere (usually the left hemisphere) results in deficits in verbal and arithmetical functions, while loss of the nondominant hemisphere leads to deficits in processing spatial information.

The most dramatic of the clinical studies have come from the laboratory of Sperry (1968) and his colleagues (Bogen, 1969; Levy, 1970; Sperry, Gazzaniga, & Bogen, 1969) who have studied patients treated for epilepsy by having the commissures connecting the left and right hemispheres surgically severed. Testing these "split-brain" patients with apparatus designed to input signals into one hemisphere at a time, Sperry and his colleagues have demonstrated the duality of consciousness. Each hemisphere can process information independently, and when there are no connections between the two hemispheres, the right brain is not aware of what the left brain is doing. The two halves of the brain sense, perceive, and conceptualize independently such that the left hemisphere excels at speech, writing, and mathematical calculation, while the right hemisphere best performs tasks involving spatial relationships and musical patterns. If spatial information is presented to the left hemisphere, it is severely limited in analysis, and the right hemisphere has use of only a few words and can perform simple addition only up to 10.

Sperry (1968) has been careful to emphasize that it is not that the two hemispheres process different types of material but rather that they process the same material differently. The hemispheres appear to be specialized for different cognitive styles. An analytic, logical mode prevails in the left hemisphere for which words and numbers are optimal tools. The right hemisphere uses a holistic, gestalt mode especially suited to process spatial relations and music. Levy (1969) suggested that the two modes of processing show indications of mutual antagonism such that processing in one mode interferes with processing in the other. For this reason, one hemisphere usually dominates at a given time. In the commissurotomy patients it has been observed that behavior is dominated by the major (left) hemisphere except in tasks for which the right hemisphere is specialized (Levy, Trevarthen, & Sperry, 1972).

To determine if cognitive function is lateralized in normal subjects, behavioral and EEG studies were undertaken. It has been demonstrated that normal adults process verbal information more efficiently in the left hemisphere and spatial information more efficiently in the right hemisphere in tasks involving reaction time to auditory (Filbey & Gazzaniga, 1969) and visual stimuli (McKeever & Huling, 1971). Dichotic listening tasks have also been used to demonstrate that performance with verbal material is superior in the left hemisphere (e.g., Bertelson & Tisseyre, 1972; Kimura, 1961; Zurif, 1974; Zurif & Mendelsohn, 1972), while performance with musical patterns is superior in the right hemisphere (e.g., Kimura, 1963a, 1967; Knox & Kimura, 1970).

ERP studies have demonstrated that in both the visual and auditory modes verbal and nonverbal stimuli produced different waveforms in the two hemispheres. For example, verbal stimuli led to higher amplitude evoked-potential waveforms than nonverbal stimuli in the left hemisphere, while the right hemisphere showed no amplitude differences for these stimuli (Buchsbaum & Fedio, 1969; Wood, Goff, & Day, 1971). When stimuli were input to the left and right visual fields, differences could be seen between verbal and nonverbal stimuli in both the left and right hemispheres (Buchsbaum & Fedio, 1970). Latency differences for clicks and verbal stimuli have also been observed in the two hemispheres, with words showing shorter latencies in the left and clicks showing shorter latencies in the right hemisphere (Cohn, 1971). L. K. Morrell and Salamy (1971) reported that evoked potentials to speech sounds were of higher amplitude when recorded over the left hemisphere than when recorded over the right hemisphere, and Matsumiya, Tagliasco, Lombrosco, and Goodglass (1972) reported that meaningful verbal stimuli produced more asymmetry between the hemispheres than did meaningless stimuli. Diffuse flashes produced higher amplitude activity in the right than in the left hemispheres (Schenkenberg, 1970), and higher amplitude responses for complex visual forms were recorded over the right than over the left hemisphere (Vella, Butler, & Glass, 1972).

Slow wave activity preceding the response has also been found to be lateralized. The motor potential over the left frontotemporal area was greater than over the right homologous area just before subjects spoke (McAdam & Whitaker, 1971). Marsh and Thompson (1972) found that CNV asymmetries over temporal and parietal areas were dependent on the set given to the subject. For example, left-hemisphere CNV was greater in amplitude in anticipation of a verbal task. While the evoked potential asymmetries are small and not always present, and while CNV asymmetries cannot always be produced (Gazzaniga & Hillyard, 1973; Marsh & Thompson, 1973a), the ERP data are relatively consistent in suggesting lateral specialization in the two hemispheres.

Studies of ongoing EEG activity recorded while verbal and spatial tasks were being performed also indicated hemispheric specialization in normal adults (Galin & Ornstein, 1972). Ratios of the power in homologous leads over temporal and parietal areas indicated that during verbal tasks (such as writing a letter) there was less power in the left hemisphere than in the right, and during spatial tasks (such as positioning blocks in a pattern) rhythmic EEG was more prominent in leads over the left hemisphere. The ratios in the alpha band showed the greatest task dependence, while the theta and beta bands showed the effect less consistently, and the delta band did not show any asymmetry dependent on the task (Doyle, Ornstein, & Galin, 1974). The interpretation of these results is that the "active" hemisphere is more desynchronized during information processing, while the hemisphere showing more power primarily in the alpha band remains in an "idling" state or less engaged in the task.

These results have been replicated and extended in studies using similar integrated ratios of activity in the alpha band (McKee, Humphrey, & McAdam, 1973; Morgan, McDonald, & McDonald, 1971) and with evoked potentials to diffuse light flashes (Galin & Ellis, 1975). When a different measure of alpha activity not combining amplitude and duration was used, task-dependent asymmetry was not found in simple tasks which did not involve learning (Chartock, Glassman, Poon, & Marsh, 1975). The investigators suggested that the combination measure of amplitude and duration may be more sensitive to brain function than only a duration measure.

Clinical and neurosurgical studies suggested hemispheric specialization, and EEG and behavior studies on normal adult subjects confirm that the right and left hemispheres of the human brain process the same information differently. Scientists are now turning to developmental approaches to determine the origin and mechanisms of lateralization and its significance in behavioral development.

A. BRAIN LATERALIZATION AND THE DEVELOPMENT OF LANGUAGE

Evidence continues to accumulate indicating that one hemisphere, typically the left hemisphere, is specialized for processing language, and recent studies of the ontogeny of brain lateralization are revising notions about the onset of language-processing capacity. As recently as the late 1960s specialists in cerebral lateralization (Bogen, 1969) and language (Lenneberg, 1967) reported that lateralization of language occurs around 2 years after birth. These reports were based on clinical data collected on patients such as left hemispherectomized infants. Lenneberg believed that lateralization of language occurred as a function of language acquisition. According to this position, prior to the acquisition of language, neither hemisphere should be more involved in the processing of verbal stimuli.

Bogen (1969) agreed, stating that the hemispheres were equipotential for language in the first years of life. These assertions became open to question when studies of the perception of language in infants indicated that receptive capacity for linguistic stimuli is present early in infancy (Eimas, 1975; Eimas, Siqueland, Jusczyk, & Vigorito, 1971; Moffitt, 1971; Morse, 1972; Trehub & Rabinovitch, 1972). Behavioral data provided evidence of language acquisition and hence possible brain lateralization long before speech production. Previous notions about lateralization were challenged to an even greater extent when Witelson and Pallie (1973) reported marked anatomical asymmetry in the brains of human neonates in brain areas associated with language (the superior surface of the left temporal lobe was greater than the right temporal lobe surface). Hemispheric asymmetries in infants were comparable to the anatomical asymmetry in adults (Geschwind & Levitsky, 1968). Wada, Clarke, and Hamm (1975) replicated this work in 100 infant and 100 adult brains and found the left temporal area to be greater in 90% of the brains. The anatomical asymmetry was greater in adults than in infants, suggesting additional development of asymmetry after birth.

The anatomical asymmetry found in neonates in a brain area of known significance for language in adults supported the hypothesis that the human newborn has a preprogrammed biological capacity to process speech sounds. Evoked potential studies of infants processing speech and nonspeech stimuli have provided the link between anatomical and behavioral data indicating that early in development the left hemisphere is more involved in the processing of speech stimuli while the right hemisphere is more involved in nonspeech processing (Crowell, Jones, Kapuniai, & Nakagawa, 1973; Molfese, Freeman, & Palermo, 1975).

AERs were recorded from the temporal regions of both cerebral hemispheres in a cross-sectional study of infants (mean age = 5.8 months), children (mean age = 6 years), and adults (mean age = 25.9 years). Asymmetry to both speech and nonspeech sounds was present in all three age groups (Molfese *et al.*, 1975). The evoked response to verbal stimuli (two speech syllables, *ba* and *da*) was of greater amplitude in the left hemispheres of 9 of the 10 infants, 10 of the 11 children, and 8 of the 10 adults. At least one of the two nonspeech stimuli (a C-major piano chord and a burst of noise) produced higher amplitude right hemisphere activity in all subjects in each of the three age groups. Figure 9 presents these effects in subjects in the three age groups. Most of the asymmetries were greater in the younger age groups—a phenomenon which Molfese *et al.* (1975) thought might result from immaturity of the corpus callosum and various commissures which interconnect the two cerebral hemispheres. The various brain commissures are among the last structures to develop

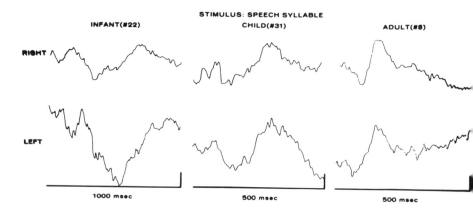

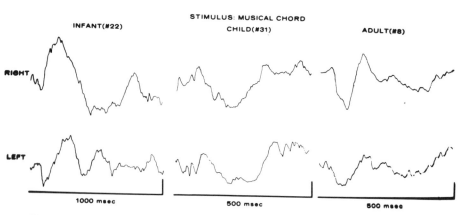

Fig. 9. The top two tracings show an infant, child, and adult's AERs to a speech syllable. The top and bottom AERs for each subject were recorded from the right and left hemispheres, respectively. The vertical scale marker for the infant is 7.5 μV and for the child and adult, 3μV. The upward direction indicates positivity. The bottom two tracings show an infant, child, and adult's AERs to the piano chord stimulus. Recording conventions are the same as in the top two tracings. (From Molfese, Freeman, & Palermo, 1975.)

and become myelinated, and myelination of the brain continues through puberty (Conel, 1941; Yakovlev & Lecours, 1967). Indeed, Gazzaniga (1970) has suggested that the immaturity of the commisures in infancy may result in infants being functionally "split-brained" with good communication between the hemispheres seen between the ages of 2 and 3. Molfese *et al.* (1975) found that the only stimuli more asymmetrical in children than in infants were words. This result is consistent with the work of Matsumiya *et al.* (1972) who found that in adults meaningful speech stimuli produced greater asymmetries than nonmeaningful stimuli. Stimuli meaningful to children produced greater asymmetries in their brains than in the brains of infants to whom the words had not yet acquired meaning.

Molfese and his associates (1975) concluded that the brain is preprogrammed to differentiate between certain types of stimuli very early in life, perhaps at or before birth. Their data suggest that the anatomical differences are functional early in life, but their cross-sectional data including an infant group ranging in age from 1 week to 10 months do not provide evidence sufficient to pinpoint the onset of functional brain asymmetry. Evidence has been presented previously to indicate that evoked potentials change dramatically with maturation over the period from birth to 10 months (see Fig. 6), and it remains for future investigations to determine the onset of functional asymmetry to speech sounds (Smolak, 1976).

In the visual mode there is evidence of occipital lobe asymmetry in newborns. Crowell and his associates (1973) presented 97 newborns (ranging in age from 36 to 59 hr) with repetitive light flashes of 3 Hz and recorded EEG at left and right occipital sites. After screening the data for eye movement artifact with electrooculogram (EOG) data, spectral analysis was performed on the EEGs to determine if cortical areas responded to the stimulation with a bilateral driving response, as is present in children and adults stimulated in this fashion (Vitova & Hrbek, 1972). The majority of the newborns showed no driving response, but in 36 of the infants (37%) driving was present. Of these 36 infants, 16 showed driving on the right side only, and 2 showed driving on the left side only. Eighteen had driving on both sides. Crowell *et al.* (1973) interpreted their results in terms of maturation, suggesting that since adults respond bilaterally, the ontogenetic sequence appears to be first no photic driving response, then unilateral, followed by bilateral photic driving. The unilateral phase may reflect the immaturity of the commissures resulting in the lack of interhemispheric integration. Also, since the right hemisphere is specialized for holistic, visual–spatial information processing, the appearance of unilateral driving predominantly in the right hemisphere may be an early index of lateralization. VERs to diffuse flashes of light in children and adults are of greater amplitude in the right than in the left hemisphere (Schenkenberg, 1970), and the unilateral driving data suggest that this asymmetry develops at or shortly after birth. Longitudinal data and data on premature infants will have to be collected to assess the hypothesis of Crowell *et al.* (1973) of the ontogeny of the driving response which they feel progresses from being absent in both hemispheres, to being present unilaterally, to being bilateral. While much is yet to be determined about lateralization of brain activity in infancy, the work of Crowell *et al.* (1973) and Molfese *et al.* (1975) provide evidence for lateral specialization functioning early in life and highlight the significance of brain electrical activity in the study of behavioral ontogeny.

B. LATERALIZATION AND SCHOOL PROFICIENCY

While recent EEG studies indicate that some lateralization of brain function exists at birth, lateralization and cerebral dominance is not complete until at least the third to sixth year (Buffery, 1971; Kimura, 1963b, 1967), and the immature brain appears to be able to reorganize lateral specialization after injury up to the age of 12 (Hecaen & de Ajuriaguerra, 1964). There is also some evidence that when lateralization is slow to develop or incomplete, cognitive difficulties arise which limit proficiency in school. Over 40 years ago Orton (1934) suggested that stuttering and dyslexia might result from poorly established cerebral specialization. Since that time a large number of investigations have been undertaken in an attempt to relate poor lateralization to cognitive difficulties with mixed results. A review of this literature led Hecaen and de Ajuriaguerra (1964) to conclude that while no convincing direct relation had been demonstrated, disorders of laterality could have played a role in a certain number of the cases.

One of the difficulties of early studies of lateralization was the unavailability of a valid measure of cerebral organization. Until recently the only generally available index of lateralization was handedness, and this measure is not always accurate. Virtually all right-handed individuals (98–99%) have left-dominant brains with language localized in the left hemisphere. The cerebral lateralization of left-handed individuals is more complex, with around 30% showing right-brain localization of language and the rest showing left-brain lateralization or less lateralization for language. Hecaen and his associates (Hecaen & de Ajuriaguerra, 1964; Hecaen & Sauguet, 1971) provided an extensive review of the neurological literature and a summary of their own clinical studies, and they concluded that left-handers show a greater cerebral ambilaterality, not only for language, but also for spatial and tactile functions. Hecaen distinguished between left-handedness which appears to be an inherited trait, running in families, and left-handedness which may be the result of perinatal injury to the left hemisphere. The familial type may or may not have reversed language lateralization, while the brain-injured type will have reversed or more bilateral cerebral representation of language. In the clinical studies, left-handers, people with little hand preference, left-handers who were "switched," or those with mixed hand and eye preference were considered likely candidates for less lateralized cerebral organization. The incidence of such people in clinical categories such as stuttering, dyslexia, and specific learning disability is usually found to be higher than in the normal population.

Working with Sperry's group of "split-brain" patients, Levy (1969) developed the "interference hypothesis" which stipulates that left and right brain modes of processing are antagonistic and interfere with one another when ongoing in the same hemisphere. This hypothesis was supported by a study of left-handed subjects who were presumed to have less lateralized language representation (Levy, 1969). Left-handed and right-handed subjects who had equal Wechsler Adult Intelligence Scale (WAIS) verbal scores were compared, and Levy found that the left-handers had significantly lower performance scores, which she attributed to interference from the presumed ambilaterality of language. Miller (1971) replicated these results. In support of Levy's verbal–spatial antagonism concept is Sperry's contention that in cases of forced sharing of the same hemisphere for verbal and spatial modes of processing (e.g., brain damage, early hemispherectomy, or congenital absence of the corpus callosum), top performance for either mode is prevented. Hemispheres committed to language are handicapped in the spatial, perceptual, nonverbal functions like geometry, drawing, and sculptural and mechanical ingenuity, and this is evident in left-handers. Sperry (1973) cited a number of studies in addition to the Levy (1969) and Miller (1971) work in which left-handers were clearly inferior on spatial tasks to support his contention that bilateral representation results in poorer capacity. While individual left-handers can have brains organized to favor nonverbal abilities (e.g., Leonardo da Vinci, Raphael, Michelangelo), more commonly the tendency is for the nonverbal functions to be handicapped in favor of the verbal.

This evidence of interference between the right and left cognitive modes provides a new kind of support for the hypothesis of Orton (1934) that lack of cerebral lateral specialization plays a major role in dyslexia and stuttering. This hypothesis has continued to sustain interest, in spite of the lack of convincing direct evidence. Recently developed EEG techniques along with dichotic listening tests can provide a much more direct and presumably more sensitive means for investigating disorders of laterality than measures based on hand, eye, or foot dominance alone. In addition to investigating the diagnostic value of EEG asymmetries in populations of preschool and school-aged children, Galin and Ornstein (1973) have speculated that the EEG techniques may provide a therapy.

When given information about a physiological rate, subjects can learn to modify that rate, and this technique (biofeedback) may be used to reduce interference between hemispheres. Galin and Ornstein (1973) discussed a pilot study undertaken by O'Malley and Conners (1972) who gave a dyslexic boy lateralized alpha feedback training. The boy showed significant changes in EEG asymmetry. Whether such EEG changes could affect reading capacity raises questions about the role of causality of EEG phenomena which cannot be answered at the present time. Undoubtedly, the potential of biofeedback of EEG asymmetries as a therapy for dyslexia will continue to be explored.

Galin and Ornstein (1973) believe that the EEG asymmetry studies have important implications for education. For example, assessment of students' preferred cognitive mode could give the student insights about his or her cognitive strengths and weaknesses. A preferred cognitive style might facilitate learning of one type of subject matter (spatial, relational) and hamper learning in another mode (verbal, analytical). A student's difficulty with one part of a curriculum might arise from an inability to change to the cognitive mode appropriate to the work being done. Once such problems are diagnosed, retraining might be undertaken.

Another dramatic implication for education was proposed by Galin and Ornstein (1973) with regard to cultural conflict and cognitive style. They discussed several studies (Bogen, DeZure, Tenhouten, & Marsh, 1972; R. A. Cohen, 1969) which suggest that different subcultures within the United States are characterized by different predominant cognitive modes. Middle-class individuals may be more likely to use the verbal–analytic mode, while urban poor individuals may be more likely to use the spatial–holistic mode. If these differences in cognitive style can be confirmed, such data might provide a partial explanation for the difficulties of urban poor children in the school system oriented toward the middle class. Some educators have recognized the importance of both modes of experiencing the world (Bruner, 1962), and programs such as Sesame Street emphasize the development of verbal–analytical and spatial–holistic skills. Galin and Ornstein (1973) proposed that training procedures (including EEG biofeedback) might be devised to help an individual child to enter both cognitive modes appropriately.

The study of EEG asymmetries might also be of use in the study of cognitive development. Since brain injuries before the age of 12 rarely result in permanent aphasia, it is reasonable to suppose that the brain is still plastic with regard to the lateralization of cognitive function up to that point. Thus, there is clear plasticity in the brains of young children after the acquisition of speech and even after the acquisition of written language. The maturation of the child's cognitive power may be paralleled by, and perhaps even depend upon, increasing lateral specialization with a resulting decrease in interference between cognitive systems. EEG measures of cognitive functioning could be powerful tools for mapping the course of this growth. These measures could also be used in diagnosing aberrations in cognitive development such as dyslexia, certain forms of which may be caused by interhemispheric interference.

C. SEX DIFFERENCES IN VERBAL AND SPATIAL INFORMATION PROCESSING AND BRAIN LATERALIZATION

Since verbal and spatial information appear to be processed most efficiently in the left and right hemispheres, respectively, and since verbal and spatial abilities are among the few behavioral capacities showing reliable sex differences, speculation has arisen regarding sex differences in brain lateralization. There are currently two opposing hypotheses regarding sex differences in brain organization. Levy and Sperry postulate greater lateral specialization in males, while Buffery and Gray (1972) argue that females are more lateralized. This issue is nearing a resolution, and EEG data provide a means to add further clarity.

Behavioral data suggest that lateralization is not complete at birth but develops in the first 5 years, and there is also evidence that lateralization is completed earlier in females than in males. Using a dichotic listening technique, Kimura (1963b) found that left-hemispheric dominance for words was present by the age of 4 in both boys and girls from professional homes, but in children from less advantaged environments left-hemispheric dominance developed by age 5 in girls and not until later among boys (Kimura, 1967). Boys with reading difficulties lag even further behind girls in the establishment of dominance, and many more boys than girls exhibit reading difficulties. Girls develop verbal skills earlier than boys, and this may be a reflection of girls' earlier establishment of left-hemisphere dominance (Buffery & Gray, 1972).

Sex differences in the development of localization of spatial abilities are not as clear. Knox and Kimura (1970) and Kimura (1969) found greater localization among males for certain spatial tasks, and the sex differences were apparent as early as age 5. Using a different task, Witelson (1976) found males to be more lateralized for spatial tasks from age 6 on. On the other hand, Buffery (1971) reported that girls were more fully lateralized on a spatial task and more advanced in the development of handedness at ages 3–4. Recent data support Buffery. Coates (1974) reported on nine studies of visual–spatial ability as measured by the Children's Embedded Figures task in preschool children. In eight of the nine studies, girls' performance was significantly better. The biggest sex difference favoring girls occurred at age 5, and it disappeared by age 6. Kogan (1976) argued that in the first 4–6 years of life girls mature more rapidly and develop stable cognitive styles at least 1 year before boys. Such data support the notion that girls lateralize earlier.

Buffery and Gray (1972) contended that earlier and stronger development of lateralization in females facilitates their verbal development. They argue, however, that spatial capacity requires less lateralized cerebral representation. Since they feel that laterality is slower to develop and less strong in males, it follows that spatial reasoning is better in men. The evidence does not support this position. For example, left-handers who are presumably less lateralized in cerebral organization perform more poorly on spatial tasks (Levy, 1969) even if all the left-handed subjects are male (Levy-Agresti & Sperry, 1968). Additionally, McGlone and Davidson (1973) found that females with some evidence of left-hemisphere specialization for spatial abilities (and hence presumably less lateralized) performed most poorly of all subject groups on spatial tasks. A unilateral right hemisphere lesion also appears to hamper spatial ability to a greater degree in males than in females, again suggesting greater lateralization for space in males (McGlone & Kertesz, 1973). Finally, recent analyses of sex differences in verbal dichotic listening tasks in adolescents and adults indicated that males are more lateralized (Lake & Bryden, 1976). Hence, it is difficult to defend Buffery and Gray's (1972) contentions that bilateral organization facilities spatial–holistic capacity or that females are more lateralized after puberty.

Sherman (1967) suggested that girls' early left-hemisphere dominance orients them to use verbal means to solve problems. Boys, on the other hand, lateralize later and thus have more time to practice gestalt-type processing. Girls' precocious verbal development precludes operation in the spatial mode, while boys' later lateralization gives them the opportunity to practice.

Waber (1976) provided partial support for such a position by presenting evidence that rate of maturation (at puberty) is related to degree of lateralization and also to spatial ability. Measuring secondary sex characteristics, Waber identified early and late maturing boys and girls in the age range of 10–14. On the basis of dichotic listening performance, late maturers appeared to be more left-hemisphere lateralized for language, and they also were superior on a battery of spatial tasks. Waber hypothesized that regardless of sex, children who mature early are less well lateralized for language. They may use their right as well as their left hemisphere to process language. Levy (1969) suggested that when the two modes of processing occur in the same hemisphere there is interference.

Thus, visual–spatial processing may be interfered with in children less well lateralized for language. Since these children may process language in both hemispheres, their proficiency in language may not be affected.

The relation of Waber's maturation rate hypothesis to lateralization in preschool years has yet to be determined. Sherman (1967) and Waber (1976) have provided maturation rate as a means to explain sex differences in lateralization and behavior, and such an explanation will undoubtedly receive much empirical scrutiny.

The bulk of recent evidence suggests that contrary to Buffery and Gray's (1972) position, adult female cerebral hemispheres may be less well specialized than male hemispheres. This is the position of Sperry (1973) and Levy (1970) who agree that strong cerebral dominance and specialization facilitate performance, while cerebral ambivalence interferes. Young girls who may be more lateralized perform better on verbal and spatial tasks until the age of 6–8 when boys begin showing superiority in spatial abilities. Slower development may facilitate lateralization, resulting in greater lateralization in males. Lateralization appears to facilitate visual–spatial reasoning, but girls, who are more bilateral for verbal abilities in adolescence and adulthood, maintain their superiority in verbal abilities throughout life (Maccoby and Jacklin, 1974). Thus, Levy's hypothesis that greater lateralization leads to superior performance appears to hold for spatial but not for verbal abilities. Adult males show greater left hemisphere lateralization for verbal abilities (e.g., Lake & Bryden, 1976), but they are not superior to females on verbal tasks. They are superior, however, on spatial abilities.

Recent EEG data on adults provide another means to assess sex differences in lateralization. Using the technique devised by Galin and Ornstein (1972) to observe lateral specialization in ongoing EEG while subjects are performing verbal and nonverbal tasks, Davidson and his colleagues have found evidence suggesting that the brains of female subjects are more lateralized. Davidson, Schwartz, Pugash, and Bromfield (1976) compared asymmetries in ongoing alpha activity in the left and right hemispheres during tasks involving whistling songs, reciting lyrics to the song, and singing the song. There was significant asymmetry between the whistle and talk conditions only in female subjects. Males and subjects with family histories of left-handedness showed no significant asymmetries. Females also showed higher amplitude right-hemisphere activity over the parietal lobes during self-induced periods of affective thinking while males did not. When males and females attempted to increase left-right asymmetry in a biofeedback task, females had more success than did males. Davidson and Schwartz (1976) also assessed sex differences in EEG during cardiac biofeedback and self-regulation of emotion. Both sexes had

EEG asymmetry when asked to regulate heart rate without biofeedback, but during the cardiac biofeedback task the female subjects shifted to more right cerebral hemisphere activity while the male subjects showed little differentiation between the two conditions. Testing 90 male and female subjects, Galin and Ornstein were unable to replicate the results of Davidson *et al.* (Galin, personal communication). In the latter study, no sex differences were found among right-handed subjects. EEG and dichotic listening tasks may assess different aspects of brain lateralization, and more research is needed to determine the relation between these measures.

The EEG work also provides another means to resolve controversies regarding sex differences in the development of laterality as well as the relationship between lateralization and the development of verbal and spatial processing capacities. Work is currently being undertaken in our laboratory using methods described by Galin and Ornstein and by Davidson and his colleagues to assess EEG lateralization in males and females aged 5–20 while they perform verbal and spatial tasks. These data, along with dichotic listening tests and tests of eye, hand, and foot preference and of language and spatial visualization abilities will be used to resolve some of the inconsistencies in the sex difference and cerebral specialization literature. We will also use EEG data to assess maturation rate in an attempt to clarify the relation of maturation rate in childhood and adolescence to sex differences in verbal and spatial abilities.

D. AGING CHANGES AND VERBAL AND SPATIAL PROCESSING

Longitudinal, cross-sectional, and sequential studies of intellectual changes in adults have suggested that verbal processes show less age decrement than do nonverbal processes (Botwinick & Birren, 1963; Cunningham & Birren, 1976; Owens, 1953, 1966; K. W. Schaie, Labouvie, & Buech, 1973; K. W. Schaie & Strother, 1968). This had led some investigators to infer that there are selective changes in cognitive functions (Botwinick, 1967; Matarazzo, 1972; Wechsler, 1958). Since the verbal and nonverbal tasks reflect to some degree processes involving the left and right hemispheres, respectively, investigators such as Thompson and Marsh speculated that the left and right brain might age at different rates. These investigators undertook EEG studies of lateralization in young and old adults and were able to demonstrate that a psychological set for verbal or spatial perception could lead to asymmetric bioelectric phenomena (Marsh & Thompson, 1972, 1973a). However, there did not appear to be any age differences in EEG asymmetry (Thompson, 1974). After extensive attempts to find age differences in EEG asymmetry as a function of age differences in spatial and verbal information processing, Thompson (1974) suggested that the hypothesis that the right and left brain aged at different rates could not be supported.

Several lines of evidence are available which suggest no differential decline of verbal and spatial processing. Elias and Kinsbourne (1974) collected data on age and sex differences in the processing of verbal and nonverbal stimuli suggesting that all cognitive abilities decline equally with advancing age, and that for proper comparison, verbal and spatial tasks must be tested using the same response mode, attention demands, and time limitations. Gaylord and Marsh (1975) measured age differences in the speed of a spatial cognitive task and found the differences to be comparable to age differences on a digit scanning task reported by Anders and Fozard (1973) and Anders, Fozard, and Lillyquist (1972). Gaylord and Marsh suggested that the similarities between processing rates on these right- and left-hemisphere tasks might indicate a similar decline in speed for all serial processing relying upon recent memory processes. Recently, Zelinski, Thompson, and Marsh (1976) reported on the behavioral data gathered in the earlier EEG and behavior studies of asymmetry (Marsh & Thompson, 1972, 1973a; Thompson, 1974). In the verbal task involving the recognition of four-letter words input into the left and right visual fields, subjects made a greater number of errors on words input into the left visual field (right hemisphere) than to the right visual field (left hemisphere). While old subjects made more errors than young subjects, there was not age × hemisphere interaction. Old subjects were not more deficient in the right hemisphere. There was no asymmetry in error rate for the spatial task. Thus, while old subjects made more errors than young subjects, the pattern of errors for young and old was similar. Zelinski *et al.* (1976) concluded that there were no data to indicate different rates of aging or selective decline on tasks controlled by one of the two hemispheres. Thus, the absence of EEG evidence for differential decline in the left and right hemispheres has led investigators to reassess the literature on age differences in rates of decline on verbal and spatial tasks and suggest that the rates of change in these two cognitive modes may not be different.

V. Conclusion

Knowledge advances when facts are rearranged and brought together in new forms of organization. Bruner (1962) acknowledged this in his essays on knowing and quoted Henri Poincare who stated that insights result from combinations that "reveal to us unsuspected kinship between . . . facts, long known, but wrongly believed to be strangers to one another" (p. 19). Bringing together research evidence from the fields of neurophysiology and developmental psychology and placing them in a life-span developmental framework provides a perspective highlighting certain points in the life span as critical for behavioral development. Such an approach also indicates a number of behavioral areas in which insights can be gained using electrophysiological techniques. Additionally, the life-span EEG and behavior data have already provided significant information. Data collected in a life-span framework have led to hypotheses about timing mechanisms in behavior and about change in neural mechanisms involved in sensation of visual, auditory, and somatosensory stimuli.

Beginning with the data which have been collected, it is apparent that taking a life-span orientation is useful. Surwillo demonstrated this by using life-span changes in the EEG alpha rhythm to test hypotheses about the timing of behavior. He has collected data on subjects ranging in age from 4 to 99 years and devised a testable model involving the EEG alpha rhythm as a central factor in timing. Whether the alpha rhythm is functionally involved in behavioral timing or whether it is simply a correlate of the mechanisms affecting the timing of behavior has not been resolved, but Surwillo's life-span approach has extended knowledge about EEG and behavior relationships and has provided a perspective and several hypotheses with which such issues can be resolved. This life-span descriptive research has been augmented with experimental work in adulthood (e.g., Beatty *et al.*, 1974; Surwillo, 1964b; Woodruff, 1975) and infancy (Karmel *et al.*, 1977; Karmel & Maisel, 1975) which may soon result in explanations about changes in behavioral timing and in attention over the life span.

The descriptive research of Beck, Dustman, and Schenkenberg is the other presently available body of life-span brain electrical activity and behavior data. These data, like those of Surwillo, provide an important initial step in understanding developmental changes in behavior. Coupled with experimental approaches examining active processing in infancy (Hofmann *et al.*, 1977), childhood (J. Cohen, 1973), and adulthood and old age (Marsh & Thompson, 1976), and with life-span studies on active information processing which have yet to be initiated, these ERP data can lead to an understanding of the neural mechanisms involved in perception and cognition and their changes with age.

Brain and behavior relationships at various points in the life span have also been explicated with developmental EEG and ERP data. Electrophysiological studies of behavior in infancy have provided a clearer, more detailed picture of the capacity and mechanisms involved in neonatal responses. From the original perspective of the infant's world as a blooming, buzzing confusion, researchers moved to the perspective which emphasized the complexity and sophistication of infant perceptual abilities. The current perspective emerging as a refinement of these earlier ideas suggests that while the neonate is capable of a number of seemingly complex behaviors, these behaviors can be mediated at a subcortical level. Cortical integration of behavior may not occur until the third month of life. These data provide evidence that neonatal capacity is qualitatively as well as quantitatively different from capacity in later infancy and childhood.

Another point in the life span at which data on EEG, ERP, and behavior relationships have provided evidence for mechanisms involved in developmental change is in old age. Studies of the LPC confirm earlier speculation than an important locus of age-related slowing is in the CNS. What is not yet clear is if the CNS slowing involves changes in functional integration coded by the alpha rhythm or if anatomical and biochemical changes independently cause the alpha rhythm and behavior to slow.

While EEG, ERP, and behavior relationships have received attention from developmentalists working in early and late phases of the life span, less developmental information is available in childhood, adolescence, and middle age. Data collected during these periods could provide a number of useful insights. EEG and ERP studies of behavior development in the first 2 years may clarify the nature of CNS changes involved in the onset of symbolic thought. ERPs also provide an excellent means to study the onset of receptive language abilities. Studies of EEG and ERPs later in childhood may extend the understanding of cognitive organization and lateralization as well as provide strategies for identification and intervention in problems of dyslexia, stuttering, and other school failures. The search for biological causes of sex differences can be expanded with the study of EEG, ERP, and behavior relationships. Hormone, EEG, and behavior interactions is a promising area which has received little attention from developmentalists. The period when the biggest hormone changes take place—early adolescence—has received almost no attention in developmental EEG research; and middle age, when the female menopause occurs, is another developmental period of import for hormone, EEG, and behavior studies as well as for studies of sex differences in EEG and behavior change.

Developmental studies of brain electrical activity and behavior relationships over the life span have provided us with new information about behavioral development and its biological foundations and have led to the confirmation and refutation of various hypotheses generated by purely anatomical or behavioral studies. This overview of life-span research on

EEG, ERP, and behavior relationships has also led to the identification of a number of periods which may be critical in terms of behavior change and to the identification of a number of topics which merit additional study. Given the demonstrated usefulness of studies of brain electrical activity and behavior relationships to extend our understanding of behavioral development, and given the demonstrated usefulness of developmental approaches at all points of the life span to expand basic knowledge in the biological and behavioral sciences, this area clearly deserves the increasing attention it appears to be receiving from developmentalists working at various points of the life span and life-span developmentalists as well.

Acknowledgments

A number of colleagues read a draft version of this chapter and provided valuable comments and new information. For this effort I wish to thank Donald Lindsley, Bernard Karmel, David Galin, Michael Lester, Walter Cunningham, Christopher Hertzog, John Rohrbaugh, and Rathe Karrer. Special acknowledgment is made to Robert Dustman, Gail Marsh, and Walter Surwillo who each provided me with a thoughtful and detailed critique.

References

Anders, T. R., & Fozard, J. L. Effects of age upon retrieval from primary and secondary memory. *Developmental Psychology,* 1973, **9,** 411–415.

Anders, T. R., Fozard, J. L., & Lillyquist, T. D. Effects of age upon retrieval from short-term memory. *Developmental Psychology,* 1972, **6,** 214–217.

Andersen, P., & Andersson, A. *Physiological basis of the alpha rhythm.* New York: Appleton, 1968.

Baltes, P. B. Longitudinal and cross-sectional sequences in the study of age and generation effects. *Human Development* 1968, **11,** 145–171.

Beatty, J. Learned regulation of alpha and theta frequency activity in the human electroencephalogram. In G. E. Schwartz & J. Beatty (Eds.), *Biofeedback theory and research.* New York: Academic Press, 1977.

Beatty, J., Greenberg, A., Deibler, W. P., & O'Hanlon, J. F. Operant control of occipital theta rhythm affects performance in a radar monitoring task. *Science,* 1974, **183,** 871–873.

Beck, E. C., & Dustman, R. E. Changes in evoked responses during maturation and aging in man and macaque. In N. Burch & H. L. Altshuler (Eds.), *Behavior and brain electrical activity.* New York: Plenum, 1975, Pp. 431–472.

Beck, E. C., Dustman, R. E., & Schenkenberg, T. Life span changes in the electrical activity of the human brain as reflected in the cerebral evoked response. In J. M. Ordy & K. R. Brizzee (Eds.), *Neurobiology of aging.* New York: Plenum, 1975. Pp. 175–192.

Benton, A. L., & Joynt, R. J. Early descriptions of aphasia. *Archives of Neurology,* 1960, **3,** 205–222.

Berger, H. Uber das Electroen-cephalogram des Menschen. III. *Archives of Psychiatry Nervenkr.,* 1931, **94,** 16–60.

Bernhard, C. G., & Skoglund, C. R. On the alpha frequency of human brain potentials as a function of age. *Skandinavisches Archiv für Physiologie,* 1939, **82,** 178–184.

Bernhard, C. G., & Skoglund, C. R. On the blocking time of the cortical alpha rhythm in children. *Acta Psychiatrica Scandinavica,* 1943, **18,** 159–170.

Bertelson, P., & Tisseyre, F. Lateral asymmetry in the perceived sequence of speech and nonspeech stimuli. *Perception & Psychophysics,* 1972, **11,** 356–362.

Birren, J. E. Age changes in speed of behavior: Its central nature and physiological correlates. In A. T. Welford & J. E. Birren (Eds.), *Behavior, aging and the nervous system.* Springfield, Ill.: Thomas, 1965. Pp. 191–216.

Birren, J. E. Toward an experimental psychology of aging. *American Psychologist,* 1970, **25,** 124–135.

Birren, J. E. Translations in gerontology—from lab to life. *American Psychologist,* 1974, **29,** 808–815.

Boddy, J. The relationship of reaction time to brain wave period: A reevaluation. *Electroencephalography and Clinical Neurophysiology,* 1971, **30,** 229–235.

Bogen, J. E. The other side of the brain. I, II, III. *Bulletin for the Los Angeles Neurological Society,* 1969, **34,** 73–105, 135–162, 191–220.

Bogen, J. E., DeZure, R., Tenhouten, W. D., & Marsh, J. F. The other side of the brain. IV. The A/P ratio. *Bulletin of the Los Angeles Neurological Society,* 1972, **37,** 49–61.

Bond, E. K. Perception of form by the human infant. *Psychological Bulletin,* 1972, **77,** 225–245.

Botwinick, J. *Cognitive processes in maturity and old age.* New York: Springer, 1967.

Botwinick, J., & Birren, J. E. Cognitive processes: Mental abilities and psychomotor responses in healthy aged men. In J. E. Birren, R. N. Butler, S. W. Greenhouse, L. Sokoloff, & M. R. Yarrow (Eds.), *Human aging: A biological and behavioral study.* Washington, D.C.: U.S. Government Printing Office, 1963. Pp. 97–108.

Botwinick, J., & Thompson, L. W. Premotor and motor components of reaction time. *Journal of Experimental Psychology,* 1966, **71,** 9–15.

Brazier, M. A. B., & Finesinger, J. E. Characteristics of the normal electroencephalogram. I. A study of the occipital-cortical potentials in 500 normal adults. *Journal of Clinical Investigation,* 1944, **23,** 303–311.

Bronson, G. The postnatal growth of visual capacity. *Child Development,* 1974, **45,** 873–890.

Bruner, J. S. *On Knowing: Essays for the left hand.* Cambridge, Mass.: Harvard University Press, 1962.

Buchsbaum, M., & Fedio, P. Visual information and evoked responses from the left and right hemispheres. *Electroencephalography and Clinical Neurophysiology,* 1969, **26,** 266–272.

Buchsbaum, M., & Fedio, P. Hemispheric differences in evoked potentials to verbal and nonverbal stimuli in the left and right visual fields. *Physiology and Behavior,* 1970, **5,** 207–210.

Buffery, A. W. H. Sex differences in the development of hemispheric asymmetry of function of the human brain. *Brain Research,* 1971, **31,** 364–365.

Buffery, A. W. H., & Gray, J. A. Sex differences in the development of spatial and linguistic skills. In C. Ounsted & D. C. Taylor (Eds.), *Gender differences: Their ontogeny and significance.* Baltimore: Williams & Wilkins, 1972. Pp. 123–157.

Busse, E. W., & Obrist, W. D. Significance of focal electroencephalographic changes in the elderly. *Postgraduate Medicine,* 1963, **34,** 179–182.

Callaway, E., & Halliday, R. A. Evoked potential variability: Effects of age, amplitude and methods of measurement. *Electroencephalography and Clinical Neurophysiology,* 1973, **34,** 125–133.

Caskey, G. M. Age changes in human predominant receptive field size. Unpublished manuscript, Temple University, 1976.

Caveness, W. F. *Atlas of electroencephalography in the developing monkey (Macaca Mulatta)*. Reading, Mass: Addison-Wesley, 1962.

Chartock, H. E., Glassman, P. R., Poon, L. W., & Marsh, G. R. Changes in alpha rhythm asymmetry during learning of verbal and visuospatial tasks. *Physiology and Behavior,* 1975, **15,** 237–239.

Ciganek, C. The EEG response (evoked potential) to light stimulus in man. *Electroencephalography and Clinical Neurophysiology,* 1961, **13,** 165–172.

Coates, S. Sex differences in field dependence-independence between the ages of 3 and 6. *Perceptual and Motor Skills,* 1974, **39,** 1307–1310.

Cohen, J. Developmental aspects of the CNV: A review. *Electroencephalography and Clinical Neurophysiology,* 1973 (Suppl. 33), 133–137.

Cohen, L. B., & Salapatek, P. *Infant perception: From sensation to cognition.* Vol. 1. *Basic visual processes.* New York: Academic Press, 1975. (a)

Cohen, L. B., & Salapatek, P. *Infant perception: From sensation to cognition.* Vol. 2. *Perception of space, speech, and sound.* New York: Academic Press, 1975. (b)

Cohen, R. A. Conceptual styles, culture conflict and non-verbal tests of intelligence. *American Anthropologist,* 1969, **71,** 826–856.

Cohn, R. Differential cerebral processing of noise and verbal stimuli. *Science,* 1971, **172,** 599–601.

Conel, J. L. *The postnatal development of the human cerebral cortex.* Vol. 1. *The cortex of the newborn.* Cambridge, Mass.: Harvard University Press, 1939.

Conel, J. L. *The postnatal development of the human cerebral cortex.* Vol. 2. *The cortex of the one month infant.* Cambridge, Mass.: Harvard University Press, 1941.

Conel, J. L. *The postnatal development of the human cerebral cortex.* Vol. 3. *The cortex of the three month infant.* Cambridge, Mass.: Harvard University Press, 1947.

Creutzfelt, O. D., Arnold, P. M., Becker, D., Langenstein, S., Tinsch, W., Wilhelm, H., & Wuttke, W. EEG changes during spontaneous and controlled menstrual cycles and their correlations with psychological performance. *Electroencephalography and Clinical Neurophysiology,* 1976, **40,** 113–131.

Crowell, D. H., Jones, R. H., Kapuniai, L. E., & Nakagawa, J. K. Unilateral cortical activity in newborn humans: An early index of cerebral dominance? *Science,* 1973, **180,** 205–208.

Cunningham, W. R., & Birren, J. E. Age changes in human abilities: A 28 year longitudinal study. *Developmental Psychology,* 1976, **12,** 81–82.

Davidson, R. J., & Schwartz, G. E. Patterns of cerebral lateralization during cardiac biofeedback versus the self-regulation of emotion. *Psychophysiology,* 1976, **13,** 62–68.

Davidson, R. J., Schwartz, G. E., Pugash, E., & Bromfield, E. Sex differences in patterns of EEG asymmetry. *Biological Psychology,* 1976, **4,** 119–138.

Davies, D. R., & Krkovic, A. Skin conductance, alpha activity and vigilance. *American Journal of Psychology,* 1965, **78,** 304–306.

Davis, P. A. The electroencephalogram in old age. *Diseases of the Nervous System,* 1941, **2,** 77.

Dawson, G. D. Cerebral responses to electrical stimulation of peripheral nerve in man. *Journal of Neurology, Neurosurgery and Psychiatry,* 1947, **10,** 134–140.

Dawson, G. D. A summation technique for detecting small signals in a large irregular background. *Journal of Physiology (London),* 1951, **115,** 2–3.

Dawson, G. D. A summation technique for the detection of small evoked potentials. *Electroencephalography and Clinical Neurophysiology,* 1954, **6,** 54–84.

Dekaban, A. *Neurology of early childhood.* Baltimore: Williams & Wilkins, 1970.

Dobson, V. Spectral sensitivity of the 2-month infant as measured by the visually evoked cortical potential. *Vision Research,* 1976, **16**, 367–374.

Doyle, J. D., Ornstein, R., & Galin, D. Lateral specialization of cognitive mode: II. EEG frequency analysis. *Psychophysiology,* 1974, **5**, 567–578.

Dreyfus-Brisac, C. The electroencephalogram of the premature infant and full-term newborn: Normal and abnormal development of waking and sleeping patterns. In P. Kellaway & I. Petersen (Eds.), *Neurological and electroencephalographic correlative studies in infancy.* New York: Grune & Stratton, 1964.

Dreyfus-Brisac, C., & Blanc, C. Electro-encéphalogramme et maturation cérébrale. *Encéphale,* 1956, **3**, 205–245.

Dreyfus-Brisac, C., Samson, D., Blanc, C., & Monod, N. L'électroencéphalogramme de l'enfant normal de moins de 3 ans. *Etudes Neo-Natales,* 1958, **7**, 143–175.

Dustman, R. E., & Beck, E. C. The visually evoked potential in twins. *Electroencephalography and Clinical Neurophysiology,* 1965, **19**, 570–575.

Dustman, R. E., & Beck, E. C. Visually evoked potentials: Amplitude changes with age. *Science,* 1966, **151**, 1013–1015.

Dustman, R. E., & Beck, E. C. The effects of maturation and aging on the wave form of visually evoked potentials. *Electroencephalography and Clinical Neurophysiology,* 1969, **26**, 2–11.

Dustman, R. E., Beck, E. C., & Schenkenberg, T. Life span changes in man. In J. E. Desmedt (Ed.), *Cerebral evoked potentials in man: The Brussels International Symposium.* London and New York: Oxford University Press, 1977.

Eeg-Olofsson, O. The development of the electroencephalogram in normal children and adolescents from the age of 1 through 21 years. *Acta Paediatrica Scandinavica Supplementum,* 1971, **208**, 1–46.

Eichorn, D. H. *Electrocortical and autonomic response in infants to visual and auditory stimuli.* Unpublished doctoral dissertation, Northwestern University, 1951.

Eimas, P. D. Speech and perception in early infancy. In L. B. Cohen & P. Salapatek (Eds.), *Infant perception: From sensation to cognition.* Vol. 2. *Perception of space, speech, and sound.* New York: Academic Press, 1975. Pp. 193–231.

Eimas, P. D., Siqueland, E. R., Jusczyk, P., & Vigorito, J. Speech perception in infants. *Science,* 1971, **171**, 303–306.

Eisdorfer, C. Arousal and performance: Experiments in verbal learning and a tentative theory. In G. A. Talland (Ed.), *Human aging and behavior.* New York: Academic Press, 1968. Pp. 189–216.

Eisengart, M. A., & Symmes, D. The effect of eye blink on the visual evoked response in children. *Electroencephalography and Clinical Neurophysiology,* 1971, **31**, 71–75.

Elias, M. F., & Kinsbourne, M. Age and sex differences in the processing of verbal and nonverbal stimuli. *Journal of Gerontology,* 1974, **29**, 162–171.

Ellingson, R. J. Electroencephalograms of normal full term newborns immediately after birth with observations on arousal and visual evoked responses. *Electroencephalography and Clinical Neurophysiology,* 1958, **10**, 31–50.

Ellingson, R. J. Cortical electrical responses to visual stimulation in the human infant. *Electroencephalography and Clinical Neurophysiology,* 1960, **12**, 663–677.

Ellingson, R. J. Cerebral electrical responses to auditory and visual stimuli in the infant (human and subhuman studies). In P. Kellaway & I. Petersen (Eds.), *Neurological and electroencephalographic correlative studies in infancy.* New York: Grune & Stratton, 1964. Pp. 78–116.

Ellingson, R. J. The study of brain electrical activity in infants. In L. P. Lipsitt & C. C.

Spiker (Eds.), *Advances in child development and behavior.* Vol. 3. New York: Academic Press, 1967. Pp. 53–97.

Ellingson, R. J., Lathrop, G. H., Danahy, T., & Nelson, B. Variability of visual evoked potentials in human infants and adults. *Electroencephalography and Clinical Neurophysiology,* 1973, **34,** 113–124.

Fantz, R. L., & Fagan, J. F. Visual attention to size and number of pattern details by term and preterm infants during the first six months. *Child Development,* 1975, **46,** 3–18.

Fedio, P. M., Mirsky, A. G., Smith, W. J., & Perry, D. Reaction time and EEG activation in normal and schizophrenic subjects. *Electroencephalography and Clinical Neurophysiology,* 1961, **13,** 923–926.

Feinberg, I. Effects of age on human sleep patterns. In A. Kales (Ed.), *Sleep physiology and pathology.* Philadelphia: Lippincott, 1969. Pp. 39–52.

Feinberg, I. Changes in sleep cycle patterns with age. *Journal of Psychiatric Research,* 1974, **10,** 283–306.

Feinberg, I., & Carlson, V. R. Sleep variables as a function of age in man. *Archives of General Psychiatry,* 1968, **18,** 239–250.

Filbey, R. A., & Gazzaniga, M. S. Splitting the normal brain with reaction time. *Psychonomic Science,* 1969, **17,** 335.

Fiorentino, M. R. *Normal and abnormal development: The influence of primary reflexes on motor development.* Springfield, Ill.: Thomas, 1972.

Freedman, N. L., Hafer, B. M., & Daniel, R. S. EEG arousal decrement during paired associate learning. *Journal of Comparative and Physiological Psychology,* 1966, **61,** 15–19.

Friedlander, W. J. Electroencephalographic alpha rate in adults as a function of age. *Geriatrics,* 1958, **13,** 29–31.

Froehling, S. *Effects of propranolol on behavioral and physiological measures in elderly males.* Unpublished doctoral dissertation, University of Miami (Florida), 1974.

Fuster, J. M. Tachistoscopic perception in monkeys. *Federation Proceedings,* 1957, **16,** 43.

Galin, D., & Ellis, R. R. Asymmetry in evoked potentials as an index of lateralized cognitive processes: Relation to EEG alpha asymmetry. *Neuropsychologia,* 1975, **13,** 45–50.

Galin, D., & Ornstein, R. Lateral specialization of cognitive mode: An EEG study. *Psychophysiology,* 1972, **9,** 225–230.

Galin, D., & Ornstein, R. Hemispheric specialization and the duality of consciousness. In H. Widroe (Ed.), *Human behavior and brain function.* Springfield, Ill.: Thomas, 1973.

Gastaut, H. The role of the reticular formation in establishing conditioned reactions. In H. H. Jasper, L. D. Proctor, R. S. Knighton, W. C. Noshay, & R. T. Costello (Eds.), *Reticular formation of the brain.* Boston: Little, Brown, 1958. Pp. 561–579.

Gaylord, S. A., & Marsh, G. R. Age differences in the speed of a spatial cognitive process. *Journal of Gerontology,* 1975, **30,** 674–678.

Gazzaniga, M. S. *The bisected brain.* New York: Appleton, 1970.

Gazzaniga, M. S., & Hillyard, S. A. Attention mechanisms following brain bisection. In S. Kornblum (Ed.), *Attention and performance IV.* New York: Academic Press, 1973. Pp. 221–238.

Geschwind, N., & Levitsky, W. Human brain: Left-right asymmetries in temporal speech region. *Science,* 1968, **161,** 186–187.

Glaser, G. H., & Levy, L. L. Photic following in the EEG of the newborn. *American Journal of Diseases in Childhood,* 1965, **109,** 333–337.

Gloor, P. *Hans Berger on the electroencephalogram of man.* Amsterdam: Elsevier, 1969. [Also *Electroencephalography and Clinical Neurophysiology,* 1969 (Suppl. 28).]

Groll, E. Central nervous system and peripheral activation variables during vigilance performance. *Zeitschrift für Experimentelle und Angewandte Psychologie,* 1966, **13,** 248–264.

Gullickson, G. R. CNV and behavioral attention to a glide-tone warning of interesting non-moving or kaleidoscopic visual or auditory patterns in 2- and 3-year-old children. *Electroencephalography and Clinical Neurophysiology,* 1973 (Suppl. 33), 145–150.

Hagne, I. Development of the waking EEG in normal infants during the first year of life. In P. Kellaway & I. Petersen (Eds.), *Clinical electroencephalography of children.* New York: Grune & Stratton, 1968. Pp. 97–118.

Harkins, S. W., Froehling-Moss, S., Thompson, L. W., & Nowlin, J. B. Relationship between central and autonomic nervous system states: Correlates of psychomotor performance in the elderly. Paper presented at the Western Psychological Association Meeting, Los Angeles, April 1976.

Harter, M. R. Effects of carbon dioxide on the alpha frequency and reaction time in humans. *Electroencephalography and Clinical Neurophysiology,* 1967, **23,** 561–563. (a)

Harter, M. R. Excitability cycles and cortical scanning: A review of two hypotheses of central intermittency in perception. *Psychological Bulletin,* 1967, **68,** 47–58. (b)

Harter, M. R., & Suitt, C. D. Visually-evoked cortical responses and pattern vision in the infant: A longitudinal study. *Psychonomic Science,* 1970, **18,** 235–237.

Harvald, B. EEG in old age. *Acta Psychiatrica Scandanavica,* 1958, **33,** 193–196.

Hecaen, H., & de Ajuriaguerra, J. *Left-handedness, manual superiority and cerebral dominance.* New York: Grune & Stratton, 1964.

Hecaen, H., & Sauguet, J. Cerebral dominance in left-handed subjects. *Cortex,* 1971, **7,** 19–48.

Hecox, K. Electrophysiological correlates of human auditory development. In L. B. Cohen & P. Salapatek (Eds.), *Infant perception: From sensation to cognition.* Vol. 2. *Perception of space, speech, and sound.* New York: Academic Press, 1975. Pp. 151–191.

Henry, C. E. Electroencephalograms of normal children. *Society for Research in Child Development, Monograph.* 1944, **9,** 1–71.

Hershenson, M. Development of the perception of form. *Psychological Bulletin,* 1967, **67,** 326–336.

Hershenson, M., Munsinger, H., & Kessen, W. Preference for shapes of intermediate variability in the newborn human. *Science,* 1965, **147,** 630–631.

Hofmann, M. J., Karmel, B. Z., & Lester, M. L. Infants' electrophysiological response in a classical conditioning paradigm. 1977. (Submitted for publication.)

Hrbek, A., & Mares, P. Cortical evoked responses to visual stimulation in fullterm and premature newborns. *Electroencephalography and Clinical Neurophysiology,* 1964, **16,** 575–581.

Hubel, D. H., & Wiesel, T. N. Receptive fields, binocular interaction and functional architecture in the cat's visual cortex. *Journal of Physiology (London),* 1962, **160,** 106–154.

Hubel, D. H., & Wiesel, T. N. Receptive fields of cells in striate cortex of very young, visually inexperienced kittens. *Journal of Neurophysiology,* 1963, **26,** 994–1002.

Jasper, H. H. Recent advances in our understanding of ascending activities of the reticular system. In H. H. Jasper, L. D. Proctor, R. S. Knighton, W. C. Noshay, & R. T. Costello (Eds.), *Reticular formation of the brain.* Boston: Little, Brown, 1958. Pp. 319–331.

Jasper, H. H. Unspecific thalamocortical relations. In J. Field (Ed.), *Handbook of physiology* (Sect. I). Washington, D.C.: American Physiology Society, 1960.

Jeffrey, W. E., & Cohen, L. B. Habituation in the human infant. In H. W. Reese (Ed.), *Advances in child development and behavior* (Vol. 6). New York: Academic Press, 1971.

John, E. R., & Thatcher, R. W. *Functional neuroscience.* Hillside, N.J.: Lawrence Erlbaum Associates, 1976.

Kahn, E. Age related changes in sleep characteristics. In E. Hartmann (Ed.), *Sleep and dreaming.* Boston: Little, Brown, 1970. Pp. 25–29.

Karmel, B. Z., Hoffmann, R. F., & Fegy, M. J. Processing of contour information by human infants evidenced by pattern-dependent evoked potentials. *Child Development,* 1974, **45,** 39–48.

Karmel, B. Z., Lester, M. L., McCarvill, S. L., Brown, P., & Hofmann, M. J. Correlation of infants' brain and behavior response to temporal changes in visual stimulation. *Psychophysiology,* 1977, **14,** 134–142.

Karmel, B. Z., & Maisel, E. B. A neuronal activity model for infant visual attention. In L. B. Cohen & P. Salapatek (Eds.), *Infant perception: From sensation to cognition.* Vol. I. *Basic visual processes.* New York: Academic Press, 1975. Pp. 77–131.

Karrer, R. (Ed.). *Developmental psychophysiology of mental retardation.* Springfield, Ill.: Thomas, 1976.

Kimura, D. Cerebral dominance and the perception of verbal stimuli. *Canadian Journal of Perception,* 1961, **15,** 166–171.

Kimura, D. Left-right differences in the perception of melodies. *Quarterly Journal of Experimental Psychology,* 1963, **16,** 355–358. (a)

Kimura, D. Speech lateralization in young children as determined by an auditory test. *Journal of Comparative and Physiological Psychology,* 1963, **56,** 899–902. (b)

Kimura, D. Functional asymmetry of the brain in dichotic listening. *Cortex,* 1967, **3,** 163–178.

Kimura, D. Spatial localization in left and right visual fields. *Canadian Journal of Psychology,* 1969, **23,** 445–458.

Knox, C., & Kimura, D. Cerebral processing of nonverbal sounds in boys and girls. *Neuropsychologia,* 1970, **8,** 227–237.

Kogan, N. *Cognitive styles in infancy and early childhood.* Hillside, N.J.: Lawrence Erlbaum Associates, 1976.

Kornfeld, C. M. *EEG spectra during a prolonged compensatory tracking task.* Unpublished doctoral dissertation, University of California at Los Angeles, 1974.

Kristofferson, A. B. Successiveness discrimination as a two-state, quantal process. *Science,* 1967, **158,** 1337–1339.

Lake, D. A., & Bryden, M. P. Handedness and sex differences in hemispheric asymmetry. *Brain and Language,* 1976, **3,** 266–282.

Lansing, R. W., Schwartz, E., & Lindsley, D. B. Reaction time and EEG activation under alerted and nonalerted conditions. *Journal of Experimental Psychology,* 1959, **58,** 1–7.

Leavitt, F. EEG activation and reaction time. *Journal of Experimental Psychology,* 1968, **77,** 194–199.

Lenneberg, E. H. *Biological foundations of language.* New York: Wiley, 1967.

Levy, J. Possible basis for the evolution of lateral specialization of the human brain. *Nature (London),* 1969, **224,** 614–615.

Levy, J. *Information processing and higher psychological functions in the disconnected hemispheres of human commissurotomy patients.* Unpublished doctoral dissertation, California Institute of Technology, 1970.

Levy, J., Trevarthen, C., & Sperry, R. W. Perception of bilateral chimeric figures following hemispheric deconnection. *Brain.* 1972. **95.** 61–78.

Levy-Agresti, J., & Sperry, R. W. Differential perceptual capacities in major and minor hemispheres. *Proceedings of the National Academy of Sciences, U.S.A.* 1968, **61,** 1151.

Lindsley, D. B. Brain potentials in children and adults. *Science,* 1936, **84,** 354.

Lindsley, D. B. Electrical potentials of the brain in children and adults. *Journal of General Psychology,* 1938, **19,** 285–306.

Lindsley, D. B. A longitudinal study of the occipital alpha rhythm in normal children: Frequency and amplitude standards. *Journal of Genetic Psychology,* 1939, **55,** 197–213.

Lindsley, D. B. Studying neuropsychology and bodily functions. In T. G. Andrews (Ed.), *Methods of psychology.* New York: Wiley, 1948. Pp. 417–458.

Lindsley, D. B. Psychological phenomena and the electroencephalogram. *Electroencephalography and Clinical Neurophysiology,* 1952, **4,** 443–456.

Lindsley, D. B. Attention, consciousness, sleep, and wakefulness. In J. Field (Ed.), *Handbook of physiology.* Vol. II. Neurophysiology. Washington, D.C.: American Physiological Society, 1960. Pp. 1553–1593.

Lindsley, D. B. The ontogeny of pleasure: Neural and behavioral development. In R. G. Heath (Ed.), *The role of pleasure in behavior.* New York: Hoeber, 1964. Pp. 3–22.

Lindsley, D. B., & Wicke, J. D. The electroencephalogram: Autonomous electrical activity in man and animals. In R. F. Thompson & M. M. Patterson (Eds.), *Bioelectric recording techniques.* New York: Academic Press, 1974. Pp. 3–83.

Loveless, N. E., & Sanford, A. J. Effects of age on the contingent negative variation and preparatory set in a reaction-time task. *Journal of Gerontology,* 1974, **29,** 52–63.

Lykken, D. T., Tellegen, A., & Thorkelson, K. Genetic determination of EEG frequency spectra. *Biological Psychology,* 1974, **1,** 245–259.

Maccoby, E. E., & Jacklin, C. *The psychology of sex differences.* Stanford, Calif.: Stanford University Press, 1974.

Marsh, G. R. Evoked potential correlates of information processing across the life span. Paper presented at the 82nd annual meeting of the American Psychological Association, New Orleans, September 1974.

Marsh, G. R. Age differences in evoked potential correlates of a memory scanning process. *Experimental Aging Research,* 1975, **1,** 3–16.

Marsh, G. R., & Thompson, L. W. Hemispheric asymmetry in slow cortical potentials as a function of verbal or nonverbal set. Paper presented at the second annual meeting of the society for Neuroscience, Houston, October 1972.

Marsh, G. R., & Thompson, L. W. Effect of verbal and non-verbal psychological set on hemispheric asymmetries in the CNV. In C. McCallum & J. R. Knott (Eds.), *Event related slow potentials of the brain: Their relation to behavior.* Amsterdam: Elsevier 1973. Pp. 195–200. (a)

Marsh, G. R., & Thompson, L. W. Effects of age on the contingent negative variation in a pitch discrimination task. *Journal of Gerontology,* 1973, **28,** 56–62. (b)

Marsh, G. R., & Thompson, L. W. Psychophysiology of aging. In J. E. Birren & K. W. Schaie (Eds.), *Handbook of the psychology of aging.* New York: Van Nostrand Reinhold, 1976. Pp. 219–248.

Martin, R. M. Effects of familiar and complex stimuli on infant attention. *Developmental Psychology,* 1975, **11,** 178–185.

Matarazzo, J. D. *Wechsler's measurement and appraisal of adult intelligence.* Baltimore: Williams & Wilkins, 1972.

Matousek, M., Volavka, J., Roubicek, J., & Roth, Z. EEG frequency analysis related to age in normal adults. *Electroencephalography and Clinical Neurophysiology,* 1967, **23,** 162–167.

Matsumiya, Y., Tagliasco, V., Lombrosco, C. T., & Goodglass, H. Auditory evoked response: Meaningfulness of stimuli and interhemispheric asymmetry. *Science,* 1972, **175,** 790–792.

McAdam, D. W., & Whitaker, H. A. Language production: Electroencephalographic localization in the normal human brain. *Science,* 1971, **172,** 499–502.

McGlone, J., & Davidson, W. The relation between cerebral speech laterality and spatial ability with special reference to sex and hand preference. *Neuropsychologia,* 1973, **11,** 105–113.

McGlone, J., & Kertesz, A. Sex differences in cerebral processing of visuo-spatial tasks. *Cortex,* 1973, **9,** 313–320.

McKee, G. B., Humphrey, B., & McAdam, D. W. Scaled lateralization of alpha activity during linguistic and musical tasks. *Psychophysiology,* 1973, **10,** 441–443.

McKeever, W. F., & Huling, M. Left cerebral hemisphere superiority in tachistoscopic word recognition performance. *Perceptual and Motor Skills,* 1971, **30,** 763–766.

Melin, K. A. The EEG in infancy and childhood. *Electroencephalography and Clinical Neurophysiology,* 1953 (Suppl. 4), 205–211.

Miller, E. Handedness and the pattern of human ability. *British Journal of Psychology,* 1971, **62,** 111–112.

Moffitt, A. R. Consonant cue perception by twenty- to twenty-four week old infants. *Child Development,* 1971, **42,** 717–731.

Molfese, D. L., Freeman, R. B., Jr., & Palermo, D. S. The ontogeny of brain lateralization for speech and nonspeech stimuli. *Brain and Language,* 1975, **2,** 356–368.

Morgan, A. H., McDonald, P. J., & MacDonald, H. Differences in bilateral alpha activity as a function of experimental task, with a note on lateral eye movements and hypnotizability. *Neuropsychologia,* 1971, **9,** 459–469.

Morrell, F. Microelectrode and steady potential studies suggesting a dendritic locus of closure. *Electroencephalography and Clinical Neurophysiology,* 1960 (Suppl. 13), 65–79.

Morrell, L. K. EEG frequency and reaction time: A sequential analysis. *Neuropsychologia,* 1966, **4,** 41–48.

Morrell, L. K., & Salamy, J. G. Hemispheric asymmetry of electrocortical responses of speech stimuli. *Science,* 1971, **174,** 164–166.

Morse, P. A. The discrimination of speech and nonspeech stimuli in early infancy. *Journal of Experimental Child Psychology,* 1972, **14,** 477–492.

Moruzzi, G., & Magoun, H. W. Brain stem reticular formation and activation of the EEG. *Electroencephalography and Clinical Neurophysiology,* 1949, **1,** 455–473.

Mundy-Castle, A. C., Hurst, L. M., Beerstecher, D. M., & Prinsloo, T. The electroencephalogram in senile psychosis. *Electroencephalography and Clinical Neurophysiology,* 1954, **6,** 245–252.

Obrist, W. D. The electroencephalogram of normal aged adults. *Electroencephalography and Clinical Neurophysiology,* 1954, **6,** 235–244.

Obrist, W. D. The electroencephalogram of healthy aged males. In J. E. Birren, R. N. Butler, S. W. Greenhouse, L. Sokoloff, & M. R. Yarrow (Eds.), *Human aging: A biological and behavioral study.* Washington, D.C.: U.S. Government Printing Office, 1963. Pp. 76–93.

Obrist, W. D. Electroencephalic approach to age changes in response speed. In A. T. Welford & J. E. Birren (Eds.), *Behavior, aging and the nervous system.* Springfield, Ill.: Thomas, 1965.

Obrist, W. D., & Busse, E. W. The electroencephalogram in old age. In W. P. Wilson (Ed.), *Applications of electroencephalography in psychiatry.* Durham, N.C.: Duke University Press, 1965. Pp. 185–205.

Obrist, W. D., Henry, C. E., & Justiss, W. A. Longitudinal study of EEG in old age. *Excerpta Medica International Congress Series,* 1961, No. 37, 180–181.

O'Hanlon, J. F., McGrath, J. J., & McCauley, M. E. Body temperature and temporal acuity. *Journal of Experimental Psychology,* 1974, **102,** 788–794.

Ohlrich, E. S., & Barnet, A. B. Auditory evoked responses during the first year of life. *Electroencephalography and Clinical Neurophysiology,* 1972, **32,** 161–169.

O'Malley, J. E., & Conners, C. K. The effects of unilateral alpha training on visual evoked responses in a dyslexic adolescent. *Psychophysiology,* 1972, **9,** 467–470.

Orton, S. T. Some studies in language function. *Research Publications Association for Research in Nervous and Mental Disease,* 1934, **13,** 614–632.

Otomo, E. Electroencephalography in old age: Dominant alpha patterns. *Electroencephalography and Clinical Neurophysiology,* 1966, **21,** 489–491.

Owens, W. A. Age and mental abilities: A longitudinal study. *Genetic Psychology Monographs,* 1953, **48,** 3–54.

Owens, W. A. Age and mental ability: A second follow-up. *Journal of Educational Psychology,* 1966, **57,** 311–325.

Pampiglione, G. Some criteria of maturation in the EEG of children up to the age of 3 years. *Electroencephalography and Clinical Neurophysiology,* 1972, **32,** 463.

Penfield, W., & Roberts, L. *Speech and brain mechanisms.* Princeton, N.J.: Princeton University Press, 1959.

Price, R. L., & Smith, D. B. D. The $P_{3(00)}$ wave of the averaged evoked potential: A bibliography. *Physiological Psychology,* 1974, **2,** 387–391.

Roffwarg, H. P., Munzio, J. N., & Dement, W. C. Ontogenic development of the human sleep-dream cycle. *Science,* 1966, **152,** 604–619.

Rose, G. H. Relationship of electrophysiological and behavioral indices of visual development in mammals. In M. B. Sterman, D. J. McGinty, & A. M. Adinolli (Eds.), *Brain development and behavior.* New York: Academic Press, 1971. Pp. 145–183.

Rose, G. H., & Lindsley, D. B. Development of visually evoked potentials in kittens: Specific and non-specific responses. *Journal of Neurophysiology,* 1968, **31,** 607–623.

Ruff, H. A., & Turkewitz, G. Developmental changes in the effectiveness of stimulus intensity on infant visual attention. *Developmental Psychology,* 1975, **11,** 706–710.

Samson-Dolfus, D., Forthomme, J., & Capron, E. EEG of the human infant during sleep and wakefulness during the first year of life: Normal patterns and their prognostic significance. In P. Kellaway & I. Petersen (Eds.), *Neurological and electroencephalographic correlative studies in infancy.* New York: Grune & Stratton, 1964.

Sanford, A. J. A. A periodic basis for perception and action. In W. P. Colquhoun (Ed.), *Biological rhythms and human performance.* New York: Academic Press, 1971. Pp. 179–209.

Schaie, J. P., Syndulko, K., & Maltzman, I. Time estimation of the elderly and performance in a forewarned reaction time task. Paper presented at the meeting of the Western Psychological Association, Los Angeles, April 1976.

Schaie, K. W. A general model for the study of developmental problems. *Psychological Bulletin,* 1965, **64,** 92–107.

Schaie, K. W., Labouvie, G. V., & Buech, B. U. Generational and cohort-specific differences in adult cognitive functioning. *Developmental Psychology,* 1973, **9,** 151–166.

Schaie, K. W., & Strother, C. R. A cross-sequential study of age change in cognitive behavior. *Psychological Bulletin,* 1968, **70,** 671–680.

Schenkenberg, T. *Visual, auditory, and somatosensory evoked responses of normal subjects from childhood to senescence.* Unpublished doctoral dissertation, University of Utah, 1970.

Schenkenberg, T., Dustman, R. E., & Beck, E. C. Changes in evoked responses related to age, hemisphere and sex. *Electroencephalography and Clinical Neurophysiology,* 1971, **30**, 163–164.

Schenkenberg, T., Dustman, R. E., Beck, E. C., Cannon, G., & Callner, D. A. Normative and clinical data on the cortical evoked potential and aging. Paper presented at the meeting of the Western Psychological Association, Los Angeles, April 1976.

Schneirla, T. C. Aspects of stimulation and organization in approach-withdrawal processes underlying vertebrate behavioral development. In D. S. Lehrman, R. Hinde, & E. Shaw (Eds.), *Advances in the study of behavior* (Vol. 1). New York: Academic Press, 1965.

Sherman, J. A. Problem of sex differences in space perception and aspects of intellectual functioning. *Psychological Review,* 1967, **74**, 290–299.

Silverman, A. J., Busse, E. W., & Barnes, R. H. Studies in the processes of aging: Electroencephalographic findings in 400 elderly subjects. *Electroencephalography and Clinical Neurophysiology,* 1955, **7**, 67–74.

Smith, D. B. D., Tom, C. E., Brent, G. A., & Ohta, R. J. Attention, evoked potentials, and aging. Paper presented at the meeting of the Western Psychological Association, Los Angeles, April 1976.

Smith, J. R. The electroencephalogram during infancy and childhood. *Proceedings of the Society for Experimental Biology and Medicine,* 1937, **36**, 384–386.

Smith, J. R. The electroencephalogram during normal infancy and childhood: I. Rhythmic activities present in the neonate and their subsequent development. *Journal of General Psychology,* 1938, **53**, 431–453. (a)

Smith, J. R. The electroencephalogram during normal infancy and childhood: II. The nature of the growth of the alpha waves. *Journal of General Psychology,* 1938, **53**, 455–469. (b)

Smith, J. R. The "occipital" and "pre-central" alpha rhythms during the first two years. *Journal of Psychology,* 1939, **7**, 223–226.

Smolak, L. M. Ontogeny of receptive language ability. Unpublished manuscript, Temple University, 1976.

Sokol, S., & Dobson, V. Pattern reversal visually evoked potentials in infants. *Investigative Ophthalmology,* 1976, **15**, 58–62.

Sperry, R. W. Hemisphere deconnection and unity in conscious awareness. *American Psychologist,* 1968, **23**, 723–733.

Sperry, R. W. Lateral specialization of cerebral function in the surgically separated hemispheres. In F. J. McGuigan & R. A. Schoonover (Eds.), *The psychophysiology of thinking.* New York: Academic Press, 1973. Pp. 209–229.

Sperry, R. W., Gazzaniga, M. S., & Bogen, J. E. Interhemispheric relationships: The neocortical commissures, syndromes of hemisphere disconnection. In P. J. Vinken & G. W. Bruyn (Eds.), *Handbook of clinical neurology* (Vol. 4). Amsterdam: North-Holland Publ., 1969. Pp. 273–290.

Stamm, J. S. On the relationship between reaction time to light and latency of blocking of the alpha rhythm. *Electroencephalography and Clinical Neurophysiology,* 1952, **4**, 61–68.

Stevens, J. R. The electroencephalogram: Human recordings. In R. F. Thompson & M. M. Patterson (Eds.), *Bioelectric recording techniques.* New York: Academic Press, 1974. Pp. 85–98.

Storm van Leeuwen, W., Bickford, R., Brazier, M., Cobb, W. A., Dondey, M., Gastaut, H., Gloor, P., Henry, C. E., Hess, R., Knott, J. R., Kugler, J., Lairy, G. C., Loeb, C., Magnus, O., Oller Daurella, L., Petsche, H., Schwab, R., Walter, W. G., & Widen, L.

Proposal for an EEG terminology by the terminology committee of the International Federation for Electroencephalography and Clinical Neurophysiology. *Electroencephalography and Clinical Neurophysiology*, 1966, **20**, 306–310.

Surwillo, W. W. Central nervous system factors in simple reaction time. *American Psychologist*, 1960, **15**, 419.

Surwillo, W. W. Frequency of the "alpha" rhythm, reaction time and age. *Nature (London)*, 1961, **191**, 823–824.

Surwillo, W. W. The relation of simple response time to brain wave frequency and the effects of age. *Electroencephalography and Clinical Neurophysiology*, 1963, **15**, 105–114.

Surwillo, W. W. The relation of decision time to brain wave frequency and to age. *Electroencephalography and Clinical Neurophysiology*, 1964, **16**, 510–514. (a)

Surwillo, W. W. Some observations on the relation of response speed to frequency of photic stimulation under conditions of EEG synchronization. *Electroencephalography and Clinical Neurophysiology*, 1964, **17**, 194–198. (b)

Surwillo, W. W. On the relation of latency of alpha attenuation to alpha rhythm frequency and the influence of age. *Electroencephalography and Clinical Neurophysiology*, 1966, **20**, 129–132.

Surwillo, W. W. Timing of behavior in senescence and the role of the central nervous system. In G. A. Talland (Ed.), *Human aging and behavior*. New York: Academic Press, 1968. Pp. 1–35.

Surwillo, W. W. Digit span and EEG frequency in normal children. *Electroencephalography and Clinical Neurophysiology*, 1971, **31**, 93–95. (a)

Surwillo, W. W. Frequency of the EEG during acquisition in short-term memory. *Psychophysiology*, 1971, **8**, 588–593. (b)

Surwillo, W. W. Human reaction time and period of the electroencephalogram in relation to development. *Psychophysiology*, 1971, **8**, 468–482. (c)

Surwillo, W. W. Latency of EEG attenuation (blocking) in relation to age and reaction time in normal children. *Developmental Psychobiology*, 1972, **5**, 223–230.

Surwillo, W. W. Word-association latency in normal children during development and the relation of brain electrical activity. *Psychophysiology*, 1973, **10**, 154–165.

Surwillo, W. W. The electroencephalogram in the prediction of human reaction time during growth and development. *Biological Psychology*, 1975, **3**, 79–90. (a)

Surwillo, W. W. Reaction-time variability, periodicities in reaction-time distributions, and the EEG gating-signal hypothesis. *Biological Psychology*, 1975, **3**, 247–261. (b)

Surwillo, W. W. Interval histograms of period of the electroencephalogram and the reaction time in twins. *Behavior Genetics*, 1977, **7**, 161–170.

Surwillo, W. W., & Titus, T. G. Reaction time and the psychological refractory period in children and adults. *Developmental Psychobiology*, 1976, **9**, 517–527.

Sutton, S., Braren, M., & Zubin, J. Evoked-potential correlates of stimulus uncertainty. *Science*, 1965, **150**, 1187–1188.

Taft, L. T., & Cohen, H. J. Neonatal and infant reflexology. In J. Hellmuth (Ed.), *Exceptional infant*. Vol. 1. The normal infant. Seattle, Wash.: Special Child Publications, 1967.

Thompson, L. W. Progress in research on brain electrical activity and aging. Colloquium presented at the University of Southern California, April 1974.

Thompson, L. W., & Marsh, G. R. Psychophysiological studies of aging. In C. Eisdorfer & M. P. Lawton (Eds.), *The psychology of adult development and aging*. Washington, D.C.: American Psychological Association, 1973. Pp. 112–148.

Thompson, L. W., & Nowlin, J. B. Relation of increased attention to central and autonomic nervous system states. In L. R. Jarvik, C. Eisdorfer, & J. E. Blum (Eds.), *Intellectual functioning in adults: Psychological and biological influences.* New York: Springer, 1973. Pp. 107–123.

Thompson, L. W., & Obrist, W. D. EEG correlates of verbal learning and overlearning in the elderly. *Journal of Gerontology,* 1966, **21,** 45–51.

Thompson, L. W., & Wilson, S. Electrocortical reactivity and learning in the elderly. *Journal of Gerontology,* 1966, **21,** 45–51.

Timiras, P. S. *Developmental physiology and aging.* New York: Macmillan, 1972.

Trehub, S. E., & Rabinovitch, M. S. Auditory-linguistic sensitivity in early infancy. *Developmental Psychology,* 1972, **6,** 74–77.

Vaughan, H. G. The relationship of brain activity to scalp recordings of event-related potentials. In E. Donchin & D. B. Lindsley (Eds.), *Average evoked potentials: Methods, results and evaluations.* Washington, D.C.: NASA, 1969. Pp. 45–75.

Vella, E. J., Butler, S. R., & Glass, A. Electrical correlate of right hemisphere function. *Nature (London),* 1972, **236,** 125–126.

Vitova, Z., & Hrbek, A. Developmental study on the responsiveness of the human brain to flicker stimulation. *Developmental Medicine and Child Neurology,* 1972, **14,** 476–486.

Waber, D. P. Sex differences in cognition: A function of maturation rate? *Science,* 1976, **193,** 572–573.

Wada, J. A., Clarke, R., & Hamm, A. Cerebral hemispheric asymmetry in humans: Cortical speech zones in 100 adult and 100 infant brains. *Archives of Neurology,* 1975, **32,** 239–246.

Walter, W. G., Cooper, R., Aldridge, V. J., McCallum, W. C., & Winter, A. L. Contingent negative variation: An electric sign of sensori-motor association and expectancy in the human brain. *Nature (London),* 1964, **203,** 380–384.

Wang, H. S., & Busse, E. W. EEG of healthy old persons—A longitudinal study. I. Dominant background activity and occipital rhythm. *Journal of Gerontology,* 1969, **24,** 419–426.

Wang, H. S., Obrist, W. D., & Busse, E. W. Neurophysiological correlates of the intellectual function of elderly persons living in the community. *American Journal of Psychiatry,* 1970, **126,** 1205–1212.

Wechsler, D. *The measurement and appraisal of adult intelligence.* Baltimore: Williams & Wilkins, 1958.

Weinbach, A. P. Some physiological phenomena fitted to growth equations: II. Brain potentials. *Human Biology,* 1938, **10,** 145–150.

Wetherford, M. J., & Cohen, L. B. Developmental changes in infant visual preferences for novelty and familiarity. *Child Development,* 1973, **44,** 416–424.

Williams, H. L., Granda, A. M., Jones, R. C., Lubin, A., & Armington, D. C. EEG frequency and finger pulse volume as predictors of reaction time during sleep loss. *Electroencephalography and Clinical Neurophysiology,* 1962, **14,** 64–70.

Witelson, S. F. Sex and the single hemisphere: Specialization of the right hemisphere for spatial processing. *Science,* 1976, **193,** 425–427.

Witelson, S. F., & Pallie, W. Left hemisphere specialization for language in the newborn. *Brain,* 1973, **96,** 641–646.

Wood, C., Goff, W. R., & Day, R. S. Auditory evoked potentials during speech perception. *Science,* 1971, **173,** 1248–1251.

Woodruff, D. S. *Biofeedback control of the EEG alpha rhythm and its effect on reaction time in the young and old.* Unpublished doctoral dissertation, University of Southern California, 1972.

Woodruff, D. S. Relationships among EEG alpha frequency, reaction time, and age: A biofeedback study. *Psychophysiology,* 1975, **12,** 673–681.

Woodruff, D. S. Assessment of age changes in the nervous system. Paper presented at the 84th annual meeting of the American Psychological Association, Washington, D.C., September 1976.

Woodruff, D. S., & Gerrity, K. M. The behavioral significance of developmental changes in the EEG alpha rhythm (Biomedical Research Support Grant Program). Unpublished manuscript, Temple University, 1976.

Yakovlev, P. I. Morphological criteria of growth and maturation of the nervous system in man. In L. C. Kolb, R. L. Masland, & R. E. Cooke (Eds.), *Mental retardation.* Baltimore: Williams & Wilkins, 1962.

Yakovlev, P. I., & Lecours, A. R. Myelogenetic cycles of regional maturation of the brain. In A. Minkowski (Ed.), *Symposium–Regional development of the brain in early life.* Oxford: Blackwell, 1967. Pp. 3–70.

Yoshii, N. Principes méthodologiques de l'investigation électroencéphalographique du comportement conditionne. *Electroencephalography and Clinical Neurophysiology,* 1957 (Suppl. 6), 75–88.

Zelinski, E. M., Thompson, L. W., & Marsh, G. R. Age differences in hemispheric processing of verbal and spatial information. Paper presented at the 84th annual meeting of the American Psychological Association, Washington, D.C., September 1976.

Zurif, E. B. Auditory lateralization; Prosodic and Syntactic factors. *Brain and Language,* 1974, **1,** 391–404.

Zurif, E. B., & Mendelsohn, M. Hemispheric specialization for the perception of speech sounds; the influence of intonation and structure. *Perception & Psychophysics,* 1972, **11,** 329–332.

Cognitive Development and Life-Span Developmental Theory: Idealistic versus Contextual Perspectives

Gisela Labouvie-Vief
DEPARTMENT OF PSYCHOLOGY
WAYNE STATE UNIVERSITY, DETROIT, MICHIGAN

and

Michael J. Chandler
DEPARTMENT OF PSYCHOLOGY,
UNIVERSITY OF BRITISH COLUMBIA,
VANCOUVER, BRITISH COLUMBIA

Abstract

The present chapter argues that contemporary treatments of life-span cognitive development may place undue emphasis on decremental changes in later life. As a result of applying youth-centered, unilinear, organismic models of development, these treatments may have selectively focused on inappropriately selected subject samples and invalid assessment procedures. It is proposed that the ensuing interpretations of adult cognitive development may need to be corrected as researchers direct their attention to uniquely adult cognitive achievements in nonartificial settings.

I. Introduction

The course of intellectual development is a stream of events in which psychologists have done a great deal of thematic horse switching. Near its source, strong, universalistic undercurrents have been reported and the pell-mell rush of cognitive development from one intellectual plane to the next has focused attention on the apparently directional character of intellectual change (Langer, 1969; Lerner, 1976; Mischel, 1971; Overton & Reese, 1973; Reese, 1973; Reese & Overton, 1970). Further along the life span, beyond the early race of childhood and adolescence changes, intellectual development has been seen as slower and more meandering, its direction obscured by situations and the topography of the sociocultural terrain. Here, earlier organismic models have been abandoned, in part, and more environmentalistic arguments have been mounted (Birren, 1963; Flavell, 1970; Reese, 1973; Woodruff, 1973, 1975). Finally, as the terminus of this intellectual course is approached, psychological theories are often abandoned altogether in favor of purely physiological accounts of hypothesized intellectual deterioration (Baltes & Labouvie, 1973; Baltes & Willis, 1977).

The view that cognitive changes in adulthood, if compared to those in childhood, are characterized by stability at best, fairly represents the gist of current interpretations of a substantial body of research on lifespan changes in intellectual functioning. In contrast to this interpretation, the present chapter will argue that this view may not be as inevitable as it may appear at first sight. Whether the course of cognitive growth be termed progressive or regressive, and whether or not it be primarily linked to the directional force of maturational changes, is often less a matter of firmly established "fact" than the particular theoretical and pretheoretical bias of those interpreting data. Thus, if one examines life-span cognition in general, and cognitive maturity and aging in particular, from a primarily child-centered perspective, the calm of maturity and arrest of old age may appear to be rather unalterable givens. If one transcends such child-centered models, however, adult cognition may present itself in an altogether different light: like vision, life-span cognition is largely a matter of perspective.

The present chapter argues that the accumulation of recent evidence regarding intellectual developments outside the periods of childhood and adolescence cannot be subsumed by existing child-oriented accounts. To support this contention it will be necessary to first make explicit the salient features of currently favored descriptions of intellectual development and to direct attention to the various idealistic assumptions which underpin much of current research (Section II). Following this initial statement is another major section (Section III) which is more methodological in focus, and which attempts to selectively criticize current research regarding life-span intellectual processes. Section IV is intended to be a synthesis, and attempts to combine these earlier theoretical and data based arguments into a contextual reinterpretation of these issues.

Some of the interpretations advanced in this chapter are, to be sure, tentative and suggestive rather than compelling; to many, indeed, they might appear to be biased and to glibly do away with a way of thinking that has emerged through literally hundreds of studies on the topic. Lest the reader be offended by such an apparently arrogant treatment of tradition, it is necessary to briefly anticipate the authors' understanding of the meaning of objectivity in the conduct of scientific research.

As Giorgi (1971) has pointed out, the concept of objectivity in psychological literature has primarily connoted methodoligical guidelines. In the hope of freeing themselves from the potentially distorting influence of personal values and biases on the conduct of their research, scientists have relied on an objective methodology to safeguard themselves against the intrusion of subjectivity. By so doing, however, they have assumed that objective methods yield objective facts in some automatic and necessary way. In this sense, they have implicitly subscribed to the idealistic notion that scientific knowledge is oriented toward the unraveling of certain absolute, a priori truths. In contrast, a recently emerging view has been the assertion of the inevitable and intricate relationship between scientific knowledge and the context—personal, historical, and ideological—from which such knowledge emerges (e.g., Buss, 1975; Gergen, 1973; Giorgi, 1971; Habermas, 1971).

From such a context-bound perspective, to achieve objectivity no longer merely means to cumulatively record the facts uncovered by research. Such activity, while a necessary part of science, does not render objective those prescientific assumptions which have suggested the phenomena to be studied, as well as hypotheses about their conduct, in the first place. Objectivity of this latter kind, on the contrary, may even demand a certain irreverence in relation to traditionally accepted interpretations and viewpoints since, as argued by Habermas (1971), this brand of objectivity requires a confrontation with the contextual relativity of truth. It is this notion of objectivity which has motivated the present chapter. Needless to say, the reinterpretations advanced here are not meant to be taken as novel objective truth claims; they are rather intended as heuristics which, in the view of the authors, should be helpful in stimulating alternative viewpoints and research avenues.

II. Idealism and Conceptions of Life-Span Cognition

The orienting assumption upon which this critique of current accounts of intellectual development is based is that these views commonly contain a residual form of idealism which sharply limits their scope and applicability to the study of life-span developmental processes. What is seen here as idealistic about most contemporary accounts of intellectual development is that they portray intellectual competence as though it were moving inextricably along some nomological path toward an ideal end state of mature adult cognition. In this sense, much current life-span cognitive theory appears to have borrowed assumptions from organismic conceptions about processes of development (Baltes & Labouvie, 1973; Baltes & Willis, 1977; Labouvie-Vief, 1978) or, at the very least, appears to have erected organismic theories as a standard against which to pin adulthood changes (e.g., Flavell, 1970; Reese, 1973).

A. ORGANICISM À LA MODE

As Barrett (1962) has pointed out, much of the intellectual effort of this century has been expended in attempting to expunge idealistic assumptions from our philosophies, our moralities, and our art. Still, in other ages and other contexts, idealism has been held out as something of virtue, and why its presence in organismic metatheory is here judged to be a flaw requires explanation. Two questions present themselves: First, in what sense are organismic theories implicitly idealistic, and second, what difference does it make if they are?

What is idealistic about most organismic accounts of cognitive development, as Pepper (1970) has pointed out, is that they define stages in the process of human development as imperfect or progressive categories aimed at and only ultimately realized in a fixed ideal goal or end state. Any adequate comprehension of a developing system requires, in this view, prior knowledge of this ultimate, ideal category. Change in such an account is construed as inherently directional, growth is understood as progress, and adulthood is regarded as success. Developmental research, in this tradition, becomes a kind of ontological ballistics, tracking growth along a unilinear trajectory toward its idealized apogee in maturity. The laws or principles of development generated in this context became prescriptive rather than descriptive and adulthood comes to play the role of a kind of platonic absolute.

The determinant order of events called for by organismic models is assumed to be a feature of events themselves, rather than of the theorists who construe them. Through this breach in relativism, a new brand of realism reenters. Facts are assumed to organize themselves, and theory becomes the enunciation of principles already present in events. Observing and documenting the course of development becomes equivalent to theorizing about it. The principle functions of the researcher, beyond simply acting as an executor to nature, are to recognize that some events reveal the underlying organic process of development more readily than do others and to selectively train attention most directly on instances which are especially telling. Even here, however, the constraints are minimal because the same organizing principles are presumably universally expressed in all the features of development on which one focuses. Similarly, cultural or other situational differences acquire the status of nuisance variables which introduce potential sources of error variance that may obscure, but not substantially alter, the genotypic course of development. Hence unilinearity and universality appear as a priori givens, and organismic theorists may tend to "disparage all evidence except humanly unattainable goal" (Pepper, 1970, p. 32).

B. DUALISTIC MODELS OF INTELLECTUAL DEVELOPMENT

In both public and professional circles routine assumptions about the aging process have been shaped largely by similar kinds of idealistic assumptions about the course of intellectual development. In either case children are pictured as swept along toward some inevitable cognitive maturity by powerful, universalistic forces that gradually spend themselves as physical maturity is approached. Cognition is then thought to knit and ossify, locking us into a kind of intellectual stalemate, thought to persist until general enfeeblement takes our minds as well as our bodies. Research efforts intended to further explicate the aging process have generally elaborated this picture by attempting to distinguish what might be called "true" or "normal" components of aging from ancillary, pathological (Birren, 1964, 1970; Botwinick, 1967), or exogenous (Jarvik and Cohen, 1973) factors.

This dualistic system for parsing the aging process, reminiscent of the idealistic distinction between the imperfect appearance of existence and the perfect reality of subsistence, has provided a framework for interpreting the mixed pattern of improvements and deterioration which characterize intellectual change throughout the adult period. Thus, those functions displaying stability or improvements throughout adulthood and old age often are held to be less telling of "true" aging processes; the truly dramatic effect of advancing age on cognitive functioning is rather thought to be revealed in those functions that do decline.

Perhaps the best known and most comprehensive variant of this dual-process model is the theory of fluid and crystallized intelligence proposed by Cattell (1963) and Horn (1970, 1976; Horn & Cattell, 1966, 1967). According to this two-factor model, crystallized intelligence refers to those cognitive processes which are imbedded in a context of cultural meaning and which are relatively "age-insensitive" (Botwinick, 1973). Fluid intelligence, by contrast, typically concerns the processing of information in a context of low meaningfulness and exhibits profound age differences between younger and older adults. This prediction of differential decline rates in crystallized and fluid intelligence subsumes an enormous body of empirical evidence (for summaries, see Baltes & Labouvie, 1973; Botwinick, 1973; Horn, 1970) and offers one explanation for the repeated demonstration that the elderly routinely perform well on tests of stored information while evidencing apparent deficits on tests of immediate memory, spatial relations, and abstract reasoning. Both these performance changes, as well as the changes in structural organization on which they are thought to rest, are said to reflect the dual interplay between life-long cumulative learning on the one hand and "normal" maturational aging on the other.

> At first [fluid intelligence] and [crystallized intelligence] are indistinguishable . . . . The accumulation of CNS injuries is masked by rapid [neurological] development in childhood, but in adulthood the effects become more obvious. Fluid intelligence, based upon this, thus shows a decline as soon as the development of CNS structures is exceeded by the rate of CNS breakdown. Experience and learning accumulate throughout development. The influence of these is felt in the development of crystallized intelligence, which increases throughout adulthood. It, too, will decline after the rate of loss of structure supporting intelligence behavior exceeds the rate of acquisition of new aids to compensate for limited anlage functions. (Horn, 1970, p. 466)

A somewhat similar model has been proposed on the basis of more strictly bio-behavioral research aimed at identifying those adulthood changes reflective of decline processes in neurophysiological and neuroanatomical structures. One common index of such maturation-based primary manifestations of aging (Birren, 1970) is psychomotor slowing, which has become associated with normal maturational rather than environmental and pathological processes on the basis of two arguments.

First, on the behavioral side, psychomotor slowing with advancing age appears to be an almost universal finding, and appears to be the parameter most impervious to variations due to disease or situational factors (Birren, 1970; Birren, Butler, Greenhouse, Sokoloff, & Yarrow, 1963; Hicks & Birren, 1970; Jarvik & Blum, 1971; Jarvik & Cohen, 1973). While the younger person's psychomotor speed is typically found to depend upon variations in experience and specific situational demands, the general quality of slowness in the older individual's behavior is suggested by the emergence of a broad and general "speed" factor (Birren, Riegel, & Morrison, 1962; Chown, 1961) not present in younger subjects. Second, the assumed implication of a physiological mechanism received some support from electroencephalographic research (Hicks & Birren, 1970; Surwillo, 1963, 1964, 1968; Woodruff, 1975). As a result, slowing is often considered a key mediating factor in intellectual development as exemplified by Birren's (1970, p. 126) statement that "slowness is the independent variable that sets limits for the older person in such processes as memory, perception, and problem-solving." A similar view is also expressed by Jarvik (1973; Jarvik & Cohen, 1973) who proposes that intellectual aging is primarily characterized by psychomotor deterioration, while other indices of cognitive performance—in particular, measures of information and verbal knowledge—may not show change or even slight increases in age groups up to the eighth decade.

When viewed from within the idealistic context which generated it, all of this evidence seems sufficiently inevitable and compelling that it might be regarded as having firmly established the obvious. The fact that the elderly no longer seem equal to the idealized accomplishments of late adolescents, that they perform best in concrete and meaning-laden rather than abstract contexts, and that they no longer keep pace with the quick tempos of their juniors all serve to make the case open and shut. Nevertheless it has been the target of extensive criticisms in the recent past (Baltes & Labouvie, 1973; Baltes & Willis, 1977; Labouvie-Vief, 1978; Schaie & Labouvie-Vief, 1974), criticisms that focused less upon the model's empirical generalizations than upon some of the unquestioned and untested surplus meaning on which it rests. What is debatable is the kind of generalizations which the available data permit. That there "is" a relationship between increasing age and decreasing competence on tests of fluid intelligence seems descriptively accurate. What is not apparent, however, is that this empirical fact warrants the normative conclusion that such a relationship "ought" to exist (Toulmin, 1971; Wartofsky, 1971), or that the usual accompaniments of aging "must," in some idealized or prescriptive sense, inevitably follow. Having made this questionable "is" to "ought" (Kohlberg, 1971) inferential leap, several equally questionable assumptions have followed.

A first such assumption commonly made by advocates of these dual-process models relates to the presumed causes of developmental progression, which are taken to be relatively impervious to external influences and to be primarily traceable to the epigenetic unfolding of maturational capacities. Second, because of their assumptive maturational base, developmental laws are seen to transcend boundaries of history, culture, and locale. Consequently, primarily contextual interpretations of older adults' difficulty with learning and cognition are deemphasized. These assumptions seem to have absolved investigators of important responsibilities for selecting assessment procedures addressed to the special needs, strengths, and capacities of the adult and have led to a heavy reliance upon child-centered, laboratory measures devoid of ecological significance.

III.   Contextual Variations in Adult Cognition

From the perspective of these criticisms, the task of assigning meaning to the well-documented age differences in cognitive performance becomes more demanding. Here, before concluding that intellectual decline is a necessary consequence of aging, one would hold out, as minimal methodological requirements, that assessment procedures be employed which fairly sample the ecology of events related to adult competence, that the population of aged persons be representatively sampled, that cohort effects not be mistaken for age-related changes, and that claims for universality not be based upon data gathered in overly narrow subcultural contexts.

If judged against these infrequently applied criteria, much of the purported evidence linking intellectual deterioration to advancing age becomes suspect. The evidence is so suspect, in fact, that it becomes possible to suggest the hypothesis that, among adults, known variations in intellectual competence are totally unrelated to age. To defend this hypothesis, an effort will be made to review available evidence in light of two minimal standards. Any research which claims to have demonstrated irreversible age-related changes in cognitive competence should be able to demonstrate (1) that the comparison groups employed were not different on important dimensions that are not inherently related to advancing age; (2) that the behaviors sampled or assessment procedures employed were not unfairly biased against one of the comparison groups, and that the differences reported were in fact irreversible, as demonstrated by unsuccessful retraining efforts. Few available studies in the literature satisfy any one, let alone both of these requirements. There is considerable evidence, however, to suggest that these are methodological considerations of first-rank importance when attempting research in a life-span context. Selective studies representative of these assessment considerations are reviewed in the following paragraphs.

A. COMPARABILITY OF COMPARISON GROUPS

When attempting to compare elderly persons with their younger counterparts to determine the specific effects of their more advanced age, several potential confounds have been identified which require careful attention. First, the elderly are often in poor health and this burden, while different from aging per se, is a common covariate which may distinguish the aged from persons of less advanced age whose health is often better. The elderly, more frequently than their younger counterparts, are approaching their own death and this factor, rather than age qua age, may differentiate them from their younger counterparts. This is particularly likely when the elderly are sought out in places where they are often grouped fro the purpose of ministering en bloc to their special health needs. Second, as a direct consequence of their years, elderly persons have experienced a different swath of history, were exposed to different formative influences, and are consequently members of a different cohort than are their less senior counterparts. Third, as a consequence of their age, elderly persons are often segregated and subjected to a variety of depersonalizing, degrading, and estranging experiences which may not fall with equal force on their younger counterparts.

1. Health Status and Proximity to Death

While the commonly reported correlation between health and cognitive status (Botwinick, 1973; Horn, 1970, 1976; Jarvik & Cohen, 1973) has been taken as supporting strong biocognitive relationships, more recent data suggest, instead, that such relationships may be secondary to pathology, poor health, and/or nearness to death. There is evidence from the literature (Obrist, Busse, Eisdorfer, & Kleemeier, 1962; Wang, 1973) which indicates that there is generally a positive correlation between the degree of brain impairment (as revealed by histopathological, pneumoencephalographic, electroencephalographic, or cerebral blood flow study) and intellectual malfunctioning in *institutionalized* patients who have various neuropsychiatric or brain disorders. Rather than serving as an appropriate model for all age-related changes in intellectual functioning, however, such findings are rather exceptional and do not apply to elderly persons who are living in the community and are in relatively good health (Birren, 1963, 1970; Eisdorfer & Wilkie, 1973; Hertzog, Gribbin, & Schaie, 1975; Obrist *et al.*, 1962).

This interpretation is also supplemented by a set of findings which have emerged from various major longitudinal projects (Eisdorfer & Wilkie, 1973; Jarvik, 1973; Palmore & Cleveland, 1976; Riegel & Riegel, 1972) in which it was possible, when subjects died, to retrospectively examine performance changes associated with death. This research shows decrement related to chronological age to be an artifactual result, since or because performance changes as a function of distance from death rather than birth. According to this evidence, individuals maintained a more or less stable level of cognitive functioning throughout their adult life span with dramatic changes occurring primarily in the (approximately 5) years immediately preceding death. In view of these findings, the continuous rate of decrement in cognitive functioning suggested by group data may arise simply out of the correlations of age and mortality, and the age-related increase in the incidence in pathological alterations that are associated with, and eventually lead to, natural death (Baltes & Labouvie, 1973; Riegel & Riegel, 1972). Data such as these would seem to imply that the validity of a maturational hypothesis is much more restricted than had been previously assumed. By contrast, it is reasonable to assume that the maturational trends implied in the fluid intelligence hypothesis need to be reinterpreted to suggest the presence of a degree of pathology. Such an assumption is, in fact, not altogether far fetched, since age differences in psychomotor speed (Botwinick & Thompson, 1971; DeVries, 1975) and fluid intelligence (Barry, Steinmetz, Page, & Rodahl, 1966; Powell, 1974; Powell & Pohndorf, 1971) may be related to poor physical exercise habits or decreased stress tolerance (Birren & Renner, 1976) rather than age per se.

2. Sociocultural Context

The conclusion that the morphogenetic features of cognitive development assumed by organismic models may break down if development is treated in a less universalistic manner and is instead related to a variety of differentiated contexts is further strengthened if these contexts are examined from a less biological, and more sociological–psychological perspective.

One of these context factors, historical change, is a relative newcomer to developmental theorizing. Its potential significance was originally suggested by methodological discussions noting that apparent developmental change may often be contaminated by the more transient effects related to historical change and epochs (Baltes, 1968; Baltes, Cornelius, & Nesselroade, 1977; Kuhlen, 1963; Schaie, 1965; Wohlwill, 1973). Indeed, the commonplace use of "time-less cross-sectional designs" (Proshansky, 1976) in developmental research virtually assumes a course of development that is only minimally affected by the particular contexts in which generations grow and age: It is this ahistoric, idealistic assumption which has motivated behavioral scientists to tack together observations derived from generations born at different historical times in a string presumed to be descriptive of universal normative developmental patterns.

A number of studies are now available which support the view that generational change does in fact represent a major source of confounding in past research on life-span cognitive development (Nesselroade, Schaie, & Baltes, 1972; Schaie & Labouvie-Vief, 1974; Schaie, Labouvie, & Buech, 1973; Schaie & Strother, 1968a, 1968b). By methodologically separating cohort and developmental change components, these studies have pointed out that much of what initally appeared to be decrement could be interpreted as generational change. Instead, within-cohort comparisons suggested that:

"most of the adult life span is characterized by an absence of decisive intellectual decrements. In times of rapid cultural and technological change it is primarily in relation to younger populations that the aged can be described as deficient, and it is erroneous to interpret such cross-sectional age differences as indicating ontogenetic change patterns." (Schaie & Labouvie-Vief, 1974, p. 319)

In general, because this research showed cohort membership, rather than age, to account for a major share of the variation between age groups, it raises the possibility that currently accepted patterns of intellectual development are not necessarily an expression of organismic ontogenetic patterns, but may instead reflect on the changing contexts in which cohorts grow and age. Such an interpretation is suggested by several observations. First, it appeared in Schaie's most recent research (Schaie & Labouvie-Vief, 1974; Schaie *et al.*, 1973) that decrements are almost entirely restricted to the postretirement phase and thus they may be in part a response to social policy issues (e.g., the timing of retirement) rather than the effects of normal aging. Second, since it is possible that ontogenetic patterns themselves covary with epochal events rather than age (Nesselroade & Baltes, 1974; Schaie & Labouvie-Vief, 1974; Schaie *et al.*, 1973), it may be quite hazardous to make even short-range generalizations about the universal applicability of obtained age functions. It is this aspect of potential developmental diversity that poses a challenge to traditional interpretations, and that needs to be incorporated into viable theories of life-span cognition.

3. *Cultural and Subcultural Differences*

By the same logic that prompted the exploration of the effects of time-linked cultural change variables, other researchers have similarly begun to investigate the role of contexts within the same slice of historical time. On most of the tests of complex abstract thinking utilized in the assessment of cognitive development, cultural differences exert a pronounced and decisive effect: whether comparisons be based upon education and socioeconomic categories (Botwinick, 1973; Charles, 1973; Hooper & Sheehan, 1976; Papalia & Del Vento Bielby, 1974), ethnic differences (Katz, 1973; Watson, 1973), or cross-cultural research (Buck-Morss, 1975; Cole & Bruner, 1971; Cole & Scribner, 1974), they usually indicate a marked covariation between cognitive performance and sociological–anthropological criteria other than age.

From a cognitive–anthropological perspective, then, it has been suggested that what has previously appeared as maturationally induced, stage-dependent behavior may often be the consequence of such variables as industrialization and modernization rather than age per se. Thus Cole (Cole & Bruner, 1971; Cole & Scribner, 1974) found that the variability in the classification behavior of Kpelle children in Liberia could be accounted for by the time of their entrance into Western-style schools. Similarly, Buck-Morss (1975) has contended that the development of formal thinking, in a Piagetian sense, may reflect a culture's commitment to abstract commodity systems rather than any universal ontogenetic process. Also, as Kagan (1972) suggests, the development of formal operational intelligence may hinge upon the presence or activation of such social catalysts as choice, conflict, and plurality.

The significance of exposure to a pluralistic system of values and ethical codes has been particularly forcefully argued in the domain of less formal, more social–cognitive reasoning. Like formal reasoning, Kohlbergian measures of moral development appear to contain a systematic culture bias (e.g., Lickona, 1976; Rest, 1974). In Keniston's (1972) view, cross-cultural differences do not seem so much a function of a cognitive lag, as the consequence of such sociological variables as mobility and contact with conflicting systems of morality. Garbarino and Bronfenbrenner (1976) espouse a similar interpretation when presenting data to indicate that postconventional moral reasoning may be specific to relatively pluralistic societies.

Thus, what at first glance may appear to be a "normal" maturationally determined ontogenetic component of aging, on closer examination often appears to reflect a system of culturally imposed "prods and brakes" (Neugarten & Datan, 1973). A favored interpretation within the area of adolescent psychology (Bandura, 1964; Gallatin, 1976; Havighurst, 1976; Mead, 1970; Muuss, 1975) and operant approaches to child development (Baer, 1973; Gewirtz, 1969; Lindsley, 1964), this view suggests that regularity in development may be accounted for not by age, but rather by a series of change-producing events (Flavell, 1970) or normative life crises (Datan & Ginsberg, 1975) which, as a result of public policy or culture-specific, age-graded expectations, become correlated with age.

From this perspective, the fact that accounts of adulthood cognitive changes—as opposed to those of childhood and adolescence on the one hand, and old age on the other—have resisted universalistic organismic descriptions is not surprising, if one concedes that during this segment of the life span the sequencing and timing of critical life events are least related to age. In retirement, however, public policy reintroduces a correlation between age and major life event. It is possible, in fact, that the contextual restraints related to retirement rather than aging ultimately may prove to be the basis of a powerful theoretical explanation of the ubiquitous post-60 decline—a hypothesis suggested by a number of recent socioecological interpretations of cognitive decrement in later life (Baltes & Labouvie, 1973; Bengtson, 1973; Labouvie-Vief, Hoyer, Baltes, & Baltes, 1974; Lindsley, 1964; Seligman, 1975). Thus, this viewpoint suggests that attention should be directed toward such factors as lifestyles (Maas & Kuypers, 1974; Neugarten, Crotty, & Tobin, 1964; Schaie & Gribbin, 1975; Schoenfeldt, 1973), patterns of social isolation and participation (Schaie & Gribbin, 1975), institutionalization (Lawton & Nahemow, 1973), and age norms (Baltes & Labouvie, 1973; Bengtson, 1973; MacDonald & Butler, 1974).

B. SAMPLING OF BEHAVIORS

It has been argued, up to this point, that the organismic assumption that all developmental events participate in the same universal laws of the same lawful universe has led to a lack of attention to a proper definition of subsamples, thus avoiding a full confrontation with diversity in life-span cognitive development. A related feature of organismic theory has similarly tended to smooth out the warps in developmental findings and to cast life-span cognition into a single mold. According to this assumption, the choice may be a rather tautological consequence of a society in which opportunities are stratified along class and age lines. If the association is examined within more homogeneous groups, measures of intelligence often fail to predict life outcomes (McClelland, 1973). Nevertheless, such indices have attained the rather autonomous status of an ultimate criterion, as exemplified in Boring's famous tautology that "intelligence is what intelligence tests measure." Indeed the assumed superiority of cognitive measures over relevant behavioral samples is so widespread a phenomenon that to this date there is no research available examining the ecological validity of measures of cognitive functioning from a life-span perspective.

The question of ecological validity is of importance not merely from the perspective of whether or not cognitive research can be applied outside highly controlled laboratory settings (Botwinick, 1973; Jenkins, 1974), but may also throw a new light on what "good" measures are as judged by other criteria. Since the validity of cognitive measures tends to be evaluated primarily on the basis of measurement and theoretical considerations, most of the current cognitive indices tend to be based on samples of achievement of extreme specialization. Insensitivity to situational variability tends to be required from both psychometric (McClelland, 1973) and developmental-theoretical considerations (Kohlberg, 1971; Wohlwill, 1973). In contrast to this view, McClelland (1973) has argued that situational *sensitivity* should be made the sine qua non of validity considerations. That is, tests should be constructed in such a way that scores *change* as a person grows in experience, wisdom, and the ability to successfully cope with life's problems.

From this perspective, the consistent finding that age differences are augmented on tasks that are highly abstract and low in meaning—far from attesting to their validity as indicators of powerful developmental dimensions—rather than regarding the particular samples of behaviors drawn is not overly critical, as long as one attends to relatively abstract features of cognition, organismic theorists (e.g., Kohlberg, 1971) propose, meaningful developmental dimensions are almost of necessity exposed. In contrast, this section will review a number of findings and arguments to suggest that developmental laws may be much less impervious to behavioral sampling, and that what appears to be relatively stable knowledge at this time may be a consequence of unrepresentative sampling of behavioral indices which yield developmental dimensions either too specialized or too unrepresentative of any given age group.

1. Ecological Validity

The last decade or so has witnessed a proliferation of writings (e.g., Buss, 1975; McClelland, 1973; Proshansky, 1970, 1976) reassessing psychological theory in the light of what Proshansky (1970) has called "phenomenon legitimacy," that is, the ability of theories to generate predictions about real-life outcomes. In this view, many theories may have sacrificed scope and relevance for internal consistency, and promoted criteria of cognition and intelligence that are relatively overspecialized, tautological, and validated by their fit to theory rather than to reality.

Despite the widespread use of intelligence tests and related cognitive measures in life-span research, for instance, the notion that such tests predict important life outcomes within a life-span framework has rarely been subjected to any critical tests. To be sure, the earlier mentioned correlation of cognitive measures with social status, education, health, age, and mortality has connoted to many (e.g., Jensen, 1973; Kohlberg,

LaCrosse, & Ricks, 1970) that such tests indeed measure what they are supposed to measure: a person's ability to adapt to life's demands. Such an interpretation is not as inevitable, however, as pointed out by McClelland (1973). As long as they are based on individuals from widely divergent social strata, such correlations raise doubts concerning their validity. In the absence of clearly demonstrated real-world correlates, statements about levels of cognitive–structural complexity may be quite misleading. On the contrary, age functions may change in a most decisive manner if tasks are devised that are high on both meaning and abstractness (Arenberg, 1968; Fozard & Poon, 1976).

2. Age-Related Validity

The problem of ecological validity and its potential biasing effect on developmental theory is further exacerbated if one entertains the notion that—quite apart from whether or not behavioral indices are said to be ecologically valid—measures of cognition which have been validated in one particular age group or in the context of one age-specific developmental theory may not necessarily maintain their validity if applied across distant age groups. There is, in fact, evidence to suggest that performance levels which first appear similar in distant age groups are less convincingly equivalent upon closer scrutiny.

In research on free classification behavior in subjects of widely varying age levels, for example, it has often been found that the elderly tend to group on a basis of complementarity rather than conventional class relations (Denney, 1974; Denney & Wright, 1975)—a classification style variably called "less abstract," "more childlike," "primitive," and "less sophisticated." Yet, as Kogan (1974) points out, such an interpretation glosses over a number of other differences in the classification basis of younger and older subjects which are not so easily captured by a decremental hypothesis. In his research, older adults also produced more inclusive (thus, more abstract) categories and in general appeared to display an unconventional imaginativeness characteristic of highly creative individuals.

A similar tendency to overassimilate the cognitive behavior of older adults to a decremental model may also be seen in research on the utilization of mediational strategies, where elderly subjects often are reported to be more rigid than younger adults. Here again, the behavior of elderly persons show quite remarkable differences from that of school-age children. While the latter tend to profit most from mediational prompts that are explicit and provided by the experimenter, the former appear to do better under conditions in which they are free to implement their own mediational link (Hulicka & Grossman, 1967; Labouvie-Vief & Gonda,

1976; Panicucci & Lavouvie-Vief, 1975; Treat & Reese, 1976). What from one perspective is called decremental, childlike, or less sophisticated, from another may also be interpreted as being more integrative, more self-initiated, and more creative (Arlin, 1975; Riegel, 1973). Thus, an alternative to the "rigidity" interpretation might rely on the ecological utility of preferred and/or salient learning strategies.

Such an ecological or contextual interpretation may be useful from several perspectives. First, it suggests that what appears to be "rigid," "inflexible" behavior may sometimes be due to a mismatch, in at least one of the age groups compared, between ecologically adaptive skills and those adaptive for the specific measurement task at hand. With the predominant bias of tasks in favor of younger subjects, so-called "decrements" may be less a function of the structural limitations of those who are older than of an improper selection of criterion tasks. This interpretation receives some support from a study by Weir (1964) that ingeniously turned around the usual age bias in a study of children and college students. In a task in which a complex, formalistic strategy actually was not asked for, it was the college students who appeared inflexible and perservered in complex but ineffective behavior. Quite similarly, when an attempt is made to render tasks more meaningful and attractive to older adults, age-trends frequently have been found to favor the middle-aged and elderly (Demming & Pressey, 1957; Fozard & Poon, 1976; Lorge, 1936).

The above argument mirrors one recently proposed by Bowers (1973), who criticized the fact that experimental methodology has tended to maximize the amount of treatment/process variance with virtually no consideration for the issue of the psychological significance of the processes thus identified. Applied to developmental research, Bowers' critique implies that the representativeness of a process or strategy in a standardization age group is not invariant across age groups. To answer such question of invariance, we must rely on multiple assessment, interlocking naturalistic and experimental research.

On a more substantive level it appears quite certain that the "ecological validity" of psychological task/treatments is not invariant across age, cohort, and cultural settings. Often, in fact, it appears doubtful at all that tests of "cognition" and "learning" measure what they are meant to measure. First, the adult and older subject tends to have a higher need for relevance and meaningfulness of tasks and may simply refuse to cooperate with tasks of low meaning (Hulicka, 1967). They may similarly have a greater need for internal self-direction (Neugarten, 1967; Woodruff & Walsh, 1975) and thus experience a sense of alienation and concern in a rigidly controlled laboratory setting (Baltes & Labouvie, 1973; Botwinick, 1973; Riegel, 1975).

3. Behavioral Plasticity

In light of this potential multiple determination of age differences, *prima facie* deficit patterns are seldom theoretically meaningful. To arrive at more valid statements, it is necessary instead to examine the responsiveness of such patterns to multiple treatment conditions (Baltes & Goulet, 1970; Baltes & Labouvie, 1973) geared at remediating whatever might be the cause of presumptive deficient performance.

A number of studies implementing this rationale have appeared over the last few years and they all suggest that the routine cognitive performance of older individuals as they function in psychological research settings may be an extremely poor indicator of what they *can* do. First, aging deficits have been quite readily alleviated on tests of speed (Hoyer, Labouvie, & Baltes, 1973), Piagetian cognition (Denney, 1974; Hornblum & Overton, 1976), and fluid intelligence (Labouvie-Vief & Gonda, 1976; Mergler & Hoyer, 1975; Panicucci & Labouvie-Vief, 1975; Plemons, Willis, & Baltes, 1975). And second, what appears upon superficial examination to be deficit may often reflect such noncognitive interference factors as anxiety (Eisdorfer, Nowlin, & Wilkie, 1970; Labouvie-Vief & Gonda, 1976), fatigue (Furry & Baltes, 1973), cautiousness (Botwinick, 1973; Okun & DiVesta, 1978), and a reluctance to guess when not sure (Birkhill & Schaie, 1975).

IV. From Context to Contextualism

Cognitive developmental theorists who have remained alert to the gradual accumulation of evidence concerning the inter- and intrasubject variability in intellectual functioning are faced with a conceptual challenge. To remain viable in the future, the need for theories to accommodate the various context variables and to deal with dialectic organism–environment relations is now widely recognized (e.g., Baltes & Schaie, 1976; Baltes & Willis, 1977; Riegel, 1975); the solutions offered, however, have spanned a range from relative conservatism to a more radical departure from traditionally idealistic assumptions.

A. DISCONTINUITY

First, one may conclude that theories of cognitive development articulated in the study of childhood remain valid, but are restricted in their scope, so that they do not adequately account for the situationally dependent character of cognition in adults and aged persons. In some ways, this is a variant of the dual-process models discussed earlier in this chapter.

The discontinuity solution involves a strategic, but limited retreat, in which only as much of the original theory is yielded as is absolutely necessary. This is, in effect, a policy of containment, by which special boundaries are drawn around specific subsets of the population to which the theory does not seem to apply. Several authors have adopted this discontinuity hypothesis as a working assumption and have posed the question of whether adult development can be assumed to reflect the same organizing principles as were once thought to characterize development from infancy to adolescence. Flavell (1970), for example, has argued that the intellectual development of children but not of adults displays the distinctive feature of being universal as well as constrained by biological–maturational factors.

While according to this view experience may introduce a significant source of variation, uniformity of growth is nevertheless virtually guaranteed because experience is assumed to operate in concert with the constraining process of biological growth. In adulthood, on the other hand, the characteristics of directionality, uniformity, and inevitability are thought to no longer apply and the explanatory utility of maturational processes is minimized. In this discontinuity hypothesis adulthood changes are not assumed to proceed in a regressive fashion which mirrors earlier progressive development, but are thought to reflect immediate, situationally specific contextual constraints (see also Bearison, 1974; Reese, 1973).

Flavell's interpretation, in fact, restates an earlier and closely related suggestion by Birren (1963), who has also argued for a discontinuous relationship between physiological indices and cognition within an ontogenetic context. According to Birren's (1963) "discontinuity hypothesis," physiological factors account for variability in adult behavior only if they reach critical abnormal ranges, as they may in individuals suffering from a pathology and/or approaching death. As long as they stay within a normal range, physiological conditions provide a necessary basis for behavior, but become determining and sufficient causes only when certain critical limits are exceeded.

The discontinuity solution has the virtue of recognizing the existence of contradictory evidence and of tolerating its presence rather than imagining, like the next solution to be discussed, that it will disappear later in the face of some technological breakthrough. The discontinuity solution, however, has several decided limitations. First, by drawing on biological deficit antecedents, it rules out evidence calling for more psychological interpretations even in late life, interpretations which acknowledge a genuine interaction between environmental, biological, and behavioral systems (Woodruff, 1973, 1975). Second, it illegitimately minimizes the treatment of variability and plasticity in early as well as late life. Thus, it displays the flaw of preserving a theory by ruling certain evidence out of court. A developmental model which elects what evidence it will or won't consider is a bit like a system of morality which one pockets when it is no longer convenient. Although shifting theories in midstream may seem to be nimble-footed, intellectually it is not particularly satisfying and fails to permit theory its most valuable function, the facility of proving itself wrong.

B. MULTISYNCHRONICITY

Rather than switching horses in midstream, it is alternatively possible to maintain that adult cognition, like the earlier stages on which it is presumably based, adheres to normative and universal forms, but that this underlying competence may either be obscured through the failure to control potential sources of situation and error variance, or may be applied with a certain degree of discretion only. How, then, is unity to be maintained in the face of the diversity documented earlier in this chapter?

First of all, the absence of an exclusively abstract, formal model of reasoning in adulthood is not a particular disaster from an organismic perspective if one concedes that unlike the model, reality demands no perfect synchrony. Both Piaget (1972) and some of his interpreters (e.g., Chandler, 1977; Flavell, 1971; Flavell & Wohlwill, 1969; Hooper & Sheehan, 1976) have pointed out that one's level of competency is not inevitably documented in reality; at any developmental level, earlier acquired skills are maintained intact in the individual's repertoire and permit a degree of multilevel operation. The task becomes, then, the explanation of failures on the part of the subjects to draw upon the more advanced of their developmental modes. In this form, the organismic model proposes a distinction between competence and performance. Immaturities of performance, in this light, may be blamed on a number of situational and methodological factors of the sort discussed earlier, such as differences in familiarity and expertise (Bearison, 1974; Piaget, 1972), cultural background (Cole & Scribner, 1974), cohort effects, and so forth.

Alternatively, it can be argued that, rather than ascribing lapses in performance to the workings of situational whims to be countered by the vigorous development of a more adequate assessment technology, multiformity is a valid principle in its own right. Solutions of this type have called attention to the fact that adaptive intelligence, rather than abstractly operating *in vacuo*, adjusts with flexibility to the structural demands of the environment (Chandler, 1977; Riegel, 1975; Turner, 1973; Youniss, 1975). Rather than ascribing developmental asynchrony to such factors as fixation or regression, this interpretation stresses the adaptive synthesis of matching one's cognitive level to the requirements of a task. Such synthetic cognitive flexibility is, in fact, considered by several authors to be the hallmark of mature adult intelligence (Birren, 1963; Chandler, 1977; Riegel, 1973).

Either of these interpretations is here seen to carry with it the advantage of calling for a greater degree of caution when arguing presumptive deficit at any point of the life span. It serves, in fact, a heuristic tool by examining the notion that any of the contextual deterrents discussed in this chapter serve to either expose noncompetence-related aspects of cognition in the comparison between age groups, or to force one's view on a more serious attention to the environment side of the subject–object equation. Nevertheless, as a life-span developmental theory, it is less than convincing.

However heuristic, the competence–performance distinction itself exemplifies a concession of idealistic theories that diversity can no longer be covered by one theoretical umbrella (Chandler, 1977; Riegel, 1975). Because idealistic theories commonly interpret the dynamics of intellectual development as the derivative consequence of temporal–structural instabilities equilibrated at the level of some "most mature" form, progressive growth in childhood is explained by constructs intrinsic to the theory, while subsequent life-span changes are explained away by principles extrinsic to the original theoretical account. Second, the presumption that development proceeds toward, and is best judged against, some monistic, idealized end state, is evaluative in the worst sense (Baratz & Baratz, 1970; Riegel, 1975). Whether maturity is a point, plateau, or multilevel affair, it is marked, in such idealistic views, by failure on all sides. The efforts of the young or culturally alien appear puny and amateurish, while the attempts of the aging or elderly are seen as hollow caricatures of youth. The application of this evaluative standard becomes, then, unremittingly pejorative, with a moment of optimal functioning bracketed by immaturity on the one hand and infirmity on the other.

C. CONTEXTUALISM AND MULTILINEARITY

Idealistically oriented organismic developmental models fare best when applied to culturally homogenized groups of children and adolescents engaged in relatively bloodless interactions with selected swaths of their impersonal, object environments. When stretched to account for development in a full life-span framework, these models are poorly suited to the task. A third alternative, and the one to be advocated in the remainder of this chapter, asserts that the accumulation of evidence regarding intellectual development outside the periods of childhood and adolescence should not be subsumed by existing idealistically oriented accounts, and that a major revision of our theoretical and metatheoretical assumptions about intellectual development is required. The best currently available alternative to traditionally idealistic, aristocratic, and child-centered accounts, in the judgment of the writers, is the family of theories which Pepper (1970) has labeled as contextual.

In many important respects contextual models are similar to more familiar organismic views. Both emphasize the centrality of change, the importance of qualitative rather than merely quantitative shifts, and the role of dialectical tensions in providing an impetus to development. Contextual theories are different from idealistic models principally with respect to the assumptions which they make regarding the directional or nondirectional character of change. Whereas organismic models presume that all developmental change is ordered and equivalent to progress, contextual theories regard change as simply that, and make no assumptions that such variations are in the service of achieving a particular goal or idealized end state. The omission of this single idealistic assumption is sufficient, according to Pepper (1970), to cause the progressive categories of organismic models to suffer a general revision in the direction of contextualism. A contextualist, in a way, is an organicist who has peered into the Platonic cave and found it empty.

Thus disillusioned, the contemporary philosophy of science has rejected the idealistic epistemological view according to which scientific progress proceeds in a cumulative fashion to expose an ever more accurate picture of the workings of the universe. In its place has moved a view of epistemology which has firmly asserted the position that scientific activity is, first and foremost, human activity (Berger & Luckmann, 1966; Habermas, 1971; Kuhn, 1970). According to this thinking, the context in which research operates is one established by researchers themselves, and so are the criteria accepted for the truth of theoretical statements.

Although this variation on a common theme may seem modest, its consequences are far reaching and imply major differences between idealistic and contextual views of cognitive development. First, although some idealistic models do permit a kind of interim pluralism—commonly expressed as qualitatively different stages of development—these alternative ways of being are typically seen as eventually homogenized into a single, monistic, adult form. Contextualism, in contrast, proposes a more pragmatic solution to such universalistic claims. From its perspective, it may be fallacious to interpret currently available theories of behavior as universally fixed; rather, they are likely to reflect norms which are relative to certain cultural contexts and thus need to be reexamined on the background of their particular historical–ideological context (Berger &

Luckmann, 1966; Buss, 1975; Gergen, 1973; Giorgi, 1971; Riegel, 1973). According to this interpretation, context variables are not merely theoretical excess baggage to be stored away in a content category. On the contrary, the relationship between context and theory is a structural one. Idealistic form *is itself content* from a contextual perspective (Buck-Morss, 1975) or, to paraphrase Jenkins (1974), *what cognition is depends upon context.*

Second, as the contextualist argues for multiformity in developmental adaptation, no *one* teleological stage is seen as capping off the process of development. Pejorative hierarchical interpretations of contextual variability hence become obsolete as well. Lack of formalized thinking, in this view, should not be interpreted merely as an undesirable by-product of deficient socialization, but reflects an inherent structural relationship between social structure variables and behavior (Berger & Luckmann, 1966; Buck-Morss, 1975; Campbell, 1975; Garbarino & Bronfenbrenner, 1976; Kohn, 1969)—a relationship which

> captures the reality that the interplay of all those variables creates different basic conditions of life at different levels of the social order. Members of different social classes, by virtue of enjoying (or suffering) different conditions of life, come to see the world differently—to develop different conceptions of social reality, different aspirations and hopes and fears, different conceptions of the "desirable." (Kohn, 1969, p. 7).

"Maturity," hence, cannot be captured by a universal epigenetic formula, but represents an equilibrium between biological and social evolutionary forces—an equilibrium that is not static or universal but rather shifts to suit cultural demands (Campbell, 1975).

Third, since contextualism suggests the identification of multilinear developmental paths leading to pluralistic goals, it proposes that the value of currently existing knowledge of life-span cognition may be more forceful from the perspective of a sociology of knowledge than from that of a universal genetic epistemology. The extensive demonstration of deficit in life-span intellectual development in this view may be the result of a lopsided growth of a field slanted toward formalistic content (Baltes & Willis, 1977). The simple beauty of the resulting overarching idealistic system may thus be a result of not having identified a parsimonious and comprehensive development, but of selectively discarding behavioral content that defies ready synthesis under an idealistic teleology (Hamlyn, 1971; Toulmin, 1971).

Thus, contextualism finally argues that developmental psychology needs to reassess its content, methodology, and theory in light of what Proshansky (1970) has called "phenomenon legitimacy." The resulting implications have been succinctly summarized by Jenkins (1974):

It is *not* true in this view that one can study any part of the "cosmic machine" to just as good an effect as any other part. The important thing is to pick the right kinds of events for your purposes. And it *is* true in this view that a whole theory can be elaborated without contributing in an important way to the science because the situations are artificial and nonrepresentative. . . . In short, contextualism stresses relating one's laboratory problems to the ecologically valid problems of everyday life. (p. 794)

V. Conclusion

In sum, this chapter has argued that much of what we know about cognitive functioning throughout the life span may be a historic happenstance. Research in life-span intellectual ontogeny has tended to derive its content and methodology via deduction from idealistic, maturational, youth-centered models. Thus led to expect dramatic and maturation-bound cognitive changes in later life, the chapter may have inappropriately attended to a number of methodological requirements. A number of Seele methodological oversights are discussed in the present chapter. First, the explanatory force of maturation-related variables appears to be evident primarily in diseased and/or institutionalized samples. Second, what appears to be dramatic decrement is often more adequately explained by the heterogeneity, in terms of historic origin and cultural context, of the age groups compound in most research. Third, the samples of behavior from which inference about the cognitive status of adults are drawn may be biased toward formalistic content of doubtful ecological validity and/or toward measurements of primary relevance to the young. Finally, little attention has been paid to the possibility—and, at this point, likelihood—of pronounced situational plasticity of intellectual functioning in older populations.

As a result, contemporary accounts of adulthood cognitive changes are biased in favor of decremental interpretations which tend to foster doubt with respect to the cognitive competence of adults and older persons. At this time it is reasonable, however, to argue that such decremental interpretations are slanted, nonrepresentative, and poorly related to the concrete, everyday, cognitive interactions of adults and older people. Thus, research in this area would profit from a pendulum swing in the opposite direction, with emphasis on induction, context, and the careful naturalistic and ethological mapping of cognitive skills in a life-span context.

At present, such a contextualist posture is here seen as having heuristic value rather than representing theoretical dogmatism. If there is any dogmatism to the contextualist's attitude, in fact, it is the assertion that he must embrace *any* potential theoretical outcome, even the possibility that all his pluralistic multilinear analyses might, after all, eventually converge and expose *one* organismic scheme.

References

Arenberg, D. Concept problem solving in young and old adults. *Journal of Gerontology,* 1968, **23,** 279–282.

Arlin, P. K. Cognitive development in adulthood: A fifth stage? *Developmental Psychology,* 1975, **11,** 602–606.

Baer, D. M. The control of the developmental process: Why wait? In J. R. Nesselroade & H. W. Reese (Eds.), *Life-span developmental psychology: Methodological issues.* New York: Academic Press, 1973.

Baltes, P. B. Longitudinal and cross-sectional sequences in the study of age and generation effects. *Human Development,* 1968, **11,** 145–171.

Baltes, P. B., Cornelius, S. W., & Nesselroade, J. R. Cohort effects in developmental psychology: Theoretical and methodological perspectives. In W. A. Collins (Ed.), *Minnesota Symposia on Child Psychology* (Vol. 11). New York: Crowell, 1977.

Baltes, P. B., & Goulet, L. R. Status and issues of a life-span developmental psychology. In L. R. Goulet & P. B. Baltes (Eds.), *Life-span developmental psychology.* New York: Academic Press, 1970.

Baltes, P. B., & Labouvie, G. V. Adult development of intellectual performance: Description, explanation, and modification. In D. Eisdorfer & M. P. Lawton (Eds.), *The psychology of adult development and aging.* Washington, D. C.: American Psychological Association, 1973.

Baltes, P. B., & Schaie, K. W. On the plasticity of adult and gerontological intelligence: Where Horn and Donaldson fail. *American Psychologist,* 1976, **31,** 720–725.

Baltes, P. B., & Willis, S. L. Toward psychological theories of aging and development. In J. E. Birren & K. W. Schaie (Eds.), *Handbook on psychology of aging.* New York: Reinhold-Van Nostrand, 1977.

Bandura, A. The stormy decade: Fact or fiction? *Psychology in the Schools,* 1964, **1,** 224–231.

Baratz, S. S., & Baratz, J. S. Early childhood intervention: The social science base of institutional racism. *Harvard Educational Review,* 1970, **40,** 29–50.

Barrett, W. The twentieth century in its philosophy. In W. Barrett & H. D. Aiken (Eds.), *Philosophy in the twentieth century.* New York: Harper, 1962.

Barry, A. J., Steinmetz, J. R., Page, H. F., & Rodahl, K. The effects of physical conditioning on older individuals. II. Motor performance and cognitive function. *Journal of Gerontology,* 1966, **21,** 182–191.

Bearison, D. The construct of regression: A Piagetian approach. *Merrill-Palmer Quarterly,* 1974, **20,** 21–30.

Bengtson, V. L. *The social psychology of aging.* New York: Bobbs-Merrill, 1973.

Berger, P. L., & Luckmann, T. *The social construction of reality.* Garden City, N.Y.: Doubleday, 1966.

Birkhill, W. R., & Schaie, K. W. The effect of differential reinforcement of cautiousness in intellectual performance among the elderly. *Journal of Gerontology,* 1975, **30,** 578–583.

Birren, J. E. Psychophysiological relations. In J. E. Birren, R. N. Bulter, S. W. Greenhouse, L. Sokoloff, & M. R. Yarrow (Eds.), *Human aging: A biological and behavioral study.* Washington, D.C.: U.S. Government Printing Office, 1963.

Birren, J. E. *The psychology of aging.* Englewood Cliffs, N.J.: Prentice-Hall, 1964.

Birren, J. E. Toward an experimental psychology of aging. *American Psychologist,* 1970, **25,** 124–135.

Birren, J. E., Butler, R. W., Greenhouse, S. W., Sokoloff, L., & Yarrow, M. R. (Eds.). *Human aging: A biological and behavioral study.* Washington, D.C.: U.S. Government Printing Office, 1963.

Birren, J. E., & Renner, V. J. *Stress and aging: Psychobiological theory and research.* Paper presented at the meeting of the Gerontological Society, New York, October 1976.

Birren, J. E., Riegel, K. F., & Morrison, D. F. Aging differences in response speed as a function of controlled variations in stimulus conditions. Evidence of a general speed factor. *Gerontologia,* 1962, **6,** 1–18.

Botwinick, J. *Cognitive processes in maturity and old age.* New York: Springer Publ., 1967.

Botwinick, J. *Aging and behavior.* New York: Springer Publ. 1973.

Botwinick, J., & Thompson, L. W. Cardiac functioning and reaction time in relation to age. *Journal of Genetic Psychology,* 1971, **119,** 127–132.

Bowers, K. S. Situationism in psychology: An analysis and a critique. *Psychological Review,* 1973, **80,** 307–336.

Buck-Morss, S. Socio-economic bias in Piaget's theory and its implication for cross-culture studies. *Human Development,* 1975, **18,** 35–49.

Buss, A. R. The emerging field of the sociology of psychological knowledge. *American Psychologist,* 1975, **30,** 988–1002.

Campbell, D. T. On the conflicts between biological and social evolution and between psychology and moral tradition. *American Psychologist,* 1975, **30,** 1103–1126.

Cattell, R. B. Theory of fluid and crystallized intelligence: A critical experiment. *Journal of Educational Psychology,* 1963, **54,** 1–22.

Chandler, M. Social cognition and life-span approaches to the study of cognitive development. In H. W. Reese (Ed.), *Advances in child development and behavior* (Vol. 11). New York: Academic Press, 1977.

Charles, D. C. Explaining intelligence in adulthood: The role of life history. *Gerontologist,* 1973, **13,** 485–488.

Chown, S. M. Age and the rigidities. *Journal of Gerontology,* 1961, **16,** 353–362.

Cole, M., & Bruner, J. S. Cultural differences and inferences about psychological processes. *American Psychologist,* 1971, **26,** 867–876.

Cole, M., & Scribner, S. *Culture and thought: A psychological introduction.* New York: Wiley, 1974.

Datan, N., & Ginsberg, L. H. (Eds.). *Life-span developmental psychology: Normative life crises.* New York: Academic Press, 1975.

Demming, J. A., & Pressey, S. L. Tests "indigenous" to the adult and older years. *Journal of Counseling Psychology,* 1957, **4,** 144–148.

Denney, N. W. Classification abilities in the elderly. *Journal of Gerontology,* 1974, **29,** 309–314.

Denney, N. W., & Wright, J. C. *Cognitive changes during the adult years: Implications for developmental theory and research.* Paper presented at the annual meeting of the Society for Research in Child Development, Denver, April 1975.

DeVries, H. A. Physiology of exercise and aging. In D. S. Woodruff & J. E. Birren (Eds.), *Aging: Scientific perspectives and social issues.* New York: Reinhold-Van Nostrand, 1975.

Eisdorfer, C., & Wilkie, F. Intellectual changes with advancing age. In L. F. Jarvik, C. Eisdorfer, & J. C. Blum (Eds.). *Intellectual functioning in adults.* New York: Springer Publ., 1973.

Eisdorfer, C., Nowlin, J., & Wilkie, F. Improvement of learning by modification of autonomous nervous system activity. *Science*, 1970, **170**, 1327–1328.

Flavell, J. H. Cognitive changes in adulthood. In P. B. Baltes & L. R. Goulet (Eds.), *Life-span developmental psychology*. New York: Academic Press, 1970.

Flavell, J. H. Stage-related properties of cognitive development. *Cognitive Psychology*, 1971, **2**, 421–453.

Flavell, J. H., & Wohlwill, J. Formen and functional aspects of cognitive development. In D. Elkind & J. H. Flavell (Eds.), *Studies in cognitive development: Essays in honor of Jean Piaget*. London and New York: Oxford University Press, 1969.

Fozard, J. L., & Poon, L. W. *Age-related differences in long-term memory for pictures*. Paper presented at the meeting of the Gerontological Society, New York, October 1976.

Furry, C. A., & Baltes, P. B. The effect of age differences in ability-extraneous variables on the assessment of intelligence in children, adults and the elderly. *Journal of Gerontology*, 1973, **28**, 73–80.

Gallatin, J. Theories of adolescence. In J. F. Adams (Ed.), *Understanding adolescence* (3rd ed.). Boston: Allyn & Bacon, 1976.

Garbarino, J., & Bronfenbrenner, U. The socialization of moral judgment and behavior in cross-cultural perspective. In T. Lickona (Ed.), *Moral development and behavior*. New York: Holt, 1976.

Gergen, K. J. Social psychology as history. *Journal of Personality and Social Psychology*, 1973, **26**, 309–320.

Gewirtz, J. L. Mechanisms of social learning: Some roles of stimulation and behavior in early human development. In D. A. Goslin (Ed.), *Handbook of socialization theory and research*. Chicago: Rand McNally, 1969.

Giorgi, A. Phenomenology and experimental psychology. In A. Giorgi, W. F. Fischer, & R. Von Eckartsberg (Eds.), *Duquesne studies in phenomenological psychology* (Vol. 1). Pittsburgh: Duquesne University Press, 1971.

Habermas, J. *Knowledge and human interests*. Boston: Beacon Press, 1971.

Hamlyn, D. W. Epistemology and conceptual development. In T. Mischel (Ed.), *Cognitive development and epistemology*. New York: Academic Press, 1971.

Havighurst, R. J. A cross-cultural view. In J. F. Adams (Ed.), *Understanding adolescence* (3rd ed.). Boston: Allyn & Bacon, 1976.

Hertzog, C., Gribbin, K., & Schaie, K. W. *The influence of cardiovascular disease and hypertension on intellectual stability*. Paper presented at the annual meeting of the Gerontological Society, Louisville, October 1975.

Hicks, L. H., & Birren, J. E. Aging, brain damage, and psychomotor slowing. *Psychological Bulletin*, 1970, **74**, 377–396.

Hooper, F. H., & Sheehan, N. W. *Logical concept attainment during the aging years: Issues in the neo-Piagetian research literature*. Unpublished manuscript, University of Wisconsin, 1976.

Horn, J. L. Organization of data on life-span development of human abilities. In L. R. Goulet & P. B. Baltes (Eds.), *Life-span developmental psychology*. New York: Academic Press, 1970.

Horn, J. L. Human abilities: A review of research and theory in the early 1970's. *Annual Review of Psychology*, 1976, **27**, 437–485.

Horn, J. L., & Cattell, R. S. Refinement and test of the theory of fluid and crystallized intelligence. *Journal of Educational Psychology*, 1966, **57**, 253–270.

Horn, J. L., & Cattell, R. B. Age differences in fluid and crystallized intelligence. *Acta Psychologica*, 1967, **26**, 107–129.

Hornblum, J. N., & Overton, W. F. Area and volume conservation among the elderly: Assessment and training. *Developmental Psychology*, 1976, **12**, 68–74.

Hoyer, W. J., Labouvie, G. V., & Baltes, P. B. Modification of response speed deficits and intellectual performance in the elderly. *Human Development*, 1973, **16**, 233–242.

Hulicka, I. M. Age differences in retention as a function of interference. *Journal of Gerontology*, 1967, **22**, 180–184.

Hulicka, I. M., & Grossman, J. L. Age-group comparisons for use of mediators in paired-associate learning. *Journal of Gerontology*, 1967, **22**, 46–51.

Jarvik, L. F. Discussion: Patterns of intellectual functioning in the later years. In L. F. Jarvik, C. Eisdorfer, & J. C. Blum (Eds.), *Intellectual functioning in adults*. New York: Springer, 1973.

Jarvik, L. F., & Blum, J. E. Cognitive declines as predictors of mortality in twin pairs: A twenty-years longitudinal study of aging. In E. Palmore & F. Jeffers (Eds.), *Prediction of life span*. Lexington, Mass.: Heath, 1971.

Jarvik, L. F., & Cohen, D. A biobehavioral approach to intellectual changes with aging. In C. Eisdorfer & M. P. Lawton (Eds.), *The psychology of adult development and aging*. Washington, D.C.: American Psychological Association, 1973.

Jenkins, J. J. Remember that old theory of memory? Well, forget it! *American Psychologist*, 1974, **29**, 789–795.

Jensen, A. R. *Educability and group differences*. New York: Harper, 1973.

Kagan, J. A conception of early adolescence. In J. Kagan & R. Coles (Eds.), *Twelve to sixteen: Early adolescence*. New York: Norton, 1972.

Katz, I. Alternatives to the personality-deficit interpretation of Negro underachievement. In P. Watson (Ed.), *Psychology and race*. Baltimore: Penguin Books, 1973.

Keniston, K. Student activism, moral development and morality. In W. R. Looft (Ed.), *Developmental psychology: A book of readings*. Hinsdale, Ill.: Dryden, 1972.

Kogan, N. Categorizing and conceptualizing styles in younger and older adults. *Human Development*, 1974, **17**, 218–230.

Kohlberg, L. From is to ought: How to commit the naturalistic fallacy and get away with it in the study of moral development. In T. Mischel (Ed.), *Cognitive development and epistemology*. New York: Academic Press, 1971.

Kohlberg, L., LaCrosse, J., & Ricks, D. The predictability of adult mental health from childhood behavior. In B. Wolman (Ed.), *Handbook of child psychopathology*. New York: McGraw-Hill, 1970.

Kohn, M. *Class and conformity: A study in values*. Homewood, Ill.: Dorsey Press, 1969.

Kuhlen, R. G. Age and intelligence: The significance of cultural change in longitudinal vs. cross-sectional findings. *Vita Humana*, 1963, **6**, 113–124.

Kuhn, T. S. *The structure of scientific revolutions* (2nd ed.). Chicago: University of Chicago Press, 1970.

Labouvie-Vief, G. Adult cognitive development: In search of alternative interpretations. *Merrill-Palmer Quarterly*, 1977, **23**, 227–263.

Labouvie-Vief, G., & Gonda, J. N. Cognitive strategy training and intellectual performance in the elderly. *Journal of Gerontology*, 1976, **31**, 327–332.

Labouvie-Vief, G., Hoyer, W. J., Baltes, M. M., & Baltes, P. B. Operant analysis of intellectual behavior in old age. *Human Development*, 1974, **17**, 259–272.

Langer, J. *Theories of development*. New York: Holt, 1969.

Lawton, M. P., & Nahemow, L. Ecology and the aging process. In C. Eisdorfer & M. P. Lawton (Eds.), *The psychology of adult development and aging*. Washington, D.C.: American Psychological Association, 1973.

Lerner, R. M. *Concepts and theories of human development*. Reading, Mass.: Addison-Wesley, 1976.

Lickona, T. Critical issues in the study of moral development and behavior. In T. Lickona (Ed.), *Moral development and behavior.* New York: Holt, 1976.

Lindsley, O. R. Geriatric behavioral prosthetics. In R. Kastenbaum (Ed.), *New thoughts on old age.* New York: Springer, 1964.

Lorge, I. The inference of the test upon the nature of mental decline as a function of age. *Journal of Educational Psychology,* 1936, **27,** 100–110.

Maas, H. S., & Kuypers, J. A. *From thirty to seventy.* San Francisco: Jossey-Bass, 1974.

MacDonald, M. L., & Butler, A. K. Reversal of helplessness: Producing walking behavior in wheel chair residents using behavior modification procedures. *Journal of Gerontology,* 1974, **29,** 97–101.

McClelland, D. C. Testing for competence rather than for "intelligence." *American Psychologist,* 1973, **28,** 1–14.

Mead, M. Culture and commitment: *A study of the generation gap.* Garden City, N.Y.: Doubleday, 1970.

Mergler, N. L., & Hoyer, W. J. *Cognitive performance of elderly adults as a function of strategy training and non-contingent social praise.* Paper presented at the annual meeting of the Gerontological Society, Louisville, October 1975.

Mischel, T. (Ed.). *Cognitive development and epistemology.* New York: Academic Press, 1971.

Muuss, R. E. *Theories of adolescence* (3rd ed.). New York: Random House, 1975.

Nesselroade, J. R., & Baltes, P. B. Adolescent personality development and historical change: 1970–1972. *Monographs of the Society for Research in Child Development,* 1974, **39**(1).

Nesselroade, J. R., Schaie, K. W., & Baltes, P. B. Ontogenetic and generational components of structural and quantitative change in adult cognitive behavior. *Journal of Gerontology,* 1972, **27,** 222–228.

Neugarten, B. L. The awareness of middle age. In R. Owen (Ed.), *Middle age.* London: British Broadcasting Corp., 1967.

Neugarten, B. L., Crotty, W. J., & Tobin, S. S. Personality types in an aged population. In B. L. Neugarten (Ed.), *Personality in middle and late life.* New York: Atherton Press, 1964.

Neugarten, B. L., & Datan, N. Sociological perspectives on the life cycle. In P. B. Baltes & K. W. Schaie (Eds.), *Life-span development psychology: Personality and socialization.* New York: Academic Press, 1973.

Obrist, W. D., Busse, E. W., Eisdorfer, C., & Kleemeier, R. W. Relation of the electroencephalogram to intellectual function in senescence. *Journal of Gerontology,* 1962, **17,** 197–206.

Okun, M. A., & DiVesta, F. J. Cautiousness in adulthood as a function of age and instructions. *Journal of Gerontology,* 1978, in press.

Overton, W. F., & Reese, H. W. Models of development: Methodological implications. In J. R. Nesselroade & H. W. Reese (Eds.), *Life-span developmental psychology: Methodological issues.* New York: Academic Press, 1973.

Palmore, E., & Cleveland, W. Aging, terminal decline, and terminal drop. *Journal of Gerontology,* 1976, **31,** 76–81.

Panicucci, C. L., & Labouvie-Vief, G. *Effect of training on inductive reasoning behavior.* Paper presented at the annual meeting of the Gerontological Society, Louisville, October 1975.

Papalia, D. E., & Del Vento Bielby, D. Cognitive functioning in middle and old adults: A review of research based on Piaget's theory. *Human Development,* 1974, **17,** 424–443.

Pepper, S. C. *World hypotheses* (2nd ed.). Berkeley: University of California Press, 1970.

Piaget, J. Intellectual evolution from adolescence to adulthood. *Human Development,* 1972, **15,** 1–12.

Plemons, J. K., Willis, S. L., & Baltes, P. B. *Challenging the theory of fluid intelligence: A training approach.* Paper presented at the annual meeting of the Gerontological Society, Louisville, October 1975.

Powell, R. R. Psychological effects of exercise therapy upon institutionalized geriatric mental patients. *Journal of Gerontology,* 1974, **29,** 157–161.

Powell, R. R., & Pohndorf, R. H. Comparison of adult exercisers and nonexercisers on fluid intelligence and selected physiological variables. *Research Quarterly,* 1971, **42,** 70–77.

Proshansky, H. M. Methodology in environmental psychology: Problems and issues. *Human Factors,* 1970, **14,** 451–460.

Proshansky, H. M. Environmental psychology and the real world. *American Psychologist,* 1976, **21,** 303–310.

Reese, H. W. Life-span models of memory. *Gerontologist,* 1973, **13,** 472–478.

Reese, H. W., & Overton, W. F. Models of development and theories of development. In L. R. Goulet & P. B. Baltes (Eds.)., *Life-span developmental psychology.* New York: Academic Press, 1970.

Rest, J. The cognitive developmental approach to morality: The state of the art. *Counseling and Values,* 1974, **18,** 64–78.

Riegel, K. F. Dialectic operations: The final period of cognitive development. *Human Development,* 1973, **16,** 346–370.

Riegel, K. F. From traits and equilibrium towards developmental dialectics. In W. Arnold (Ed.), *Nebraska Symposium on Motivation.* Lincoln: University of Nebraska Press, 1975.

Riegel, K. F., & Riegel, R. M. Development, drop, and death. *Developmental Psychology,* 1972, **6,** 306–319.

Schaie, K. W. A general model for the study of developmental problems. *Psychological Bulletin,* 1965, **64,** 92–107.

Schaie, K. W., & Gribbin, K. *The impact of environmental complexity upon adult cognitive development.* Paper presented at the third biennial conference of the International Society for the Study of Behavioral Development, Guildford, England, July 1975.

Schaie, K. W., & Labouvie-Vief, G. Generational versus ontogenetic components of change in adult cognitive behavior: A fourteen-year cross-sequential study. *Developmental Psychology.* 1974, **10,** 305–320.

Schaie, K. W., Labouvie, G. V., & Buech, B. U. Generational vs. cohort-specific differences in adult cognitive functioning: A fourteen-year study of independent samples. *Developmental Psychology,* 1973, **9,** 151–166.

Schaie, K. W., & Strother, C. R. A cross-sectional study of age changes in cognitive behavior. *Psychological Bulletin,* 1968, **70,** 671–680. (a)

Schaie, K. W., & Strother, C. R. The effects of time and cohort differences on the interpretation of age changes in cognitive behavior. *Multivariate Behavior Research,* 1968, **3,** 259–294. (b)

Schoenfeldt, L. F. Life history subgroups as moderators in the prediction of intellectual change. In L. F. Jarvik, C. Eisdorfer, & J. E. Blum (Eds.), *Intellectual functioning in adults.* New York: Springer, 1973.

Seligman, M. E. P. *Helplessness.* San Francisco: Freeman, 1975.

Surwillo, W. W. The relation of simple response time to brain wave frequency and the effects of age. *Electroencephalography and Clinical Neurophysiology,* 1963, **15,** 105–114.

Surwillo, W. W. The relation of decision time to brain wave frequency and to age. *Electroencephalography and Clinical Neurophysiology,* 1964, **16,** 510–514.

Surwillo, W. W. Timing of behavior in senescence and the role of the central nervous system. In G. A. Talland (Ed.), *Human aging and behavior.* New York: Academic Press, 1968.

Toulmin, S. The concept of "stages" in psychological development. In T. Mischel (Ed.), *Cognitive development and epistemology.* New York: Academic Press, 1971.

Treat, N. J., & Reese, H. W. Aging, pacing and imagery in paired-associated learning. *Developmental Psychology,* 1976, **12,** 119–124.

Turner, T. Piaget's structuralism. *American Anthropologist,* 1973, **75,** 351–373.

Wang, H. S. Cerebral correlates of intellectual functioning in senescence. In L. F. Jarvik, C. Eisdorfer, & J. E. Blum (Eds.), *Intellectual functioning in adults.* New York: Springer, 1973.

Wartofsky, M. W. From praxis to logos: Genetic epistemology and physics. In T. Mischel (Ed.), *Cognitive development and epistemology.* New York: Academic Press, 1971.

Watson, P. (Ed.). *Psychology and race.* Baltimore: Penguin, 1973.

Weir, M. W. Developmental changes in problem solving strategies. *Psychological Review,* 1964, **71,** 473–490.

Wohlwill, J. F. *The study of behavioral development.* New York: Academic Press, 1973.

Woodruff, D. S. The usefulness of the life-span approach for the psychophysiology of aging. *Gerontologist,* 1973, **13,** 467–472.

Woodruff, D. S. A physiological perspective on the psychology of aging. In D. S. Woodruff & J. E. Birren (Eds.), *Aging: Scientific perspectives and social issues.* New York: Reinhold-Van Nostrand, 1975.

Woodruff, D. S., & Walsh, D. Research in adult learning: The individual. *Gerontologist,* 1975, **15,** 424–430.

Youniss, J. Another perspective on social cognition. In A. D. Pick (Ed.), *Minnesota Symposia on Child Psychology* (Vol. 9). Minneapolis: University of Minnesota Press, 1975.

Human Ability Systems[1]

John L. Horn
DEPARTMENT OF PSYCHOLOGY,
UNIVERSITY OF DENVER,
DENVER, COLORADO

Abstract

Important phenomena pertaining to the nature and development of human abilities are considered in theories about intelligence. In these it is recognized that many, many abilities are positively interrelated and that measures based on collections of abilities show a quasi-simplex pattern of relationships over most of the life span. Analyses of interrelationships among large samples of abilities have indicated some 30 or so primary abilities which, in turn, indicate six broad dimensions of intellectual functioning. These involve mixtures of basic processes of memory, use of concepts and aids, control mechanisms, and activation of

[1] Research in this chapter was supported by the Army Research Institute, Grant Number DAHC 19-76-G-0019, and the National Science Foundation, Grant Number R01 MH28455-01. I thank Jan Keenan for helpful suggestions.

schemata, metaknowledge systems, and executive functions. One of these dimensions provides rough indication of organization of basic processes brought about by acculturation, as realized through influences associated with selection/deselection, positive transfer, avoidance learning, the configurations of interpersonal groupings of significant others, and the climate for inquiry, as well as physiological factors. This is referred to as crystallized intelligence, Gc, an indicator of one's appropriation of the intelligence of a culture. A second major dimension represents an organization of mental resources produced by incidental learning and physiological influences that operate largely independently of those of acculturation. This is fluid intelligence (Gf). Other dimensions indicate organizations of perceptual mechanisms associated with sensory modalities, visualization and audition, and short-term acquisition, storage, and retrieval functions, as these affect manifest abilities. The knowledge systems represented by these dimensions are augmented and become automated and restructured in ever more intricate ways over the course of development. Abilities that reflect this expansion of knowledge base, intricacy of structuring and automation (as roughly recorded in Gc) increase with age throughout life. Abilities that reflect loss of physiological substrate and rigidities brought on by expansion and systematization of knowledge systems (as accumulated in Gf) decline with age, most noticeably in adulthood.

I. Conceptions of the Concept of Intelligence

The human begins life as a simple undifferentiated cell, but contained within this tiny cell is a potential of profound wonder. Similarly, a life begins in an environment of homogeneous constancy, but the range of environmental variations that can be experienced (in some threescore, and more, of living) is so immense that one must marvel at what is possible. A myriad of such influences, dynamically operating from within and relentlessly pressing from without, defines the individuality of each of us—and there is a myriad of us. And time moves on. Even some of the salient features of the environments of one historical period are absent in the environments before and after, replaced by different salient features. The species evolves, the range of genetic potentials—the genome— changes, subtly but perhaps profoundly. Do we really know? Now comes the intrepid behavioral scientist into this swirl of possibilities and uncertainties to describe and explain how individuals develop and individual differences are created. Is it clear that compared with our ignorance what truthfully can be said about human abilities and their development is as a whisper in a gale?

Almost everyone talks as if there is a "something" called intelligence in respect to which there are nontrivial individual differences. Almost everyone talks as if they know what this "something" is (namely, that which they have in abundance) and what it is not (that in which they are lacking). This is the starting point for specifying a theory about human intelligence, for the scientist in this instance cannot ignore the wisdom of common sense. But this raises a fundamental problem: There is a vast and complex array of behavior that is said (by someone) to be indicative of intelligence. Many aspects of sensing, perceiving, thinking, problem solving, adapting, comprehending, communicating, reacting, etc., can be regarded as in some sense a manifestation of intelligence. But what is necessary? What is sufficient? What is unique? What is redundant? What can be disregarded? What must be present? In short, what is the sine qua non of that which we so confidently speak of as intelligence in our everyday judgments about ourselves and others?

For some, the answers to these questions are rather easy. Intelligence is life achievement, as indicated by earning (or even stealing) money, gaining an education, speaking several languages, or simply "doing well." In the context of this chapter, however, and probably in any truly scientific theory about intelligence, this is not the answer. There is no necessary reason why individual differences in intelligence, as defined scientifically, will have much to do with individual differences in achievements in a complex society such as our own. Indeed, results from several studies have suggested that the major differences between people in life achievements in income, prestige standings, and even education are due more to factors of circumstance and luck than to differences in personal attributes considered collectively, including the intellectual ability attributes (Jencks, Smith, Acland, Bane, Cohen, Gentis, Heyns, & Michelson, 1972; Lundberg, 1968; Mayeske, Okada, Beaton, Cohen, & Wisler, 1973; Mosteller & Moynihan, 1972). This is not to say that intellectual abilities are unrelated to life achievements. Rather it is to say, simply, that life achievement is not a univocal indicant of intelligence or even the criterion that scientific measures of intellectual abilities necessarily must predict. A science of human abilities must be specified in terms of operations of measurement, confirmed findings based on these measurements, and the concepts of theories that adequately account for the essential features of confirmed findings.

For the empiricist, answers to questions about the sine qua non of intelligence can be sought in study of the diversity of behavior that is said to be indicative of this attribute. And for the empiricist who also desires to pin conclusions to objective results that can be replicated by others, the answers can be sought with analyses of behavior observed under standard conditions. Our principal systematic understanding of intellectual abilities has come from the study of problems, puzzles, questions—i.e., tests in general—that can be administered in much the same way to substantial samples of people. This is the kind of understanding with which we are concerned in this chapter.

A.   SOME EVIDENCE JUSTIFYING USE OF THE CONCEPT

The diversity of indicants of intelligence remains after we have moved away from unqualified acceptance of common sense notions about intelligence to a consideration of the tests that have been devised to indicate this attribute. Literally thousands of tests have been invented to measure what someone labels "intelligence" or a quality "essential to intelligence." A remarkable result of research with these tasks is that, with very rare exception, the performance so assessed are positively correlated, both when several tests are administered at one time and when the times between measurements extend over years (provided that the first measurement is not in infancy). It is remarkable, too, that these many and diverse test measures usually correlate positively with performances that are said in common parlance to indicate intelligence, performances of the kind indicated in school achievements of a variety of kinds, on-the-job success, money earned, prestige, etc. This fact, probably perceived in common sense almost as well as it has been recorded in research literature, is a principal pillar of support for hypotheses (and these take many forms) stipulating a general attribute of intelligence, here referred to as G.

Another interesting bit of evidence indicating G among the diversity of abilities is found in results showing positive intercorrelations among the *means* for ability tests in different schools sampled in a fairly representative manner, as in Project TALENT (1962). This evidence can be interpreted as indicating that systematic samplings of children for different schools, or the influences (learnings) produced by schools, operate in respect to a general factor. The correlations in this case are considerably higher than those typically found for the same abilities in sampling over individuals. Humphreys (1976) points out, for example, that the means for Reading Comprehension and Mechanical Information correlate in excess of .9 in samples of schools, but only about .3 to .4 in samples of school-age children. The high correlations for schools suggest that influences other than those represented by G (produced by, or producing, G) are relatively weak.

B.   INTERPRETATIONS OF G

But what does the evidence for G represent developmentally and in terms of human functioning? As concerns the latter, one interpretation is that G indicates a "something," such as mental energy in Spearman's (1927) classic theory, which, although it may appear in many forms (even as energy in the physical sense may be manifested in kinetic, heat, and other forms), nevertheless is the underlying influence that produces the abilities that are seen to intercorrelate positively. It is as if G were a true score component running through many possible manifestations of obtained scores that also involve random processes (cf. Lord & Novick, 1968). Usually in this kind of theory, G is assumed to be a major (systematic) cause of observed abilities. Usually, also, it is regarded as a structure–process determined by the particular assortment of genes that one receives at conception. Much evidence suggests that a substantial proportion of the variance of G—perhaps as much as 80%—is inherited (Jensen, 1973). This theory might thus be referred to as the single inherited cause (SIC) conception of G.

Ordinarily it would be recognized in this kind of theory that the structure–process condition (laid down by heredity) can itself be changed, as, for example, by injury. Such alteration would change the true score, so not all of the true score variance (between individuals) would be due to heredity. Also, usually such theory would acknowledge that the abilities of G must be learned and that there are individual differences in the availability and quality of learning, so there will be perturbations from the true score in fallible measures based on particular (in practice often arbitrary) samples of the abilities that are the outcomes of learning.

But the facts represented by G needn't be interpreted in accordance with the SIC conception. The existing evidence can be interpreted in several rather different ways (e.g., Baltes & Nesselroade, 1973; Humphreys, 1976; Watson, 1975; Zajonc, 1976). For example, G might represent a collection of different capacities, each having an independently determined genetic basis, but each being of some value in developing many of the manifest abilities measured with tests. Primary memory (PM) and Gestalt closure (GES) capacity might be separately inherited and both of use in learning to read and learning to do arithmetic. A person high in PM but low in GES could learn reading and arithmetic by virtue of PM, but one high in GES and low in PM could as well learn reading and arithmetic by exercise of GES. The outcome would be a positive correlation between arithmetic and reading tests, but this outcome would have been produced by two distinct causal processes. And, of course, the causal influences need not be inherited: PM and GES could correspond to capacities produced exclusively by particular experiences (particular training) in early childhood. This possibility is seen concretely in simulation studies (e.g., Baltes & Nesselroade, 1973) in which the "causes" for observed patterns of interrelationships among abilities are assumed to be environmental and then are approximately reproduced by use of a simulation model based on the stated assumptions. Other variations on this theme will be played below in discussion of a simplex model.

The major point here is that although G represents some lawful, well-established findings about human abilities, it does not mandate any particular interpretation of the findings. Adequate theories about human abilities should take account of G, and theories that do not do this can be faulted for this failure, but there is still room for choice among different theories that do provide plausible interpretations of G. The compellingness of such theories should depend on the extent to which they recognize, and explain, other established evidence pertaining to the development and expression of human abilities.

There have been many, many studies in which intelligence has been defined operationally, i.e., measured by adding together a subject's subscores (often representing merely pass versus fail) on several somewhat different tasks or tests. Scores obtained in this way are called omnibus measures of intelligence (Cronbach, 1970). Different intelligence tests—as the Stanford-Binet, Wechsler, Lorge-Thorndike, etc.—and the same test used at different age levels, involve different collections of tasks or subtests and thus yield operationally different omnibus measures of intelligence. This fact is important to keep in mind when evaluating evidence from several studies said to involve measures of intelligence but employing different tests or the same test at different age levels.

Given the fact that different intelligence tests provide operationally different measurements, it is interesting, and a notable piece of evidence, that the correlations between the different omnibus measures often have been found to be high relative to relationships typically found in the behavioral sciences (Littell, 1960). Related here also are findings indicating that when a total score is obtained over several subtests of what are called achievement tests,[2] such scores correlate about as highly with omnibus intelligence measures obtained with different tests as the latter correlate with each other, and vice versa (Humphreys, 1974). In other words, a broad collection of school achievements is as indicative of the intelligence measured with one omnibus intelligence test as is the collection of abilities measured with another omnibus intelligence test. The general point is that intelligence, as measured in most of the popular omnibus tests, is a collection of achievements. Several theories of abilities, notably the SIC theories, stipulate that the major thread of common influence running through different achievements is one stemming from a single capacity for developing intelligence. In "nativistic" theories this single capacity is physiological structure determined by biological heredity. In "environmentalistic" theories the capacity is learned skills determined by societal influences. It seems that most scien-

---

[2]For example, the American College Testing Progrm (ACT), the Cooperative School and College Ability Tests (SCAT), and the Sequential Tests of Educational Progress (STEP).

tists who have studied the evidence favor theories that are somewhere between the extremes of "nativism" and the "environmentalism."

Also of interest in this context are findings indicating that the correlations between omnibus measures of intelligence decrease regularly as the time between measurements increases (Anderson, 1940; Humphreys, 1960). Measures obtained with the Stanford-Binet test at 5 years of age correlate about .85 with measures obtained with the same test at 6 years of age, but the scores for the 5-year-olds correlate only about .80 with their scores at age 8, and by age 16 the correlation has dropped to .50. This is referred to as the simplex, or near-simplex, pattern of time-lag intercorrelations for omnibus measures of intelligence. Although the evidence for such a pattern throughout the life span is sketchy, it seems that a near-simplex pattern will indeed characterize the interrelationships between omnibus measures of achievement obtained from early childhood until late adulthood.

There can be considerable discussion about the meaning of the simplex pattern. For example, it can result because the collections of abilities measured in omnibus tests change from one age level to another. Many of the same tasks and subtests, measuring much the same abilities, are involved in the measurements obtained at adjacent age levels, but the extent of such overlap decreases as the gap between age levels increases. Thus less and less of a common core of abilities might be assessed as differences between age levels increases. This could be the reason for the simplex pattern.

Another possibility was advanced by Anderson (1940). He suggested that the pattern might reflect individual differences in the development of abilities. His hypothesis is perhaps best described with a mathematical model. If the manifested ability, M_{ij}, of person $i = 1, ..., N$ at developmental period $j = 1, ..., k, m, ..., n$ is a result of increments I_{ij} produced in the different developmental periods, then abilities measured in periods that are close together can be expected to have more increments in common than those measured in periods that are distant. $M_{i2} = I_{i1} + I_{i2}$ will have more in common with $M_{i3} = I_{i1} + I_{i2} + I_{i3}$ than with $M_{i4} = I_{i1} + I_{i2} + I_{i3} + I_{i4}$, for example. The correlation between adjacent measures at j and k will thus be high and the correlations between the widely separated first and last measures will be low. If these conditions prevail, a simplex will result.

The initial increment (ability) in this kind of theory is usually designated to be a physiologically determined capacity of some sort. It can be either large, relative to the influences represented by increments, or it can be small (see Roff, 1941). The increments themselves may be thought of as experiential units or maturational accretions or combinations of both.

These two theories to account for simplex patterns cannot be distinguished in terms of the model alone, without forging links between the increment terms of the model and empirical representation of these in the form of subtest changes and/or changes in the experiences of people. These links have yet to be forged.

II. Multiple Ability Theories and Evidence

While the evidence for, and utility of, a concept of G should not be discounted, still it should be recognized that many of the tasks, subtests, and achievement measures that intercorrelate positively to indicate the G influence are not highly correlated. In particular, the intercorrelations among such measures are typically smaller than the reliabilities of measurement. Similarly, the squared multiple correlation (SMR) of prediction of one such measure by a linear combination of the others is often less than the internal consistency reliability (r^2_{xt}, representing the true score variance) of the measure. Moreover, a few of the intercorrelations among abilities are not significantly different from zero and some are even negative (Guilford, 1964). These facts indicate that there are somewhat separate—what the multivariate psychologist refers to as independent[3]— influences operating to produce one kind of ability in distinction from another.

A. PRIMARY ABILITIES

One line of research aimed at dealing with these facts has used the mathematical/statistical methods of factor analysis in efforts to isolate the

[3]Independence in this sense should not be, but often is, equated with the concepts of zero correlation or orthogonality or conditional probability equal to zero. The multivariate psychologist will allow that two abilities are independent even if the correlation between them is substantial (they contain elements in common) provided that each involves nonerror elements specific to itself. For collections of abilities, and in particular data, the requirement of independence can be specified by a demand that the internal consisting, r^2_{xt}, of an ability be notably (statistically and in terms of variance) larger than the SMR prediction of that ability from other abilities. In theory, independent abilities may be correlated in the universe of inference (the population), but correlated zero in samples drawn from the population (as when orthogonal factoring is imposed to represent influences believed to be functionally related), or the abilities may be assumed to be uncorrelated in the population but be expected to be correlated nonzero in samples drawn from the population [as in some of Thurstone's (1947) discussion of sample selection in respect to one or more variables]. In process theories of abilities, as in the present writer's work, manifest abilities are said to result from combinations of several basic influences, and different manifest abilities will result from some (but not all) of the same influences.

major kinds of abilities resulting from the multitude of influences that operate in conception and throughout development. The results of this research have been summarized in several available reviews (e.g., French, 1951; French, Ekstrom, & Price, 1963; Guilford, 1967; Guilford & Hoepfner, 1971; Horn, 1972: Pawlik, 1966). The reviews indicate that the major proportion of the reliable individual differences observed with hundreds (perhaps thousands) of ability tests can be accounted for (predicted, described, understood) in terms of a relatively small number of basis variables, called factors. It is not certain just how small this small number is, but a conservative estimate is 20 and a generous estimate is 80. Here we will talk about 30 basis variables. These variables need not represent abilities, as such. Also, a factor analytic resolution into basis variables can be done with any of an infinity of different sets of the same number of basis variables. With these provisos, however, the results of multiple factor analyses with ability tests are said to indicate some 30 independent (see footnote 3, p. 218) primary mental abilities (or functions of intelligence). The suggestion is that a comprehensive description of intelligence should involve 30 (or perhaps more) separate primary abilities, each based on a different set of determiners, each possibly indicating a separate cognitive function or pointing to a distinct kind of developmental influence.

B. STRUCTURE AMONG PRIMARY ABILITIES

A system of 30 primary abilities is considerably easier to comprehend than a system of all the tests that have been devised to indicate important aspects of human cognition. But at this stage of knowledge it is difficult to specify separate functional and developmental theories, based on research findings, even for only 30 separate abilities (or cognitive processes). Simpler systems are desired. A number of such systems have been proposed. Some of the pros and cons of different classifications of these systems have been discussed in other readily available publications (e.g., Cattell, 1971; Horn, 1972, 1977). One conclusion from these analyses is that systems specifying a subdivided hierarchy of abilities seem to be rather widely accepted by researchers in this domain of study. One exemplar of this kind of system is the theory of fluid (Gf) and crystallized (Gc) intelligence. A discussion of this theory will serve to illustrate some of the major kinds of results and ideas considered in multiple-ability hierarchical theories.

Gf–Gc theory derives in part from factor analytic study of the intercorrelational structure among primary abilities, but it also deals with the development of abilities and with some of the ideas and findings pertaining to classical distinctions between sensation, perception, memory, and cognition.

In terms of this last-mentioned distinction, the theory argues at a general level that most human behavior involves intelligence to some degree, but that the behavior evoked by some kinds of tasks is much more indicative of the intelligence that is characteristic of the mature human than is the behavior evoked by other kinds of tasks. Intellectual functioning is probably involved to some degree, for example, in sensorimotor performances of the kind displayed by a skilled athlete or a piano virtuoso or an infant child. Somewhat more characteristic of mature human intelligence, however, is the kind of performance involved in perceiving a geometric figure as a whole or maintaining the melody or tempo of simple musical composition. Indicating a still higher level of intellectual function are association learning performances. And the most characteristically human indications of intelligence are to be found in performances in which complex relationships must be comprehended and implications must be derived from these awarenesses. Almost any task that indicates a person's abilities in attending to stimuli, perceiving relationships, and drawing conclusions will indicate, in part, individual differences in intelligence. But such tasks will involve other functions as well, and in some tasks the variance associated with such "other" functions is considerably greater than the variance associated with intelligence; moreover, there are developmental differences in the use and availability of these functions.

Factor analytic study of the interrelationships among exemplars of primary mental abilities (including analyses of the Wechsler subscales) has provided some indications of an operational basis for distinguishing between the major functions of the hierarchy outlined above. Results from several of these studies have been summarized in Table I. The factors of this table represent broad regularities occurring across a wide variety of tests and tasks and items. The table is illustrative, not comprehensive or fully definitional. It indicates only some, not all, of the kinds of behaviors and performances involved.

The regularity that stands out most prominently in factor analytic studies is that which points to a distinction between two broad factors, either of which can be readily accepted as indicating intelligence as this term is commonly used. The two may be described roughly as follows:

1. *Gf* is characterized by processes of perceiving relationships, educing correlates, maintaining span of immediate awareness in reasoning, abstracting concept formation, and problem solving. It is measured in unspeeded as well as speeded tasks involving figural symbolic or semantic content, but tasks in which relatively little advantage accrues from intensive or extended education and acculturation.

TABLE I

Summary of Results Indicating the Nature of *Gf* and *Gc* and Related Functions[a]

Abilities measured in	Intellectual factor						
	Gc	*Gf*	*Gv*	VPT	SAR	*Gs*	*Sp*
Broad range vocabulary	70						
Common word discriminations	60	30					
Remote associations	60			30			
General information	70						
Verbal Analogies	50	20					
Common word analogies	30	30					
Esoteric word analogies	60						
Syllogistic reasoning	30	30					
Word problem reasoning	30	30					
Mechanical knowledge	50	20	20				
Tools	50		20				
Mechanical principles	30	30	30				
Meaningful association memory	30	30			40		
Letter series	20	40					
Matrices		40	20				20
Paper folding		30	40				
Hooper visual organization		40	20				
Gestalt closure		20	40				
Embedded figures			50				
Associations for a word	20			60			
Uses for objects	20			60			
Things fitting a definition				60			
Finding letters *a*						60	
Comparing numbers						60	
Matching forms						60	
Span memory (backward)	20	30			40		
Primacy	30	20			60		
Recency		30			50		
Permuted clustering recall		30		20	50		
Slow writing		30			50		
Sorting prior to recall	30	30			60		
Question asking efficiency	30	30			30		
Quickness correct response							60
Quickness incorrect response	30						60

[a] Numbers in table are rough averages respresenting factor correlations obtained over several studies of Horn and associates.

2. *Gc* also involves the processes of perceiving relationships, educing correlates, reasoning, etc., just as does *Gf*, and *Gc*, too, can be measured in unspeeded tasks involving various kinds of content (semantic, figural, symbolic), but the content of the tasks that best characterize *Gc* indicates

relatively advanced education and acculturation either in the fundaments of the problem or in the operations that must be performed on the fundaments.

To say that the two forms of intelligence are operationally defined by separate sets of abilities and tasks can be a bit misleading. For one thing the task sets are limited relative to the complexities of the attributes. Each form of intelligence, *Gf* and *Gc*, is a conglomerate or compound of several abilities or cognitive functions only some of which have been indicated by research completed at the present time. For example, to define *Gf* in a fully adequate operational manner would require not only a combination (properly weighted) of the primary abilities indicated in Table I as being markers for the factor, but also primary abilities yet to be discovered or yet to be entered into studies of the *Gf* dimension. For another thing the abilities and tasks that indicate *Gf* or *Gc* do not have univocal relationships to one or the other form of intelligence. The Induction primary ability, for example, or a Letter Series task that helps to define this primary, has its main correlation with *Gf,* but it is also correlated with *Gc.* Similarly many memory tasks are associated with both *Gf* and *Gc,* as well as with a broad memory function, SAR, to be discussed later in this chapter.

When a task correlates substantially with more than one factor, it is said to permit the operation of alternative mechanisms. This means that individuals can cope with the task by use of one function (e.g., *Gf*) or alternatively by use of another function (e.g., *Gc*). One individual may perform well on a verbal analogies test by virtue of knowing the meaning of many of the words (a part of *Gc*), but without reasoning terribly well, but another person who does not know the meaning of many of the words may do equally well by virtue of superior reasoning (a part of *Gf*). Many such combinations of relatively high and low *Gf* and *Gc* (as well as the other factors to be discussed below) may be involved in putative measures of intelligence.

There is an important practical consequence of the fact that several abilities must be involved in both *Gf* and *Gc* and the fact that no task is univocally related to either dimension. These facts mean that neither dimension can be well represented by measurement through only one test. One must use several tests, representing several primary abilities, to obtain a measure that approximates the breadth of either one of these forms of intelligence. Results from studies in which only one test or two tests have been used to define *Gf,* for example, should be interpreted very cautiously and in the light of these qualifications. The results obtained with a matrices test as a measure of *Gf,* for example, can pertain primarily to the visualization function that this test involves, not to the *Gf* that is also assessed in this test.

The other major factors found among broad samples of primary abilities appear to represent, on the one hand, perceptual functions associated with sensory modalities, as in seeing or hearing and, on the other hand, functions pertaining to acquisition, storage, and retrieval over long and short periods of time.

The *Gv* factor of Table I represents a broad visualization function. This involves imagining the way objects may change as they move in space, maintaining orientation with respect to objects in space, keeping configurations in mind, finding the Gestalt among disparate parts in a visual field, and maintaining flexibility concerning other possible structurings of elements in space.

Similarly a broad auditory function, *Ga,* has been indicated in several studies (Horn, 1974, 1976a; see also Stankov & Horn, unpublished work). This is characterized by ability in detecting subtle sound differences (e.g., sonar beeps) when noise interferes or when the sounds are distorted, sensitivity to rhythms in sounds, capacity for retaining sound percepts in immediate awareness in order to compare them for similarity with other sounds, and keenness in distinguishing different patterns of sounds. The function is well measured with tests of Distorted Speech, Masked Speech Comprehension, and Auditory Reasoning.

Memory in some sense of the term is intimately involved in almost all expressions of ability, but research results indicate that it is useful to distinguish between several forms and processes of memory. Results of the kind shown in Table I indicate individual differences in two broad forms of memory, each independent of the other and independent of the *Gf, Gc, Gv,* and *Ga* functions described previously. One of these memory functions, here symbolized VPT (verbal productive thinking), involves recall from the distant past. It might be labeled long-term memory (LTM) except that in the research literature LTM often refers to memory over much shorter periods of time than is involved in VPT. Also, it is not known that this factor represents long-term recall of materials that are not verbally tagged, such as memory for places or shapes or episodes (Tulving, 1972). Operationally, the factor indicates facility in producing verbal responses in tasks that require one to list similarities, improvements, or alternative uses of common objects, write about consequences or problems associated with unusual events, write interpretations of lines or simple figures or topics, or provide multiple connotations of a given word. The function is often referred to as indicating creativity, but there is doubt about whether it is any more related to widely accepted criteria of creativity than are the other dimensions referred to here (Horn, 1976a).

The major broad factor of memory indicates a unity among short-term acquisition and retrieval (SAR) processes. It involves acquisition, storage, and retrieval over periods of a few seconds or minutes. A variety of tests of span-memory, paired-asociates recall, serial-learning recall, and recognition memory define the factor operationally. This variety includes spatial and verbal, and nonsense and meaningful materials. Although several subfactors of SAR have been identified in individual differences research (French *et al.,* 1963; Kelley, 1964), and still others have been suggested by research in which individual differences are considered only secondarily (as in Kintsch, 1970), it seems that these are interrelated in a fairly general function such as is adumbrated by SAR.

In some theories, notable the well-known theory of Jensen (1971), this broad SAR factor is said to represent a form of intelligence that is described as similar to *Gf.* However, the evidence is now fairly clear in indicating that while *Gf* does indeed contain variance in common with the variables that define SAR, there is a reliable distinction between a dimension that is defined primarily by SAR variables and the *Gf* dimension. Hence, whether or not SAR is regarded as a form of intelligence (and a claim of this kind can be made for each of the functions mentioned above, as well as for SAR), it should be recognized as representing a function in which individual differences are distributed independently of those in *Gf.*

The *Gs* and *Sp* factors of Table I are less firmly established than the other dimensions, with the possible exception of *Ga.* Basically, they represent the fact that speediness in a variety of ability tasks is at least somewhat independent of accuracy. Gs involves quickness in simple repetitive tasks in which almost everyone would get almost every item correct if the tasks were not speeded. It is questionable, however, whether perceptual speed tests, in which the person must quickly scan material to find a particular symbol, involve the same speediness as is measured by quickness in printing or writing or marking. Simple reaction time to a point stimulus (a light or sound) appears to be largely unrelated to any of these speediness measures or any of the other intellectual abilities.

The *Sp* in Table I is really not a factor in the usual sense but instead merely provides a summary statement of results from a couple of recent, as yet unpublished, studies (Horn, 1976b, 1976c). The results were obtained by scoring all items of several tests for number correct, number attempted but incorrect, and time to obtain both correct and incorrect answers. Considered in respect to seven tests representing *Gf* and *Gc,* the time scores (both for correct and incorrect responses) were found to have small correlations, relative to their reliabilities, with operationally independent measures of accuracy (number correct) on the same and similar tests.

III. Processes Involved in Manifest Abilities

Before trying to make sense out of the vast literature pertaining to the development of abilities, it is wise to recognize a distinction of the kind

Horn (1976a) adumbrated under the headings of "macrolevel" and "microlevel" abilities. This particular dichotomous classification is a bit Procrustean, but it can help to alert one to attend to a continuum of levels of analysis of behavior. This extends from detailed description of specific behaviors to general description of heterogeneous classes of behavior.

A. NARROW AND BROAD MEASURES

Without specifying the many different features of various possible psychometric models for assessing an ability (e.g., see Horn, 1963; Lord & Novick, 1968; White, 1973), it can be recognized that implicitly most ability tests have been designed to (1) contain an order of difficulty of tasks (items), (2) represent a diversity of possible expressions of (indicants of) the ability attribute, and (3) permit some redundancy of observations to reduce error. But tests vary considerably in the extent to which one or the other of these three conditions prevail. A vocabulary test regarded as a measure of verbal comprehension, for example, involves emphasis on redundancy. Different difficulty levels are represented in such a test, and at each level there is sampling of many equivalent items. Counting correct responses to such items allows error to cancel and measurement to converge on an expected value (true score) for each subject (Lord & Novick, 1968). For reasons of convenience in expression, this kind of test will be referred to as *narrow*.

A narrow test of verbal comprehension can be contrasted to the measurement sought in a test in which some of the items require selection of a synonym for a word, some require selection of an antonym, some require written short answers to questions about an essay, some require production of a word to represent a particular idea, etc. This kind of test puts emphasis on diversity of possible expressions of verbal comprehension at some expense, as it were, to the error reduction that can be achieved with redundancy. This kind of task will be referred to as *broad* or *diverse*.

When the emphasis in a test is on diversity of content, one can argue that the objective of measurement is to ensure that the ability is not highly specific to a particular task, i.e., is not narrow. This can be viewed as one of the conditions to be satisfied in attaining external validity, as discussed recently by Schaie (1976).

In a general way, this objective has been emphasized in the kind of research described as "studies of human abilities" (or the like) in contrast to the research identified under headings such as "studies of cognitive processes" or "the nature of human information processing" (e.g., as represented in the books of Broadbent, 1958; Kintsch, 1970; Norman, 1969). No invidious comparisons are intended by this distinction or, indeed, seem warranted. But it is important to note the distinction, and thereby remain aware of the breadth of the variables represented by different operations of measurement in different studies. What is called "memory" or "verbal ability" or "spatial ability" in one study may be only one of several components of what is called by the same name in another study.

B. DIRECT ATTAINMENT AND RECALL
ATTAINMENT TESTS

When there is order of difficulty in an ability test, a score on the test can represent (in part) the level of complexity with which an individual can successfully cope (the level before insight fails). In some tests level of complexity (in this sense) corresponds roughly to the number of relationships that one must perceive and resolve in order to comprehend a pattern that inheres in the relationships. Once such comprehension is achieved, it can be retained for some time. If the same set of relationships is presented again, one needn't redevelop comprehension of the pattern; one can simply recognize it as a pattern previously comprehended. These considerations lead to another dichotomous classification representing a continuum, namely one distinguishing (1) tests in which there is emphasis on measurement of the thinking process in the immediate task and (2) tests in which the emphasis is on recognition of comprehension previously attained. In a rough way, but only a rough way, this is the distinction represented by *Gf* in contrast to *Gc*. Here, rather arbitrarily (but see below), the first kind of test will be referred to as a direct attainment (DAT) test and the second kind of measure will be labeled a recognition of attainment (REC) test.

An example of the way in which the DAT/REC distinction is used is provided in a description of notable similarities in, and differences between, a vocabulary (VOC) test and a concept formation (CF) test. Both are measures of ability to attain concepts. In the CF test the subject demonstrates this ability (usually with conjunctive concepts) over trials in which he is required to correctly identify exemplars (things having the defining properties of the concept) and nonexemplars. Each such task in a CF test is, in a sense, a miniature version of the process whereby individuals become aware of such "real-life" concepts as "dog" or "courage." The test is thus a fairly direct (DAT) measure of the complexities with which one can cope in forming concepts. In contrast, in a VOC test one is required to indicate understanding of a concept such as "courage." This is indirect REC measurement of concept formation. It indicates whether or not, in the past, one had adequately dealt with the complexities of comprehending a concept and can now bring that previous solution into awareness.

One may note that the VOC test can indicate not only concept attainment ability, but also individual differences in exposure to exemplars and nonexemplars, recall memory, and other things. These latter influences on test score can be regarded as extraneous biases in the measurement of concept attainment ability. Such extraneous influences may be reduced to some extent by good sampling over items and use of appropriate item format, but they can never be entirely eliminated. Extraneous influences also affect measurement with the CF test. For example, attentiveness and short-term memory are measured in such a test but can be regarded as extraneous to concept attainment ability, as such (as exercised in "real life," say). The main point is that each form of measurement can indicate the same ability—concept attainment—and each is subject to perturbations and errors of measurement, some of which may be shared with other tests and some of which may be unique to a particular test.

C. THINKING PROCESSES

Concept formation in a great variety of areas of experience, and assessed in many different DAT and REC tests, constitutes a major component of the abilities measured in the research that was briefly reviewed in previous sections of this chapter. But also prominently involved in the measurements of this research is variance produced by what may be referred to as strategies or generalized solution instruments or aids—that is, techniques for arriving (more and less efficiently) at resolutions of complexities or solutions to problems. For example, the techniques of alegebra enable one who knows them to efficiently solve problems that he otherwise couldn't solve or couldn't solve as efficiently. This is an example of a *cultural aid* transmitted by acculturation. Some ability measurement is aimed fairly directly at DAT and REC assessment of cultural aids. But each of us develops on our own a repertoire of techniques for dealing with complexities of a variety of kinds. These techniques are referred to as *idiosyncratic aids*. To some extent tests of reasoning and thinking assess the utility and efficiency of idiosyncratic aids.

Established findings in research on information processing, attention, and perception suggest that the broad measures obtained with ability tests involve a number of basic processes in addition to concept formation and aid development. For example, it seems that the development of what Keele (1973) and Kintsch (1970) have described as *control processes* is integral to individual differences assessed with ability tests. A control process is somewhat similar to an aid. It, too, is a strategy, but one used (with more and less efficiency) to achieve retention, as in rehearsal. For example, one can come to believe that by repeating material over and over he can learn (i.e., memorize) it. This might be called a maintenance strategy of rehearsal. It is useful over relatively short periods of time, as when one strives to keep a telephone number in mind as he moves across a crowded room, but it is not a very good way to learn anatomy or history. For these latter, one needs to employ control processes for achieving meaningful organization in material, ways of classifying elements into chunks that "make sense," and procedures for integrating material (as well described in Norman, 1969). Norman (1977) has also described metaknowledge processes used to monitor thinking, as when we use knowledge about memorizing to check to see if we are memorizing in an efficient manner, and supervisory processes involved in deploying our thinking resources, as when we decide that it is futile to use simultaneous scanning (attempting to comprehend all contingencies) in a particular concept attainment task and shift instead to a strategic hypothesis testing system.

These are but a few of many possible process concepts that can be of use in understanding the concept of intelligence, or the concepts of different kinds of intelligence, as in *Gf–Gc* theory, or indeed the concepts of primary mental abilities or of tests. In general, the process concepts described in this section derive from narrow operational definitions relative to the broad measurements obtained with ability tests. Thus they pertain to microlevel abilities relative to the macrolevel abilities of *Gf–Gc* theory. But analysis can almost always be further refined and, indeed, the processes described above can be partitioned, as it were, into subprocesses. It seems that some of these subprocesses may be very important for our understanding of the development of abilities, particularly in the very early years of life and in aging in adulthood.

D. MEMORY PROCESSES

To attain a concept or activate an aid or exercise a control process, one usually must become rather pointedly aware of the fundaments of the problem at hand. To put it simply, one must become aware that there is a "something" before one can be expected to comprehend that this particular "something" is a dog. The processes of thus becoming aware are described under headings such as "mechanisms of attention," "perception," and "memory." Here they will be discussed under the last-mentioned heading largely because memory is frequently regarded as the most important process involved in intelligence.

Existing evidence indicates that there is functional independence and independent individual differences in three temporally specified forms of memory, namely: (1) memory over periods of 20 sec or less, here termed primary memory (PM); (2) memory over periods of more than 20 sec but less than months or years, here termed secondary memory (SM); and (3) memory over periods of months and years, here termed tertiary memory (TM). Again the trichotomy is a bit Procrustean: Memory is perhaps best regarded temporally as involving subprocesses ranging all the way from nonvolitional, echoic, very, very short-term acquisition, storage, and retrieval up to highly volitional, associated, organized, very, very long-term retention and retrieval (Broadbent, 1958; Glanzer & Cunitz, 1966; Keele, 1973; Mandler, 1967; Murdock, 1960; Norman, 1970; Waugh & Norman, 1965). Also, for some purposes it is useful to talk about memory as episodic in contrast to semantic (Tulving, 1972), visual in contrast to auditory (e.g., Hundall & Horn, 1977), and in other ways, but these ideas will not be used very much in the present treatment.

One can remember a telephone number long enough to dial it, but usually it is forgotten almost as soon as the phone begins to ring. This is PM. Retention is for a very short period of time and little meaningful organization is perceived among the elements retrieved. Information retained over very short periods of time tends to be filed and retrieved in terms of what Broadbent (1966) has referred to as "sensory descriptors," for example, features of the input modality (eye, ear), time (first, second), and place (left ear, right ear) of arrival.

Retrieval of information over periods of time longer than about 20 sec seems to be based (more and more as recall time interval is increased) on use of what Broadbent (1966) described as "meaningful descriptors" such as are represented by categories of logic or subject matter disciplines—for example, animal, vegetable, mineral. Such descriptors can also be seen to indicate organization imposed on the material that is recalled (for review, see Mandler, 1967). If one can organize elements into meaningful categories, such as odd numbers and even numbers, then if one recalls a category, he usually recalls most of the elements in that category (up to a limit of about 4 elements unless there is further organization). Retrieval of this kind (over minutes or longer) indicates SM. As the time between learning exposure and retrieval increases, to an ever-greater extent the logical organization that one imposes on information determines whether or not the material is retrieved (Bower & Clark, 1969). Also, as time between learning exposure and retrieval increases, to a greater extent one fills in the gaps, so to speak, and "recalls" information that wasn't present in learning, as such, but is consistent with the organization system one had imposed on the learning materials (Bartlett, 1932; Jenkins, 1974; Tulving, 1962).

PM and SM together seem to be subfunctions of the span memory measured in tests that have helped to define the SAR dimension described in Section II. The mean for span is about 6 or 7; the standard deviation is about 2. These statistics define what Miller (1956) referred to as a magical number 7 ± 2. This represents a kind of short-term limit on the information one can retain within the span of immediate awareness. It is sometimes referred to as the information-processing capacity of the human. Our recent work indicates that individual differences in the PM and SM subfunctions can be reliably ($r_{xx} > .70$) and independently ($r_{xy} < .40$) measured. The mean for PM appears to be about 3 ± 1 and that for SM about 4 ± 1. Thus, the magical number 7 ± 2 appears to be composed of two magical numbers, 3 and 4, each having a plus and minus range of about 1.

There is suggestive evidence (e.g., see Bitterman, 1965) that the capacities of memory reach asymptote at relatively early stages of phylogenetic and ontogenetic development. That is, primary memory may be about the same in 8-year-old children as in young adults and, similarly, the great apes (chimpanzees, gibbons) and the dolphin appear to have primary memory spans comparable to those of humans. In this sense PM (and perhaps SM too) does not appear to be, in itself, an advanced form of expression of human intelligence, even as it may be essential to intellectual functioning. Just as the ability to see is essential to the process of solving visual problems and yet the goodness of problem solutions need not relate to the keenness of seeing, so the ability to retain low association material in immediate awareness can be essential to solving many intellectual problems and yet the span of PM need not relate to the goodness of the solutions realized for these problems. For many intellectual tasks, failures to reach insightful solutions occur primarily as a consequence of limits in perceiving relationships, and organizing these, not because of limited functioning of PM.

The processes of perceiving relationships among the fundaments of a stimulus array (as in concept formation) and using these in the eduction of consequences (as in problem solving) seem to be principal characteristics of human intelligence. These processes seem to be involved also in the organization that is characteristic of SM. Thus, the suggestion is that SM should relate rather more to *Gf* and *Gc* (or other indicants of intelligence) than does PM. Some of our recent (unpublished) work suggests that this is true. However, such assertions should be interpreted very cautiously. SM is only a short way along the continuum of memory processes from PM. Also many influences external to ability traits are known to affect memory measurements—influences associated with mood, motivation, and attention.

Of relevance in this regard are some recent findings of Botwinick and Storandt (1974), also found in our recent unpublished work (Horn, 1976c). These results suggest that a very simple measure of slow writing—trace a figure as slowly as you can—has substantial correlation with a short-term memory factor similar to the SAR dimension described in Table I. There is little reason to suppose that the slow writing task involves memory, as such, but it does seem to involve willingness or ability to concentrate.

In the research completed at this time TM is perhaps best represented by the measures that cluster in the broad factor labeled VPT, as was suggested earlier. The tasks that define this dimension require the subject to produce many concept labels (words) in accordance with rather loosely specified criteria (things "round"). The measure may be the number of concepts recalled (and written), the number of "distinct" concepts, the number of "unique" concepts, or something similar to these examples. By and large it seems that all such variations on scoring indicate, at a general level, the same VPT factor in distinction from *Gf, Gc*, SAR, *Gv*, etc.

It may be useful to distinguish between rate of retrieval in TM recall and something analogous to the size of store of available concepts. Investigators such as Mednick (1962) and Wallach and Kogan (1965) have pointed out that if over several time periods one records the number of associations (NA) to a given stimulus word, then NA decreases at a decelerating rate as time increases, many responses being given in the first few seconds but fewer and fewer being given as time goes on. This is depicted in Fig. 1 with cumulative curves (derived from some of our

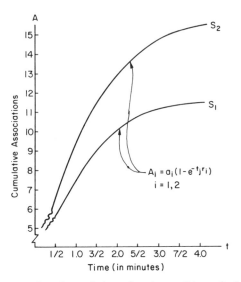

Fig. 1. Cumulative number of associations after elapse of time t_j for individuals of type S_1 and S_2. See text for further explanation.

recent empirical work) for two "types" of individuals ($i = 1, 2$). As is indicated in the figure, the data can be described with an exponential function in which A_i is the cumulative number of associations after elapse of time t_j, a_i represents approach to an asymptote, perhaps interpretable as size of store of available concepts, and r_i represents rate of approach to the asymptote, perhaps interpretable as rate of retrieval (production) for TM. It is not clear yet that this distinction between a_i and r_i is useful for descriptions of individual differences in abilities. The working hypothesis of our unpublished research (Horn, 1976b, 1976c) is that a_i is similar to active vocabulary, in distinction from the passive vocabulary measured in the usual synonyms test, and thus should be rather closely linked to Gc, while the r_i component might represent a retrieval function that fades with aging in adulthood and thus might be an aspect of Gf.

IV.   Ability Development over the Life Span

The processes and abilities described in previous sections are little more than the bare bones of the beautiful and complex bodies we recognize in mature expressions of intelligence. Where is the shape and hue of this body? One thing for certain, it is difficult to discern in our (i.e., psychologists) descriptions. But we can catch glimpses of it in attempts to describe knowledge systems and the organization among different kinds of abilities, concepts, aids, control systems, and the like. Such descriptions are found in interpretations of broad factors, such as Gf and Gc, and in the concepts created in an effort to talk about these. The idea of schemata (or schema) is an important concept of this kind. It helps to clarify some aspects of development, notable differences between the abilities of infancy, childhood, and adulthood.

A.   CONCEPTS OF DEVELOPMENT

The term schemata is used in a variety of ways. It will be used here as a generic label for organized systems of knowledge that are available to a person (i.e., can be regarded as "stored," so to speak, in tertiary memory). In terms of generality a schemata may range from something as specific as a concept or aid all the way up to a belief system as complex as one's world view. The thought is that as development proceeds from infancy into childhood and adulthood, such knowledge systems are modified in several more or less definable ways. This is what development is all about. But how are they modified, how are individual differences in such systems created and, then finally, what can we see as the practical outcome of these modifications in manifest human abilities?

Again (as in our discussion of processes) it must be recognized that there are different levels of analysis of the development of knowledge systems. Fischer (1976), for example (representing the Piagetian school), provides a high power focus on a very small segment of development, namely, that in infancy and early childhood. In this kind of treatment there can be detailed description of how such things as mimicking and circular reactions lead from a simple system to more complex systems in month-to-month development. But to provide a bird's eye view of development over the life span, one must consider pervasive kinds of changes and influences that occur over large segments of development. For this purpose, terms such as accretion, restructuring, and tuning, as used by Norman (1977) to describe skill development, are helpful.

Accretion refers to the addition of new information to a knowledge system. The concepts, aids, and control systems described earlier are major elements of this new information. Throughout development, from birth to death, such elements are added.

Restructuring represents the idea of developing different ways to organize and access the information of schemata. Just as librarians file books in a variety of ways to aid our search for a book when it is needed, so we file and cross-reference our knowledge system in many ways so that we may better retrieve information when it is needed (Broadbent, 1966). This reorganization occurs again and again as development proceeds and so even with accretion making the system ever larger, it is possible for access to elements in the system to be ever more efficient.

Tuning represents the idea that schemata can improve (in any of several ways, for any of several purposes) with practice. In general the more practice occurs, the more a schemata becomes automated and the less one has to think, as it were, in activating it. In the early stages of acquiring facility in reading, for example, one proceeds very slowly, checking every word and perhaps losing the thought of a sentence before it is read to the end. With tuning, however, it becomes possible to see entire lines and sentences at a glance. The skill thus becomes automated even as one reads for meaning. But practice, as such, is not enough to finely tune a schemata. There must be practice of a kind that improves. Some people practice reading a great deal for many years and yet do not learn to read as well as one, expertly tutored, who learns the tricks of reading most efficiently. In both cases the facility in reading becomes automated, but in one case it becomes automated at a higher level than in the other case. Over the course of development some schemata become ever more finely tuned, others rise to an automated level and stay at that level, and still others become more or less automated and then slip back to less automated form. And, of course, some people never develop schemata that are well developed by other people.

B.   LEARNING AS A FACTOR IN ABILITY DEVELOPMENT

The accretion, restructuring, and tuning of knowledge and skill systems can all be said to involve learning in a broad sense of this term. One might well suppose, therefore, as many theorists have, that the ability to learn, or learning, is what intelligence is all about. But we have seen that not all that goes under the name of learning is closely related to expressions of intelligence. Classical conditioning learning, for example, seems to occur no more easily in highly intelligent adults than in those of low intelligence and this seems to be true also for many variations of instrumental conditioning (Guilford, 1967). Indeed, it seems that most forms of learning over short periods of time bear only very low (but positive) relationships to various omnibus measures of intelligence (see Guilford, 1967; Hundall & Horn, 1977). The kind of learning that seems to be most related to intelligence is, not surprisingly, that which is assessed in tests of the kind that previously were described as DAT tests. As noted, these can be seen to involve the perception of patterns of relationships, the holding of these in awareness as a basis for, in effect, asking about consequences (forming hypotheses), and checking to see if anticipated consequences are in fact realized. To a considerable extent childhood development of intellect, and perhaps adulthood development as well, is characterized by change from an A state that involves (1) noting relatively few patterns of relationships in a stimulus array, (2) forming relatively simple scenarios of consequences of a set of conditions, (3) applying rather limited checks on the adequacy of a prediction or proposed explanation; to a B state that involves (1) complicating even seemingly rather simple patterns of relationships, (2) anticipating hugely complex possible outcomes of even rather simple situations, (3) trying out a great variety of possible checks to see if one or another explanation is sound. This movement from A to B is, on the one hand, a description of the way the learning of intelligence develops and, on the other hand, a description of the kind of learning that seems to produce intelligence.

C.   INFLUENCES ON DEVELOPMENT

But all of this is rather circular, of course. What things affect the kind of learning that is intelligence; what leads to more and better restructuring, more and better tuning, more and better accretion? Such development is conditioned by a myriad of influences operating over a huge number of time frames. The replicable structures we see in primary mental abilities and the *Gf, Gc,* etc., dimensions of intelligence are outcomes of lawful patterns of these influences, but it is difficult to infer backward from the outcomes to clear descriptions of the causes. The following, however, appear to be among the general, and most potent, classes of influences affecting the development of the *Gc* and *Gf* forms of intelligence. Subdivisions of these classes of influence can also be seen to be prominent in the development of abilities that are narrower than *Gf* and *Gc* as, for example, verbal comprehension or numerical skill (see Horn, 1970).

1. Acculturation

Education, even in the most formal sense of this term, no doubt accounts for much development and differentiation of intellectual abilities, particularly in childhood. But this term does not encompass all of the shaping of intellectual abilities that occurs through the pervasive influences of the dominant culture. For example, connotations of the term education usually do not include the idea that family groupings that are generally accepting and supportive of the achievement values of a culture provide (for children) a different climate for learning the lore of the culture than do family groupings in which those things regarded as most worth achieving stand in inverse order to the order of values (priorities) in the dominant culture. In *Gf–Gc* theory the term acculturation is used to represent a broad category of the influences such as those last mentioned, as well as those of education. Acculturation thus represents all of those influences that tend to shape each individual's intelligence in a mold prescribed, as it were, by the culture.

2. Incidental Learning

The major educational efforts of parents and teachers, in the home and in schools, are directed at producing acculturation, but there is learning in addition to this. Typically, for example, parents and teachers do not teach much about the "street lore" that enables a child to get around quickly in a neighborhood and, in general, function effectively in the environment outside the school and home. Such acquisition is referred to as incidental learning to distinguish it from the learning of acculturation.

Although most tests constructed to measure aspects of intelligence have not been designed to measure the abilities that are acquired through incidental learning, nevertheless these abilities can facilitate test performance, particularly in certain kinds of tests. For example, if through incidental learning one acquires exceptional ability in getting around the mazes of a city, then this ability can be manifested in paper and pencil tests of the kind that measure the Visualization (Vz) primary ability.

3. Climate for Inquiry

As noted, the kind of learning that seems to be most indicative of intelligence is active, questioning, hypothesis-generating, hypothesis-testing. This describes an attitude toward the learning process—indeed, an attitude toward one's existence. It seems that such an attitude may be essential to the development of some of the finest features of intelligence. Some conditions in which one may develop are conducive to the development of such attitude, others are not. Variations in such conditions may be likened to the variations in the climates in which plant growth takes place. Such "climate" is an important aspect of acculturation, as noted above.

It seems likely that the climate for inquiry is an important factor in intellectual development, but not a great deal is known about the "climatic" features that are most important at each major stage of intellectual growth. It is known that some very high levels of intellectual ability have developed in environments that must be classified as "disadvantaged," while some individuals raised in what are regarded as "advantaged" conditions do not attain high levels of ability. But what are the crucial factors that distinguish these cases? We do not know with certainty, but a few of these are indicated in the sections that follow.

4. Positive Transfer

Learning one concept or aid makes it easier to learn related concepts and aids (although there are a number of qualifiers to this assertion). Learning Spanish makes it easier to learn Italian. In concept learning one can learn aids that facilitate other concept learning even when the concepts, as such, are not very similar. The "learning sets" of Harlow's well-known experiments, for example, represent aids in paired-associates learning that were applied to the learning of quite different sets of associations. Schemata are comprised of such combinations of aids and concepts.

As Ferguson (1956) pointed out in pioneering work on this theme, the effect of positive transfer over the rather long course of development of abilities in childhood (and thereafter) must be to group together expressions of similar abilities in individual differences. Thus to some extent, positive transfer through acculturation can account for the fact that abilities to do division and solve word problems correlate with the same factor (the R, General Reasoning, primary ability).

5. *Selection and Deselection*

For a variety of reasons too extensive to try to list here, individuals drift into, are placed in or, in general, simply are found in programs in which a variety of concepts and aids are inculcated that are not necessarily similar (in the positive transfer sense of similarity) but form a group (schemata) that is different from the schemata acquired in programs in which other individuals are found. For example, some individuals are exposed to rather extended acculturation associated with a particular form of religion, while other individuals encounter virtually none of this kind of acculturation. One might learn some Latin, some music, and some history under the aegis of the church, for example. The abilities that are formed under this kind of influence constitute a grouping that may look as if it resulted from positive transfer, but is due instead to the fact that those who learn one ability of the group tend to learn the others, while those who do not receive this form of learning do not acquire the abilities of the group.

6. *Labeling*

When one is selected for some programs of acculturation, he also is labeled. One selected for the "exceptional child" program of a particular educational system, for example, might also tend to be affixed with a label such as "exceptional child," or one less euphemistic than this. And there are other reasons why one can be labeled in one way or another. The child placed in a program for "exceptionals" is exposed to a different program of training than an individual not so placed, but in addition the individual may take on a concept of self associated with the label (in conformance with, or in opposition to). Others with whom he is in frequent contact may react to his label and thus tend to "call out" particular forms of behavior from him (see Finn, 1971, on the so-called Pygmalion effect). These factors can notably influence a wide variety of achievements. Thus labeling can help to produce individual differences in broad groupings of abilities, such as those of Gc.

7. *Avoidance Learning*

In one sense this is the other side of positive transfer. More generally, however, it represents a rather broad category of influences associated not only with learning to avoid circumstances in which certain kinds of learning can occur, but also learning not to learn even when placed in these circumstances. Girls in our culture may thus tend to learn not to learn mathematics, for example. Since an actively curious and motivated desire to learn is necessary for truly efficient and rapid learning, avoidance of areas of acculturation can very much restrict ability development. When certain areas of learning are avoided by some and not by others then, over an extended period of development, this can tend to produce individual differences in broad groupings of abilities.

8. Interpersonal Configurations

Zajonc (1976) recently brought together, from several sources, evidence suggesting that a child's ability development is systematically influenced by the number of, and intellectual maturity of, the persons with whom the child has principal contact during formative years. A child who is persistently exposed to several adults will have more opportunities to learn adult verbal expressions, for example, than a child whose major contacts over an extended period of development are with other children.

Zajonc has used this idea to help explain data showing: (1) decreases in children's ability scores with increase in birth order and size of family, (2) lower scores for twins than nontwins, (3) higher scores for children in home settings in which adults in addition to the parents (e.g., the grandparents) also reside, (4) change in standardized high school and college achievement scores (SAT, ACT) associated with change in birth rates. With increase in the birth rate between 1946 and 1950, for example, there was decrease in SAT scores obtained between 1964 and 1968.

9. Values of Significant Others

A general expression of the idea of configurational influences should contain references to configurations representing the dominant values the child encounters in interactions with parents and peers, in neighborhoods and in schools. For example, Lesser, Fifer, and Clark (1965) present evidence indicating that children raised in Jewish homes tend to score high on verbal comprehension relative to spatial abilities, but that children brought up in American-Chinese homes tend to score high in spatial abilities relative to verbal comprehension (for more of this kind of evidence for home and subcultural influences on the formation of abilities, see Hill, 1967; Levinson, 1961; Werts, 1967).

10. Physiological Influences

Physiological, particularly neurological, structures can be seen to affect intellectual development and to be affected by it. In the first instance, how well one can comprehend, learn, etc., is determined by the functioning, and adequacy of functioning, of the physiological substratum. Call this the effective physiological base for intellectual development (EPB). But the experience occasioned by comprehension, learning, etc., changes physiological structures and functions, and in a sense these changes are irreversible. Call this the incremental effect on the physiological base (IPB). Thus EPB at time i plus the IPBs between times i and j can yield the EPB at time j. One's knowledge or lack of knowledge at any point in development is related to IPB and thus to future EPB. Knowledge can help one to avoid deleterious agents: One who knows that carbon monoxide inhalation can destroy neural tissues can use this knowledge to effectively avoid loss of EPB.

At any given point in development the EPB is a major factor in manifest expressions of intelligence, and in further development of intelligence, i.e., IPB. Any injuries or illnesses that depress EPB in the short run may affect the long run development adversely, by putting the person behind, so to speak, normal development. An injury that destroys parts of the EPB decreases the absolute capacity for dealing with complexities at all times following the injury. Although it is easiest to see these kinds of influences in terms of adverse affects produced by injuries and illnesses, particularly salubrious health and other factors that favorably affect neurological functioning (e.g., certain drugs, exercise) may enhance EPB in the short run and/or IPB over time.

Although EPB determines, to some extent, how well one utilizes accultural opportunities and the latter affects IPB, physiological and acculturational influences can operate largely independently, particularly in childhood and very old age. Illnesses and injuries that affect central nervous system functioning can occur at any time in development, before or after quite variable amounts of acculturation. The effects of such injury at time t_1 can limit further acculturation at times t_{1+i} (for $i = 1, ..., n$), but this can be unrelated to amount of acculturation preceding t_1.

D. OUTLINES OF DEVELOPMENT

At birth the infant has no concepts, no aids, no schemata, no meta-knowledge, no supervisory systems. Indeed, even some of the most elementary processes of intelligence may be missing from the limited repertoire of behavior the infant can display. For example, even SM must be lacking if one has no associational structure to which a stimulus can be related. Thus even elementary pattern recognition is lacking in the infant. In sort, the infant can display relatively little of the kind of behavior that, at later ages, is identified as indicating intelligence.

One might refer to this as "adultcentricism" (analogous to ethnocentricism) in the definition of intelligence, but to do so is merely to suggest a rather unfavorable connotation for a condition of existence. Intellectual abilities are complex outcomes of development. They can no more exist prior to substantial periods of development than mammals can evolve on the moon. Since little development can have occurred in the early periods of development, little that rightly can be called intelligence can appear in infancy.

It may seem odd, but this basic fact has not been well comprehended in psychology until recently. It seems that one reason for this is that nativism and biological–medical conceptions of intelligence have dominated in thinking about intellectual abilities. This has led people to look for the homunculus of intelligence in the infant child. This has also led to development of measures that are often interpreted as if they indicated intelligence in infancy but in fact pertain primarily to whether a child is healthy, has intact sensory and motor capabilities, and is alert. Such measures might relate to behavioral measurements of intelligence, but there are reasons why they should not. In any case they are not descriptive of the behaviors of intelligence.

One reason tests based on biological conceptions of intelligence—e.g., sensorimotor tests—should not relate to intelligence is that in childhood and adulthood such measures (as seen in athletic ability) have only a very low (but positive) relationship to most forms of intellectual ability. In principle, sensorimotor alertness in infancy could be a necessary, or even a sufficient, condition for later intellectual development and thus it could be a strong predictor of intelligence in childhood and adulthood. But analyses of the existing evidence argue that this is not the case (Hofstaetter, 1954; Horn, 1968, 1976a; Lewis & McGurk, 1972; McCall, Hogarty, & Hurlbert, 1972; Pease, Wolins, & Stockdale, 1973). Measures of sensorimotor alertness are reliable, they indicate gross physical and physiological retardation, and they may usefully indicate precursors of intelligence (although as yet there is little evidence to support this hypothesis), but they do not tell us much about intelligence, as such, or enable us to predict very much about intellectual development. Indeed, there is evidence to suggest that when gross cases of retardation are excluded from the sampling, precocity in sensorimotor development in infancy may be contraindicative of intelligence measured in childhood and thereafter (Kagan & Klein, 1973; McCall *et al.,* 1972; Werner & Bayley, 1966).

1. Earliest Indicants of Intellectual Abilities

The objective of measuring precursors of intelligence in infancy is very appealing, however, and there is some work suggesting how this might be done. Watson (1975) and Horn (1976a) have provided recent summaries of this work, so it will be mentioned here only briefly.

The work of McCall *et al.* (1972) suggests that indicants of manipulative exploration in the first 6 months of life predict imitation behavior in the next 6 months of infancy, that this latter portends verbal labeling in the early part of the second year, and that this in turn predicts grammatical use and comprehension of language in the period from 18 to 24 months of age. The measures of development in the first year of life were unrelated to measures of intellectual development in the preschool and early school period, but the measures obtained in the second year of life did, in some cases indicate later intellectual development. This kind of path analysis thus provides a basis for a theory about independent stages of intellectual development, as in some of the work stemming from Piagetian formulations (for critical evaluations of some of this work, see Horn, 1976a).

Watson's (1975) review and his own research suggest that measures of conditioning in infancy may provide precursor indicants of subsequent intellectual development. Again it is known that simple conditionability (instrumental as well as classical) has only a very low (but positive) relationship to the intellectual abilities of childhood and adulthood. It may be rather closely related to the learning represented by primary and secondary memory, however, and as such could well provide early indications of processes on which intellectual development is, in part, based. Watson's work suggests that this is true.

It may be useful to consider Watson's approach in the context of work by Kagan (1972) and Campos (1975) on the nature of attentiveness in infants. This work suggests that by using physiological reactions to stimuli and conditions (the visual cliff), it may be possible to measure the extent to which an infant is forming hypotheses, as it were, and checking to see if information fits in his early formed schematas. If such capabilities can be assessed in infancy, the resulting measures should be indicative of intellectual development at later ages.

2. *Childhood into Adulthood*

The formal educational system provides the framework of organization for most of the acculturation that occurs from late infancy into early adulthood. Positive transfer, avoidance learning, selection and deselection, and labeling operate in tandem and iteratively, each reinforcing the other, to mold the schemata of one person into a different shape than that of another. One who is selected for, and does not turn off, the most accelerated and advanced programs of acculturation accumulates, restructures, and tunes to automation a great variety of knowledge and metaknowledge systems that have little more in common than that they have been developed, saved, and cherished within a particular culture. The motley collection of knowledge systems adumbrated in the factor of Gc can be only a very primitive indicator of individual differences in the variegated structure that is the intelligence of a culture. But Gc is what we have today as our measure of this, a glimmering at least of an incredibly complex pattern.

Yet some important aspects of intelligence develop somewhat independently of the shaping of acculturation. Intellectual resources that are not harnessed by acculturation are left free for incidental learning. As Toynbee pointed out in his monumental treatise on *A Study of History* (1934–1954), people develop on the fringes of cultures. There they appropriate a potpourri of intelligences of different cultures. This may, but need not, facilitate assimilation of the dominant culture, and may even interfere with this. Injuries and illnesses destroy some of the neurons that provide the functional basis for elementary mnemonic and pattern recognition processes. Such changes also decimate elements of the neuron assemblies that support schemata. All of these various influences can operate after or before or, in general, independently (see footnote 3, p. 218) of massive and lean doses of acculturation. Only the shadowy outlines of the complex pattern of abilities that emerges from these influences can be seen in the factor structure that defines *Gf,* but again this seems to provide at least a glimmering.

The earliest expressions of intelligence are probably determined primarily by physiological factors, and these may mainly represent genetically determined structure and process (for indications of other kinds of influences, see Loehlin, Lindzey & Spuhler, 1975). Such influences are common to the development of both *Gf* and *Gc*. The two factors are thus virtually indistinguishable in infancy. This means that the quasi-simplex pattern for both *Gf* and *Gc* can be specified with the same equation in the earliest stages of development. But as development continues from infancy through childhood and into adulthood, some of the increments that are added and some of the decrements that are subtracted in one form of intelligence are not added and subtracted in the other.[4] In this manner two

[4]The term decrement is here used rather loosely to represent not only the fading or loss of a skill previously learned, but also interference in acquisition and expression of a schemata. As a schemata (idea about something) becomes elaborated and automated, it can interfere with development of a schemata pertaining to some of the same phenomena. These are the rigidities of logic tight compartments, and the like. Increments in established schemata in *Gc* may thus prevent increments in *Gf* and vice versa. It is better to refer to this as interference, but in the interest of conciseness of notation in Equations (1) and (2) it is lumped with the ideas of decrement. Interference could be a major factor in reducing the correlation between *Gf* and *Gc*, perhaps particularly in adulthood.

William James, as far back as 1902, in *The Varieties of Religious Experience,* Lecture 5, rather nicely expressed this idea or rigidities (as well as several of the other ideas outlined in this chapter) in his likening of the growth of the mind to the spread of grease spots. "Our minds grow," he said, "in spots; and like grease spots, the spots spread. But we let them spread as little as possible: we keep unaltered as much of our old knowledge, as many of our old prejudices and beliefs, as we can. We patch and tinker more than we renew. The novelty soaks in; it stains the ancient mass, but it is also tinged by what absorbs it."

overlapping quasi-simplex patterns develop. At any given point in development, this outcome may be specified as:

$$Gc_i = A_i + p_{1i} + \ldots + p_{ji} \qquad\qquad + a_{ni} + \ldots + a_{si} + c_{ti} + \ldots + c_{vi} \qquad (1)$$

$$Gf_i = A_i + p_{1i} + \ldots + p_{ji} + f_{ki} + \ldots + f_{mi} + a_{ni} + \ldots + a_{si} \qquad\qquad\qquad (2)$$

| Common physiological increments/ decrements | Specific *Gf* increments/ decrements | Common acculturational increments/ decrements | Specific *Gc* increments/ decrements |

The common initial condition, A_i, and the common p_{hi} and a_{qi} increments/decrements represent the overlap, or common measurement, or correlation of *Gf* and *Gc*. As defined in the studies completed up to this time, this correlation becomes about .50 by the preadolescent period of development (Cattell, 1967, 1971; Horn & Cattell, 1966). This indicates that about 25% of all the components of fallible estimates of *Gf* and *Gc* (including error components, not entered in the equations, as well as A_i and increment/decrement components) are common to the two forms of intelligence—i.e., A_i, p_{hi}, and a_{qi}.

As the number of specific elements represented in the equations increases relative to the number of common elements, the correlation between *Gf* and *Gc* will decrease. Although the evidence of relevance for considering this possibility is far from unambiguous, it is in a general way supportive of the idea that the *Gf–Gc* correlation decreases throughout childhood (Reinert, 1970; Schmidt & Crano, 1974).

The issues in this regard are complex enough for childhood development, but they become even more complicated when one focuses on adulthood. It can be argued that in this period decrements of specific elements will increase relative to decrements of common elements. For example, those ahead in acculturation will tend to slip back, forgetting some of the esoteria they had previously mastered. Similarly, some behind in acculturation in childhood may "catch up." Such influences would tend to increase the proportion of elements in common between *Gf* and *Gc* (relative to the proportions of specific elements) and thus increase the correlation between the two dimensions. There is some suggestion that this may best represent the results obtained with fallible ability measurements (Cunningham, 1976; Reinert, 1970). On the other hand, it is not unreasonable to suppose that the ratio of specific to common elements represented in the equations should increase throughout most of adulthood, in which case the *Gf–Gc* correlation should decrease in this period (as in Cunningham & Clayton, 1973). At present the evidence is much too equivocal to provide clear answers to questions of this kind.

3. The Mature Years

As development proceeds from adolescence into young adulthood, through the mid-years and into old age, the major impetus for acculturation shifts from the education system, to a system associated with employment, and finally to a system that almost seems to lack conjunctive elements and therefore is defined disjunctively in terms of what it does not have that is characteristic of vocational and educational systems. It is relatively easy to specify the domain of elements inculcated through acculturation in childhood, but difficult to do this for the vocational period of adulthood, and still more difficult to do it for the retirement period.

The definition of the intelligence of the culture thus seems to become more and more diffuse as later and later periods of development are specified in adulthood. It becomes more and more difficult to specify the major kinds of schemata, metaknowledges, executive systems, etc., that should characterize the more mature expressions of adult intelligence. The tests that have indicated Gc and Gf abilities (and the distinction between Gf and Gc) in adulthood may be mainly only atavistic carryovers from ability definitions of childhood, not very good indications of adult intelligence. This opinion has been expressed many times, and is of rather ancient vintage, but not much has been done to heed it. Recent papers by Riegel (1973) and Schaie (1976) may address the issue in ways that will yield new adulthood measures, however.

Many of the positive influences on ability development should act throughout adulthood. Accretion, restructuring, and tuning can work to increase abilities into old age and, indeed, existing evidence, even though based on tests that may be considerably less than optimally appropriate, indicates that many Gc abilities are more adequately organized, more finely tuned and, in general, better in older than in youger adults. Verbal comprehension (as partially indicated by size of vocabulary), general information, reasoning based on advanced knowledge and highly developed aids, and verbal fluency in recall from tertiary storage all seem to increase with age in adulthood, particularly when speediness and educational differences are controlled statistically (for reviews, see Horn, 1970, 1975, 1976a). In general it seems that to the extent that existing tests measure such things as: (1) breadth of concepts, aids, etc., within schemata, (2) number of schemata as such, (3) intricacy of interrelationships among schemata, (4) accessibility of concepts (as in VPT; see also Drachman & Leavitt, 1972), (5) range of metaknowledge, and (6) complexity of executive control systems, then the measures indicate increase, or at least not decrease, in ability over a major part of the adulthood period of development.

But there are good reasons to suppose that some abilities will decline with age in adulthood. Some of these reasons have been alluded to previously in mention of the physiological influences on development of ability systems (for reviews of this evidence, see Bromley, 1974; Gershon & Raskin, 1975; Horn, 1970). As age increases in a steady state of exposure to possibilities for loss of neural structure, there is increasing probability that one will have been exposed to conditions that reduce the neural substrate of support for intellectual functions. There may be intrinsic catabolic influences that work to destroy the neural substrate or the effectiveness of its function. Neural tissue is not regenerated after the earliest period of development. Present evidence suggests that brain weight decreases by about 15% over a period from age 20 to age 70. This could affect both the most elementary subfunctions of intelligence, such as PM, and the most developed structures, as if some of the neural elements of support for a schemata were to be lost.

But not all decline in intellectual abilities need be attributed to loss of physiological base: There are psychological reasons for decline. We have already referred to the rigidities that result when knowledge systems become elaborated and automated (see footnote 4, p. 242). Abilities to shift to new knowledge systems may thus be hampered. Also, as systems such as schemata become larger, they can become more difficult to access. Restructuring and tuning can mitigate this problem, but eventually, assuming that the storage system has finite capacity, the problem of overload must arise. When this occurs, a variety of inefficiencies can result. Functioning may slow down, more circuitous pathways to access may have to be used, more confusions may arise, etc. Such events may correspond to the slownesses, the confabulations, and the confusions that are noted in common sense observations of adulthood intellectual change. And, indeed, recognizing again that available tests provide only rough guidelines, the evidence from a number of studies indicates aging decline in several of the abilities of *Gf* (and SAR). Indicating such decline, for example, are measures of reasoning (of several kinds, as assessed in unspeeded letter series, matrices, and common word analogies tests), measures of associative and span (PM + SM) memory, and measures of perceptual speediness. Evidence of overload breakdown is provided in studies showing aging decline in complex reaction time (but not simple reaction time), and tasks in which the subject must store information while monitoring thinking activities. Other behavioral indicants of *Gf* decline are (as identified in Botwinick, 1977; Horn, 1970, 1976a) increases in distractability, confusion of parts of a problem, abandonment of difficult problems, acceptance of inconsistent solutions, inabilities in distinguishing characteristics of a class, inappropriateness of classifications, inattention to form (in contrast to content) of an argument, and decrease in information taken in per chunk. Some of the more specific aspects of these changes are identified in the discussion to follow.

   a.   Speediness issues.   The results from many studies have shown that in a wide variety of tasks older adults tend to work more slowly than younger adults. As noted above, perceptual speediness measures show this decline. These are tasks in which the subject must find a particular symbol or check to see if one symbol is the same as another. This can be viewed as elementary pattern recognition speed. Some measures of motor speed, as in performing a small muscle or large muscle task, also show aging decline.

   There is considerable evidence that older individuals hear less well and see less well than younger individuals, and there are suggestions that slowness in perceptual and motor tasks may relate mainly to defects in hearing and/or seeing. Since many intellectual tasks are speeded, at least somewhat, there is reason to believe that the aging decrements in performance on these tasks are not due to loss of intellectual functions, as such, but to decreases brought on by creeping defect in peripheral sensory processes. This is a difficult set of questions to answer properly, but to the extent that existing evidence is relevant, it suggests that not all of the aging decrement in intellectual abilities is due to processes that are peripheral to central intellective functioning. Some of the decline seen in Gf measures seems to represent loss of intelligence that is not well explained as being only performance loss associated with sensory defect, changes in attitude toward intellectual tasks, or similar nonintellective factors.

   Three kinds of evidence have cast doubt on assertions that aging decrement in intellectual abilities is due only to peripheral functions. One kind of evidence derives from studies in which decrement is found for tests that are given under unspeeded (or only very lowly speeded) conditions. Much of the evidence derived from use of the Wechsler scales is of this kind (Matarazzo, 1972), but so is evidence derived from other tests. For example, Horn and Cattell (1967) found that when Matrices and Letter Series measures of Gf were administered under conditions in which all subjects attempted all items, the aging decrements recorded with these measures were virtually the same as were indicated for other Gf tests administered in the usual way (time limits imposed and items given in order from easy to difficult). These results have been verified in our recent (as yet unpublished) studies (Horn, 1976b, 1976c).

   Of relevance in this regard is the fact that the items of tests are often presented in order of difficulty (from easy to difficult), and the time limits are worked out in a way designed to ensure that most test respondents are performing at a near-chance level before time is called. Studies in which the performances of young and old subsamples are compared on the first part and the last part of a test should be interpreted cautiously relative to these considerations (cf. Cunningham, 1976). For example, if a sample of older subjects perform as well as a sample of younger subjects on the first part of a test, but complete fewer items and for this reason perform less well on the last part of the test, it doesn't follow necessarily that this indicates that speediness peripheral to central intellective functioning is responsible for the age-related effect. For any subject (of any age), as the problem difficulty approaches and passes the level with which the person can cope, the central processing time expended in efforts to solve the problem tends to increase (Horn, 1976b, 1976c). Thus slow work on a problem can indicate mainly that the problem is difficult for the person in question or, to put the matter the other way around, that the person's ability is lacking. The decline in *Gf* that has been recorded in unspeeded or lowly speeded performances is based on tests in which the difficulty level of the items is sufficient to ensure that most subjects will be unable to solve some problems no matter how long they work at solution (Horn, 1976b, 1976c; Horn & Cattell, 1967).

A second kind of evidence derives from studies in which both speediness and accuracy are measured separately in intellectual tasks and the two separate measures are related to aging. Welford (1958) has brought together a wealth of evidence of this kind and more recent reviews have been provided by Botwinick (1977), Arenberg (1973), Horn (1970, 1975, 1976a, 1976b, 1976c), and others. This evidence indicates that while speediness often declines with age, so too do nonspeeded aspects of performance. In particular, as the difficulty of problems increases, there is increase in working time and consequent decrease in performance of older as compared with younger subjects.

In the third kind of study bearing on this issue, it is recognized that although many kinds of speediness may decline with age in adulthood, these may not be related to performance on ability tests and thus may not account for the observed decline in these latter performances. In studies of this kind measures of motor speediness (MS) and simple reaction time (SRT) are obtained and analyses are directed at determining if the differences measured in this way will account for the age-related differences indicated for *Gf* or other abilities. The evidence derived in this way indicates that when the effects associated with SRT and MS are controlled by partial correlation or covariance analyses, the age decrements for *Gf* (or SAR) are not eliminated: the reliably measured individual differences in SRT and MS do not account for the measured age differences in abilities of the kind represented in *Gf* and SAR (Horn, 1976b, 1976c; Horn & Cattell, 1967).

Complex reaction time (CRT) does seem to account for some of the aging decrement in *Gf* tests, however. A CRT task is one in which a subject must anticipate several contingencies and/or do one of several different things. In one such task, for example, subjects sort cards according to the four suits and according to whether a card is a court card or not. As task complexity of this kind increases, age decrements become more pronounced and such decrements become related to those recorded in *Gf* tasks. Several findings suggest that the decrement in this regard is shown mainly in the processes of initiating a response—i.e., digesting, as it were, the stimulus in relation to the contingencies, and utilizing this food for thought to energize a response (for review, see Horn, 1976a). This could reflect the fact that the more complex knowledge systems of older people (relative to younger ones) are nearer to, and thus more susceptible to, overload.

Decline in perceptual speed or pattern recognition speed also seems to be related to *Gf* decline. The age decrements found with this kind of task are not notably reduced by controlling for writing speed or similar measures of motor speediness. It seems that the intellectual age-declining function indicated with this factor is one involving facility in becoming aware of, and maintaining keen awareness of, stimulus elements that may be of relevance for dealing with the complexities of a problem (Horn, 1975, 1976a, 1976b, 1976c).

b. Memory functions. As everyday observations suggest, there is aging decline in short-term memory functions (Arenberg, 1973; Arenberg & Robertson-Tchabo, 1977; Botwinick, 1977; Botwinick & Storandt, 1974; Craik, 1977; Horn, 1970, 1976a; Reese, 1976; Walsh, 1975). Many questions can be asked, however, about just what aspects of the SAR factor decline and about how, and how much, this relates to *Gf* decline.

Short-term memory can be seen to involve apprehension, acquisition, retention, retrieval, and production. Each of these processes may be further analysed into subfunctions. For example, there is a vast literature pertaining to acquisition strategies and patterns of attention in apprehension. A defect seen in memory, measured merely in terms of recall or not (as in the items of most memory tests), can indicate defect in one but not the other of these processes and subprocesses, or (as seems most likely) defects in a combination of the more elementary functions. Also, memory is time based, so one can ask about not only the amount of material retrieved, say, but also the rate of retrieval (as in Fig. 1), and the same may be said also for apprehension, acquisition, etc. Issues in this regard may be crossed, also, with others pertaining to whether the task is to recall or recognize, to pair associate or serially organize, etc. Thus, there are many things to consider in evaluating aging decline in memory and the relation of this to *Gf* decline.

Very short-term span memory (PM + part of SM) declines with age and is lowly related to both *Gf* and *Gc*. Our recent (unpublished) work indicates that both components of span memory, PM and SM, decline and account for part (but not all) of the age decrements of *Gf*. Anders and Fozard (1973), using the Sternberg search paradigm, found that both the slope and the intercept of the time-to-identify function increased with age. The slope is interpreted as rate of comparison operations, a part of SM, and the intercept is said to indicate encoding time, a part of PM. Both primacy (indicating SM) and recency (indicating PM) show decline with age. Partialing PM alone in the *Gf*–age relationship reduces the absolute value of the negative correlation, but partialling SM further reduces this relationship. This suggests that both nonassociative, echoic memory and associated "meaningful" memory are involved in manifest measures of intellectual decline. The former is conceptually, and as regarded in the research literature, similar to the elementary pattern recognition, attentional process mentioned previously in discussing the aging decline of perceptual speediness. It was noted in a previous section also that ability to write slowly relates to the SAR function. We have found in our studies that this measure of concentration (or the like) also declines with age and accounts for some of the *Gf* aging decline. Whether this is primarily in PM or SM is not yet clear from our work, however.

In part, then, *Gf* decline may relate to a rather elementary capacity for focusing attention or maintaining concentration. However, it seems that some of the decline must be associated with capacities for imposing organization on stimulus materials, capacities that become somewhat more prominent in SM measures than in PM measures. With increase in age there is decrease in the number of meaningful associations generated among stimulus elements (words, phrases, signs, symbols, sentences, etc.), and this is accompanied by loss of recall over periods of minutes or longer (for reviews, see Arenberg, 1973; Horn, 1970, 1976a). As recorded with the Sternberg paradigm, the older person takes a longer time to assimilate (i.e., inspect and/or anticipate) the stimulus elements of a problem, but this does not seem to be due only to inability to become aware of the separate elements, as such. Rather it seems to be due to inability to comprehend the relational aspects of the stimulus pattern. For example, if an association prompt is supplied in a recognition memory task, the older person displays awareness of the associated element nearly as quickly as the younger person (Hultsch, 1971). It is primarily only when performance is dependent on awareness of the relations among several elements of a task that age differences become notable.

In sum, then, it seems that decline of intelligence is accompanied by an elementary loss of capacity for maintaining focused awareness of the elements of a problem and a more fundamental loss of capacity for perceiving relationships among the problem elements. The former is recorded in perceptual speed and attention tests, as well as in measures of PM. The latter is manifested in failure to organize materials in the manner required for efficient SM performance, but is indicated more fundamentally in failure to solve problems in which several relationships must be apprehended and used as a basis for drawing conclusions that can constitute a problem solution. This is recorded most accurately in tasks in which acculturational skills are of relatively little value (i.e., in the tasks of the *Gf* factor).

   c. A few cautions. All research results, and efforts to integrate these in treatments such as this one, should be regarded with fair skepticism, of course, but such caution may be particularly called for in evaluation of developmental studies. In such studies there are major problems in achieving comparability of samples at different stages of development, and there are still other major problems associated with insuring comparability of measurement at different ages.

   The first set of issues has been discussed rather fully in recent papers by Baltes and Schaie (1976) and Horn and Donaldson (1976), and in the references cited in these articles. The issues are complex. It would take more space than is available here to develop them adequately. However, a simple conclusion one can draw from these analyses is that one must tolerate much ambiguity in research on age differences and aging changes. There are simply too many reasonable and yet opposing interpretations of existing evidence to permit unequivocal conclusions.

   Consideration of the measurement problems of developmental research also should inspire caution in interpreting conclusions of the kind cited in previous sections. As noted before, a test used with older persons may measure something rather different from what is measured with the same test used with younger persons. This problem has many facets. For example, several studies reviewed by Welford (1958) have indicated that in speed/accuracy trade-offs in ability tasks, the elderly relative to the youthful tended to favor accuracy. Moreover, this strategy may be rather volatile. At least Hoyer, Labouvie, and Baltes (1973) showed that the speed/accuracy trade-off can be manipulated with relatively simple incentives: They found that they could notably increase older adults' speediness on ability tasks by rewarding speed with trading stamps. No doubt differences in strategies account for some of the manifest differences in the performances of younger as compared with older persons. Labouvie-Vief and Gonda (1976), for example, recently showed that the performances of elderly persons on *Gf* tasks could be altered with training designed to develop self-monitoring strategies. Such results need not be interpreted as indicating absence of aging decline in the functions underlying test performances, but they do suggest that performance is affected by strategy and thus provide a basis for an hypothesis that age differences are due primarily to strategy differences (that might be rather easily modified), not to functional differences.

Finally, it should be noted that age differences are calculated in terms of averages at each age level, and a mean, in the rather small samples at each age in many developmental studies, can be affected notably by a relatively few cases. A few persons showing decline can depress a mean notably even when most individuals show no decline. The same may be said also, of course, for a trend line showing aging increments. The curve for the average need not describe the curve for an individual.

V. Final Word

The findings and theories and hypotheses considered in this chapter are only rough examples of what is known about the organization and development of intellectual abilities. More of relevance for study in this area has been omitted than has been mentioned. Recent and rather detailed reviews are available to help correct this deficiency; for example, Arenberg (1973), Botwinick (1977), Botwinick and Storandt (1974), Butcher (1968), Butcher and Lomax (1972), Cattell (1971), Eysenck (1973), Green (1974), Guilford and Hoepfner (1971), Horn (1970, 1972, 1975, 1976a, 1977), Matarazzo (1972), and Resnick (1976). Even these, however, considered collectively, do not do full justice to the vastness of the results and the intricacies of the issues in this field of study. The point is that human abilities are difficult to understand, and the reader should regard this chapter as, at best, only a bird's eye view of some very complicated terrain.

References

Anders, T. R., & Fozard, J. L. Effects of age upon retrieval from primary and secondary memory. *Developmental Psychology,* 1973, **9**, 411–415.

Anderson, J. E. The prediction of terminal intelligence from infant and preschool tests. *39th Yearbook National Society for Studies in Education,* 1940, **1**, 385–403.

Arenberg, D. Cognition and aging: Verbal learning, memory, and problem solving. In C. Eisdorfer & M. P. Lawton (Eds.), *The psychology of adult development and aging.* Washington, D.C.: American Psychological Association, 1973.

Arenberg, D., & Robertson-Tchabo, E. A. Learning and aging. In D. E. Birren & W. K. Schaie (Eds.), *The handbook of the psychology of aging.* New York: Reinhold-Van Nostrand, 1977.

Baltes, P. B., & Nesselroade, J. R. The developmental analysis of individual differences on multiple measures. In J. R. Nesselroade & H. W. Reese (Eds.), *Life-span developmental psychology: Methodological issues*. New York: Academic Press, 1973.

Baltes, P. B., & Schaie, K. W. On the plasticity of intelligence in adulthood and old age: Where Horn and Donaldson fail. *American Psychologist,* 1976, **31,** 720–723.

Bartlett, F. C. *Remembering*. London: Cambridge University Press, 1932.

Bitterman, M. E. The evaluation of intelligence. *Scientific American,* 1965, **212,** 92–100.

Botwinick, J. Aging and intelligence. In J. E. Birren & K. W. Schaie (Eds.), *Handbook of the psychology of aging*. New York: Reinhold-Van Nostrand, 1977.

Botwinick, J., & Storandt, M. *Memory, related functions and age*. Springfield, Ill.: Thomas, 1974.

Bower, G. H., & Clark, M. C. Narrative stories as mediators for serial learning. *Psychonomic Science,* 1969, **14,** 181–182.

Broadbent, D. E. *Perception and communication*. Oxford: Pergamon, 1958.

Broadbent, D. E. The well ordered mind. *American Educational Research Journal,* 1966, **3,** 281–295.

Bromley, D. B. *The psychology of human aging* (2nd ed.). London: Penguin Books, 1974.

Butcher, H. J. *Human intelligence: Its nature and assessment*. London: Methuen, 1968.

Butcher, H. J., & Lomax, D. E. (Eds.). *Readings in human intelligence*. London: Methuen, 1972.

Campos, J. J. Heart rate. In L. Lipsett (Ed.), *Psychobiology: The significance of infancy*. Potomac, Md.: Lawrence Erlbaum Associates, 1975.

Cattell, R. B. The theory of fluid and crystallized intelligence checked at the 5–6 year-old level. *British Journal of Educational Psychology,* 1967, **37,** 209–224.

Cattell, R. B. *Abilities: Their structure, growth and action*. Boston: Houghton-Mifflin, 1971.

Craik, F. I. M. Age differences in human memory. In J. E. Birren & W. K. Schaie (Eds.), *The handbook of the psychology of aging*. New York: Reinhold-Van Nostrand, 1977.

Cronbach, L. J. *Essentials of psychological testing* (3rd ed.). New York: Harper, 1970.

Cunningham, W. R. Fluid intelligence vs. the intellectual speed hypothesis. *Proceedings of the 84th Annual Convention of the American Psychological Association,* 1976.

Cunningham, W. R., & Clayton, V. "Fluid" and "crystallized" intelligence in the elderly. *Proceedings of the 81st Annual Convention of the American Psychological Association,* 1973, **8**(2), 771–772.

Drachman, D., & Leavitt, J. Memory impairment in the aged: Storage versus retrieval deficit. *Journal of Experimental Psychology,* 1972, **93,** 302–308.

Eysenck, H. J. (Ed.). *The measurement of intelligence*. Baltimore: Williams & Wilkins, 1973.

Ferguson, G. A. On transfer and the abilities of man. *Canadian Journal Psychology,* 1956, **10,** 121–131.

Finn, J. D. Expectations and the educational environment. *Review of Educational Research,* 1971, **42,** 387–399.

Fischer, K. W. *A theory of cognitive development: Seven levels of behavior and understanding* (Research Report). Denver: University of Denver, Department of Psychology, 1976.

French, J. W. The description of aptitude and achievement tests in terms of rotated factors. *Psychometric Monographs,* 1951, No. 5.

French, J. W., Ekstrom, R. B., & Price, L. A. *Manual for kit of reference tests for cognitive factors*. Princeton, N.J.: Educational Testing Service, 1963.

Gershon, S., & Raskin, A. (Eds.). *Genesis and treatment of psychologic disorders in the elderly*. New York: Raven, 1975.

Glanzer, M., & Cunitz, A. R. Two storage mechanisms in free recall. *Journal Verbal Learning and Verbal Behavior,* 1966, **5,** 351–360.

Green, D. R. (Ed.). *The aptitude-achievement distinction.* New York: McGraw-Hill, 1974.

Guilford, J. P. Zero intercorrelations among tests of intellectual abilities. *Psychological Bulletin,* 1964, **61,** 401–404.

Guilford, J. P. *The nature of human intelligence.* New York: McGraw-Hill, 1967.

Guilford, J. P., & Hoepfner, R. *The analysis of intelligence.* New York: McGraw-Hill, 1971.

Hill, J. P. Similarity and accordance between parents and sons in attitudes toward mathematics. *Child Development,* 1967, **38,** 777–791.

Hofstaetter, P. R. The changing composition of intelligence: A study in F technique. *Journal of Genetic Psychology,* 1954, **85,** 159–164.

Horn, J. L. Equations representing combinations of components in scoring psychological variables. *Acta Psychologica,* 1963, **21,** 184–217.

Horn, J. L. Organization of abilities and the development of intelligence. *Psychological Review,* 1968, **75,** 242–259.

Horn, J. L. Organization of data on life-span development of human abilities. In L. R. Goulet & P. B. Baltes (Eds.), *Life-span development psychology.* New York: Academic Press, 1970. pp. 423–466.

Horn, J. L. The structure of intellect: Primary abilities. In R. M. Dreger (Ed.), *Multivariate personality research.* Baton Rouge, La.: Claitor, 1972.

Horn, J. L. Theory of functions represented among auditory and visual test performances. In J. R. Royce (Ed.), *Contributions of multivariate analysis to psychological theory.* New York: Academic Press, 1974. pp. 203–239.

Horn, J. L. Psychometric studies of aging and intelligence. In S. Gershon & A. Raskin (Eds.), *Genesis and treatment of psychologic disorders in the elderly.* New York: Raven, 1975.

Horn, J. L. Human abilities: A review of research and theories in the early 1970's. *Annual Review of Psychology,* 1976, **27,** 437–485. (a)

Horn, J. L. *Progress report on a study of speed, power, carefulness and short-term learning components of intelligence and changes in these components in adulthood* (Army Research Institute, Grant No. DAHC 19-/74-5-0012). Denver: University of Denver, 1976. (b)

Horn, J. L. *Progress report on learning components of intelligence and adulthood development* (National Science Foundation, Grant No. GB-/41452). Denver, University of Denver, 1976. (c)

Horn, J. L. The nature and development of intellectual abilities. In R. T. Osborne, C. E. Noble, & N. Weyl (Eds.), *Human variation: The biopsychology of age, race and sex.* New York: Academic Press, 1977.

Horn, J. L., & Cattell, R. B. Refinement and test of the theory of fluid and crystallized intelligence. *Journal of Educational Psychology,* 1966, **57,** 253–270.

Horn, J. L., & Cattell, R. B. Age differences in fluid and crystallized intelligence. *Acta Psychologica,* 1967, **26,** 107–129.

Horn, J. L., & Donaldson, G. On the myth of intellectual decline in adulthood. *American Psychologist,* 1976, **31,** 701–719.

Hoyer, J. A., Labouvie, G. V., & Baltes, P. B. Modification of response speed deficits and intellectual performance in the elderly. *Human Development,* 1973, **16,** 233–242.

Hultsch, D. F. Adult age differences in free classification and free recall. *Developmental Psychology,* 1971, **4,** 338–342.

Humphreys, L. G. Investigations of the simplex. *Psychometrika,* 1960, **25,** 313–323.

Humphreys, L. G. The misleading distinction between aptitude and achievement tests. In D. R. Green (Ed.), *The aptitude-achievement destination.* New York: McGraw-Hill, 1974.

Humphreys, L. G. A factor model for research on intelligence and problem solving. In. L. B. Resnick (Ed.), *The nature of intelligence.* Hillsdale, N.J.: Lawrence Erlbaum Associates, 1976.

Hundall, P. S., & Horn, J. L. On the relationships between short-term learning and fluid and crystallized intelligence. *Applied Psychological Measurement,* 1977, **1**, 11–22.

Jencks, C., Smith, M., Acland, H., Bane, M. J., Cohen, D., Gentis, H., Heyns, B., & Michelson, S. *Inequality: A reassessment of the effect of family and schooling in America.* New York: Harper, 1972.

Jenkins, J. J. Remember that old theory of memory? Well, forget it! *American Psychologist,* 1974, **29**, 785–795.

Jensen, A. R. A two-factor theory of familiar mental retardation. *Proceedings of the 4th International Congress on Human Genetics,* 1971, pp. 263–271.

Jensen, A. R. *Educability and group differences.* New York: Harper and Row, 1973.

Kagan, J. Do infants think? *Scientific American,* 1972, **226**, 74–82.

Kagan, J., & Klein, R. E. Cross-cultured perspectives on early development. *American Psychologist,* 1973, **28**, 947–961.

Keele, S. W. *Attention and human performance.* Pacific Palisades, Calif.: Goodyear, 1973.

Kelley, H. P. Memory abilities: A factor analysis. *Psychometric Monographs,* 1964, No. 11.

Kintsch, W. *Learning, memory, and conceptual processes.* New York: Wiley, 1970.

Labouvie-Vief, G., & Gonda, J. N. Cognitive strategy training and intellectual performance in the elderly. *Journal of Gerontology,* 1976, **31**, 327–332.

Lesser, H. S., Fifer, G., & Clark, D. H. Mental abilities of children from different social-class and cultural groups. *Monographs of the Society for Research in Child Development,* 1965, **30** (4, Serial No. 4).

Levinson, B. M. Subcultural values and IQ stability. *Journal of Gerontological Psychology,* 1961, **98**, 69–82.

Lewis, M., & McGurk, H. Evaluation of infant intelligence: Infant intelligence scores—true or false? *Science,* 1972, **178**, 1174–1177.

Littell, W. M. The Wechsler intelligence scale for children: Review of a decade of research. *Psychological Bulletin,* 1960, **57**, 132–156.

Loehlin, J. C., Lindzey, G., & Spuhler, J. *Race differences in intelligence.* San Francisco: Freeman, 1975.

Lord, F. M., & Novick, M. R. *Statistical theories of mental test scores.* Reading, Mass.: Addison-Wesley, 1968.

Lundberg, F. *The rich and the super-rich.* New York: Lyle Stuart, 1968.

Mandler, G. Verbal learning. In G. Mandler & P. Mussen (Eds.), *New directions in psychology* (Vol. 3). New York: Holt, 1967. pp. 1–50.

Matarazzo, J. D. *Wechsler's measurement and appraisal of adult intelligence* (5th ed.). Baltimore: Williams & Wilkins, 1972.

Mayeske, G. W., Okada, T., Beaton, A. E., Cohen, W. M., & Wisler, C. E. *A study of achievement of our nation's students.* Washington, D.C.: U.S. Government Printing Office, 1973.

McCall, R. B., Hogarty, P. S., & Hurlbert, N. Transitions in infant sensorimotor development and the prediction of childhood IQ. *American Psychologist,* 1972, **27**, 728–748.

Mednick, S. A. The associative basis of the creative process. *Psychological Review,* 1962, **69**, 220–232.

Miller, G. A. The magical number seven, plus or minus two: Some limits on our capacity for processing information. *Psychological Review,* 1956, **63,** 81–97.

Mosteller, F., & Moynihan, D. P. (Eds.). *On equality of educational opportunity.* New York: Vintage Books, 1972.

Murdock, B. B. The immediate retention of unrelated words. *Journal of Experimental Psychology,* 1960, **60,** 222–224.

Norman, D. A. *Memory and attention.* New York: Wiley, 1969.

Norman, D. A. (Ed.). *Models of human memory.* New York: Academic Press, 1970.

Norman, D. A. *Research considerations in the assessment of the (impaired) elderly.* Paper presented at the Conference on Cognition and Aging, Battelle Research Center, Seattle, January 1977.

Pawlik, K. Concepts in human cognitions and aptitudes. In R. B. Cattell (Ed.), *Handbook of multivariate experimental psychology.* Chicago: Rand McNally, 1966.

Pease, D., Wolins, L., & Stockdale, D. F. Relationship and predictions of infant tests. *Journal of Genetic Psychology,* 1973, **122,** 31–35.

Project TALENT. *Studies of the American high school.* Pittsburgh: Project TALENT, 1962.

Reese, H. W. The development of memory. In H. W. Reese & L. P. Lipsitt (Ed.), *Advances in child development and behavior* (Vol. 11). New York: Academic Press, 1976.

Reinert, R. Comparative factor analytic studies of intelligence throughout the human life-span. In L. T. Goulet & P. B. Baltes (Eds.), *Life-span developmental psychology.* New York: Academic Press, 1970.

Resnick, L. B. (Ed.). *The nature of intelligence.* Hillsdale, N.J.: Lawrence Erlbaum Associates, 1976.

Riegel, K. F. *Dialectic operations: The final period of cognitive development.* Princeton, N.J.: Educational Testing Service, 1973.

Roff, M. A statistical study of the development of intelligence test performance. *Journal of Psychology,* 1941, **11,** 371–386.

Schaie, K. W. External validity in the assessment of intellectual development in adulthood. *Proceedings of the 84th Annual Convention of the American Psychological Association,* 1976.

Schmidt, F. L., & Crano, W. D. A test of the theory of fluid and crystallized intelligence in middle- and low-socioeconomic-status children: A cross-lagged panel analysis. *Journal of Educational Psychology,* 1974, **66,** 255–261.

Spearman, C. *The abilities of man.* New York: Macmillan, 1927.

Thurstone, L. L. *Multiple-factor analysis.* Chicago: University of Chicago Press, 1947.

Tulving, E. Subjective organization in free recall of "unrelated" words. *Psychological Review,* 1962, **69,** 344–354.

Tulving, E. Episodic and semantic memory. In E. Tulving & W. Donaldson (Eds.), *Organization and memory.* New York: Academic Press, 1972.

Wallach, M. A., & Kogan, N. *Modes of thinking in young children.* New York: Holt, 1965.

Walsh, D. A. Age differences in learning and memory. In. D. S. Woodruff & J. E. Birren (Eds.), *Aging: Scientific perspectives and social issues.* New York: Reinhold-Van Nostrand, 1975.

Watson, J. S. Early learning and intelligence. In M. Lewis (Ed.), *Origins of intelligence.* New York: Plenum, 1975.

Waugh, N. C., & Norman, D. A. Primary memory. *Psychological Review,* 1965, **72,** 89–104.

Welford, A. T. *Aging and human skill.* London and New York: Oxford University Press, 1958.

Werner, E. E., & Bayley, N. The reliability of Bayley's revised scale of mental and rotar development during the first year of life. *Child Development,* 1966, **37,** 39–50.

Werts, C. E. Paternal influence on career choice. *National Merit Scholarship Corporation Research Reports,* 1967, **3,** 19.

White, P. O. Individual differences in speed, accuracy, and persistence: A mathematical model for problem solving. In H. J. Eysenck (Ed.), *The measurement of intelligence.* Baltimore: Williams & Wilkins, 1973.

Zajonc, R. B. Family configuration and intelligence. *Science,* 1976, **197,** 227–236.

Development of Females from Childhood through Adulthood: Career and Feminine Role Orientations

Aletha Huston-Stein

DEPARTMENT OF HUMAN DEVELOPMENT,
UNIVERSITY OF KANSAS,
LAWRENCE, KANSAS

and

Ann Higgins-Trenk

SCHOOL OF EDUCATION,
HARVARD UNIVERSITY,
CAMBRIDGE, MASSACHUSETTS

Abstract

Women's patterns of family and work roles are examined with attention to their antecedents in childhood and to developmental processes in early and middle adulthood. Age and cohort differences in sex role stereotypes are reviewed. Historical changes in women's roles during the past 30 years are examined in conjunction with an analysis of historical changes in sex role definitions, expectancies of both women and men concerning women's roles, and a variety of sociocultural factors that might account for changes in women's life patterns. Many social barriers to changes in women's roles remain, perhaps accounting for the fact that women continue to be employed predominantly in low status jobs.

Individual differences among women are also discussed in order to identify important influences on development. Childhood socialization of nontraditional behaviors and interests forms one clear antecedent of adult achievement orientation. Both developmental continuities and change in adulthood are considered with an attempt to derive hypotheses about ongoing processes of individual development. Finally, the consequences of different life patterns for women's self-esteem, life satisfaction, and mental health are considered with particular attention to those qualities which permit women to integrate a variety of roles successfully.

I. Introduction

The changing role of the American woman is so widely discussed in the literature and mass media that it has become almost a cliché. During the last 30 years, dramatic changes have taken place in women's participation in the labor force and, correspondingly, in their participation in home and family roles, particularly child rearing. The purpose of this chapter is to examine the developmental patterns followed by women across the life span with particular attention to the impact of social and historical changes. This broad topic is delimited in the following ways. First, we are focusing on women's participation in two major roles: work and family. We are concerned with early socialization toward assumption of one or both of these roles and with the patterns of actual adoption followed by adult women. Second, the discussion is concerned primarily with American women. Cross-cultural comparisons are made occasionally in order to illustrate a point, but no effort is made to cover the literature on women in other nations systematically. Finally, the time period on which we are focusing is the three decades since World War II. In some instances, data from earlier periods are introduced, but most of the available literature deals with the postwar period.

The questions examined in this chapter are organized into two major sections. In Section II, developmental patterns are examined with particular attention to age- and cohort-related changes; in Section III, historical changes and sociocultural influences are examined. Some of the questions addressed include: Are there age-related changes in people's understanding of sex roles? Does the attractiveness of traditional femininity change with age? Are there cohort differences in sex role attitudes that may be related to historical change? What are the various sequences or patterns followed by females with respect to participation in work and family roles? How have these changed over time? Have the sex role stereotypes in the society kept pace with the changes in women's behavior? Are young females being socialized in a way that is functional for their adult lives, or are they being taught sex role definitions that are outdated? Do the aspirations and expectations of females fit current reality or the likely reality of their future lives? What events or experiences pose demands for which females have not been prepared through socialization (e.g., college, divorce, the women's movement)? What are the major sociocultural influences on women's development? Do these influences affect different cohorts differently? Through what channels are they communicated (e.g., mass media)? In summary, the purpose of Section III is to determine developmental patterns and historical changes in life patterns followed by women, and to attempt to explain these changes through examination of sex role definitions and sociocultural variables.

In Section IV, individual differences in the patterns followed by women are discussed. It is not sufficient to describe the stages, roles, and institutions through which people pass; there are wide individual variations in normative patterns that need to be explained through examination of variables that differentiate women who are full-time homemakers, who return to work after having children, who maintain a continuous work pattern while marrying and having children, who remain single, and who follow other life patterns. Developmental continuities and developmental changes are examined with particular attention to the timing and sequencing of marriage, motherhood, education, and employment. Early socialization by parents as well as the influence of peers, schools, and family members are considered as possible sources of women's development.

Recent discussions of developmental theory and methods from a life-span perspective have highlighted a number of issues and assumptions that are pertinent to this examination of the development of women (cf. Baltes & Schaie, 1973; Goulet & Baltes, 1970; Nesselroade & Reese, 1973). In particular, the concept of development has been expanded beyond a concern with age-correlated changes to include behavior changes over time based on historical or sociocultural antecedents (Baltes, Cornelius, & Nesselroade, 1977). These models permit examination of a variety of sources of developmental change—ontogenetic, environmental, sociocultural—and help one to move away from the more unifocused approaches that have often appeared in the literature. For example, theorists of adult development have focused on age-correlated events or experiences, such as menopause, empty nest, or marriage, that they assume are watershed experiences for all women. Child development theorists have emphasized either ontogenetically based cognitive changes or environmental influences that are not necessarily related to chronological age. Life-span theorists and sociologists have brought greater attention to social, cultural, and historical changes as they influence the development of individuals (e.g., Baltes & Willis, 1976; Elder, 1975; Huston-Stein & Baltes, 1976; Riley, 1976).

In this chapter, a variety of sources of change are considered as possibilities in the interpretations of the literature. Those normative changes that are correlated with age and/or cohort are examined first; historical changes in women's behavior and in social role definitions and stereotypes about women are then examined with attention to possible sociocultural antecedents of these changes.

II.   Age and Cohort Differences in Role Choices

There are some relatively consistent, age-related patterns of sex role development that occur across a wide range of cohorts particularly during childhood and adolescence. These patterns suggest that ontogenetic change and/or age-correlated experiences are sources of early sex role learning. Cross-sectional age or cohort differences among adults seem more likely due to historical changes in the socialization experiences of different cohorts. Adults in different periods of their lives may also be influenced differently by current cultural change.

A.   AGE-CORRELATED PATTERNS IN CHILDHOOD

Knowledge of sex role stereotypes appears consistently during early childhood and increases gradually with age to an apparent asymptote. For example, preschool girls state highly sex-stereotyped occupational aspirations—teacher, nurse, or mother (Looft, 1971; Papalia & Tennent, 1975; Thornbur & Weeks, 1975). In different cohorts of children ranging from 3 to 7 years old, older females chose more feminine activities than younger ones (Hartup & Zook, 1960; Kohlberg & Zigler, 1967). At 6 or 7 years of age, most children knew what behaviors were sex-stereotyped (Emmerich, 1959; Kagan, Hosken, & Watson, 1961). By adolescence, there were fewer differences among age groups (Urberg & Labouvie-Vief, 1976), but some studies have found more clear knowledge of subtle sex role definitions among late adolescents than among elementary school children (Baruch, 1975; Stein, 1971; Stein & Smithells, 1969).

Although knowledge of sex stereotypes increases monotonically with age, attraction or preference for the female role appears to *decrease* during the elementary and adolescent years. A corresponding increase in attraction to masculine activities characterizes cohorts studied over a 50-year period. In a reanalysis of Terman's data on samples ranging from 8 to 20 years old, Kohlberg and Zigler (1967, p. 106) found that older females had more masculine interests than younger ones. Their own subjects also showed increased preference for a masculine model with age. In both studies, brighter females at a given age had more masculine preferences than those with average ability. In other studies, older girls preferred more masculine activities (Sutton-Smith, Rosenberg, & Morgan, 1963), more often preferred their fathers as models (Baruch, 1975), and viewed the female role less positively and the male role more positively (Smith, 1939) than younger females.

These age changes are relatively independent of time of measurement. Given their consistency, it is surprising that they have not been emphasized in earlier writing; most often they have been treated as aberrant failures to confirm hypotheses. Two interpretations for these data are plausible. The cognitive developmental level of very young children may make them prone to highly stereotyped thinking. As thought becomes more flexible and abstract in middle childhood and adolescence, it may be easier for children to understand and tolerate deviation from stereotypes. Second, with simple accumulation of experience over time, knowledge of stereotypes may be increased and refined. At the same time, children may increasingly appreciate the greater value and recognition attached to masculine activities in American society. The fact that brighter children shift to masculine preferences earlier than less bright females may indicate that they learn societal norms more quickly.

The developmental pattern of decreasing attraction to feminine activities and increasing preference for masculine activities has implications for the concept of role conflict that is usually invoked to describe the incompatibility of adult family and work roles. These data suggest that conflict begins in childhood with the girl's growing recognition that the role society prescribes for her is not a socially valued one. Children have faced this conflict for many years if our interpretation of the data collected in the 1920s and 1930s is correct. The recent social changes that give women more latitude to achieve and to engage actively in a career may be reducing rather than increasing the role conflicts experienced by many females because newer sex role prescriptions are more consistent with activities that are rewarded in the society.

B. AGE–COHORT DIFFERENCES AMONG ADULTS

Cross-sectional age–cohort differences also appear in the adult years. Older adults generally have more traditional attitudes about appropriate activities for women than young adults. Older people are less likely to approve of working mothers (Boedecker, 1975; Etaugh, 1973, Nye, 1974d), to have egalitarian attitudes about women (Yorberg & Arafat, 1975), and are more likely to advocate large families and early marriage (Boedecker, 1975).

These findings appear more likely to be a function of cohort differences in experience than of changes associated with age. For example, in one comparison of two similar samples of middle-aged women studied in 1955 and 1974, respectively, the earlier cohort thought women should marry younger than the later one (Boedecker, 1975). Older cohorts experienced more traditional sex role definitions during early socialization than younger ones. In addition, older people have made life choices about childbearing and work that are not reversible. As their choices more often followed a traditional pattern, they may be more resistant to changing cultural attitudes about women's roles than are young adults who still have more options from which to choose. Considerably more data incorporating systematic variations of cohort, age, and time of measurement (Baltes, 1968; Schaie, 1965; Schaie & Baltes, 1975) are needed to evaluate the hypothesis that the developmental patterns observed in adulthood are primarily a function of historical changes.

Different explanatory processes appear to account for age changes in childhood and adulthood. Cognitive developmental changes and age-related exposure to social norms appear to be important processes in children's sex role development. In adulthood, environmental variables and sociocultural change appear to be more important. With a few exceptions, the latter are not associated consistently with chronological age. One implication of this view is that the developmental changes described are not necessarily unidirectional because sociocultural change is not unidirectional.

C. SUMMARY

Children learn sex role stereotypes during the preschool years; with increasing age, their knowledge of stereotypes is increased and refined reaching an apparent asymptote in adolescence. Girls' preference or attraction to feminine activities, however, declines during middle childhood and adolescence while attraction to masculine activities increases. These age trends appear in cohorts sampled over approximately 50 years. Both cognitive developmental changes and accumulated exposure to societal values are suggested as sources of these developmental changes. Among adults, older cohorts have more traditional views of the female role than younger cohorts when measured at one point in time. These cohort differences seem to result from historical and cultural change rather than from age-related change.

III. Historical Changes in Role Choices

A. WORK AND FAMILY PATTERNS

1. Work

From the turn of the century until 1940, 20% of women 14 years old and older worked and they were characteristically young, single, and poor. Since 1940 there has been a steady increase in the number of white, married women in the work force (Nye, 1974d; VanDusen & Sheldon, 1976). The percent of married women who were employed rose at a fairly even rate from 15% in 1940 to 43% in 1974.

More important, women are increasingly engaging in outside employment during periods of their lives when they have demanding child-rearing responsibilities. Earlier in the century, the typical female worker was young; many women discontinued employment after marriage or at least after the birth of a child and did not return. During World War II the middle-aged women with no children at home first broke the previous pattern of working women as young and single. During the 1950s a wave of married women with school-age children began work, and by the late 1960s the greatest influx of women into the labor market was those with preschool children (Chafe, 1976). Clearly, a great many American women are combining employment with performing their roles as mother and homemaker at a very demanding period of their family life. This recent pattern—that women are either maintaining continuous employment during the years when they are marrying and having children, or they are returning to the job market when their children are still quite young—has not been sufficiently noted (Oppenheimer, 1973).

Continuous employment is particularly common for well-educated women. In 1970, 56% of the women with college degrees and 71% of those with work beyond the bachelor's degree were employed as compared with 31% of those with 8 years of schooling or less. While these differences may be partly a reflection of cohort differences in education, they are consistent with other data. For example, in a 1966 national sample of women who had graduated from college 7 years earlier, 91% of those with a doctorate, 71% of those with a master's degree, and 45% of those with a baccalaureate were employed (Wells, 1966).

Historically, black women were much more likely to be gainfully employed than were white women. Today black women still are more likely than white women to work outside the home, and young black women at various educational levels more often expect to work and aspire to careers than do white women (Fichter, 1971; Lott & Lott, 1963). Educated black married women have fewer children than comparable white women (Bram, 1974).

2. Changes in Women's Status and Roles

Employment outside the home does not necessarily change the social status of women. Knudson (1966) argues that women's status has declined since the 1930s; the increases in employment have occurred in relatively low status, poorly paid jobs, primarily white collar clerical work. The percentage of women workers in professional and managerial positions remained relatively steady from 1940 to 1960. The difference between salaries of men and women continues to be dramatic (median earnings of women in 1974 were $6,772 compared with $11,835 for men).

Perhaps equally important for the individual lives of women over time is the fact that assuming an outside occupational role does not bring significant changes in performance of home and family roles. Women who work outside the home also have the major responsibility for child care and for operating the household. For example, in a national sample of American adults, employed women spent an average of 3 hours and 40 min a day on housework, household obligations, and child care; employed men spent 1 hour and 15 min on such activities (Robinson, 1971). The reduction of home work is not the usual concomitant of increased market work for women (Kreps & Leaper, 1976). Even among couples where both are highly trained professionals with full-time positions, the wife assumes primary responsibility for the house and the children (Holmstrom, 1973; Poloma & Garland, 1971a). In one of these studies, the husband's participation in child care is called "baby-sitting" and his assumption of housework is labeled "helping around the house"—a clear indication of where the responsibility lies.

3. Marriage and Childbearing

Following the war until about 1960, young women were more likely to marry, they married younger, they had children earlier, and they had more children than comparable cohorts in earlier time periods. Sometime in the late 1950s or early 1960s, these trends reversed. Since that time, women are more likely to remain single in early adulthood, they marry later, they have fewer children, and they have their children later. Women born during the postwar baby boom began the reversal by marrying a year or two later (average age at marriage in 1950 was 20.3 years, in 1960 20 years, and in 1974 21.1 years). The birth rate demonstrated similar increases following the war with a peak of 25 births per 1,000 in 1957; since that time, it has dropped steadily to a rate slightly lower than that of the 1930s (16 births per 1,000).

Modell, Furstenberg, and Strong (1977) suggest that during and after the Great Depression the traditional economic criteria for timing of marriage and parenthood no longer existed, and the youth of the 1940s and 1950s were the first generation to gain the ability to schedule decisions according to their personal timetables. Paradoxically, these young people scheduled their lives in close synchronization with each other creating strong norms for the appropriate age at which to marry and the appropriate time after marriage to begin a family. For instance, the number of years within which three-fourths of a cohort marries has been cut in half from the turn of the century (18.9) years to the present (8.3 years). In 1960, 70% of married women had one child within 2 years of getting married. It was not until 1965 that the spread of age at marriage and conscious postponement of the birth of children increased, thus ending the effect of the Depression and World War II on family life-styles.

One outcome of these trends in women's lives is that many more young women are childless. The data suggest that a higher proportion will remain childless permanently than in the immediately preceding time periods. For instance, the percentage of ever-married women who were childless in three age groups in 1960 was: 15–19 = 44%, 20–24 = 24%, 25–29 = 13%. In 1974: 15–19 = 56%, 20–24 = 41%, 25–29 = 20%. About one-fourth of those in the latter category expected to remain childless.

Still another significant change is the increased rate of divorce and the fact that divorce occurs more often at an early age. For example, in 1960, the modal age of divorced persons was over 45; by 1974, there were more divorced persons under 45 than over (VanDusen & Sheldon, 1976). At the current rate of divorce more than a quarter of the women who are now about 30 years old have ended or will end their first marriage in divorce (Glick & Norton, 1973). A very high proportion of divorced women are employed (70%; 62% of those with preschool children).

4. Education

Until 1974 women's educational attainment in average number of years completed exceeded that of men (in 1952 women completed 12.0 years and men 10.4 years of school); in 1974 both sexes completed about 12.5 years of school. Educational/vocational training continues to be relatively segregated by sex. In post-high school vocational training 95% of the health courses and 79% of the commercial (clerical) courses are taken by women and 98% of the technical, industrial, and trade courses are taken by men (Kreps & Leaper, 1976).

In the past 5 years, the proportion of women entering college and professional training has increased relative to males. For instance, there has been a 30% increase in college enrollment of women compared with a 12% increase for men (VanDusen & Sheldon, 1976). The percentage of women enrolled in law schools and medical schools, while still small, has increased steadily since 1960. In addition, more women are in college during the age range from 25 to 34 years (VanDusen & Sheldon, 1976). Again, it appears that women are less likely to spend a significant period of their early adult lives in full-time homemaking; during the age period when they are most likely to have young children, they are going to school in greater numbers than in earlier periods.

5. *Changes in Women's Life Patterns*

Two features of these historical trends suggest striking changes in the life patterns of women during the past 30 years. The modal pattern is no longer one in which women are solely homemakers and mothers throughout their adult lives. Perhaps more interesting, it is becoming increasingly common for women to maintain relatively continuous patterns of involvement in outside employment and/or education even during the period of their lives when they are involved in the care of young children. Of course, living ouside marriage during some parts of adult life either through remaining single or being divorced is also a part of many more women's life patterns. Finally, there has been a shift in the past 15 years toward greater involvement in occupational roles and less involvement in family and maternal roles.

The second striking aspect of these trends is that the increase in education and employment has been almost linear and steady since the war, while the changes in marriage and family patterns have been curvilinear. Until 1960, employment of married women increased at the same time that women were marrying earlier, having more children, and generally assuming more family responsibilities. Since 1960, the family commitments of women have declined, and employment has continued to rise. Thus, one cannot make any simplistic statements concerning the relation between a woman's assumption of family roles and her likely involvement in outside employment.

B. ATTITUDES, STEREOTYPES, AND EXPECTANCIES ABOUT FEMALES

Our search for the antecedents and consequences of these historical changes in the life patterns of females begins with an examination of the beliefs and stereotypes about women in the society and correspondingly the attitudes and expectancies that females have for their own lives. The first question is whether beliefs and attitudes have changed over time in a way that corresponds to the changes in women's behavior. Obviously, any cause-and-effect relation between changes in belief and behavior is probably complex and multidirectional. Nevertheless, if the social stereotypes about appropriate behavior for women are not congruent with the likely future lives of today's children, then young females are being socialized in a maladaptive way for roles that are different from those they will have to assume as adults.

1. Female Expectancies and Stereotypes

There have been changes over time in sex role stereotypes and in female's expectancies about their life patterns that correspond to the changes in behavior already discussed, but in some cases the stereotypes appear to lag well behind reality. Samples of college women questioned in 1971 more often expected to obtain graduate degrees and to pursue a career, usually in combination with marriage, than had earlier cohorts (Cross, 1971; Komarovsky, 1973; Lockheed, 1975). Similarly, fewer members of recent cohorts expected to be solely housewives and mothers or thought that women should confine themselves to home and family. By 1970, the modal response of young women about their future had shifted from homemaker to an interrupted career pattern (a career with some years spent at home when children are young) (Almquist, 1974b; Cross, 1971; Komarovsky, 1973). The number who expected to pursue a continuous career, usually in combination with marriage, was 20% in both 1950 and 1971 in one college (Komarovsky, 1973). In one of the few longitudinal studies of developing career aspirations through the college years, about 20% were career-committed throughout college, but another 22% converted and aspired to careers by their senior year (Angrist, 1972).

There have been parallel decreases during the past 15 years in women's expected involvement in marriage and childbearing. For instance, in 1955, 38% of ever-married women in the 18–24 age group expected to have four or more children; in 1974, the figure was 8%. Among college women, the number who wish to remain childless has also increased (Bram, 1974).

More recent cohorts of females also describe themselves as less conforming to traditional feminine personality attributes. Female students in 1971 were less likely than those in 1950 to say that they try to hide their intellect or try to make a man feel he is superior intellectually (Komarovsky, 1973). Samples of women tested from 1954 to 1966 showed increased frequency of self-orientation as opposed to other orientation (Gump, 1972). Self-orientation in this research was associated with career orientation and negatively related to traditional femininity.

On the whole, then, it appears that the aspirations and plans of young women, at least those who attend college, have reflected the changing social conditions and life patterns of women over the past two decades. Women increasingly plan to be employed, either continuously or with some interruption during the years when children are young. The number of children expected has declined, corresponding fairly closely to changing patterns of actual family size.

2. *Male Expectancies about Women's Roles*

While young women appear to be adapting to changing social conditions, young men have different expectations about the patterns their wives will follow. Exact percentages vary across locales, but very few college men (4–7%) want their wives to work continuously or express any willingness to alter their own lives or careers to provide work opportunities for their wives. From 40 to 60% favor an interrupted career pattern, but most often this means they think the wife should not work until children have completed school. A large number do not want their wives to work, especially after children are born (Almquist, 1974a; Komarovsky, 1973; McMillin, 1972). Although many men want an intellectually equal companion with her own interests and talents, few seem aware of the need for such women to have a career rather than an occasional job, and most do not recognize the difficulties inherent in long interruptions of a career.

3. *Sex Role Stereotypes*

Despite the changes in women's employment, achievement patterns, and expectations, stereotypes of females as incompetent, emotional, unable to handle high level jobs, and generally inferior persist to a remarkable degree. Both men and women students associate many undesirable characteristics with women (Herman & Sedlacek, 1973; Ross & Walters, 1973). Students and others rated magazine articles and art works as less competent when they believed a woman had produced them than when the same works carried a man's name (Goldberg, 1968; Pheterson, Kiesler, & Goldberg, 1971). Exceptions occurred when the articles concerned childrearing or when the art works were described as prize winners (Pheterson *et al.,* 1971).

Women are less preferred in college admissions (Walster, Cleary, & Clifford, 1971) and by employers (Clifford & Looft, 1971; Fidell, 1970; Rosen & Jerdee, 1974) than men with identical qualifications, particularly when both fall in the average range of performance. Although one recent study failed to find differences in ratings given hypothetical male and female job applicants by high school and college students, the authors' argument that their results reflect changing sex role stereotypes may be premature (Soto & Cole, 1975).

Stereotypes of females as incompetent, emotional, and the like continue to operate in many areas. When a woman has clearly superior ability or recognized status, she is not stereotyped, but the "average" female is viewed less favorably than the "average" male. Perhaps the relative absence of stereotyping of the superior female explains the finding that college students rated career women more favorably than other types of women (Peterson, 1975) and rated a female with masculine interests more favorably than one with feminine interests (Kristal, Sanders, Spence, & Helmreich, 1975). However, women with "masculine" personality characteristics and women who reject femininity by wishing to remain childless continue to be negatively stereotyped (Bram, 1974; Kristal *et al.*, 1975; O'Leary, 1974; Shields, 1973).

4. Media Portrayals of Females

Television and children's books—two of the most potentially powerful socializing influences for young children—are among the most intransigent purveyors of traditional sex role stereotypes. On television, married women are portrayed as caring for husband, hearth, and children; employed women are usually single and typically work in traditionally female occupations such as secretary, nurse, and teacher (DeFleur, 1964; Kaniuga, Scott & Gade, 1974; Stein & Friedrich, 1975). Children's literature, especially for preschool children, is equally out of touch with the reality of women's lives (Nilsen, 1971). Among recent winners of a major prize for children's books, employed women were virtually absent, and motherhood was presented as a full-time, lifelong job. The three women who were not mothers were a fairy godmother, a fairy, and an underwater maiden (Weitzman, Eifler, Hokada, & Ross, 1971).

The media could play an important role in stimulating or facilitating social change rather than lagging behind it. In Finland, between 1966 and 1970, there was a planned media campaign stressing women's equality. Of representative samples across that nation questioned in 1966, 50% expressed egalitarian attitudes about women; in 1970, 80–90% of similar samples gave egalitarian responses (Haavio-Manila, 1972).

5. Stereotypes in Social Science

At the opposite extreme from popular stereotypes, but perhaps equally important influences on social institutions and parents, are the beliefs and stereotypes in the writings of social scientists. Helson (1972) built a telling case for the proposition that social scientists have shifted from negative to positive evaluations of career-oriented females in the past 25–30 years. In earlier writings, she argued, negative, abnormal traits of career women were emphasized while more recent works have interpreted many of the same empirical findings with a positive bias. Similarly, writings on working mothers appear to have shifted from a purely defensive posture of examining the possible harmful effects of maternal employment to a consideration of possible positive benefits for women and their families (Hoffman & Nye, 1974; Nye & Hoffman, 1963).

Although social scientists appear to have caught up with the times, there was some lag. Helson (1972) considered the 1966 book on educated women by Ginsberg as the beginning of the positive trend. Attempts to study achievement motivation in women first appeared in the mid-1960s (Stein & Bailey, 1973). The shift from the assumption that "appropriate" sex roles were most desirable to a focus on androgyny (Bem, 1972; 1975), and sex role transcendence (Hefner, Rebecca, & Oleshansky, 1975) are even more recent. By the time social scientists recognized the phenomenon of changing sex roles, behavior changes had been going on for some time.

6. Influence of Stereotypes on Female Development

Few direct links between social stereotypes and individual development can be found, but the overall patterns exhibited by females in our culture suggest that they are influenced from an early age by stereotypes concerning female competence. Such influence is likely to result both from discriminatory treatment by others and from internalization of the stereotypes by females themselves. In an earlier review (Stein & Bailey, 1973), evidence was assembled showing that females have lower expectancies of success across many tasks, lower levels of aspiration, more anxiety about failure, less willingness to risk failure, and more feeling of personal responsibility when failure occurs than males. These differences appear during middle childhood and appear to increase with age.

The sexes also differ in the causes that they attribute to success and failure. Attributions can be classified in four categories: ability, effort, task difficulty, and luck (Weiner, 1974). The first two are internal to the person; the latter two are external. Earlier research indicated that girls more often attributed success and failure, particularly failure, to internal causes than boys (Crandall, Katkovsky, & Crandall, 1965). In a more recent study of children (Dweck & Reppucci, 1973), girls attributed failure to lack of ability, whereas boys more often thought failure was due to lack of effort or luck. Conversely, college students attributed male success to ability and female success to effort or luck (Feldman-Summers & Kiesler, 1974; Frieze, 1975). When females perform traditionally masculine activities, their successes are even more likely to be attributed to unusual effort or luck (Taynor & Deaux, 1973) and they are blamed more for their failures (Shaw & McMartin, 1975). On the whole, it appears that females accept the stereotyped view that they are less competent, particularly in "masculine" activities. They attribute success to unusual effort or situational factors, yet they consider failure as due to ability.

How might this pattern of attributions arise from existing stereotypes? Perhaps evaluations of female performance by teachers and parents are more arbitrary and use less explicit criteria than evaluations of males. Girls may learn that in some situations they are judged according to lower standards than those used for boys (based on the idea that girls cannot be expected to do as well); in other situations they may have to perform better to gain recognition because people discount their performance as a result of luck rather than ability. These experiences could lead girls to a pattern of caution until a situation is clear before risking action.

C. SOCIOCULTURAL INFLUENCES ON WOMEN'S LIFE PATTERNS

The historical changes in women's patterns of adopting family and work roles and in the attitudes about women's roles that have occurred in American society suggest that sociocultural changes should be examined as antecedents. Some social changes are consistent with the changing life patterns of women. What is more striking is the number of social conditions that continue to present barriers to women's employment or to combining family and work roles. In some respects, we emerged from this analysis feeling surprised that women have made such dramatic changes in their lives given the lack of societal supports.

Two social changes have paralleled the increase in women's employment since World War II: increasing *demand for female labor* and a *rising divorce rate*. Oppenheimer (1973) pointed out that the demand for female workers increased greatly in the postwar years because the number of available jobs in predominantly female occupations (e.g., teachers, nurses, clerical workers) increased at a higher rate than those in many male occupations. At the same time, the supply of unmarried females was low, so there was considerable inducement for married women to enter the labor market. In recent years, female professional jobs, especially teaching, have declined, so most of the demand for female labor is in low status occupations (VanDusen & Sheldon, 1976).

The divorce rate hit a peak in the few years following the war, then dropped and has been steadily rising since that time. Divorce can be both an antecedent and a consequence of women's employment. The capacity to support herself may give a woman more freedom to end an unhappy marriage and, obviously, divorce often forces a woman to earn a living because she must support herself and her children. The divorce rate has not yet peaked and, although it will do so within the next decade or two if the marriage rate remains constant (Glick & Norton, 1973), there is no reason to expect a decline. Moreover, each cohort is experiencing a larger percentage of divorces at earlier ages resulting in a continuing increase in the number of single women with children to support.

In an earlier section, it was pointed out that women's employment has increased monotonically since World War II, but rates of fertility and early marriage have followed a curvilinear pattern with a peak in the late 1950s. The demand for female labor and the divorce rate have paralleled the monotonic trend of employment patterns. Two other social changes have accompanied the drop in family role involvement since 1960: the *women's movement* and *concern about overpopulation*. Each of these trends may, of course, be both cause and effect of the changes in women's behavior. Feminist organizations have achieved some reduction in legalized discrimination in education and hiring. In the past 5 years, for instance, the percent of women students in medical and law schools has increased considerably (VanDusen & Sheldon, 1976). Equally important, however, may be the less tangible results of the movement in providing social support for women who deviate from traditional roles and who fight unfair treatment.

The concern about overpopulation has generated some social pressure and propaganda that probably contribute to the declining birth rate. Fertility is negatively correlated with married women's employment (Hoffman, 1974). From a developmental perspective, a woman whose first one or two children reach school age may now be more likely to seek employment rather than deciding to have another baby. The possibility for reversing these trends is illustrated on some Israeli kibbutzim where women returned to performing traditional roles after an earlier period of sex role equality at least partly because of pressure to populate the kibbutz by bearing more children (Mednick, 1975).

1.   Barriers to Changing Women's Roles

Despite the trends discussed, the barriers to women's participation in the work world, particularly in combination with raising a family, are still considerable. Discrimination in education and employment has been reduced, but by no means eliminated (Astin & Bayer, 1975; VanDusen & Sheldon, 1976). Furthermore, women's perception of discrimination increases with exposure to it in the market place (Gould & Pagano, 1972). Hence, perception of discrimination may be a more important barrier to continuing and advanced achievement by women who are already invested in a career than it is to initial entry into the labor market.

Another barrier recurrent in our history, particularly in times of high unemployment, is the specious belief that men should have priority for jobs because they are breadwinners for families while women work merely to supplement a family income. The fallacy of this argument is clearly illustrated by the fact that three-fifths of the female labor force in 1974 was comprised of women who were unmarried, divorced, separated, widowed, or whose husbands earned less than $7,000 a year (U.S. Department of Labor, 1974). Female-headed households are much more likely than male-headed households to fall below the poverty threshold; hence, a disproportionately high number of children in this country are growing up in poverty (VanDusen & Sheldon, 1976). Like all discriminated-against groups, women are hurt more severely by economic recession than men. In the recent recession, unemployment increased more among women than men (VanDusen & Sheldon, 1976).

2. *Structure and Demands of Available Occupations*

Because most married women or women with children must fulfill the roles of housewife and mother, the ease with which an occupation can be integrated with family roles affects a woman's chances for pursuing it. Many professional and managerial occupations demand extreme amounts of time, travel, and assignment of priorities to the job. Some almost require a spouse "helpmate" to fulfill the job role (Papanek, 1973). This is more true of some professions that involve employment in an institutional context such as a university or a large corporation than of professions such as medicine where one can operate as an independent entrepreneur. One of the likely reasons that teaching is selected by so many married women is the time schedule that permits them to be home when their children are not in school. Even though lower status occupations demand less commitment, many of them have long, inflexible hours which make the fulfillment of family responsibilities difficult. For instance, if mother and father both have to be at work at 8:00 and the children leave for school at 8:45, who fills that time gap?

The occupational structure has not been modified to any significant degree by creation of part-time jobs or job sharing—patterns that would permit women (and/or men) to meet family obligations. Gronseth (1972) argues that as long as the husband role continues to be primarily defined as one of economic provider by industrial and capitalist institutions of Western societies and is buttressed by existing attitudes of its appropriateness, normality, and desirability, the career plans and potential achievements of women necessarily will remain secondary and, thus, underdeveloped.

3. Child Care

Despite the considerable rise in employment of mothers with young children, child-care facilities have remained scarce and inadequate. For instance, day-care centers provided for only 10% of all preschool children of working mothers in 1970 (Moore & Sawhill, 1976). Adequate child care might permit more women with large families to be employed. Hoffman (1974) pointed out that the negative correlation between fertility and employment does not exist in countries where there are strong extended family systems that presumably supply child care readily.

D. SUMMARY

Historical and cultural changes over time appear to be major influences on patterns of assuming home and work roles. Since World War II, there have been dramatic increases in women's participation in the labor market and in higher education. More important, married women are entering roles outside the home earlier in the family life cycle—many of them during their children's preschool years. Although the increase in married women's employment has been linear, the changes in family role participation have been curvilinear; early marriage and a high birth rate reached a peak in the late 1950s and have declined since that time. Hence, the relationship of employment and family commitments is not simply an inverse one.

A variety of sociocultural influences have been examined in relation to these trends in women's lives. Although the expectancies and attitudes of women about their involvement in work and family roles have changed with their actual engagement in these roles, negative sex role stereotypes concerning feminine competency and interests remain strong and pervasive. These stereotypes are manifested in discriminatory behavior by employers and in reluctance by many men to accept changes in women's roles. They pervade the early socialization experiences of young girls, particularly in children's books and television programs. Moreover, females of all ages appear to internalize the stereotypes to some degree with the result that they lack confidence in their abilities and attribute their successes and failures to causes beyond their control.

Sociocultural barriers to women's achievement take the form of discrimination and a set of social structures that make being responsible to a family and career/job incompatible (e.g., the occupational structure, lack of good child care, the continuation of traditional familial roles). The large increase in women's employment has been attributed by some analysts to the increased demand in female jobs and to the climbing divorce rate since the war. In recent years, the women's movement, concern with overpopulation, and legal actions for equal opportunity have added force, but the continuing barriers to women's achievement may partially account for the fact that women continue to be employed primarily in dead-end, poorly paid jobs.

E.   WHAT ABOUT THE FUTURE?

The numbers of women working and of educated women working are increasing so rapidly, it is difficult to predict even a few years into the future. Moreover, the number of women receiving bachelor's degrees is expected to increase by two-thirds between 1968 and 1980 (twice the rate for men), and the proportion of women in medical, law, and architectural schools have more than doubled in the early 1970s, creating a pool of potential career women unknown heretofore. Estimates for the future indicate that the average woman's work life will be only about a decade shorter than that of men (Kreps, 1976).

Three questions arise in light of the increasing participation of women in the labor force. Will women in the future work at jobs or engage in careers? Will they continue to occupy the lower rungs of the occupational status ladder in jobs with low salaries and little possibility of advancement, or do recent trends signal an expansion by women into a variety of job and career roles?

Second, what roles will define marriage and the nuclear family as institutions? Nye (1974b) surveyed evidence that the therapeutic and recreational roles of marriage are becoming more important, while the responsibility to kin in the extended family and housekeeping in the nuclear family are becoming optional components. Bearing and rearing children are also becoming less central features of marriage.

Third, who will rear the children? In a society that prizes individual freedom as highly as does ours, it seems that primary responsibility for bearing and rearing children will continue to be carried out through the private decisions of individuals and families. However, the practical burden of child care may shift to the domain of educational and day-care institutions.

If the feminist movement continues to challenge traditional structures and becomes more successful in its attempt to reach all segments of our society, and if the economic conditions of inflation and recession are kept under control so job scarcity and unemployment do not mushroom, then innovations in the marriage/work world interface may create qualitatively different life patterns for both women and men. As more women assume careers, the primary functions of marriage will be procreative, recreative,

and emotional support-giving among family members. Ideally, couples
will bear children and families will live together in the way they choose,
but being a mother will not imply complete responsibility for the daily
care of children and/or adults.

IV. Individual Differences in Development among Women

In the preceding section, normative differences among cohorts, historical time periods, and age groups were examined in an effort to determine
some of the important influences on women's development. As we assume that development is multidirectional and strongly influenced by
social–environmental factors, examination of individual differences
among females is another potentially fruitful way to ferret out sources of
developmental change. The focus here is on those factors that contribute
to differential patterns or sequences of assuming family and work roles.
That is, following Wohlwill's (1970) suggestion, changes with age are
viewed as the dependent variable to be explained wherever the data
permit such an approach. More often, it is necessary to piece together
information from many studies in an effort to draw tentative inferences
about changes over time.

The stability and sequencing of developmental patterns are examined in
the following discussion with attention both to continuity of individual
development and to processes of developmental change. Then the
socializing influences of family, schools, and peers on the development of
traditional or nontraditional role orientations are discussed.

A. DEVELOPMENTAL CONTINUITIES

Women who are career-oriented or achievement-oriented as adults are
likely to exhibit related personality characteristics such as aggressive-
ness, dominance, objectivity, independence, assertiveness, and adven-
turousness. These attributes define the socially valued elements of mascu-
linity rather completely. Such women are also more often interested in
traditionally masculine activities than homemakers (Bachtold, 1973;
Bachtold & Werner, 1971, 1972, 1973; Broverman, Vogel, Broverman,
Clarkson, & Rosenkrantz, 1972; Hoffman, 1974; Tangri, 1972, Welch,
in press). Although achievement-oriented women have more masculine
attributes, they are not less feminine or less skilled in performing marital
and maternal roles (Birnbaum, 1975; Broverman *et al.*, 1972; Crandall &
Battle, 1970; Welch, in press).

Individual differences in achievement orientation and in attraction to traditionally feminine activities are remarkably consistent from middle childhood through adulthood. In two samples studied longitudinally at the Fels Research Institute, achievement striving in adulthood was highly correlated with observed achievement behavior in middle childhood and early adolescence (Crandall & Battle, 1970; Kagan & Moss, 1962). Achievement behavior was more consistent over time than any other attribute studied. In these and other longitudinal studies, career orientation in adolescence and young adulthood was related to masculine play interests in childhood (Crandall & Battle, 1970; Tyler, 1964), interest in masculine subject matter (Sears & Barbee, 1975), and independence (Kagan & Moss, 1962). One implication of the continuity from childhood to adulthood is that childhood socialization experiences are important antecedents of women's choices throughout their lives.

Stability during early adulthood is indicated in a survey of approximately 6,000 women graduates of 153 colleges who were studied immediately after their graduation in 1957 and again in 1964 (Wells, 1966). Stated career plans at graduation were good predictors of subsequent employment and of career plans 7 years later. Of those who said they wanted a career in 1957, 59% gave the same response in 1964 while 5% said they did not plan to work. Of those with no plans to work outside the home in 1975, 9% wanted a career in 1964 and 41% had no plans to work.

B. DEVELOPMENTAL CHANGES

1. Sequences in Young Adulthood

Although many of the antecedents of young women's decisions about careers and families occur in childhood, early adulthood is a critical period. Behavioral choices about marriage and childbearing are made that are not easily reversed and that strongly influence the subsequent course of development. Women who choose not to marry during this period or who plan to have no children become more invested in a career than those who marry and plan a family (Bram, 1974; Wells, 1966). Although a woman may remain single partly because of strong career interests, the work experience that she has because of her need to support herself may also lead to some developmental changes in the direction of increasing involvement in her career. For example, some of the professional women interviewed by Poloma and Garland (1971a) said that they had originally pursued professional training because they were not yet married.

At any educational level, women with preschool children are less likely to be employed than those with older children or without children (Astin, 1971; Nye, 1974d; Wells, 1966). The later a woman makes this transition, the more education she is likely to have completed and the more job experience she is likely to have had (Harmon, 1970; Wells, 1966). Both the amount of education and the amount of early job experience affect the probability that a woman will continue her career during her childrearing years or that she will reenter employment. For example, in a 12-year follow-up of college entrants, those who were committed to a career had married later, had their first child approximately 2 years later, had fewer children, and had completed more advanced education than those who were not committed to a career (Harmon, 1970). A small group of married professional women studied in midlife had typically deferred childbearing until 5 or more years after marriage (Holmstrom, 1973). Women doctorates who worked full time after completing their degrees were more likely to continue career involvement than those who did not (Astin, 1971). In another survey, employed married women with children had more early job experience in higher status occupations than did homemakers (Weil, 1971).

These data indicate that the *timing* of marriage, childbearing, education, and work have long-term implications for the life patterns of women. At one extreme, the probability of thwarted education and poverty accompanying adolescent motherhood is very high (Bacon, 1974). The causal relations involved are undoubtedly multidirectional. Initial differences in orientation to family and career roles probably affect young women's choices. However, once a choice is made, particularly having a child, the range of options becomes more limited, or at least some become more difficult to pursue. Although the majority of college women now anticipate both a career and marriage, they are often unrealistic about the difficulties of combining child rearing with a career (Shields, 1973). Many may make choices affecting their future life patterns without adequate understanding of the implications of those decisions.

Developmental change may also result from the experience, sense of competence, and status gained in the work world if a woman does delay childbearing. Although she may enter advanced education or employment without a firm commitment to a career, her involvement in her work may increase over time. For example, Austrian women with white collar jobs increasingly regarded the work world as indispensable for their lives the longer they combined employment with family responsibilities (Haller & Rosenmayr, 1971).

2. *Dynamics of Development—The Fall of Cinderella*

Despite the difficulties, increasing numbers of married women are returning to higher education or to employment after they have children, and increasing numbers are experiencing divorce which often coincides with reentry into education or vocation. These women have higher career commitment than women who receive their education earlier in their lives. For instance, divorced women, widowed women, and women who attained college degrees after their children were born were more likely to be employed and more often planned a continuing career 7 years after graduation than other married women or single women (Wells, 1966). In a national survey of 33,000 graduate students, divorced women also had higher levels of commitment and productivity than married or single women despite the fact that 70% of them had at least one child (S. D. Feldman, 1973).

The higher career commitment of divorced and older married women may result partly from self-selection. Those who are achievement-oriented may be more likely to make the considerable effort and sacrifice involved in returning to school while maintaining family responsibilities. Analogously, in some instances, career aspirations may be one precipitating factor in a divorce. However, these data may also reflect a dynamic process of development with some parallels to the notion of midlife crisis for men (Brim, 1976). Young girls in America have traditionally been socialized in the Cinderella myth. Prince Charming will sweep them away, give them some babies, and all will live happily ever after. Marriage and motherhood will be the ultimate life satisfactions. For some, the myth works moderately well, but for many, the reality brings disillusionment and a search for other avenues of fulfillment.

Divorce is the most dramatic confrontation with the failure of the Cinderella myth, but disillusionment also occurs for many who remain married. Women who choose further education or employment after such a process probably do so with more serious intent and more sense of the long-term meaning for their lives than those who still believe that their ultimate satisfaction lies in home and motherhood.

C. SOCIALIZATION INFLUENCES

One implication of the continuity of achievement orientation from childhood to adulthood is that childhood socialization experiences are important antecedents of women's choices throughout their lives. The influence of parents, peers, and schools on development in childhood and adolescence and socializing influences in adulthood are discussed in the following section.

1. Maternal Employment

The most consistent and well-documented correlate of career orientation and departure from traditional feminine roles is maternal employment during childhood and adolescense. Daughters of employed mothers (i.e., mothers who were employed during some period of the daughter's childhood or adolescence) more often aspire to a career outside the home (Almquist & Angrist, 1971; Hoffman, 1974; Stein, 1973), get better grades in college (Nichols & Schauffer, 1975), and aspire to more advanced education (Hoffman, 1974; Stein, 1973). College women who have chosen a traditionally masculine occupation more often had employed mothers than those preparing for feminine occupations (Almquist, 1974b; Tangri, 1972). In two studies where exceptions to these findings occurred, daughters of employed mothers did not differ in career aspirations, but did have more favorable attitudes about careers for women (Baruch, 1972; Lipman-Blumen, 1972). The apparent modeling influence of an employed mother is not a recent phenomenon. It appears across cohorts, and it appears for both children and adults. In several studies, adult career women more often had employed mothers during their childhood than comparable groups of homemakers (Astin, 1971; Birnbaum, 1975; Hoffman, 1974; Shelton, 1968).

Daughters of employed mothers also have less stereotyped views of the feminine role than daughters of homemakers (Baruch, 1972; Broverman *et al.*, 1972; Etaugh & Gerson, 1974; Hoffman, 1974; Miller, 1975). Their definitions of the feminine role are typically broader, including more traditionally masculine activities and attributes, as well as those usually defined as feminine. For example, daughters of working mothers rated "women" higher than did daughters of homemakers on Broverman *et al.*'s (1972) masculine "competency" cluster; their ratings on the feminine "warmth–expressiveness" cluster did not differ.

Parallel differences in females' personality attributes are associated with maternal employment, at least when the mother is involved in her career. In some studies, females whose mothers were employed had more masculine attributes such as dominance, achievement orientation, and independence (Hoffman, 1974; Stein, 1973). In two others, however, there was no difference or the difference was in the reverse direction (Baruch, 1973; Broverman *et al.*, 1972). In the Baruch (1973) study, those who said their mothers would have liked a career did rate themselves as more masculine. The mother's involvement or commitment to a career may be a more important influence than the sheer fact of employment outside the home.

Not only do working mothers provide less traditional feminine models for their children, but it appears that daughters are more likely to emulate them. Studies of children ranging from kindergarten to college age indicate that daughters of employed mothers more often name their mother as the person they wish to be like than daughters of unemployed mothers (Baruch, 1974; Hoffman, 1974; Miller, 1975).

While the findings concerning maternal employment are consistent across ages and cohorts, they may be restricted to middle-class women who are employed in relatively high status jobs. Few studies of working class or blue collar mothers are available. As the satisfactions and rewards of employment are fewer and the burdens are greater for working-class women, their daughters may derive a less favorable opinion about working outside the home from observing their mothers. Among working-class families, daughters of employed mothers may expect to be employed out of necessity, but they may find pursuit of an occupation a less attractive goal than middle-class females.

2. Maternal Child Rearing Practices

In an earlier review of the literature on the socialization of achievement orientation in females, one of the present authors summarized the data in the following way:

> Perhaps the major theme that emerges from the socialization data is that the child-rearing practices that are conducive to feminine sex typing are often antagonistic to those that lead to achievement-oriented behavior. A female child is most likely to develop achievement behavior and independence when her parents are moderately warm, moderately to highly permissive, and when they reinforce and encourage achievement efforts. Some concomitant features of the practices in families of highly achievement-oriented females are moderate punitiveness, high demands on the child, and acceleration attempts by the mother. (Stein & Bailey, 1973, p. 362) Copyright 1973 by the American Psychological Association. Reprinted by permission.

Fundamentally, mothers of achievement-oriented females foster growing emotional independence rather than dependency. When these children reach adolescence and adulthood, they are less close to their families of origin than more traditional females (Douvan & Adelson, 1966; Hoffman, 1974; Kagan & Moss, 1962, Tangri, 1972).

The variables discussed thus far may be viewed as influences that increase the female child's motivation and aspiration for a career outside the home, but it is unclear in what way they affect the attractiveness of home and family roles. As the predominant pattern desired by young college women currently is a combination of career and family roles, it is conceivable that the attractions of one may increase without diminishing the attractions of the other.

The rejection of family roles implied by the wish not to marry or to remain childless appears to be associated with negative experiences during childhood concerning marriage and motherhood. Adolescents who did not want to marry often came from working-class families where they had had many household and child-care responsibilities (Douvan & Adelson, 1966). Young adults who wanted to remain childless and older gifted women who had not had children remembered their parents' marriages as less happy and more conflictful than groups who wanted or had children (Bram, 1974; Houseknecht, 1974; Sears & Barbee, 1975). In some instances, they also thought children had had a negative effect on their parents' marriage. This set of antecedents, however, most likely is independent of those leading to attraction to career and occupational roles (Almquist, 1974b).

3. *Influence of Fathers*

Some authors have argued that fathers play a more critical role than mothers in sex role socialization of both males and females (Johnson, 1963). The data on career-oriented women support the proposition that paternal encouragement of achievement can be an important antecedent of achievement orientation (Hoffman, 1974; Poloma & Garland, 1971a, 1971c; Tangri, 1972). Fathers of high occupational status more often encourage achievement for their daughters, particularly when the girl is the oldest child or when there are no sons.

It is more common for fathers to train their daughters in traditional femininity and to show greater concern with the affective and interpersonal development of their daughters than with achievement-related behavior. Fathers who were observed teaching their young daughters paid more attention to the social aspects of the situation than to the child's performance (Block, 1977). Across 17 samples in six countries (Block, 1977), parents' behaviors were in agreement in the following ways. Both parents emphasized achievement, competition, independence, and taking personal responsibility more for sons than daughters. Parents encouraged "ladylike" behavior in females. Fathers emphasized the affective aspects of achievement situations for daughters and were sorry to see them grow up. In another sample of adolescents, parents formed high educational aspirations more readily for males than for females (Williams, 1972).

These data indicate that fathers (and mothers) more often train their daughters in traditional feminine behavior than in achievement-related skills. Other studies indicate that such training by the father has effects; young girls whose fathers encourage feminine behavior display more traditional sex typing (Fling & Manosevitz, 1972; Hetherington, 1967; Mussen & Rutherford, 1963).

4. *Peer and School Influences*

Schools and peers most frequently reinforce traditional feminine patterns, but there is a growing body of evidence that when they do offer encouragement for achievement orientation, it has an influence on female students. In two observational studies, teachers in preschool and elementary school classes reinforced "feminine" behavior and discouraged typically male behaviors (Fagot & Patterson, 1969; Meyer & Thompson, 1956). During the high school years, when critical choices are made about college attendance and occupational selection, counselors and teachers have often failed to encourage female students to think seriously about a career. Terman and Oden (1959) estimated that the failure of gifted females to attend college was more often due to lack of recognition and encouragement in school than it was to parents' failures. The persistence of these attitudes in recent times is suggested by the finding that vocational counselors had more traditional views about occupations for females than did widely varying samples of women (Medvine & Collins, 1973).

This information is discouraging in view of the finding that high school girls' educational aspirations were affected by teachers' expectations more than boys' aspirations, perhaps partly because parents have less often provided clear expectations for daughters than for sons (Williams, 1972). Career choices of females graduating from New York City high schools in 1969 were highly traditional; 53% wanted to be teachers, nurses, or secretaries (Berman, 1972).

Schools can have an influence on change in the sex role definitions and aspirations of females. Elementary school children in "modern" schools with individualized curricula had less stereotyped sex role concepts than children in "traditional" schools (Minuchin, 1965). A Psychological Education Project conducted in Minneapolis involved high school courses and experiences designed to promote the cognitive and ego development of young women. After a one-term course, females scored at higher levels on Kohlberg's moral maturity hierarchy and on Loevinger's ego development scale. There was also a shift from stereotypic to introspective and differentiated thinking about sex roles and women's rights (Erickson, 1977). These results indicate the potential of schools and, hence, their responsibility for enhancing the development of young women.

In the college years, individual encouragement by one or two faculty members is often an important impetus to high aspirations for women. At college graduation, career-committed women had more often worked with a professor in their field on independent study projects and more often felt that their professors considered them outstanding students (Almquist, 1974b). The personal experiences of both of the present authors as well as of many other professional women indicate that strong encouragement by one or two faculty members can be a critical determinant of the decision to pursue advanced professional status.

Peer groups also apparently serve as reference or support groups for either traditional or nontraditional patterns. By adolescence, a female selects peers partly on the basis of their similarity to her own views. In general, career-oriented college women report that their female friends have been influential in their values and career decisions (Almquist & Angrist, 1971; Levitt, 1971; Tangri, 1972). They also report using male peers as models more often than traditionally oriented females (Angrist, 1972). On the other hand, career-oriented women are less intensely involved in heterosexual relationships with male peers in the college years than are noncareer-oriented females. In several studies, career-oriented women dated as much as traditional women, but were less often seriously involved with a man (i.e., going steady, engaged, or married) (Almquist & Angrist, 1971; Gump, 1972; Tangri, 1972).

Once a woman marries, the attitudes of her husband about her working outside the home influence her choices (Holmstrom, 1973; Poloma & Garland, 1971a, 1971b; Wells, 1966). Willingness by the husband to share in some domestic roles, albeit rarely to share equally, appears to be essential for a woman to pursue a demanding professional career in combination with marriage, particularly when there are children (Holmstrom, 1973). It is unclear to what degree women select husbands whose attitudes about women's employment and childbearing are consistent with their own inclinations. In one study of English couples (Bailyn, 1970), however, those who were least happily married were the couples in which the wife wanted to combine a career with her family life and the husband held traditional views about sex role separation in marriage. Similarly, Ridley (1973) found that working couples were least happy when both were more work-oriented than family-oriented; they were most satisfied when neither was very involved with work or when one was moderately work-oriented. These findings suggest the inherent difficulty of being involved in both work and family life for anyone (males as well as females) in the present societal structure.

Socialization of achievement orientation for a female probably requires at lease one "unusual" influence, be it a parent, a school program, or a particularly potent peer or adult model. In the absence of "intervention" on some level the culture breeds a traditional female. For instance, a father's encouragement may be particularly influential if the mother has followed a traditional pattern. School programs may have greater influence for females whose parents have not provided encouragement for achievement, and so on. Any one or some combination of these influences seems necessary for most women to depart from the feminine stereotype with which they are surrounded.

D. PSYCHOLOGICAL CONSEQUENCES OF ROLE CHOICES

In the preceding sections, possible developmental continuities and processes in childhood and early adulthood were identified, and some of the socialization experiences related to role choices were discussed. Ideally, one would follow with an examination of the resulting developmental processes throughout life for women who choose different patterns of home and work roles. Instead, the data provide global information about the level of satisfaction, self-esteem, and mental health for women who have followed various paths. Inferences about developmental processes can be made only indirectly. In addition, some information is available concerning the factors that mediate women's satisfaction with their role choices.

1. Satisfaction and Self-Esteem

In surveys of large samples, women who are married have higher life satisfaction and lower levels of depression than unmarried women (Radloff, 1975; Spreitzer, Snyder, & Larson, 1975). However, the advent of children in a marriage is associated with a lowering of satisfaction with the marriage and possibly with life generally. Many studies of marital satisfaction indicate that children lead to lower levels of satisfaction for both partners than occurs in comparable samples without children (H. Feldman, 1971; Spanier, Lewis, & Cole, 1975). It appears, however, that the negative effects of children on women's satisfaction become less pronounced as children get older (Spanier *et al.,* 1975). One wonders hopefully whether children ultimately add to older women's life satisfaction.

The effects of employment on life satisfaction are less clear-cut. In two surveys, no differences between housewives and employed married women appeared (Radloff, 1975; Spreitzer *et al.,* 1975). When individuals were studied in slightly more depth, employed women were more satisfied with their lives than housewives (Hoffman & Nye, 1974; Nye, 1974a). In one survey (Brimbaum, 1975), middle-aged career women, whether single or married, had higher self-esteem than homemakers in almost every domain. The married career women even felt more adequate as mothers. Some groups are exceptions to this generalization. Older women with blue collar jobs and women with more than three children were less satisfied when they were employed than when they were full-time housewives (Nye, 1974a). A Norwegian study (Traeldal, 1973) found that homemakers' life satisfaction remained stable across ages but that employed women's life satisfaction increased with the increasing age of the women surveyed.

Among lower class women, marital satisfaction is lower for those who are employed than for housewives (Feld, 1963; Nye, 1963, 1974b, 1974c). In the middle class, employed women report the same levels of satisfaction with their marriages as homemakers (Hoffman, 1975). Numerous factors probably contribute to this difference. Lower class women have less interesting and less lucrative jobs. Husbands of employed lower class women earn less than the husbands of unemployed women; these husbands are also seen as less adequate (Nye, 1974c). It is possible that women in the lower class see the need to supplement the husband's income as a sign of his inadequacy as a male; husbands may also interpret the wife's employment in this vein with resulting resentment and tension.

These social class differences in satisfaction suggest that when women experience problems associated with combining family and work roles, these are more a function of role overload than of role conflict. Because lower class women have less flexible jobs and less household help than middle-class employed women, their problems may more often stem from role overload and lack of enough time than from intrinsic incompatibility between roles. In several studies (e.g., see Hall, 1972, 1975; Katz, 1975), not having enough time was cited by married women, regardless of their life situation, as exacerbating role conflicts, particularly for those who worked full time. Married professional women with children interviewed by Holmstrom (1973) also reported the lack of time as their major problem; many of them had every minute of the day and evening scheduled with no room for slack.

2. Factors Mediating Women's Response to Employment and Motherhood

Individual predispositions probably affect women's levels of satisfaction with maternal and work roles. There are some data suggesting that orientation to traditional feminine activities is associated with satisfaction in the homemaker role. For a national sample of women, marital happiness was correlated with motivation to achieve in homemaking activities. Women with high motivation for career achievement more often considered marriage restrictive (Veroff & Feld, 1970). H. Feldman (1971) found that women who scored high on "maternalism" and who had traditional role differentiations in their marriages increased in marital satisfaction after the birth of a baby; other women showed a decline. In another study, dissatisfied homemakers scored lower on a scale designed to measure adequacy of parenting than did employed mothers (whether or not they were satisfied) or satisfied homemakers (Yarrow, Scott, De Leeuw, & Heinig, 1962).

Coping style and ability appear to affect a woman's satisfaction with combining career and family roles. Hall (1972, 1975) identified three styles of coping based on open-ended responses of married college graduates in various life-styles. Type I coping is an active structural role definition. The person mutually agrees with those people dependent upon the services of the various roles on new role definitions and expectations and often integrates roles. Type II coping is a personal role redefinition. The person changes her perceptions of the demands and expectations rather than negotiating directly with those who obtain the services. Type III coping involves no conscious strategy for planning and organizing, just working harder to meet all the demands. The third style is defensive and not really coping in the usual sense of the term.

Women who used at least one strategy from Type I were significantly more often satisfied with their lives than those who used no Type I coping. Using Type III defensive methods or having no conscious strategy showed the strongest negative correlation with satisfaction (Hall, 1972).

Cross-sectional data from women of different ages revealed no relation of type of coping to life stage. The kind of coping used seemed to depend upon the woman and her particular life situation. Katz (1975) reported that working married women with children who had nontraditional sex role training as children used more efficient and active methods for resolving role conflicts. They delegated tasks to others and did other tasks less frequently. Women who were traditionally reared viewed holding a job as something they could do only if it did not interfere with their family life; hence, they more often fell in Hall's Type III coping category.

E. SUMMARY

Childhood socialization of achievement orientation, independence, and nontraditional interests form a basis for adult role orientation. From middle childhood to adulthood; achieving females display personality attributes that include the more positive aspects of both the feminine and masculine stereotypes. Socialization in a nontraditional direction may be influenced by parents—maternal employment and encouragement of achievement and paternal encouragement—by school programs and by peers in adolescence and adulthood. In the sociocultural environment that has existed heretofore, a young female needed at least one strong impetus to nontraditional patterns, whether it was a parent, a school influence, or a significant peer group in order to depart from traditional femininity.

Adolescence and early adulthood seem to be watershed periods in a woman's life because she makes decisions concerning the timing of marriage, childbearing, education, and work that are not easily reversed. Regardless of the developmental processes that lead her to make such choices, the decisions themselves have long-term consequences. Women who marry early, particularly if they have a child early, are less likely to reenter the labor market or are likely to do so at a later age than those who delay childbearing. While individual differences in sex role orientation probably influence the timing of marriage and motherhood, performing these roles may in turn affect career options and aspirations. Developmental change may also result from work experience for women who delay their families.

Those women who return to higher education or careers after marrying and having children, whether they remain married or are divorced or widowed, show particularly high levels of commitment. A developmental process is suggested by which experience with marriage and motherhood leads to disillusionment with the romanticized images purveyed by the culture and to a search for other avenues of self-fulfillment. In the present cultural milieu, marriage is associated with higher overall satisfaction than not being married, but having children leads to decreases in satisfaction, particularly within the husband–wife relationship. Employed women have higher levels of life satisfaction and feelings of adequacy and of self-esteem than full-time homemakers. However, the psychological benefits of employment are greater for the educated middle class, and the liabilities are greater for lower class women.

It appears that dissatisfaction and conflict about combining family and work roles result more from role overload than from role conflict. That is, time pressure rather than concern about violating social norms appears to cause the most problems for employed mothers. Women with a strong orientation to traditional feminine activities are more satisfied with home and maternal roles than those with other interests. Employed women who cope actively with time pressures and conflicts by redefining their own and their families' responsibilities are more satisfied than those who attempt to meet all demands or have no planned coping strategy. These findings suggest that future research should be focused on the ongoing developmental changes that are involved in women's performance of home and/or work roles. Intervention research, in particular, could be profitably directed toward identifying and teaching effective coping techniques for women to use in dealing with the rapidly changing life patterns that characterize American women.

V. Summary and Conclusions

Women's patterns of family and work roles have been examined from a variety of perspectives in an effort to gain understanding of the processes and influences on development throughout the life span. Although the entire life span is of interest, we have placed greater emphasis on the earlier years than on late life, primarily because most of the literature available deals with children and young or middle-aged women. The specific points made are summarized at the end of each major section above. In this final summary, conclusions of particular interest are emphasized.

In the last 30 years, the majority of women have shifted from a life pattern devoted primarily to homemaking and motherhood to a pattern in which those activities are combined with employment outside the home. Many of the current generation of young women are engaging in outside employment almost continuously even during their children's earliest years. Many others are rejecting marriage and/or motherhood altogether. The implications of this pattern for changes in male–female relationships, for children's experiences as they grow up, and for the structure of the occupational world could be very great. It is our hope that fundamental social change will result, but our optimism is guarded when other elements of the current situation are examined. Although women are often employed, they have made few advances toward more equal job status or salaries. The discrepancy between men and women in the employment world remains almost unchanged. Social stereotypes continue to portray women as incompetent, passive, and lacking in ability. Socialization processes throughout life encourage women to incorporate those stereotypes so that they achieve less than men both because of their internalized beliefs about themselves and because of externally imposed discrimination. All of these factors suggest that the social changes frequently discussed may be considerably less dramatic than they initially appear. Nevertheless, long-term changes may come about as women become more invested in their occupational activities and more conscious of the potentials and the barriers within those roles.

The continuous nature of developmental change is an intriguing and recurring theme in our examination of the literature; yet, it is peculiarly neglected in most empirical studies. In most of the theory and literature currently available there is either a static perspective that essentially involves predicting how people will remain the same, or there is a crisis perspective in which developmental transitions at particular points in time are emphasized. It is probably true that change is more rapid in some periods of one's life than in others, but surely there is a process of continuous developmental change throughout the life span that needs to be better understood. How does a person change as result of staying home as a housewife and mother for several years? How does she change as a result of engaging in a particular kind of job? People enter into these activities with a very partial understanding of what will be involved; yet they may be greatly affected by the experiences gained in them.

We hope to see more research directed toward understanding the continuing developmental changes associated with different kinds of life experiences. Finally, the small amount of literature concerned with identifying coping skills that enable women to perform a variety of roles successfully is a good beginning toward interventions that could help women adapt to the changing social circumstances in which they live.

References

Almquist, E. M. Attitudes of college men toward working wives. *Vocational Guidance Quarterly*, 1974, **23**, 115–121. (a)

Almquist, E. M. Sex stereotypes in occupational choice: The case for college women. *Journal of Vocational Behavior*, 1974, **5**, 13–21. (b)

Almquist, E. M., & Angrist, S. S. Role model influences on college women's career aspirations. In A. Theodore (Ed.), *The professional woman*. Cambridge, Mass: Schenkman, 1971.

Angrist, S. S. Changes in women's work aspirations during college or work does not equal career. *International Journal of Sociology of the Family*, 1972, **2**, 1–11.

Astin, H. S. Factors associated with the participation of women doctorates in the labor force. In A. Theodore (Ed.), *The professional woman*. Cambridge, Mass.: Schenkman, 1971.

Astin, H. S., & Bayer, A. E. Sex discrimination in academe. In M. T. S. Mednick, S. S. Tangri, & L. W. Hoffman (Eds.), *Women and achievement*. New York: Wiley, 1975.

Bachtold, L. M. Similarities in personality profiles of college and career women. *Psychological Reports*, 1973, **33**, 429–430.

Bachtold, L. M., & Werner, E. E. Personality profiles of women psychologists: Three generations. *Developmental Psychology*, 1971, **5**, 273–278.

Bachtold, L. M., & Werner, E. E. Personality characteristics of women scientists. *Psychological Reports*, 1972, **31**, 391–396.

Bachtold, L. M., & Werner, E. E. Personality characteristics of creative women. *Perceptual and Motor Skills*, 1973, **36**, 311–319.

Bacon, L. Early motherhood, accelerated role transition, and social pathologies. *Social Forces*, 1974, **52**, 333–341.

Bailyn, L. Career and family orientations of husbands and wives in relation to marital happiness. *Human Relations*, 1970, **23**, 97–114.

Baltes, P. B. Longitudinal and cross-sectional sequences in the study of age and generation effects. *Human Development*, 1968, **11**, 145–171.

Baltes, P. B., Cornelius, S. W., & Nesselroade, J. R. Cohort effects in developmental psychology: Theoretical and methodological perspectives. In W. A. Collins (Ed.), *Minnesota Symposium on Child Psychology* (Vol. 11). Minneapolis: University of Minnesota Press, 1977.

Baltes, P. B., & Schaie, K. W. (Eds.). *Life-span developmental psychology: Personality and socialization*. New York: Academic Press, 1973.

Baltes, P. B., & Willis, S. L. Toward psychological theories of aging and development. In J. E. Birren & K. W. Schaie (Eds.), *Handbook of aging series*. New York: Reinhold-Van Nostrand, 1976.

Baruch, G. K. Maternal influences upon college women's attitudes toward women and work. *Developmental Psychology*, 1972, **6**, 32–37.

Baruch, G. K. Feminine self-esteem, self-ratings of competence, and maternal career commitment. *Journal of Counseling Psychology*, 1973, **20**, 487–488.

Baruch, G. K. Maternal career-orientation as related to parental identification in college women. *Journal of Vocational Behaivor*, 1974, **4**, 173–180.

Baruch, G. K. Sex-role stereotyping, the motive to avoid success, and parental identification. *Sex Roles*, 1975, **1**, 303–309.

Bem, S. L. *Psychology looks at sex roles: Where have all the androgynous people gone?* Paper presented at the Symposium on Women, University of California, Los Angeles, May 1972.

Bem, S. L. Sex-role adaptability: One consequence of psychological androgyny. *Journal of Personality and Social Psychology,* 1975, **31**, 634.

Berman, Y. Occupational aspirations of 545 female high school seniors. *Journal of Vocational Behavior,* 1972, **2**, 173–177.

Birnbaum, J. A. Life patterns and self-esteem in gifted family oriented and career committed women. In M. T. S. Mednick, S. S. Tangri, & L. W. Hoffman (Eds.), *Women and achievement.* New York: Wiley, 1975.

Block, J. H. Another look at sex differentiation in the socialization behaviors of mothers and fathers. In *Psychology of women: Future directions of research.* New York: Psychological Dimensions, 1977. To be published.

Boedecker, A. L. *The real, the ideal, and the norm: Age-sex norms in women's early adult development.* Unpublished master's thesis, Pennsylvania State University, College of Human Development, 1975.

Bram, S. *To have or have not: A social psychological study of voluntarily childless couples, parents-to-be, and parents.* Unpublished doctoral dissertation, University of Michigan, Department of Sociology, 1974.

Brim, O. G., Jr. Theories of the male mid-life crisis. *Counseling Psychologist: Counseling Adults,* 1976, Special Issue.

Broverman, I. K., Vogel, S. R., Broverman, D. M., Clarkson, F. E., & Rosenkrantz, P. S. Sex-role stereotypes: A current appraisal. *Journal of Social Issues,* 1972, **28**(2), 58–78.

Chafe, W. H. Looking backward in order to look forward: Women, work and social values in America. In J. M. Kreps (Ed.), *Women and the American economy: A look to the 1980's.* Englewood Cliffs, N.J.: Prentice-Hall, 1976.

Clifford, M. M. & Looft, W. R. Academic employment interviews: Effect of sex and race. *Educational Researcher,* 1971, **22**, 6–8.

Crandall, V. C., & Battle, E. S. The antecedents and adult correlates of academic and intellectual achievement effort. In J. P. Hill (Ed.), *Minnesota Symposia on Child Psychology* (Vol. 4). Minneapolis: University of Minnesota Press, 1970.

Crandall, V. C., Katkovsky, W., & Crandall, V. J. Children's beliefs in their own control of reinforcements in intellectual-academic achievement situations. *Child Development,* 1965, **36**, 91–109.

Cross, K. P. *Beyond the open door: New students to higher education.* San Francisco: Jossey-Bass, 1971.

DeFleur, M. L. Occupational roles as portrayed on television. *Public Opinion Quarterly,* 1964, **28**, 57–74.

Douvan, E., & Adelson, J. *The adolescent experience.* New York: Wiley, 1966.

Dweck, C. S., & Reppucci, N. D. Learned helplessness and reinforcement responsibility in children. *Journal of Personality and Social Psychology,* 1973, **25**, 109–116.

Elder, G. H., Jr. Age differentiation and the life course. *Annual Review of Sociology,* 1975, **1**, 165–190.

Emmerich, W. Young children's discriminations of parent and child roles. *Child Development,* 1959, **30**, 403–419.

Erickson, V. L. Beyond Cinderella: Ego maturity and attitudes toward the rights and roles of women. *Counseling Psychologist,* 1977, **7**, 83–88.

Etaugh, C. F. Attitudes of professionals toward the married professional woman. *Psychological Reports,* 1973, **32**, 775–780.

Etaugh, C. F., & Gerson, A. Attitudes toward women: Some biographical correlates. *Psychological Reports,* 1974, **35**, 701–702.

Fagot, B. I., & Patterson, G. R. An *in vivo* analysis of reinforcing contingencies for sex-role behaviors in the preschool child. *Developmental Psychology,* 1969, **1**, 563–568.

Feld, S. Feelings of adjustment. In F. I. Nye & L. W. Hoffman (Eds.), *The employed mother in America*. Chicago: Rand McNally, 1963.

Feldman, H. The effects of children on the family. In A. Michel (Ed.), *Family issues of employed women in Europe and America*. Leiden: Brill, 1971.

Feldman, S. D. Impediment or stimulant? Marital status and graduate education. In J. Huber (Ed.), *Changing women in a changing society*. Chicago: University of Chicago Press, 1973.

Feldman-Summers, S., & Kiesler, S. B. Those who are number two try harder: The effect of sex on attributations of causality. *Journal of Personality and Social Psychology*, 1974, **30**, 846–855.

Fichter, J. H. Career expectations of Negro women graduates. In A. Theodore (Ed.), *The professional woman*. Cambridge, Mass.: Schenkman, 1971.

Fidell, L. S. Empirical verification of sex discrimination in hiring practices in psychology. *American Psychologist*, 1970, **25**, 1094–1097.

Fling, S., & Manosevitz, M. Sex typing in nursery school children's play interests. *Developmental Psychology*, 1972, **7**, 146–152.

Frieze, I. H. Women's expectations for and causal attributions of success and failure. In M. T. S. Mednick, S. S. Tangri, & L. W. Hoffman (Eds.), *Women and achievement*. New York: Wiley, 1975.

Glick, P. C., & Norton, A. J. Perspectives on the recent upturn in divorce and remarriage. *Demography*, 1973, **10**, 301–314.

Goldberg, P. A. Are women prejudiced against women? *Trans-Action*, 1968, **5**, 28–30.

Gould, J. S., & Pagano, A. Sex discrimination and achievement. *National Association of Women Deans and Counselors Journal*, 1972, Winter, 74–82.

Goulet, L. R., & Baltes, P. B. (Eds.). *Life-span developmental psychology: Research and theory*. New York: Academic Press, 1970.

Gronseth. E. The family in capitalist society and the dysfunctionality of the husband provider role. In J. M. Henslin & L. Reynolds (Eds.), *Social institutions as appendages to market society*. New York: McKay, 1972.

Gump, J. P. Sex-role attitudes and psychological well-being. *Journal of Social Issues*, 1972, **28**(2), 79–92.

Haavio-Manila, E. Sex-role attitudes in Finland, 1966–1970. *Journal of Social Issues*, 1972, **28**(2), 93–110.

Hall, D. T. A model of coping with role conflict: The role behavior of college educated women. *Administrative Science Quarterly*, 1972, **17**, 471–486.

Hall, D. T. Pressures from work, self, and home in the life stages of married women. *Journal of Vocational Behavior*, 1975, **6**, 121–132.

Haller, M., & Rosenmayr, L. The pluridimensionality of work commitment: A study of young married women in different social contexts of occupational and family life. *Human Relations*, 1971, **24**, 501–518.

Harmon, L. W. Anatomy of career commitment in women. *Journal of Counseling Psychology*, 1970, **17**, 77–80.

Hartup, W. W., & Zook, E. A. Sex-role preferences in three- and four-year-old children. *Journal of Consulting Psychology*, 1960, **24**, 420–426.

Hefner, R., Rebecca, M., & Oleshansky, B. Development of sex-role transcendence. *Human Development*, 1975, **18**, 143–158.

Helson, R. The changing image of the career woman. *Journal of Social Issues*, 1972, **28**(2), 33–46.

Herman, M. H., & Sedlacek, W. E. Sexist attitudes among male university students. *Journal of College Student Personnel*, 1973, **14**, 544–548.

Hetherington, E. M. The effects of familial variables on sex typing, on parent-child similarity, and on imitation in children. In J. P. Hill (Ed.), *Minnesota Symposia on Child Psychology* (Vol. 1). Minneapolis: University of Minnesota Press, 1967.

Hoffman, L. W. Effects on child. In L. W. Hoffman & F. I. Nye (Eds.), *Working mothers*. San Francisco: Jossey-Bass, 1974.

Hoffman, L. W. *Working women and the family*. Paper presented at the Study Group on the Interacting between the Family and Society, sponsored by the Society for Research in Child Development, Ann Arbor, Michigan, October 1975.

Hoffman, L. W., & Nye, F. I. (Eds.). *Working mothers*. San Francisco: Jossey-Bass, 1974.

Holmstrom, L. L. *The two-career family*. Cambridge, Mass.: Schenkman, 1973.

Houseknecht, S. *Social psychological aspects of voluntary childlessness*. Unpublished master's thesis, Pennsylvania State University, Department of Sociology, 1974.

Huston-Stein, A., & Baltes, P. B. Theory and method in life-span developmental psychology: Implications for child development. In H. W. Reese & L. P. Lipsitt (Eds.), *Advances in child development and behavior* (Vol. 11). New York: Academic Press, 1976.

Johnson, M. Sex role learning in the nuclear family. *Child Development*, 1963, **34**, 319–333.

Kagan, J., Hosken, B., & Watson, S. Child's symbolic conceptualization of parents. *Child Development*, 1961, **32**, 625–636.

Kagan, J., & Moss. H. A. *Birth to maturity*. New York: Wiley, 1962.

Kaniuga, N., Scott, T., & Gade, E. Working women portrayed on evening television programs. *Vocational Guidance Quarterly*, 1974, **23**, 134–137.

Katz, M. *Sex role training and coping behavior in a role conflict situation: Homemaking-career conflicts*. Paper presented at the meeting of the American Psychological Association, Chicago, 1975.

Knudson, D. D. The declining status of women: Popular myths and the failure of functionalist thought. *Social Forces*, 1966, **48**, 183–193.

Kohlberg, L., & Zigler, E. The impact of cognitive maturity on the development of sex-role attitudes in the years 4 to 8. *Genetic Psychology Monographs*, 1967, **75**, 89–165.

Komarovsky, M. Cultural contradictions and sex roles: The masculine case. In J. Huber (Ed.), *Changing women in a changing society*. Chicago: University of Chicago Press, 1973.

Kreps, J. M. (Ed.). *Women and the American economy: A look to the 1980's*. Englewood Cliffs, N.J.: Prentice-Hall, 1976.

Kreps, J. M., & Leaper, R. J. Home work, market work, and the allocation of time. In J. M. Kreps (Ed.), *Women and the American economy: A look to the 1980's*. Englewood Cliffs, N.J.: Prentice-Hall, 1976.

Kristal, J., Sanders, D., Spence, J. T., & Helmreich, R. Inferences about the femininity of competent women and their implications for like-ability. *Sex Roles*, 1975, **1**, 33–40.

Levitt, E. S. Vocational development of professionals: A review. *Journal of Vocational Behavior*, 1971, **1**, 375–385.

Lipman-Blumen, J. How ideology shapes women's lives. *Scientific American*, 1972, **226**, 34–42.

Lockheed, M. E. Female motive to avoid success. A psychological barrier or a response to deviancy? *Sex Roles*, 1975, **1**, 41–50.

Looft, W. R. Sex differences in the expression of vocational aspirations by elementary school children. *Developmental Psychology*, 1971, **5**, 336.

Lott, A. J., & Lott, B. E. *Negro and white youth: A psychological study in a border-state community*. New York: Holt, 1963.

McMillin, M. R. Attitudes of college men toward career involvement of married women. *Vocational Guidance Quarterly*, 1972, **20**, 8–11.

Mednick, M. T. S. Social change and sex-role inertia: The case of the kibbutz. In M. T. S.

Mednick, S. S. Tangri, & L. W. Hoffman (Eds.), *Women and achievement.* New York: Wiley, 1975.

Medvine, A., & Collins, A. *Occupational prestige and its relationship to traditional and non-traditional views of women's roles* (Res. Rep. No. 9–73). College Park, Md.: University of Maryland, Counseling Center, 1973.

Meyer, W. J., & Thompson, G. G. Sex differences in the distribution of teacher approval and disapproval among sixth-grade children. *Journal of Educational Psychology,* 1956, **47,** 385–397.

Miller, S. M. Effects of maternal employment on sex role perception, interests, and self-esteem in kindergarten girls. *Developmental Psychology,* 1975, **11,** 405–406.

Minuchin, P. Sex-role concepts and sex typing in childhood as a function of school and home environments. *Child Development,* 1965, **36,** 1033–1040.

Modell, J., Furstenburg, F. F., Jr., & Strong, D. The timing of marriage in the transition to adulthood: Continuity and change, 1860–1975. *American Journal of Sociology,* 1977, in press.

Moore, K. A., & Sawhill, I. V. Implications of women's employment for home and family life. In J. M. Kreps (Ed.), *Women and the American economy: A look at the 1980's.* Englewood Cliffs, N.J.: Prentice-Hall, 1976.

Mussen, P., & Rutherford, E. Parent-child relations and parental personality in relation to young children's sex-role preferences. *Child Development,* 1963, **34,** 589–607.

Nesselroade, J. R., & Reese, H. W. (Eds.). *Life-span developmental psychology: Methodological issues.* New York: Academic Press, 1973.

Nichols, I. A., & Schauffer, C. B. *Self-concept as a predictor of performance in college women.* Paper presented at the 83rd Annual Convention of the American Psychological Association, Chicago, September 1975.

Nilsen, A. P. Women in children's literature. *College English,* 1971, **32,** 918–926.

Nye, F. I. Marital interaction. In F. I. Nye & L. W. Hoffman (Eds.), *The employed mother in America.* Chicago: Rand McNally, 1963.

Nye, F. I. Effects on mother. In L. W. Hoffman & F. I. Nye (Eds.), *Working mothers.* San Francisco: Jossey-Bass, 1974. (a)

Nye, F. I. Emerging and declining family roles. *Journal of Marriage and the Family,* 1974, **36,** 238–245. (b)

Nye, F. I. Husband-wife relationship. In L. W. Hoffman & F. I. Nye (Eds.), *Working mothers.* San Francisco: Jossey-Bass, 1974. (c)

Nye, F. I. Sociocultural context. In L. W. Hoffman & F. I. Nye (Eds.), *Working mothers.* San Francisco: Jossey-Bass, 1974. (d)

Nye, F. I., & Hoffman, L. W. (Eds.). *The employed mother in America.* Chicago: Rand McNally, 1963.

O'Leary, V. E. Some attitudinal barriers to occupational aspirations in women. *Psychological Bulletin,* 1974, **81,** 809–826.

Oppenheimer, V. K. Demographic influence on female employment and the status of women. In J. Huber (Ed.), *Changing women in a changing society.* Chicago: University of Chicago Press, 1973.

Papalia, D. E., & Tennent, S. S. Vocational aspirations in preschoolers: A manifestation of early sex role stereotyping. *Sex Roles,* 1975, **1,** 197–199.

Papanek, H. Men, women, and work: Reflections on the two-person career. In J. Huber (Ed.), *Changing women in a changing society.* Chicago: University of Chicago Press, 1973.

Peterson, M. J. The asymmetry of sex role perceptions. *Sex Roles,* 1975, **1,** 267–282.

Pheterson, G. I., Kiesler, S. B., & Goldberg, P. A. Evaluation of the performance of women as a function of their sex, achievement, and personal history. *Journal of Personality and Social Psychology*, 1971, **19**, 114–118.

Poloma, M. M., & Garland, T. N. Jobs or careers? The case of the professionally employed married woman. In A. Michel (Ed.), *Family issues of employed women in Europe and America*. Leiden: Brill, 1971. (a)

Poloma, M. M., & Garland, T. N. The married professional woman: A study in the tolerance of domestication. *Journal of Marriage and the Family*, 1971, **33**, 531–540. (b)

Poloma, M. M., & Garland, T. N. The myth of the egalitarian family: Familial roles and the professionally employed wife. In A. Theodore (Ed.), *The professional woman*. Cambridge, Mass.: Schenkman, 1971. (c)

Radloff, L. Sex differences in depression: The effects of occupation and marital status. *Sex Roles*, 1975, **1**, 249–265.

Ridley, C. A. Exploring the impact of work satisfaction and involvement on marital interaction when both partners are employed. *Journal of Marriage and the Family*, 1973, **35**, 229–237.

Riley, M. W. Age strata in social systems. In E. Shanas & R. Binstock (Eds.), *Handbook of aging and the social sciences*. New York: Reinhold-Van Nostrand, 1976.

Robinson, J. B. Historical changes in how people spend their time. In A. Michel (Ed.), *Family issues of employed women in Europe and America*. Leiden: Brill, 1971.

Rosen, B., & Jerdee, T. H. Influence of sex-role stereotypes on personnel decisions. *Journal of Applied Psychology*, 1974, **59**, 9–14.

Ross, S., & Walters, J. Perceptions of a sample of university men concerning women. *Journal of Genetic Psychology*, 1973, **122**, 329–336.

Schaie, K. W. A general model for the study of developmental problems. *Psychological Bulletin*, 1965, **64**, 92–107.

Schaie, K. W., & Baltes, P. B. On sequential strategies in developmental research: Description or explanation? *Human Development*, 1975, **18**, 384–390.

Sears, P. S., & Barbee, A. H. *Career and life satisfaction among Terman's gifted women*. Paper presented at the Terman Memorial Symposium on Intellectual Talent, Johns Hopkins University, Baltimore, November 1975.

Shaw, J. I., & McMartin, J. A. Personal and situational determinants of attribution of responsibility for an accident. *Goteborg Psychological Reports*, 1975, **5**(20), 1–13.

Shelton, P. B. Achievement motivation in professional women. *Dissertation Abstracts*, 1968, **28**(10), 4274A.

Shields, S. A. *Personality trait attribution and reproductive role*. Unpublished master's thesis, Pennsylvania State University, Department of Psychology, 1973.

Smith, S. Age and sex differences in children's opinions concerning sex differences. *Journal of Genetic Psychology*, 1939, **54**, 17–25.

Soto, D. H., & Cole, C. Prejudice against women: A new perspective. *Sex Roles*, 1975, **1**, 385–393.

Spanier, G. B., Lewis, R. A., & Cole, C. L. Marital adjustment over the family life cycle: The issue of curvilinearity. *Journal of Marriage and the Family*, 1975, **37**, 263–275.

Spreitzer, E., Snyder, E. E., & Larson, D. Age, marital status, and labor force participation as related to life satisfaction. *Sex Roles*, 1975, **1**, 235–247.

Stein, A. H. The effects of sex role standards for achievement and role preference on three determinants of achievement motivation. *Developmental Psychology*, 1971, **4**, 219–231.

Stein, A. H. The effects of maternal employment and educational attainment on the sex-typed attributes of college females. *Social Behavior and Personality*, 1973, **1**, 111–114.

Stein, A. H., & Bailey, M. M. The socialization of achievement orientation in females. *Psychological Bulletin*, 1973, **80**, 345–366.

Stein, A. H., & Friedrich, L. K. Impact of television on children and youth. In E. M. Hetherington (Ed.), *Review of child development research* (Vol. 5). Chicago: University of Chicago Press, 1975.

Stein, A. H., & Smithells, J. Age and sex differences in children's sex role standards about acheivement. *Developmental Psychology,* 1969, **1**, 252–259.

Sutton-Smith, B., Rosenberg, B. G., & Morgan, E. F., Jr. Development of sex differences in play choices during preadolescence. *Child Development,* 1963, **34**, 199–126.

Tangri, S. S. Determinants of occupational role innovation among college women. *Journal of Social Issues,* 1972, **28**(2), 177–199.

Taynor, J., & Deaux, K. When women are more deserving than men: Equity, attribution, and perceived sex differences. *Journal of Personality and Social Psychology,* 1973, **28**, 360–367.

Terman, L. M., & Oden, M. H. *Genetic studies of genius* (Vol. 5), *The gifted group at mid-life: Thirty-five years' follow-up of the superior child.* Stanford, Calif.: Stanford University Press, 1959.

Thornbur, K. R., & Weeks, M. O. Vocational role expectations of five-year-old children and their parents. *Sex Roles,* 1975, **1**, 395–396.

Traeldal, A. The work role and life satisfaction over the life-span. Paper presented at the Biennial meeting of the International Society for the Study of Behavioral Development, Ann Arbor, Michigan, August 1973.

Tyler, L. E. The antecedents of two varieties of vocational interests. *Genetic Psychology Monographs,* 1964, **70**, 177–227.

Urberg, K. A., & Labouvie-Vief, G. Conceptualizations of sex roles: A life-span developmental study. *Developmental Psychology,* 1976, **12**, 15–23.

VanDusen, R. A., & Sheldon, E. B. The changing status of American women: A life cycle perspective. *American Psychologist,* 1976, **31**, 106–116.

Veroff, J., & Feld, S. *Marriage and work in America: A study of motives and roles.* New York: Van Nostrand, 1970.

Walster, E., Cleary, T. A., & Clifford, M. M. The effects of race and sex on college admissions. *Sociology of Education,* 1971, **44**, 237–244.

Weil, M. W. An analysis of the factors influencing married women's actual or planned work participation. In A. Theodore (Ed.), *The professional woman.* Cambridge, Mass.: Schenkman, 1971.

Weiner, B. *Achievement motivation and attribution theory.* Morristown, N.Y.: General Learning Press, 1974.

Weitzman, L. J., Eifler, D., Hokada, E., & Ross, C. Sex-role socialization in picture books for preschool children. *American Journal of Sociology,* 1971, **77**, 1125–1150.

Welch, R. L. A comparison of working and non-working housewives on two personality characteristics. *Psychology of Women Quarterly,* in press.

Wells, J. A. *College women: Seven years after graduation. Resurvey of women graduates— Class of 1957* (Bulletin No. 292). Washington, D.C.: U.S. Department of Labor, Women's Bureau, 1966.

Williams, T. H. Educational aspirations: Longitudinal evidence on their development in Canadian youth. *Sociology of Education,* 1972, **45**, 107–133.

Wohlwill, J. F. The age variable in psychological research. *Psychological Review,* 1970, **77**, 49–64.

Yarrow, M. R., Scott, P., De Leeuw, L., & Heinig, C. Childrearing in families of working and non-working mothers. *Sociometry,* 1962, **25**, 122–140.

Yorberg, B., & Arafat, I. Current sex role conceptions and conflict. *Sex Roles,* 1975, **1**, 135–146.

Possessions: Toward a Theory of Their Meaning and Function throughout the Life Cycle

Lita Furby

DEPARTMENT OF PSYCHOLOGY,
UNIVERSITY OF OREGON,
EUGENE, OREGON

Abstract

Research on the origins and nature of possessiveness is reviewed from a life-span developmental perspective. A summary of possession among nonhumans is presented, followed by a review of possession among differing human cultures. A more detailed discussion is then presented of recent empirical work on the development of possession and ownership in our culture. The focus is on the meaning or definition of possession, and on its motivational determinants. Preliminary steps toward a theory of the nature of possession are discussed, with particular emphasis on effectance and personal control in one's environment as a critical explanatory variable. A number of specific implications for the function of possessions at various stages of the life cycle are also examined. The infancy of research on this topic is stressed throughout.

I. The Problem

Why are people possessive? What role do possessions play in the lives of human beings?

Heretofore, most treatments of this topic have been appendages to political, economic, legal, philosophical, or historical treatises. Such treatments are generally inadequate when dealing with the *psychology* of possession and acquisitiveness, because they tend to make quite sweeping assumptions about the origins and development of possessive motives and behaviors. Robert Heilbroner (1975) stated the problem as follows:

> The elementary responses and drives of the constituents of the political, social, or economic processes described by the social sciences remain beyond the explanatory power—even beyond the conceptual grasp—of these disciplines. There is no sociological or economic theory of individual human action. Sociology, economics, and political science simply assume the presence of certain behavioral attributes of individuals and then seek to elucidate the consequences of the interaction of these attributes. Economics is the most ambitious of these efforts, building complex models of a deductive kind on the presumed acquisitive behavior of mankind; but economics has no theory of acquisitiveness as such, or no answer to the question of whether this important behavioral trait is the production of a certain social milieu or a transhistoric property of an invariant "human nature." (p. 416–417)

In 1932 Beaglehole had made essentially the same observation as Heilbroner, and as a result he attempted to gather and analyze all of the existing evidence dealing with the relation of property to human nature. He presented his analysis of the relevant biological, psychological, and anthropological literature in his book, *Property: A study in social psychology*. While he did an impressive job of compiling the relevant information at that time, the task of drawing valid and significant conclusions proved to be very difficult. Given the absence of any direct attempts to study possession in humans, Beaglehole's analysis was limited in that he could only offer speculative theoretical suggestions based mainly on animal studies and anecdotal anthropological reports.

The fundamental question to be examined here is a motivational one—what causes or determines possession-related behavior in human beings? Any such investigation of motivation will necessarily examine the biological and instinctual bases as well as the social and environmental determinants of the behavior in question. In so doing, one must be particularly sensitive to the nature and significance of the interaction between "nature" and "nurture," for it is becoming increasingly clear that the subtleties and varieties of this interaction can usually teach us more about human behavior than either factor examined in isolation.

Early in this century, a human "instinct of acquisition" was posited by a number of writers (James, 1890; LeTourneau, 1892; McDougall, 1916;

Rivers, 1920). The instinctual approach to human nature was soon severely criticized, and Beaglehole argued strongly against an instinctual explanation of possessiveness. The current definition and theory of instincts is much more complex and subtle than the earlier views, and it shies away from attempting an enumeration of the instincts in humans at the present time (Fletcher, 1966). Nevertheless, concepts of human nature, lay and scientific alike, have continued to contain a strong belief in innate determinants of acquisitiveness. " 'Man, by nature, desires to own and hold property' is a venerable assertion of human nature and one of the most closely analyzed and most frequently cited assumptions of human nature in the history of human thought" (Wrightsman, 1974, p. 18).

Such assumptions about innate determinants of motives and behaviors have far-reaching consequences. As Wrightsman (1974) points out:

> Although they are distinct and separate constructs, theories of human nature and theories of society are very closely tied together. These ties are not incidental. The bonds are clearly inferential and psychological. For example, if man is believed to be malleable in nature, then it becomes the function of government to mold men in socially desirable ways. But, if on the other hand, man is seen as endowed by nature with certain innate qualities, then it is the function of government to protect man's right to act in his own individual way (Weyant, 1971). (p.14)

Thus, for example, it is argued by some that capitalism is the most desirable economic system because it is the best suited to the universal desire for private gain, the latter being a fundamental human trait (Friedman, 1962). Those arguing for alternative economic systems often question the universality and innateness of this motive, maintaining that desire for private gain has its origins in certain environmental experiences, and not in any innate characteristics (Schmitt, 1973). Clearly, a thorough study of the origins, development, and functions of possession and ownership will have very important implications for social theory.

Casual observation suggests that possession also plays a central role in the psychological development of the individual. Possessiveness seems to be manifested in a very large percentage of human activity—a great deal of energy is focused on possession and ownership, at least in our society. It thus seems that major advances might be made in our understanding of individual human motivation and behavior if we would undertake a careful study of the psychological importance and function of possession to the individual throughout development.

In addition to the implications this topic has for both social and psychological theory, there may soon be very pressing practical applications of our knowledge in this area. Such titles as *The end of affluence* (Ehrlich & Ehrlich, 1974), *The next crisis: Universal famine* (Mallory, 1974), *The scarcity society* (Ophuls, 1974), and *Shortages and the social system* (Boulding, 1974) all underline one common message: We will soon face conditions of scarcity of material goods—conditions very different from the present level of affluence. While the prediction of scarcity may or may not prove correct, the large number of scholars and scientists sharing this view suggests we should consider it seriously. Indeed, Otto (1975) has even pleaded that "our socialization machinery needs practical cook book level material on how to live in a period of scarcity" (p. 14).

II. Review of the Evidence

In examining a topic as broad in scope as the nature and function of possession and ownership among human beings, we are necessarily concerned with individuals in different cultures and at different times in history. While our research question is restricted to possessiveness in humans, in attempting to understand questions of "human nature" it is advisable to also examine other species for possible evolutionary precursors of the phenomena under study. Thus, this problem must ultimately encompass all three dimensions used in a life-span developmental psychology as outlined by Baltes and Goulet (1970): species, cultures, and generations.

In this section, I will first summarize (a) the existing work with respect to possession among nonhuman species, and (b) the comparative evidence on possession among different human cultures. I will then discuss in more detail the results of recent empirical work examining the development of possession and ownership in our own culture. In the final section, I will propose some elements of a tentative theoretical framework in which this work may be interpreted from a life-span perspective.

A.   PROPERTY AMONG NONHUMANS

Comparative psychology argues for a study of possession among animals other than humans, in the belief that we may learn something about possession among humans in the process. Beaglehole (1932) carried out considerable work in this area. He examined and discussed in great detail the behavior of certain animals, representative of a number of different species. In so doing, he assumed that the existence of property[1] among

---

[1]The terms "property" and "possessions" are considered to be synonymous for our purposes. In discussing Beaglehole's work, "property" will be employed since that is the term he used.

animals is manifested by active defense against attempted aggression or spoilation—a disposition to defend against the interference of others. The adequacy of this definition is certainly questionable. Does possession require strong defense against attack? Any animal may act possessively toward a particular object in numerous ways, and yet never defend that object against attack, for example, when the animal is on the very lowest rung of the dominance hierarchy. On the other hand, there may be instances of defense against attack which in no other way indicate a property relation. However, the definitional problem is an almost insurmountable one, since the very meaning of possession and property is part of the research question itself. (This issue will be treated in greater detail below.)

By examining the life patterns and activities of certain kinds of insects, birds, and mammals, Beaglehole (1932) concluded that acquisition among most animals is restricted to the realm of food storage. The latter is an instinctive reaction to the scarcity of food, particularly in wintertime, just as there are other instinctive reactions to the severe conditions of the winter. The acquisition and storage of food is simply a means of avoiding one of the dangers of winter.

The few exceptional cases of *storing objects other than food* are explained by (a) curiosity and interest which is aroused by bright, portable objects (among birds), (b) "nest-building impulses" (among rodents), and (c) the desire to use objects for adornment and playthings (among apes). While the assumed innate "curiosity and interest" and "desire for adornment" seem almost as mysterious as the desire to possess which they are invoked to explain, Beaglehole's main point is that objects are possessed by animals solely because they fulfill certain specific needs and desires. Those cases of *defense of territory* are seen as part of a larger configuration directed toward the satisfaction of "sexual and parental impulses."

Beaglehole (1932) summarizes the results and implications of his examination of property among animals as follows. The psychological basis of property among animals is not an instinct of acquisition. Rather, it lies in the tendency of animals to appropriate objects which will satisfy basic organismic needs. An animal will acquire food, and a nest, and a mate, all because they satisfy instinctive needs. When their acquisition is threatened, those objects will be defended, and in that respect they are a primitive form of property. However, according to Beaglehole any possessive behavior with respect to such objects is not motivated by an acquisitive instinct per se, but by the desire to satisfy other instinctual needs.

Although Beaglehole's review of the evidence is basically a sound one, he does speak of "mental appropriation" and "sentiments of ownership" without offering any definition of these concepts. This is unfortunate, since it is the nature of these very concepts which he purports to be studying. With the exception of these few lapses in his usually critical analysis and careful interpretation of the data, Beaglehole's (1932) general conclusions regarding property among animals seem warranted: Animals appropriate objects which serve some basic need such as food, reproductive functions, etc., but there is apparently no instinct of acquisition per se, and no innate tendency to hoard, collect, or acquire for the sake of acquiring alone. What we may see as property among animals is simply the result of the organism's efforts toward self-provision and self-perpetuation.

While a careful examination of property among nonhumans is certainly of some interest, its significance has been questioned by Hallowell (1943):

> Neither the *de facto* control exercised by animals over certain objects, nor the aggressive defense of them, is itself evidence that property as an institution exists among them. . . . All we observe is the utilization of possession in the sense of physical custody of certain objects which bear a relation to the biological needs of the organism or group of organisms. (p. 248)

Hallowell's argument certainly has some merit, although his central concern was property *rights*—property as a social institution—while my topic of inquiry is the much broader concept of possession in general. In any case, we see that there is a limit to what we can learn about the origins and function of possession among humans by studying property among nonhumans.

B. ANTHROPOLOGICAL APPROACHES

1. A Comparative Review of Possession among Adults

Comparative anthropology argues for an examination of possession and ownership among many different cultures, in the belief that such a method is the only way one can pursue nomothetic questions—questions searching for universal principles of human behavior. The research problem before us is certainly a nomothetic one, yet it has never been examined in detail by anthropologists. While the absence of any attempt by anthropologists to study the nature of possessiveness and acquisitiveness in humans may come as a surprise to the reader, there is actually little reason to expect such nomothetic comparisons. Throughout this century anthropologists have concentrated the great majority of their efforts on descriptive ideographic case studies (Harris, 1968). The establishment of the Human Relations Area Files[2] (HRAF) was an attempt to foster more nomothetic studies, but a recent examination of anthropology journals shows that 80% of all research reported there still consists of case studies, and only 5% contains a comparative, nomothetic approach (Rohner, 1976).

There have been several general studies of the economic and property systems among a variety of different cultures (Ellwood, 1927; Herskovits, 1940; Hoebel, 1968; LaFargue, 1890; LeTourneau, 1892; Lowie, 1920; Thurnwald, 1937). However, it is Beaglehole, a psychologist, who has provided us with the only existing attempt at a comparative anthropological study of possession with the goal of drawing universal conclusions about human nature. He examined property among what he termed "primitive peoples." As was the case in studying property among lower animals, one must face the problem of defining what we mean by possession and ownership. Although Beaglehole (1932) seemed oblivious to difficulties inherent in this task when he defined property among nonhumans, he recognized the near impossibility of maintaining a single definition of property for different human societies. He recognized that not only does ownership have a different connotation in primitive compared to civilized societies, but it also undoubtedly has a different meaning for different types of primitive cultures. Nevertheless, Beaglehole did offer a definition of property as the "appropriation to persons capable of enjoying them, of goods or values satisfying fundamental needs" (p. 132). Such a definition is not very useful in that the buck is simply passed from the word "property" to the word "appropriation." One can, of course, pass the buck still further. Beaglehole went on to define appropriation as the establishment of an "enduring and intimate relation" between the individual and the object in question. The key, obviously, is what *kind* of relation. As will be seen below, recent work has included a more thorough exploration of the nature of this relation. However, Beaglehole was content with the above definition of ownership in his cross-cultural work, and his results are worth reviewing here in that light.

---

[2]The Human Relations Area Files is a catalogue of indexed ethnographic summaries (descriptions of cultures) filed under a uniform set of topical headings. All source material (book, article, etc.) for a given ethnic or political unit is coded in the margin with respect to the topic each passage deals with. Every page of a source is thus analyzed. The result is a collection of detailed ethnographic information on over 250 cultures, annotated according to a system of over 710 different categories of cultural information. Obviously, this represents an invaluable resource for investigations of a nomothetic nature.

A good deal of Beaglehole's (1932) analysis concerns magic and animism in the belief systems of many different cultures. Examination of possession and ownership in these cultures leads him to the conclusion that the "native" sees personal property as somehow assimilated to the self. A part of the individual's "life-spirit" is integrated into the object, and that object is believed to be a part of the self. Beaglehole (1932) proposes this principle as a basic psychological characteristic of humans. However, he goes on to offer numerous examples of the wide variety of systems of ownership in different societies, and of the dependence of property values on environmental and social patterns. He argues that the form of property in any given social group is the result not only of the above-mentioned integration of the self with objects. It also depends on the established cultural patterns of the group, which in turn depend on many historical and economic factors.

Although Beaglehole presents convincing evidence for the second half of his argument—the importance of sociocultural factors in shaping human behavior with respect to possession and ownership—his assertion that humans have a tendency to integrate part of their self with objects which they use is more speculative. This is an interesting hypothesis, but it is entirely unclear whether such a tendency is universal, and also whether it reflects strong biological forces or simply cultural learning. Thus, while Beaglehole's discussion of property among "primitive peoples" is quite informative, it is far from satisfactory for answering the general question about the origins and development of possession and ownership. He suggests one innate psychological basis for property, but his argument is unconvincing; and he suggests that environmental influences are important in shaping various forms that ownership takes within different societies—hardly a controversial conclusion.

2. A Cross-Cultural Look at the Socialization of Possession

Beaglehole's study was limited to examining *adult* behavior with respect to possession and ownership in different societies. However, even more germane to our research question would be an examination of the socialization practices which *children* experience with respect to property in different societies—what happens during childhood to contribute to adult behavior toward possessions? One approach to answering this question is a study recently carried out by Furby (1974) using the HRAF (see footnote 2, p. 303) as source material. The purpose of examining the HRAF was to find some indication of either (a) such wide cultural variability in the enculturation[3] and development of possessive behavior that enculturation practices could be suggested as the major determinant of possession and ownership in any given society, or (b) some kind of universal conditions or behaviors which could suggest the possibility of some fairly fundamental need or desire to possess.

The entire set of files was searched for any material dealing with the "transmission of cultural norms" (coded as #867 in the files). The latter includes the transmission of notions of property and ownership, although it also encompasses many other kinds of norms and values as well. Mention of some aspect of the socialization of enculturation of possession and ownership, sharing, generosity, possessiveness, etc., was found in 38 cultures.

Generally speaking, this material consisted of only a sentence or two, at most a paragraph or two, mentioning children's possessions, or sharing behavior, or child-rearing techniques with respect to ownership and possession. The large majority of references stated or implied that children are naturally possessive and acquisitive and that society must inculcate something different if so desired. However, the age at which, and the ease with which, generosity and sharing are obtained seems to vary widely. Thus, most of the material was too general and fragmented for any solid conclusions. Nevertheless, several types of information uncovered are worth noting.

a. Enculturation techniques. An examination of the actual techniques used by adults to enculturate attitudes and cognitions about property in different societies revealed some common themes (techniques occurring in at least five or six different societies):

1. Children are taught the boundaries of land by *observing* the settling of disputes among adults.

2. They are subjected to *public chastisement and ridicule* of those with very little, or those who don't share.

3. They experience *physical punishment* for breaking others' possessions, or for not sharing.

4. They have their *own finances,* own plot of land to cultivate, own fish to sell, etc.

5. They hear *fables and stories* with lessons about sharing, working hard for possessions, etc.

Given the nature of the data, no conclusions can be drawn as to the

[3]Williams (1972) distinguished between (a) "socialization"—the process of transmitting human culture, and (b) "enculturation"—the process of transmitting a particular culture.

importance of each of these techniques as a determinant of possessive and acquisitive behavior. But the fact that each of them has been reported in at least several different cultures suggests that they are deserving of further systematic study.

b.   The relationship between food and possession.   A considerable number of the references to the enculturation of possession were closely linked to references to the enculturation of eating. While it is unclear what the nature or importance of this relationship is, the list of dual references to food and possession with respect to enculturation practices, presented in Table I (see p. 308), suggests the possibility that much of the socialization of property and ownership takes place with respect to behavior toward food. In other words, the experiences a child has with respect to food (i.e., enculturation with respect to food) may be related to, perhaps a determinant of, the development of concepts and behaviors and attitudes with respect to possession and ownership.

This notion, of course, is not a novel one. Freudian theory argues that the infant's first possession is the mother's breast, and since at some point the infant is denied the breast, s/he desires to possess other objects instead as substitutes (Isaacs, 1933). While the results of this cross-cultural study are unclear about the nature of the relation between enculturation with respect to food and enculturation with respect to possession, this topic is certainly worthy of further research.

c.   Margaret Mead on the Manus.   In her ethnography of the Manus, Margaret Mead (1930) touched upon an analysis which may have considerable significance for the socialization of possession and ownership in most, if not all, societies. This potential universality is of great importance, given the nomothetic task at hand. Mead (1930) proposed that: "In many societies (and maybe in *all*) children's walking means more trouble for the adults. Once able to walk, the children are a constant menace to property, breaking dishes, spilling the soup, tearing books, tangling the thread" (p. 32). Now, it is also around 18–24 months that American parents report the sudden and vigorous emergence of "This is mine" behavior. One is thus led to consider the coincidence of (a) walking and the resulting danger to adult (or others') property, and (b) the emergence of observable and adamant possessive behavior in the young child. Mead's (1930) description of the Manus child at this age is relevant:

> But in Manus where property is sacred and one wails for lost property as for the dead, respect for property is taught children from their earliest years. Before they can walk they are rebuked or chastised for touching anything which does not belong to them . . . . All of our possessions . . . were safe from the 2- and 3-year-olds who would have been untamed vandals in a forest of loot in most societies. . . . There was no attempt to make it easy for the child . . . nothing is put out of the child's reach. The

mother spreads her tiny brightly colored beads out on a mat or in a shallow bowl, right on the floor within the reach of the crawling baby and the baby is taught not to touch them. . . . A good baby is a baby which never touches anything; a good child is one who never touches anything and never asks for anything not its own. These are the only important items of ethical behavior demanded of children. (p. 32–33)

It appears that the Manus were simply doing an earlier, and apparently more effective, job of what almost all societies attempt to do sooner or later, and to a greater or lesser degree: to keep children (and adults) from harming or damaging or disturbing material objects. This may be a very important situation (potential danger to property) combined with an enculturation goal (individual does not damage material goods) leading to the development of a sense of private property and the attitudes and cognitions and behaviors comprising possessiveness, and this situation and the accompanying enculturation goal might be very close to universal.

Mead (1930) goes on to describe how:

The slightest breakage is punished without mercy. . . . Any breakage, any carelessness, is punished. The parents do not condone the broken pot which was already cracked and then wax suddenly furious when a good pot is broken, after the fashion of American parents who let the child tear the almanac and the telephone book and then wonder at its grieved astonishment when it is slapped for tearing up the family Bible. [The Manus simply do the same thing more effectively and efficiently than we do.] The tail of a fish, the extra bit of taro, the half rotten betel nut, cannot be appropriated with any more impunity than can the bowl of feast food. (p. 33)

The concern of the adult Manus seems to clearly be damage or destruction of property, and the same concern may well be at the root of our own enculturation with respect to possessiveness, but it is just seen in a purer and more exaggerated form in the Manus.

In summary, one reasonable hypothesis seems to be that when children start walking, they become a much greater menace to the objects around them than they had been previously. As a result, the adults (and others) around them greatly increase behaviors directed toward preventing damage or destruction of that property. The latter include physically taking objects from the child's grasp, physical punishment, verbal punishment, expounding on "that's mine," "that's not yours," "don't touch, that doesn't belong to you," "here, take this toy which is yours, and don't touch mommy's things," etc. As a result, the child gets a heavy dose of the possession and ownership lesson for that particular culture.

While this analysis may help in understanding the socialization of possession and ownership, it does not shed much light on the relative importance of socialization as compared with other possible determinants of possessive behavior. However, Mead's analysis will be combined with certain elements of motivational theory to constitute a major portion of

TABLE I

Dual References to the Enculturation of Food and Possession
in Human Relations Area Files

1. In Korea, sweets are given by grandparents as special treats to their grandchildren. [22;3]*a*

2. In China the children of the rich (before the Revolution) spend and squander freely, and "what's true with regard to money is even more true with regard to other habits of consumption. Rich children tend to indulge in excessive eating; poor children constantly have to tighten their belts." [26;330]

3. In Afghanistan, "Weaned children are still favored as to snacks, and it is realized that they are extravagant in spending money on sweetmeats." [6;88]

4. In Tellensi, "This emphasis on just sharing among siblings begins in childhood, first when siblings sit down to eat from a common dish, and then in children's play groups" where they divide up a small animal they have killed just as their parents divide up sacrificial meat. [3;260]

5. For the Tiv, "The most important social prohibitions early taught to children are that they must not ask other people for food and that they must not steal," the former usually not being a problem because food is usually offered to them. [22;369]

Also, "A child should be generous and offer to share his food." [22;379]

6. In Mbundu, "Children are beaten if they . . . steal food." [3;213]

7. In Bemba, "Food's also something that has to be shared, and in this attitude our Bemba baby is definitely trained even in the first years. . . . As the Bemba child gets older there is a third attitude he has to acquire, i.e., that food is something over which his older brothers and sisters have definite rights." [2;197]

8. In Lovedu, "Great importance is attached to the sharing of food . . . even small children are made to share tid-bits." [2;110]

9. In Ojibwa, "A mother would put some food into a dish and tell her child to take it to the neighbors and so teach the child to give and share." [15;98]

10. In Mandau, "A son was informed at an early age of his father's fasting and war record and was taught to believe that the family's possession of property and good health was attributable to the father's fasting, respect for sacred objects, and kindness to the old people." [2;47]

11. In Yurok, "They are told to take in a little food with their spoon, to put it into their mouth slowly, to put the spoon back into the eating basket, and to chew slowly and thoroughly, meanwhile thinking always of becoming rich. . . . Nobody is supposed to talk during the meal, so that everyone can concentrate on thoughts of wealth.

In this compulsive way an attitude toward wealth is conditioned (in connection with the oral zone but not at the oral stage) which later on allows the Yurok to think of wealth at any time in an almost hallucinatory way. . . . In this way also an attitude is conditioned which encourages the Yurok to subordinate drive as such to the pursuit of wealth so that later on it will be not only his appetite for food which he learns to restrain for the sake of amassing wealth, but also his sexual desires." [4;286]

12. In Tapahumara, "The hungry child who opens the storage bins of his parents has committed a 'theft.'" [10;187]

13. In Oranda, "The sharing of food is drilled into the children from earliest infancy; both sexes are taught the lesson until it is deeply ingrained. Later they are taught to whom food must first be given, and to whom next and next." [39;21]

(continued)

14. Among the Manus, "The rule against asking for food is part of the training in respect for property." [1;96]

15. In New Ireland, children are told fables, one example of which tells of children who drowned because they ate bananas that had been forbidden them." [1;93]

16. In Maori, "Generosity and hospitality are admired virtues, thus, when a child was given some delectable article of food, an elder might ask him for a portion thereof in order to accustom the child to be unselfish." [1;395]

17. In Araucanians, "Children are taught to give and to share. On one occasion a mother showed a handerchief that I had given to her six-year-old son and then led him by the hand to the storage space in the ruka, put an egg into each of his hands, pushed him forward toward me, and had him give me the eggs and say, 'This is for you.'" [10;52]

a Note: In [X;Y], X refers to the source number, and Y to the page, of the Human Relations Area Files source.

the theoretical propositions presented below on the origins and determinants of possession and ownership.

3. The Tasaday

One additional source of anthropological evidence related to possession and ownership became available in 1971 with the discovery of the Tasaday tribe in the Philippines. This group of approximately 25 individuals lives in the dense jungle of the island of Mindanao. They are particularly fascinating to students of human behavior because they had apparently had no contact with the "outside world" for at least 700 years prior to their recent discovery. They were "untouched" by Western, or any other society, and therefore totally free from any influence of our behavior and values with respect to possessions. For this reason, it is informative to examine possession and ownership among this group.

Considerable information is available in the written reports of several anthropologists (Fernandez & Lynch, 1972) and in the recent book by a photojournalist (Nance, 1975). Since none of the individuals visiting the Tasaday have systematically obtained information with respect to possessions, only brief anecdotal evidence is available.

The Tasaday have very few artifacts. The jungle they live in is so rich that food gathering is a relatively simple task that requires few implements. The several stone tools that they do use are generally made right at the time they are needed, and then abandoned. It is interesting how well this situation matches speculations by Soergel on the nature of property among prehistoric humans:

> Soergel thinks that during the paleolithic period, property with respect to materials, tools, and utensils applied not so much to the objects themselves as to the know-how necessary to make them. He considers it necessary to recognize that neolithic hunters remade their tools according to their needs at each new place of residence, and when

they moved on they did not take the tools with them. (From Thurnwald, R., 1932, "Economics in Primitive Communities" by permission of the Oxford University Press, translation mine)

Although the Tasaday are not hunters who change their dwelling place often, it is apparently more trouble than it's worth to transport the implements they make in the jungle. They simply make new ones whenever they need them. As a result, there appears to be no ownership of these implements—or at least no ownership as we know it. Soergel (in Thurnwald, 1937) suggested that the know-how to make implements may be considered as property, but we don't have the necessary evidence to evaluate that possibility for the Tasaday.

While it appears that there was very little private ownership as we know it among the Tasaday before their contact with the outside world,[4] the kind of information presently available is far too fragmentary and anecdotal to be very informative for a more general understanding of possession and ownership in humans.

C.   A LIFE-SPAN APPROACH

A third possible research strategy is to focus on the foundations and functions of possession in humans at different periods throughout the life span. In light of the difficulties discussed above in even defining possession and ownership, and the problems in establishing general principles of property-related behavior in humans by using either comparative psychological or comparative anthropological methods, this third alternative is especially important.

Two studies have recently been carried out which focus on life-span analysis of the nature of possession.[5] The first consisted of relatively detailed interview data obtained from a total of 120 subjects, 20 at each of six age levels (kindergarten, second, fifth, eighth, eleventh grades, and college undergraduates). The results from a content analysis of these data with respect to seven general topics (the meaning or definition of possession, the nature of possessables, the onset and termination of possession, use and sharing of personal possessions, reasons for and fairness of

[4]One artifact which had been given to the Tasaday after their discovery was necklaces. Some time after they had been given these, it was noticed that they were no longer in evidence. When asked about them, the Tasaday replied that "they're in a safe place." We have no idea, of course, how many other things might also be in that "safe place."

[5]Because of the vastness of this topic, these studies were limited to possession of material objects in an attempt to delimit a research problem of manageable size. Obviously, a complete understanding of possession must eventually deal with nonmaterial possessions as well.

personal possession, judgments about unequal distribution of possessions, and feasibility and evaluation of collective possession) have been presented elsewhere (Furby, Harter, & John, 1975).

Subsequent to that initial study, a considerably larger study was undertaken encompassing both a wider age range (including 40- to 50-year-olds) as well as three different culture groups (American, Israeli kibbutz, and Israeli city). The design, procedure, and results of this study are also described in detail elsewhere (Furby, 1976a, 1976b, 1976c, 1977, 1978a, 1978b).

Consistent with "the first task of a developmental discipline" as discussed by Baltes and Goulet (1970), a major goal of these studies has been to identify and describe age differences and similarities in the nature of possession. The emphasis on *description* of developmental change was necessitated by the lack of previous research in this area. *Explanation* of developmental change will have to await further empirical (and in particular, longitudinal) studies, although some speculation about cause-and-effect relationships is offered in what follows.

The discussion in this section summarizes the highlights of the results of the above studies for American children and adults.[6] The following section (III) relates these results, as well as the cross-species and cross-cultural evidence presented above, to some preliminary thoughts on a general theoretical analysis of possessiveness throughout the life span.

1. The Meaning of Possession

What does it mean to possess something? We saw above how critical this definitional problem is, when we examined property among nonhumans as well as when we discussed possession and ownership in a cross-cultural perspective. Indeed, it was extremely difficult to establish a definition for what we mean by possession, and yet such a definition is clearly central to any systematic study of the phenomena of interest. It thus is clear that a major task of the initial work in this area is to discover what the defining dimensions and characteristics of possession and ownership are. Others have come to an analogous conclusion in closely related areas such as the study of territoriality (Kaufman, 1971).

In the above-mentioned studies, subjects were asked what it means that something is theirs or belongs to them. This was discussed both in general terms as well as with respect to specific objects they possessed.

The two most frequently mentioned features of possession were *use of*

---

[6]Although this work has included two other cultural groups (Israeli kibbutz and Israeli city), both groups were quite limited in age range (5- and 10-year-olds only) and thus contribute little to the life-span analysis presented here.

the object and *the right to control use*. This suggests that control over the use of an object is the most salient defining characteristic of possession for all ages studied to date. Both use and rights to control use contain an important element of control. If I am the one who uses an object, I certainly exercise considerable control over it; if I have the *right* to control use, I exercise even more control, not only over the object but also over other individuals. The importance of this dimension is consistent with general definitions of property and ownership. Control is at least one aspect of Webster's (1974) definitions for "possession," for "ownership," and for "property." And legally, property is "the right to control, to exploit, to use, or to enjoy wealth or possessions" (Maciver, 1945–1946).

The supreme importance of control over use has profound implications for any theoretical interpretation of the origins and function of possession. One is immediately reminded of the large body of work currently devoted to effectively interacting with one's environment as a major motivational force. Investigators have variously focused on such aspects as personal causation (deCharms, 1968), feelings of competence and self-determination (Deci, 1975), locus of control (Rotter, 1966), effectance motivation (White, 1959), learned helplessness (Seligman, 1975), and freedom (Brehm, 1972), but all represent variations on a single theme, namely, that human beings are motivated to produce effects and interact competently in their environment. Possessions may well be one major manifestation of effectance motivation. This possibility will be elaborated upon below.

For all but the youngest subjects (kindergarteners), the fact that possessions *make possible some activity or enjoyment* for the owner was frequently mentioned as a defining characteristic of ownership, and this factor took on increasing importance from second grade through middle age. In this sense, possessions appear to be seen as means to an end— they allow one to do what one wants. Again, note the personal control element that is implied in this dimension. Possessions enable one to have the effect and to engage in the activities one desires.

Another principal characteristic of ownership was the *acquisition* process. This was important at all ages, although it shifted from being a passive process for the youngest subjects (another buys or gives) to an increasingly active one beginning in fifth grade (owner buying or working for). This developmental shift from passive or other-initiated to active or owner-initiated means of acquisition may have important implications for the meaning or nature of possession at different age levels. Subjects indicated that *passive* means of acquisition result in positive affect for the object in that it has sentimental value. Also, the other person must like me, and I am aware of their sacrifice. In other words, receiving an object from someone else has certain implications about the interpersonal relationship between two individuals, and the receiver is dependent to a certain extent on the giver. A number of anthropologists have invested considerable time and energy analyzing the social functions of gift-giving and gift-receiving. In particular, Mauss' (1924) *The Gift* posited the principle of reciprocity as the basis for relationships of solidarity between individuals as well as groups: "Food, women, children, possession, charms, land, labor, services, religious offices, rank—everything is stuff to be given away and repaid" (pp. 11–12). Levi-Strauss (1949) has elaborated upon the social importance of reciprocity, and has even posited a fundamental and universal need for gift-giving and gift-receiving.

Active means of acquisition, on the other hand, are reported by subjects to require that the individual expend effort and/or obtain sufficient money—certain prerequisites have to be filled. But as a result, possession and use rights are seen as more complete. In this context, it is interesting to note that early adolescents reported some difficulty in believing they own anything at all, since their parents are the source of most possessions, and also have ultimate authority over them. The younger child does not seem to question his ability to possess things independently from parents, but the early adolescent seems to see independent, active acquisition of personal possessions as critical to ownership. The shift from passive to active means of acquisition takes place at an age when self-identity and independence from parents are of major concern. Active, owner-initiated acquisition of possessions would certainly be one way to increase one's sense of competence and decrease one's dependence on others (and thus lack of control). In this vein, Isaacs (1949) has argued that:

> The wish to be *potent* in giving is very clear in much of the behavior of little children. For if one has the wherewithal to give, one is indeed both safe and good. One is no longer the helpless ruling infant, dependent upon the gifts of others, and driven by helpless anxieties or rage and jealousy. One is now the omnipotent parent, full of good things, safe from unsatisfied desire, and all powerful to help others (viz. one's children). It is more blessed to give than receive, because to be able to give is *not to need.* It is (in unconscious meaning) to be omnipotently safe and good. (p. 259)

Isaacs' emphasis is on the benefits of *giving,* but the contrast she describes with the state of *receiving* supports the importance of this transition from passive to active means of acquisition as a transition to increased control over one's environment. However, an important distinction should be noted between this factor and that of control over *use:* The acquisition process is an aspect of the *onset* of possession, whereas the right to control use characterizes the *state* or condition of possessing.

One dimension mentioned fairly frequently by only the youngest subjects was the owner's *having or keeping the object*. This was a salient
dimension throughout elementary school, but not at the older ages. It is
unclear whether this reflects purely a custodial aspect of possession or
whether there is also an implication of control over use. In light of the fact
that use per se (in contrast to *rights* to use) was also relatively more
salient for the youngest children than for older children or adults, it
appears that simple use, contact, and custodianship may be a significant
defining characteristic of possession at this age, quite apart from any
rights to use or keep. This is reminiscent of Beaglehole's (1932) examples
of cultures in which anything that is used or touched by an individual is
then considered to be hers/his. He gave the example of a cup which, once
it has touched one's mouth, is considered to be one's personal property
by certain Africans. While Beaglehole interpreted this phenomenon as
due to an innate tendency to integrate part of the self with anything that is
contacted by an individual, it would seem that the critical feature here
may again be one of personal control. If I am the one who generally uses
and/or keeps something, I certainly control it in a very real and significant
way, even though the ultimate *right* to control it may lie elsewhere.

An alternative explanation emphasizes the *associational* aspect of possession. Something is mine by virtue of being associated with my person
(as opposed to other persons). Gesell and Ilg's (1946) observations are
consistent with this interpretation; they note that already at 18 months of
age, the child sees a definite association between an owner and his/her
possession which is manifested by taking the objects to its owner. They
interpret this as part of the child's knowledge of where things belong and a
concomitant desire to put them in their places. Thus, we must entertain
the possibility that the purely associational relation between a person and
an object is an important aspect of possession in the very young child.

In this vein, it is interesting to note Luria's (1973) evidence for the
possible localization in the brain of such an associational function. Certain
lesions in the right hemisphere result in

> *incorrect identification* or in the attribution of the wrong *ownership*. One such patient,
> for example, even recognized a shawl and could distinguish the flowers woven on it,
> but she did not recognize it as *her own* and helplessly asked: "Whose shawl is this?"
> Another patient, with an extensive atrophic lesion in the right occipital region, when
> shown a picture of some soldiers on a tank exclaimed: "Why, of course, it is all my
> family, my husband, sons and sisters." (p. 126–127)

This intriguing evidence probably raises more questions than it answers,
but it does underscore the associational element in ownership which we
may be inclined to overlook because it is taken so much for granted.

The owner's *responsibility for the care* of possessions was a frequently mentioned definition of possession by late elementary school subjects, and remained a very salient feature for older ages. While younger subjects seldom mentioned this notion, by fifth grade parents are undoubtedly trying to impress children with the importance of taking care of their own things, and this might explain the emergence of this dimension at that age. These results are consistent with Gesell and Ilg's (1946) assertion that some children as young as age 7 begin to take better care of their possessions, but this is by no means a very common characteristic until 9 or 10 years of age.

The other main factor becoming apparent at fifth grade was the owner's *positive affect for the object*—owning something means you like it. This factor takes on importance at the age when active means of acquistion become more common. In contrast to younger children for whom acquisition is a passive process (they depend on others to give or buy them things), in late elementary school children begin to participate in the selection and acquisition process. Thus, their positive affect for the object is a logical prerequisite and apparently a more central feature of possession.

It is only for the 40- to 50-year-olds that *legal aspects* of possession were frequently mentioned features of its meaning. This is consistent with the fact that they are the only age group studied having much experience with the legal system with respect to property. The other dimension unique to this older age group was *pride and satisfaction* in owning something—possessions represent an accomplishment. This may reflect their considerable experience with the work ethic and social rewards for material accumulation and "conspicuous consumption" (Veblen, 1899) so prevalent in our society. As Otto (1975) put it, "We have a classic operant model working on a grand scale in our society that rewards those who over-acquire and punishes those who do not acquire . . . [due to] our preoccupation with achievement and success" (p. 6).

2. Motivation for Possession

Why do people possess things? To what degree are the acquisition and accumulation of possessions important or central to one's existence and happiness, and for what specific reasons? In the studies reviewed here, subjects were asked why people in general own things, and why they themselves have personal possessions.

The two most frequently mentioned reasons people have personal possessions were (a) to *make possible certain activities, convenience, or enjoyment,* and (b) *positive affect* for the object. Both of these factors were important at all age levels. With respect to the instrumental function—possessions make possible certain activities and pleasures—in addition to the value of those activities and pleasures per se, there may also be a value to the *freedom* that results when one or more desired outcomes are available. It has been suggested that "in any situational context, the individual attempts to organize his environment so that it *maximizes* his freedom of choice" (Proshansky, Ittleson, & Rivlin, 1970). Or, viewed from a slightly different angle, "a person is motivationally aroused any time he thinks one of his freedoms has been threatened or eliminated. This motivational arousal, called 'psychological reactance' (Brehm, 1966), moves a person to try to restore his freedom" (Brehm, 1972).

While the definition of "freedom" is complex (see Steiner, 1970; Wilke, 1976), one critical characteristic is the ability to obtain desired outcomes—possessions enable me to do what I want. Thus, my ice skates enable me to play hockey (which I enjoy); my washing machine enables me to wash clothes when and how I want (which gives me pleasure); my car enables me to transport myself to distant places whenever I want (which is desirable). In sum, this dimension of possession seems to consist of *the ability to effect desired outcomes in one's environment.* As mentioned earlier, there is currently considerable research on the motivation for causal efficacy and personal control in one's environment; its relationship to the motivation for possession will be discussed further in the theoretical formulations presented below.

By fifth grade, the owner's *need* for the object was also a frequent reason given for why people have personal possessions, and this became the most frequently mentioned reason for high school subjects, but dropped somewhat in importance for 40- to 50-year-olds. This dimension represents the fairly straightforward assertion that a person possesses certain objects because they are necessary to the individual's welfare. Need is at the essence of Beaglehole's (1932) final theoretical formulation of the motivation for personal possession. He argues that the germ of acquisitive behavior is an "innate impulse to grasp and to handle all those objects which in some manner or other serve to satisfy the fundamental needs" (p. 279). Isaacs (1949) expressed the same basic argument: "I want to own it because if I do not it may not be there when I need it, and my need will go unsatisfied" (p. 225).

Such an analysis seems to depend on the existence of conditions of scarcity in order to account for the motivation for personal possession. If there were 100% certainty that the object would always be there when needed, and thus one's need would never go unsatisfied, then presumably there would be no motivation for possession. In other words, it is conditions of scarcity which motivate personal possession. "The insecurity engendered by material scarcity leads to the acquisition of property as an attempted insulation from the natural world" (Whitebook, 1972, p. 22).

This argument has been common in the literature (Lewinski, 1913; Schlatter, 1951; Whitebook, 1972), but its validity has yet to be tested in any systematic or rigorous fashion. It has been demonstrated that scarcity enhances the value of an object (Fromklin, Olson, Dipboye, & Barnaby, 1971; Worchel, Lee, & Adewole, 1975), but it is unclear whether it also enhances the desire to possess the object. While many subjects see possession as serving the function of assuring the satisfaction of one's needs, the importance of this dimension is somewhat tempered by the very low frequency of "availability for use" as a reason given for personal possession. The scarcity hypothesis would imply that ensuring availability per se is the critical variable; however, subjects' statements that the owner "needs" the object may just be a somewhat less articulate way of saying the same thing.

By high school age, an additional major reason for why people possess was that personal possessions imply *social power and status,* and this factor was also important for 40- to 50-year-olds. Of moderate frequency for subjects of both these ages was also the statement that possessions are *extensions of the individual* and help define individuality. Together, these two factors imply that possessions enhance one's self-image. Establishing a distinctive self-identity is certainly a social phenomenon—it must be done vis-à-vis other individuals. Since possessions are viewed as an extension of one's person, and since society values possessions and consumption (Otto, 1975), then the value of one's person is enhanced by possessions. This formulation implies several basic psychological processes at work, and it seems advisable to examine both of these aspects in more detail.

Consider first the assertion that possessions make people feel important and imply social power and status. Previous investigators have suggested that the social implications and functions of ownership are central to understanding possession:

> The mode of property holding exercises a direct organizing function. It assigns certain primary relations between man and man. It places men in positions of relative dependence and relative power. . . . Differences of property are always differences of power. (Maciver, 1945–1946, pp. 6 and 16)

Hallowell (1943) has argued that "property as a social institution implies a system of relations among individuals" (p. 119). He shows how this is the case no matter what society one is dealing with. Isaacs (1949) has stressed this same point in discussing possessiveness in children:

> I do not believe that the relation between a person and a physical object, whether it be a toy, a utensil, a weapon, a dwelling place, an ornament or a conventional unit of currency, is ever a simple affair between a person and a thing; it is always a triangular relation between at least *two* people and the thing in question. The object is a pawn in

the game, an instrument for controlling and defining the relation between two or more persons. (p. 256)

Apparently, by high school age, individuals are becoming aware of this aspect of ownership. They seem to agree with Maciver that property is not only an extension of the personality—it is also "an extension of one over the personality of others" (1945–1946, p. 6). Snyder (1972) has also presented evidence that material possessions are an important criterion of prestige among high school students. Relatedly, several studies (Carroll, 1968; Horrocks & Mussman, 1973) have shown that individuals of less than optimal social status (e.g., lower socioeconomic class, mentally retarded) desire more material possessions that those of higher status.

While the ability to interact effectively with one's environment has been a recurrent theme in the discussion thus far, I have generally focused on interaction with the inanimate environment. However, the dimension of social power and status suggests another aspect of competence which may be served by possession—social competence, or a sense of efficacy in interaction with other individuals (see White, 1963). The motivational formulations referred to above which deal with personal causation and competence should not be limited to interactions of the individual with the inanimate world. Clearly, being able to produce desired effects in one's social environment is of equal importance, and the two worlds are in any case inextricably intertwined, as demonstrated by recent work on social power (Uleman, 1972), social competence (Vance, 1973), and social attributional processes (summarized in Cialdini & Mirels, 1976).

The second assertion of the above analysis was that possessions are extensions of the individual, and thus aid in defining one's individuality. Indeed, possessions have been seen by various writers as important to the self-definition process at all ages. In observing the play behavior of 1- to 2-year-olds, Bronson (1975) remarked that, "It is as if 'I' was being partly defined by exploration of the notion of what is 'mine' or under 'my' control" (pp. 145–146). Similar assertions are made about adult behavior by existential philosophers, who argue that self-affirmation is achieved through the power to negate something external to the self (deBeauvoir, 1949; Sartre, 1946), negation of something being one potent form of control over it. William James (1890) also postulated a close relation between the self and one's possessions:

It is clear that between what a man calls *me* and what he simply calls *mine,* the line is difficult to draw. We feel and act about certain things that are ours very much as we feel and act about ourselves. Our fame, our children, the work of our hands, may be as dear to us as our bodies are, and arouse the same feelings and the same acts of reprisal if attacked. . . . In its widest possible sense, however, a man's Self is the sum total of all that he can call his, not only his body, and his psychic powers, but his clothes and his house, his wife and his children, his ancestors and friends, his reputation and words, his land and horses and yacht and bank account. (p. 291–292)

Furthermore, there are several empirical studies indicating that some possessions are explicitly considered a part of the self for at least some individuals (Dixon & Street, 1975; Prelinger, 1959).

At the root of the relation between one's possessions and one's concept of self, Beaglehole (1932) postulated a "close magico-animistic connection." This is his notion, which I discussed above when examining his anthropological evidence, that there is a tendency to integrate part of the self with any object that one uses. It is a kind of animistic feeling which constitutes an invisible bond between the individual and an object he sees as his own. Beaglehole's analysis is insightful, but he never goes beyond this innate tendency toward animism as the ultimate explanation of the nature of possession. It is profitable, however, to examine the relationship between one's possessions and one's concept of self in the light of theories of motivation which stress the importance of a sense of personal causation, competence, and control.

Consider first the mechanisms involved in developing a sense of self. Most descriptions of this process are rather general statements to the effect that the young child slowly learns to distinguish *me* from *not-me*. Exactly how that learning takes place is rarely discussed, although it is clearly of extreme importance. Seligman (1975) has made one of the few attempts to explain this process in more detail:

> What does distinguish the self from the world, after all? Those things that are part of *me* yield very high correlations when I voluntarily move them: I decide my hand is part of me, not part of others, because motor commands are almost invariably followed by the sight and feeling of the hand stretching out. Indeed, a contingency analysis that discovers synchrony between a given motor command and a given feedback seems the most likely way that we learn which motor command produces a particular response. To his grief each infant learns that mother is not part of self, but part of the world: the synchrony between motor commands and the sight of mother moving around is much less than a perfect correlation—although it is not zero except in the most impoverished environment. I suggest that those "objects" become self that exhibit near-perfect correlation between motor command and the visual and kinesthetic feedback; while those "objects" that do not, become the world. Then, of course, begins the lifelong struggle to raise the correlation of the world's changes with motor commands—the struggle for control [pp. 141–142. From *Helplessness: On Depression, Development and Death.* M.E.P. Seligman, W. H. Freeman and Company, © 1975].

Given this framework for understanding the self, it is reasonable to hypothesize that an object is considered a part of the self to the degree to which it is under the individual's control. Furthermore, the results discussed above have repeatedly suggested that a central defining dimension of possession is the owner's ability to control an object—to actively cause things to happen to that object. Thus, the concept that possessions are an extension of the self (and thus help to define individuality), is consistent with this formulation. Possessions are an extension of my self because (a) possessions are objects which I can effect as I wish and (b) one aspect of the definition of my self consists of those objects in the world which I can control. Within this framework, James' statements above about the confounding of *me* and *mine* become much more understandable. While he seems to have only grasped the merger on a phenomenological level, the analysis proposed here attempts to delineate the nature of the process resulting in such a confounding.

One factor that was frequent among high school and 40- to 50-year-old subjects was the fact that possessions provide *security*. However, the nature of this security is unclear. One plausible hypothesis is that personal possessions provide substitutes where other needs or desires have not been met. Thus, a child may be given a toy to *go* play with, or a piece of candy to *go* eat, instead of being given the attention s/he seems to be demanding. It could be that in this way the child learns that s/he cannot effect and obtain the attention s/he desires, but at least s/he can have some material pleasure instead. The adult, in attempting to encourage the child in independent activity by giving some *thing* to occupy the child, may be simultaneously communicating that objects are substitutes for interpersonal interaction. While empirical evidence on this issue is scant, two studies (Cameron, Conrad, Kirkpatrick, & Bateen, 1966; Cameron & Mattson, 1972) have found that individuals who own pets report that they like other people less, and that they are liked less by other people than individuals who do not own pets. It should also be noted that possessions may provide security in the sense that one can count on them consistently for certain pleasures, whereas one may not be able to count on other people for *consistent* emotional fulfillment.

III.   Theoretical Overview and Discussion

A.   STEPPING STONES TOWARD A THEORY OF THE NATURE OF POSSESSIONS

Perhaps the most salient theme related to possession which emerged from the discussion above is the *individual's ability to produce effects in the environment*—to experience causal efficacy and control. Both the meaning of, and the motivation for, possession and ownership seem to depend significantly on a sense of effectance or control.

The literature on motivation contains convincing evidence that the human organism (and other animals as well) is inherently motivated to influence the environment—that it is pleasurable and rewarding to experience a causal relationship between one's actions and changes in the environment. Earlier writers spoke simply of the "joy in being a cause" (Groos, 1901) or "the gratification at being a cause" (Preyer, 1888–1889). Others referred to a general pleasure in activity for its own sake (Bühler, 1918; French, 1952; Murray & Kluckhohn, 1953; Woodworth, 1958). More recently, a number of authors have presented more elaborate and refined theoretical formulations of an internal motivation for effectance and control. Unfortunately, control is not a simple notion, but rather encompasses a number of different facets: the experience of a positive correlation between one's actions and changes in the environment, the belief that one can obtain *desired* outcomes by acting on the environment, the freedom to choose among several different outcomes, to name just a few. Different authors have focused on different aspects of control (see Brehm, 1966, 1972; deCharms, 1968; Deci, 1975; Erikson, 1963; Nuttin, 1973; Rotter, 1966; Seligman, 1975; Steiner, 1970; White, 1959, 1963). Despite their differences, there is general agreement that human beings are motivated to produce effects in their environment, and that a generalized sense of competence in dealing with the environment is pleasurable.[7]

The other recurrent theme related to possession is the individual's concept of the self. Again, both the meaning of, and the motivation for, possession seem to be intimately related to the sense of one's self. I have deliberately avoided the task of defining what the self is, and I will continue to skirt this issue. Although it is a much discussed concept in the literature, and the central figure in a number of psychological and sociological theories (Allport, 1955; Cooley, 1902; Hilgard, 1949; James, 1910; Lecky, 1945; Rogers, 1951; Sarbin, 1952; Snygg & Combs, 1949; Sullivan, 1953), a satisfactory definition is still lacking. However, it is generally agreed that "there can be no argument but that the subjective feeling state of having a self is an important empirical phenomenon that warrants study in its own right" (Epstein, 1973, p. 405).

Although not attempting a complete definition of the sense of self, Seligman's (1975) formulation constitutes a very useful approach to understanding at least one aspect of the self. He has proposed that "those 'objects' become self that exhibit near-perfect correlation between motor command and the visual-kinesthetic feedback; while those 'objects' that

---

[7]What an individual *does* with a sense of control (or the underlying motivation) is a distinct and separate question. When and where one chooses to actually effect some change in the environment (from getting the food from the table to one's mouth, to destroying the land and lives of another nation) is undoubtedly determined by such factors as socialization experiences, the state of other motivational systems, etc., but this is a topic which has thus far lacked any systematic research effort.

do not, become the world" (pp. 141–142).[8] It is this aspect of the self, it seems to me, which is helpful in understanding possession and ownership.

Control is critical, in this formulation, to developing one's concept of the self: That over which I exercise perfect control becomes a part of my sense of self. In proposing this analysis of the self, Seligman had no intention of attempting a refined and detailed theory of the self. Rather, his focus was on studying perceptions of control or of helplessness, and his discussion of the sense of self was very brief, being only tangential to his main theme. Thus, in suggesting the following modification of his formulation, I am not correcting an error in his analysis so much as suggesting what I think is a necessary refinement.

The world does not fall into two distinct categories of things, those over which I have perfect control and those over which I have little control. Rather, the world consists of a continuum of control. I may, for example, have near-perfect control over the movements of my hand, somewhat less but still very considerable control over the movements of my arm swinging a tennis racquet, a moderate degree of control over the laughter of a close friend, only limited control over the ringing of my telephone, and no control at all over the dice in Las Vegas. Although I want to argue for the existence of such a continuum, I am not suggesting exactly how the totality of objects in the world are distributed on that continuum. In fact, I think that they are distributed differently for different people, and that both individual and development differences in the shape of that distribution are important determinants of motivational differences in possessiveness. The point is, however, that a given object can potentially fall anywhere along the continuum from perfect control (a perfect correlation of 1.00 between my actions and the intended[9] consequences of my actions) to complete absence of any control (a zero correlation between my actions and the intended consequences).

I propose that the central feature of possession—its principal defining characteristic, as well as the major motivational force behind it—is causal efficacy or control over aspects of one's environment. There is ample evidence that organisms are motivated to produce environmental effects, and the adaptive functions of control over the environment in an evolutionary context are obvious. But what exactly is the relation between possession and this intrinsic effectance motivation? The significance of

---

[8]Weigert's (1975) definition of the "substantive self" is very related to Seligman's, although his theory is too detailed and complex to be treated in a summarial fashion here.

[9]Intentionality, of course, is a difficult concept for the experimental psychologist. However, it is increasingly clear not only that it is central to understanding human behavior, but also that it can be dealt with in a meaningful fashion (Kvale, 1976; Kvale & Grenness, 1967; Naroll, 1976; Schmitt, 1973; Weigert, 1975).

possession seems to lie in the very high degree of control it entails. The magnitude of the control I exert over my possessions is of the same order as the control I exert over my body. Thus, possessions are included in one's concept of the self. Possession offers the opportunity to experience a sense of effectance, internal control, or personal causation. Other than one's physical body, there is little in the world which affords the opportunity for effective responding the way possessions do. Since the organism is generally motivated to engage in effective and competent responding, possessions naturally become of great significance for both behavior and affect. I should point out that the latter variable—affect—has generally been slighted in the literature on motivation to control one's environment. The "joy" in being a cause and the "pleasure" derived from mastery are often referred to in passing, and even demonstrated experimentally in certain contexts (Harter, 1974), but the nature of the positive affect involved is rarely explored in any depth. Seligman's (1975) treatment of this topic is insightful:

> After all, what is the evolutionary significance of mood? Presumably, sentient organisms could just as well be constructed without mood—complex computers are. What selective pressure produced feeling and affect? It may be that the hedonic system evolved to goad and fuel instrumental action. I suggest that *joy accompanies and motivates effective responding;* and that in the absence of effective responding, an aversive state arises, which organisms seek to avoid. It is called depression. It is highly significant that when rats and pigeons are given a choice between getting free food and getting the same food for making responses, they choose to work (Carder & Berkowitz, 1970; Jensen, 1963; Neuringer, 1969; Singh, 1970; Stolz & Lott, 1964). Infants smile at a mobile whose movements are contingent on their responses, but not at a noncontingent mobile (Watson, 1971). Do hunters hunt from a lust to kill or mountain climbers scale peaks for glory? I think not. These activities, because they entail effective instrumental responding, produce joy. (p. 98, italics added)

Within the context of the present formulation, this suggests that joy and pleasure accompany possessing an object because possessing entails a high degree of effective responding with respect to that object. And possession and ownership *in general* are accompanied by positive affect, just as is the *generalized* sense of effectance which White (1963) has labeled "competence."

The affective component of control over one's environment is interesting to consider in light of the empirical results presented above. One aspect of possession which seemed to be of considerable importance was the owner's positive affect for the object. This dimension is clearly of a different nature than the instrumental control dimension—it focuses on an emotion or feeling the owner experiences with respect to the object. It seems reasonable to propose that the frequency with which subjects mention positive affect as a dimension of both the meaning and motivation for possession reflects the importance of the positive affect which accompanies effective responding involved in possessing. This dimension, then, may be yet another manifestation of the relation between effectance motivation and possession.

B. IMPLICATIONS AND FURTHER INQUIRY

1. An Hydraulic Model

The effect of impediments to effective responding is an area that needs further investigation. Is effectance motivation unlimited, and is it independent from one's effectance experiences in another area? In other words, if I have considerable control over objects (or events) A, B, and C, do I have as much desire to control object D as does the individual who does *not* have control over A, B, and C? I think some sort of a trade-off exists, and many individual and group differences with respect to possession and ownership may reflect differences in the degree of control people have over other aspects of their lives. Edney (1976) has recently argued that control may be closely related to territoriality. He presents data demonstrating that the more controlling a person is in a given situation, the less personal space s/he needs. Edney suggests that the dynamics of territoriality may follow a priniciple of: the less one has, the more one wants. Given the similarity between territoriality and possessiveness, Edney's work has important implications here, although I would suggest that it may be *control* which follows an hydraulic model, rather than territoriality or possession per se.

Relevant to this trade-off notion is Isaacs' (1949) report of apparent changes in possessiveness that result from psychoanalysis:

> In the analysis of both adults and children, we find that their attitudes to material possessions frequently change a great deal during the course of analysis. This change is often in the direction of a lessening of the strength of the wish to own. (p. 256)

It is, of course, unclear what has taken place during analysis to affect such a change. Isaacs implies that loss and gain of love must be the critical variable. But certainly degree of perceived control over various aspects of one's life is also a candidate for investigation.

There is some recent evidence indicating that, in situations where personal control is considerably limited (e.g., nursing homes and mental institutions), the greater the opportunity for personal possessions, the more positive is the individual's attitude and the more successful in rehabilitation (Bot, 1968; Morgan & Cushing, 1966). It is as if possessions permit a healthy degree of personal control or competence, in a relatively uncontrollable environment, and thereby foster positive attitudes and adaptive behavior. This offers one example of how developmental differences in the manifestations of effectance motivation, and in the realization of competence, may help us to understand developmental differences in possessiveness. Just as the young child benefits from increased control, the aged individual suffers from loss of control as a result of changes in work and family status, income, and sometimes physical conditions (Schulz, 1976). This is a developmental phenomenon which we may be able to prevent or alleviate (optimization being the third major task of developmental theory as discussed by Baltes and Schaie, 1973) by increasing the opportunity for personal control in old age. Personal possessions may be only one of many ways to increase a sense of personal control (and not necessarily the most desirable).

Both the analysis presented here and recent empirical work suggest that a sense of personal control is the critical variable, rather than possessions per se. Schulz (1976) has demonstrated that an individual's control[10] over the occurrence and timing of visitors in a retirement home has positive consequences for physical and psychological status. Such results suggest directions we might consider in attempting to make "the radical change away from the *psychology of more* toward a *psychology of enough*" (Looft, 1971). Quantity of material possessions may be less important for psychological well-being when the exercising of personal control is possible in other areas of one's life.

There is an interesting implication of this analysis for research using social indicators of well-being. Campbell (1976) recently argued that:

> If we are primarily concerned with describing the quality of the life experience of the population, we will need measures different from those that are used to describe the objective circumstances in which people live. We will have to develop measures that go directly to the experience itself. (p. 118)

His argument is based on the fact that economic and social indicators of well-being showed marked increases between 1957 and 1972, but the percentage of people who said they were "very happy" decreased, especially for the very affluent.

It may well be that a measure of sense of personal control would be a far more useful indicator of the quality of one's life experience than is quantity of material possessions.

2. *Acquisition and Perceived Ability to Possess*

An important issue to be explored is possible developmental differences in the degree to which the individual is motivated to actually effect control

---

[10]Although predictability of visits was as effective as controllability, the former includes at least a cognitive control component (see Averill, 1973).

as opposed to simply perceive the possibility of control. A number of writers have argued that one is motivated to secure the *possibility* of effecting a certain (or several) outcome(s) (Brehm, 1966, 1972; Liebhart, 1973; Proshansky *et al.,* 1970; Steiner, 1970; Wilke, 1976). When is *actually* owning and controlling an object important and when is simply the *perceived ability* to own it the critical motivating force? The work reviewed above showing that scarcity enhances the value of an object suggests that the *possibility* of owning may often be very important, irrespective of actually owning. I think this dimension is the key to understanding the importance of the transition from passive to active acquisition. The reason acquisition is so central to possession is not simply the fact that it defines its onset, but it also represents an important element of control itself. The distinction between active and passive acquisition is very salient because of its implications for the perceived ability to own: If I depend on passive, other-initiated means of acquisition, whether or not I possess something is out of my control. But if I can acquire possessions through my own actions alone, then a whole new world of possibilities is open to me. Given Skinner's (1971) stance on the existence of freedom (or lack thereof!) it is interesting that he, too, has argued for the importance of active acquisition:

> The question is not who should have how much of what, but, rather how they are to get what they have. . . . It has been too easy to put possession ahead of acquisition and to miss the importance of strength of behavior and its relation to contingencies of reinforcement. (1976, pp. 8–10)

3. *Possession of People*

The formulation presented here has interesting implications for the possession of people. The critical feature of possession is control. What does it mean, then, that one person "belongs to" another—what does it mean that we feel "possessive" toward important individuals in our lives"? It means they respond (positively) to our actions—we control them in the sense that our actions effect desired outcomes. If I emit an action—embracing you—and you respond with a desired outcome—embracing me—then I possess you, according to the present formulation. If, at some point, when I embrace you, you no longer embrace me in return, and instead your embracing behavior seems to be under someone *else's* control, then I have lost control, and thereby lost possession of you. It seems plausible that at least one element of jealousy can be understood as the negative affect resulting from this loss of control. It is no accident that we are "jealous" when we lose our influence on another person to some third party, and we are also "jealous" when someone else has possessions we wish we had—in both cases we are denied control over something, while at the same time observing someone else who does have that control.[11]

I hasten to emphatically declare that I am in no way *advocating* control as *either necessary or desirable* in interpersonal relations. But irrespective of any evaluative judgments of this point, I think it is clear that the vast majority of people in our society at present do desire control over their "loved ones," and they *do* feel jealous when they don't have control. It is this existing phenomenon which I am analyzing here.

4. Life-Span Considerations

From a life-span developmental perspective, the above discussion suggests both differences *and* similarities in possessiveness at different periods of the life span. One theme is common at all ages thus far studied: control over possessions and over their use. One major objective of life-span developmental psychology is "the integrative conceptualization of the totality of ontogenetic behavioral changes" (Baltes & Goulet, 1970, p. 13). It is proposed here that effectance motivation, or the desire for personal control in one's environment, is one promising concept around which possessive behavior (and perhaps a good deal of the rest of human experience) might be integrated.

We have also seen that there are a number of developmental *differences* in the meaning and function of possession, those differences being a function of (a) *organismic* variables (the relative strength and different manifestations of effectance motivation), (b) *stimulus* variables (specific environmental experiences with respect to possession), and (c) *response* variables (the existence of other behaviors which provide a sense of personal control and effectance). These are the principal elements, when viewed concurrently and historically, around which a developmental research paradigm can profitably be organized (Baltes & Schaie, 1973).

Given the basic theoretical formulation, a number of life-span and developmental implications deserve detailed consideration. In fact, with possession and ownership so central to our daily activities and to our social institutions, the number of potential implications is very large. However, much more empirical work will be needed before we can adequately account for (explain and predict) developmental differences in possessive behavior. While there is a growing body of literature on both the historical and concurrent determinants of sense of personal control

---

[11]It is interesting to note Margaret Mead's (1972) reference to her father as "rivalrous as men often are in situations in which someone else seems to be controlling a person whom they believe they have the right—and may also have failed—to control" (p. 141).

(for particularly fine examples, see Gurin & Gurin, 1976; Otto & Featherman, 1975), analogous work will be needed on the determinants of possession and ownership.

It must be emphasized that we have only begun to attack this general research question, and the theoretical formulations are offered only as beginning steps—the skeleton on which further work can build. Much is still unknown. In particular, the interview studies on which much of this theoretical analysis is based are necessarily limited. The interview is certainly not an age-invariant instrument. In addition, it focuses on the cognitive-attitudinal domain and only explores nonverbal behavior in an indirect fashion. More direct studies of possessive behavior will undoubtedly add important dimensions to the present analysis. For example, Passman's (1976) work on toddlers' attachment objects suggests that a critical dimension of such possessions as security blankets and favorite toys may be their suitability for clinging. Thus, clinging behavior may be an aspect of possessiveness during this age period which the interview method does not reveal. Effectance motivation happens to be the first major explanatory variable we have identified in this area, but there are certainly others of considerable importance which must be added to the model as our research progresses. Crosby's (1976) model of egoistical relative deprivation suggests the kind of theoretical integration that is possible in a tangentially related area, once the empirical groundwork has been laid (although her model is limited to concurrent explanatory variables).

Finally, the studies summarized here deal with a restricted age range. While representing the ages between 5 and 20 years quite well, the only other age for which we have direct information is middle-aged adults. It is certainly equally important to examine possession and ownership between the 20- to 40-year age period, as well as beyond middle age and on into retirement. Likewise, it is paramount to study possession in children younger than 5 years of age. With respect to possession among very young children, observational work has begun with 1- to 2-year-olds (Furby, 1977b), and more work is certainly needed here as well.

It must also be kept in mind that the empirical work discussed in this chapter has been based on cross-sectional data only. To date, we have no longitudinal studies of possession and ownership. Clearly, this is a direction in which future work must develop, given the limitations of one-shot, cross-sectional studies (Baltes, 1968; Schaie, 1965).

5. *Universality*

In examining the anthropological evidence above, I discussed the hypothesis that an important period with respect to possession in all societies may be the age at which the child begins to walk. At that age, the child suddenly becomes a much greater menace to all available objects than s/he had been previously. Effectance motivation is one of the principal determinants of behavior from birth, but it results in much more physically *active* manifestations at this age. At the same time, feelings of efficacy may be suddenly thwarted as a direct result of increased activity. With the integrity of so many objects threatened by the child's attempts to explore them, adults spend considerable time and effort *preventing* the child from carrying out certain actions. Since so many of the 18-month-old's actions are potentially destructive to material things, his or her attempts at effective responding are often prevented or interrupted by adults. The result may be that the child has an increased investment in those objects which s/he *can* control—s/he becomes particularly involved in exercising control over them. American parents typically report a barrage of "that's mine" by the 2-year-old, and one Israeli informant referred to this as the "possessive age." Simultaneously, the child is provided with models of possessive behavior by individuals in the immediate environment, and s/he begins to learn society's rules about possession and ownership—there are some things mommy can control, some things sister can control, and there are some things I can control.

I suspect that this basic situation for the 1- to 2-year-old may exist in every culture. Every toddler's mobility presents a danger to certain objects in the physical environment (the pot on the fire in some cases and the china vase in others), and every society makes some attempts to restrict the toddler's potentially harmful actions. It seems quite possible that this constitutes a universal experience leading to the development of a sense of possession. It cannot be overemphasized, however, that the present model relies heavily on data on possessive behavior as it presently exists in our culture, and thus a careful analysis of the societal and cultural determinants of possession and its underlying motives will be critical to a more general theory in this area. Such an analysis must necessarily deal with the fact that our social interactions are governed by the rules of possessive individualism (Macpherson, 1962): We assume that to be human means to be the proprietor of one's capacities, to be free to sell those capacities, and to be independent of the will of others. The individual owns her person and owes nothing to society for it. S/he enters relations only voluntarily and with goals of self-interest. Such an image of humans is quite valid for the capitalistic market economy in which we live, where private possessions and commodity exchange are central features of social interaction. However, the strong emphasis on individual independence and autonomy—on personal control and competence—may not be appropriate for all social classes in our society (see Israel, 1978), let alone for other societies which have a less individualistic economic structure (e.g., China) and/or a more dialectic view of the degree to which individuals and the environment mutually control each other (e.g., certain native American cultures).

Because the recent empirical studies of possession have been carried out in Western, industrialized cultures, the theoretical analysis presented here necessarily deals with the phenomenon of possession among this portion of humankind—it attempts to describe and understand the meaning of and motivation for possession as it now exists in our culture. Considerable cross-cultural evidence of an anecdotal nature has been reviewed here, but there is a need for empirical studies, particularly among cultures that seem to have a very different view of the individual's place in society and in nature. Studies in these cultures may either tell us quite a different story about possessions (and their relation to effectance motivation and self-concept), or they may simply confirm the universality of much of the above analysis. Data gathered from such divergent cultures will also help us to understand the institutional or structural aspects of possession. For example, Seagrim (1976) has suggested that possessions in our own society may serve as social structures which "form the very warp and woof of our society," by imposing obligations, causing conflicts, affecting family relationships, etc., much as kinship structures do for other cultures such as the Australian aborigines. Although offered strictly as an interesting hypothesis, this represents a very provocative and fruitful direction which should be explored by future work in this area.

IV. Summary

Few would contest the observation that possessive attitudes and behaviors are evident in a large percentage of human activity, at least in our society. It thus is natural to ask questions about (a) the *nature* of possessiveness, (b) its *origins,* and (c) its *development* throughout the life span.

The multidimensionality of possession has made it an unattractive research topic for the empirical scientist. Until recently, it received only speculative theoretical attention, mainly from political scientists, philosophers, and historians. The latter contributed little to furthering our understanding of the psychology of possessiveness and acquisitiveness, particularly when systematic empirical studies are seen as critical to such an understanding.

Consistent with a life-span developmental approach, we began by searching for possible evolutionary precursors of possessiveness. A review of existing anecdotal evidence on possession among nonhuman species (a) highlighted the difficulty of *defining* possession, and (b) led to the tentative conclusion that animals appropriate objects solely because the latter are related to basic physiological needs such as hunger and reproduction.

We then moved to a comparative review of the existing ethnographic evidence on possession and ownership in different human societies. This led to several interesting hypotheses about the origins and functions of possessive behavior, but the lack of any systematic data-gathering on this topic precluded the possibility of any general conclusions. Furthermore, as was the case for possession among nonhumans, cross-cultural comparisons of possession among humans again underlined the difficulty of defining what possession means.

Given the above considerations, there was a clear need to empirically establish the defining characteristics or dimensions of the phenomenon of interest, possession among humans. In so doing, a life-span perspective on the question seemed mandatory: What is the *nature* of possession *throughout the life span?* Several recent studies were reviewed which have focused on identifying and describing developmental differences and similarities in the nature of possession. An analysis of their results led to a number of age-specific hypotheses as well as to the beginnings of a general theoretical formulation about the origins and function of possession. The latter identifies the owner's ability to control an object as one central defining characteristic of possession. As a result, it is postulated that effectance or competence motivation is a major motivation for possessive behavior: The possibly universal desire to experience causal efficacy leads to attempts to control objects in one's environment. Further, since one's concept of the self is at least partially defined by that which one controls, it is hypothesized that possessions are one constituent of a sense of self—they are experienced as an extension of the self.

This formulation has numerous and far-reaching implications, some of which were discussed here. However, we have also seen that empirical work on possession is in its infancy. Only the *nature* of possession has been examined thus far, and given its proven multidimensionality, a considerable amount of systematic study of both the *origins* and the development throughout the life span of this phenomenon will be required before we can adequately describe and explain individual and developmental differences and similarities in possessive behavior.

Acknowledgments

The comments of Mary Rothbart, Mary Wilke, Lewis Goldberg, Robyn Dawes, Carol Ryff, Susan Harter, Gavin Seagrim, and Harry Garfinkle contributed to improving earlier drafts of this article. Preparation of the manuscript was supported by a National Institutes of Mental Health Postdoctoral Research Fellowship.

References

Allport, G. W. *Becoming.* New Haven, Conn.: Yale University Press, 1955.

Averill, J. R. Personal control over aversive stimuli. *Psychological Bulletin,* 1973, **80,** 276–303.

Baltes, P. B. Longitudinal and cross-sectional sequences in the study of age and generation effects. *Human Development,* 1968, **11,** 145–171.

Baltes, P. B., & Goulet, L. R. Status and issues of a life-span developmental psychology. In L. R. Goulet & P. B. Baltes (Eds.), *Life-span developmental psychology: Research and theory.* New York: Academic Press, 1970.

Baltes, P. B., & Schaie, K. W. On life-span developmental research paradigms. In P. B. Baltes & K. W. Schaie (Eds.), *Lifespan developmental psychology: Personality and socialization.* New York: Academic Press, 1973.

Beaglehole, E. *Property: A study in social psychology.* New York: Macmillan, 1932.

Bot, B. W. The nursing-home patient and his environment. *Gawein,* 1968, **16,** 163–186.

Boulding, K. E. Shortages and the social system. *Science,* 1974, **184,** 255–257.

Brehm, J. W. *A theory of psychological reactance.* New York: Academic Press, 1966.

Brehm, J. W. *Response to loss of freedom: A theory of psychological reactance.* Morristown, N.J.: General Learning Press, 1972.

Bronson, W. C. Developments in behavior with age-mates during the second year of life. In M. Lewis & L. A. Rosenblum (Eds.), *Friendship and peer relations.* New York: Wiley, 1975.

Bühler, C. *Die geistige Entwicklung des Kindes.* Jena: Fischer, 1918.

Cameron, P., Conrad, C., Kirkpatrick, D. D., & Bateen, R. J. Pet ownership and sex as determinants of stated affect toward others and estimates of others' regard of self. *Psychological Reports,* 1966, **19,** 884–886.

Cameron, P., & Mattson, M. Psychological correlates of pet ownership. *Psychological Reports,* 1972, **30,** 286.

Campbell, A. Subjective measures of well-being. *American Psychologist,* 1976, **31,** 117–124.

Carder, B., & Berkowitz, K. Rats' preference for earned in comparison with free food. *Science,* 1970, **167,** 1273–1274.

Carroll, M. N. "Junk" collections among mentally retarded patients. *Journal of Mental Deficiency,* 1968, **73,** 308–314.

Cialdini, R. B., & Mirels, H. L. Sense of personal control and attributions about yielding and resisting persuasion targets. *Journal of Personality and Social Psychology,* 1976, **33,** 395–407.

Cooley, C. H. *Human nature and the social order.* New York: Scribner's, 1902.

Crosby, F. A model of egoistical relative deprivation. *Psychological Bulletin,* 1976, **83,** 85–113.

deBeauvoir, S. *Le deuxième sexe.* Paris: Gallimard, 1949.

deCharms, R. *Personal causation: The internal affective determinants of behavior.* New York: Academic Press, 1968.

Deci, E. L. *Intrinsic motivation.* New York: Plenum, 1975.

Dixon, J. C., & Street, J. W. The distinction between self and not-self in children and adolescents. *Journal of Genetic Psychology,* 1975, **127,** 157–162.

Edney, J. Territoriality and control: A field experiment. *Journal of Personality and Social Psychology,* 1976.

Ehrlich, R., & Ehrlich, A. H. *The end of affluence: A blueprint for your future.* New York: Ballantine, 1974.

Ellwood, C. *Cultural evolution: A study of social origins and development.* New York: Century, 1927.

Epstein, S. The self-concept revisited: Or a theory of a theory. *American Psychologist,* 1973, **28,** 404–416.

Erikson, E. H. *Childhood and society* (2nd ed.). New York: Norton, 1963.

Fernandez, C. A., & Lynch, F. The Tasaday: Cave-dwelling food gatherers of South Cotabato, Mindanao. *Philippine Sociological Review,* 1972, **20,** 279–330.

Fletcher, R. *Instinct in man.* New York: Schocken, 1966.

French, T. M. *The integration of behavior* (Vol. 1). Chicago: University of Chicago Press, 1952.

Friedman, M. *Capitalism and freedom.* Chicago: University of Chicago Press, 1962.

Fromkin, H. L., Olson, J. C., Dipboye, R. L., & Barnaby, D. A commodity theory analysis of consumer preferences for scarce products. *Proceedings of the 79th Annual Convention of the American Psychological Association,* 1971, **46,** Abstract No. 15918.

Furby, L. Socialization practices with respect to possession and ownership: A study using the Human Relations Area Files. *Oregon Research Institute Research Bulletin,* 1974, **14,** No. 20.

Furby, L. Collective possession and ownership: A comparative cross-cultural study of its judged feasibility and desirability. *Oregon Research Institute Research Bulletin,* 1976, **16,** No. 9. (a)

Furby, L. Inequalities in personal possessions: Explanations for and judgments of the unequal distribution of material goods among children and adults. *Oregon Research Institute Research Bulletin,* 1976, **16,** No. 11. (b)

Furby, L. The socialization of possession and ownership among children in three cultural groups: Israeli kibbutz, Israeli city, and American. In S. Modgil & C. Modgil (Eds.), *Piagetian research: Compilation and commentary* (Vol. 8). Windsor, Eng.: NFER Publ., 1976. (c)

Furby, L. *A proposal for behavior observational studies of possessiveness in young children.* Unpublished manuscript, University of Oregon, 1977.

Furby, L. Possession in humans: A developmental study of its meaning and motivation. *Social Behavior and Personality,* 1978, in press. (a)

Furby, L. The acquisition of personal possessions among children and adults. *International Journal of Behavioral Development,* 1978, in press. (b)

Furby, L. Sharing: Decisions and moral judgments about letting others use one's possessions. *Psychological Reports,* 1978, in press. (c)

Furby, L., Harter, S., & John, K. The nature and development of possession and ownership: A cognitive-attitudinal study of 5 to 21 year-olds. *Oregon Research Institute Research Monograph,* 1975, **15,** No. 4.

Gesell, A., & Ilg, F. *The child from five to ten.* New York: Harper, 1946.

Groos, K. *The play of man.* New York: Appleton, 1901.

Gurin, G., & Gurin, P. Personal efficacy and the ideology of responsibility. In B. Strumpel (Ed.), *Economic means for human needs.* Ann Arbor, Mich.: Institute for Social Research, 1976.

Hallowell, A. I. The nature and function of property as a social institution. *Journal of Legal and Political Sociology,* 1943, **1,** 115–138.

Harris, M. *The rise of anthropological theory.* New York: Crowell, 1968.

Harter, S. Pleasure derived from cognitive challenge and mastery. *Child Development,* 1974, **45,** 661–669.

Heilbroner, R. Marxism, psychoanalysis, and the problem of a unified theory of behavior. *Social Research,* 1975, **42,** 414–432.

Herskovits, M. J. *The economic life of primitive peoples.* New York: Knopf, 1940.

Hilgard, E. R. Human motives and the concept of the self. *American Psychologist,* 1949, **4,** 374–382.

Hoebel, E. A. *The law of primitive man.* New York: Atheneum, 1968.

Horrocks, J. E., & Mussman, M. C. Developmental trends in wishes, confidence, and the sense of personal control from childhood to middle maturity. *Journal of Psychology,* 1973, **84,** 241–252.

Isaacs, S. *Social development in young children.* London: Routledge, 1933.

Isaacs, S. Property and possessiveness. In T. Talbot (Ed.), *The world of the child.* Garden City, N.Y.: Doubleday, 1967. (Originally published, 1949.)

Israel, J. From level of aspiration to dissonance or what the middle class worries about. In A. R. Buss (Ed.), *The social context of psychological theory: Towards a sociology of psychological knowledge.* New York: Irvington, 1978, in press.

James, W. *Principles of psychology.* New York: Macmillan, 1890.

James, W. *Psychology: The briefer course.* New York: Holt, 1910.

Jensen, G. D. Preference for bar-pressing over "free-loading" as a function of the number of rewarded presses. *Journal of Experimental Psychology,* 1963, **65,** 451–454.

Kaufman, J. H. Is territoriality definable? In A. H. Esser (Ed.), *Behavior and environment: The use of space by animals and men.* New York: Plenum, 1971.

Kvale, S. Facts and dialectics. In J. F. Rychlak (Ed.), *Dialectic: Humanistic rationale for behavior and development.* Basel: Karger, 1976.

Kvale, S., & Grenness, C. E. Skinner and Sartre: Towards a radical phenomenology of behavior? *Review of Existential Psychology and Psychiatry,* 1967, **7,** 128–150.

LaFargue, P. *The evolution of property from savagery to civilization.* London: Swan Sonnerschein, 1890.

Lecky, P. *Self-consistency: A theory of personality.* N.Y.: Island Press, 1945.

LeTourneau, C. *Property: Its origin and development.* London: Walter Scott, 1892.

Levi-Strauss, C. *Les structures élémentaires de la parenté.* Paris: Presses Universitaires de France, 1949.

Lewinski, J. *The origin of property and the formation of the village community.* London: Constables, 1913.

Liebhart, E. H. Choice as a value. *European Journal of Social Psychology,* 1973, **3,** 485–489.

Looft, W. R. The psychology of more. *American Psychologist,* 1971, **26,** 561–565.

Lowie, R. *Primitive society.* New York: Boni & Liveright, 1920.

Luria, A. R. *The working brain: An introduction to neuropsychology.* London: Allen Lane, 1973.

Maciver, R. M. Government and property. *Journal of Legal and Political Sociology,* 1945/1946, **4,** 5–18.

Macpherson, C. B. *The political theory of possessive individualism.* London and New York: Oxford University Press, 1962.

Mallory, M. T. The next crisis: Universal famine. *National Observer,* March 30, 1974.

Mauss, M. *The gift.* New York: Free Press, 1954. (Originally published, 1924.)

McDougall, W. *An introduction to social psychology* (11th ed.). Boston: J. W. Luce, 1916.

Mead, M. *Growing up in New Guinea.* New York: Morrow, 1930.

Mead, M. *Blackberry winter.* New York: Morrow, 1972.

Morgan, R., & Cushing, D. The personal possessions of long-stay patients in mental hospitals. *Social Psychiatry,* 1966, **1,** 151–157.

Murray, H. A., & Kluckholn, C. Outline of a conception of personality. In C. Kluckholn, H. A. Murray, & D. M. Schneider (Eds.), *Personality in nature, society and culture.* New York: Knopf, 1953.

Nance, J. *The gentle Tasaday.* New York: Harcourt, 1975.

Naroll, R. *Cause and effect as servo elements.* Paper presented at the fifth annual meeting of the Society for Cross-Cultural Research, New York, February 1976.

Neuringer, A. Animals respond for food in the presence of free food. *Science,* 1969, **166,** 399–401.

Nuttin, J. P. Pleasure and reward in human motivation and learning. In D. E. Berlyne & R. B. Madsen (Eds.), *Pleasure, reward, preference: Their nature, determinants, and role in behavior.* New York: Academic Press, 1973.

Ophuls, W. The scarcity society. *Harpers,* April 1974.

Otto, L. B. *Socialization and acquisitiveness.* Paper presented at the National Science Foundation Conference on Societal Implications of Energy Scarcity: Social and Technological Priorities in Steady State and Constricting Systems, Portland, Oregon, June 1975.

Otto, L. B., & Featherman, D. L. Social structure and psychological antecedents of self-estrangement and powerlessness. *American Sociological Review,* 1975, **40,** 701–719.

Passman, R. H. Arousal reducing properties of attachment objects: Testing the functional limits of the security blanket relative to the mother. *Developmental Psychology,* 1976, **12,** 448–449.

Prelinger, E. Extension and structure of the self. *Journal of Psychology,* 1959, **47,** 13–23.

Preyer, W. *Mind of the child.* New York: Appleton, 1888–1889.

Proshansky, H. M., Ittleson, W. H., & Rivlin, L. G. Freedom of choice and behavior in a physical setting. In H. M. Proshansky, W. H. Ittleson, & L. G. Rivlin (Eds.), *Environmental psychology.* New York: Holt, 1970.

Rivers, W. H. R. *Instinct and the unconscious.* London: Cambridge University Press, 1920.

Rogers, C. R. *Client-centered therapy.* Boston: Houghton, 1951.

Rohner, R. *Advantages of the comparative method of anthropology.* Paper presented at the fifth annual meeting of the Society for Cross-Cultural Research, New York: February 1976.

Rotter, J. B. Generalized expectancies for internal versus external control of reinforcements. *Psychological Monographs,* 1966, **80** (Whole No. 609), 1–28.

Sarbin, T. R. A preface to a psychological analysis of the self. *Psychological Review,* 1952, **59,** 11–22.

Sartre, J.-P. *L'être et le néant.* Paris: Gallimard, 1946.

Schaie, K. W. A general model for the study of developmental problems. *Psychological Bulletin,* 1965, **64,** 92–107.

Schlatter, R. *Private property: The history of an idea.* New Brunswick, N.J.: Rutgers University Press, 1951.

Schmitt, R. The desire for private gain: Capitalism and the theory of motives. *Inquiry,* 1973, **16,** 149–167.

Schulz, R. Some life and death consequences of control. In J. Carroll & J. Payne (Eds.), *Cognition and social behavior.* Hillsdale, N.J.: Lawrence Erlbaum Associates, 1976.

Seagrim, G. Personal communication, October 18, 1976.

Seligman, M. E. P. *Helplessness.* San Francisco: Freeman, 1975.

Singh, D. Preferences for bar pressing to obtain reward over free-loading in rats and children. *Journal of Comparative Physiological Psychology,* 1970, **73,** 320–327.

Skinner, B. F. *Beyond freedom and dignity.* New York: Knopf, 1971.

Skinner, B. F. The ethics of helping people. *Humanist,* January/February 1976, pp. 7–11.

Snyder, E. E. High school student perceptions of prestige criteria. *Adolescence,* 1972, **6,** 129–136.

Snygg, D., & Combs, A. W. *Individual behavior.* New York: Harper, 1949.

Steiner, I. D. Perceived freedom. In L. Berkowitz (Ed.), *Advances in experimental social psychology* (Vol. 5). New York: Academic Press, 1970.

Stolz, S. B., & Lott, D. F. Establishment in rats of persistent response producing a net loss of reinforcement. *Journal of Comparative and Physiological Psychology,* 1964, **57,** 147–149.

Sullivan, H. S. *The interpersonal theory of psychiatry.* New York: Norton, 1953.

Thurnwald, R. *L'économie primitive.* Paris: Payot, 1932.

Uleman, J. S. The need for influence: Development and validation of a measure, and comparison with a need for power. *Genetic Psychology Monographs,* 1972, **85,** 157–214.

Vance, E. T. Social disability. *American Psychologist,* 1973, **28,** 498–511.

Veblen, T. *The theory of the leisure class.* New York: Macmillan, 1899.

Watson, J. S. Memory and "contingency analysis" in infant learning. *Merrill-Palmer Quarterly,* 1971, **17,** 139–152.

Webster's new collegiate dictionary. Springfield, Mass.: Merriam, 1974.

Weigert, A. J. Substantive self: A primitive term for a sociological psychology. *Philosophy of Social Science,* 1975, **5,** 43–62.

Weyant, R. G. *Helvétius and Jefferson: Studies in human nature and government in the eighteenth century.* Paper presented at the annual convention of the American Psychological Association, Washington, D.C., September 1971.

White, R. W. Motivation reconsidered: The concept of competence. *Psychological Review,* 1959, **66,** 297–333.

White, R. W. Ego and reality in psychoanalytic theory. *Psychological Issues,* 1963, **3,** (Monograph No. 11).

Whitebook, J. American revolution and socialist tradition: A review of post scarcity anarchism. *Liberation,* 1972, **16,** 20–27.

Wilke, M. Freedom and control: A conceptual analysis. *Oregon Research Institute Research Bulletin,* 1976, **16,** No. 5.

Williams, T. R. *Introduction to socialization.* St. Louis, Mo.: Mosby, 1972.

Woodworth, R. S. *Dynamics of behavior.* New York: Holt, 1958.

Worchel, S., Lee, J., & Adewole, A. Effects of supply and demand on ratings of object value. *Journal of Personality and Social Psychology,* 1975, **32,** 906–914.

Wrightsman, L. S. *Assumptions about human nature: A social-psychological approach.* Monterey, Calif.: Brooks, Cole, 1974.

Author Index

Numbers in italics refer to the pages on which the complete references are listed.

A

Ackoff, R. L., 59, 60, *79*
Acland, H., 213, *254*
Adelson, J., 281, *291*
Adewole, A., 317, *336*
Ainsworth, M. D. S., 12, 18, 19, 20, 24, 25, 26, 27, 28, 33, 35, *39, 44*
Albertini, B. V., 93, *107*
Aldridge, V. J., 145, *178*
Allport, G. W., *79*, 321, *332*
Almquist, E. M., 267, 268, 280, 282, 283, 284, *290*
Anders, T. R., 163, *166*, 249, *251*
Andersen, P., 113, *166*
Anderson, E. P., 24, 29, *40, 41*
Anderson, J. E., 217, *251*
Andersson, A., 113, *166*
Angrist, S. S., 267, 280, 284, *290*
Angyal, A., 59, *80*
Antonucci, T., 18, *39*
Arafat, I., 262, *296*
Arbib, M. A., 60, *80*
Arenberg, D., 195, *204*, 247, 248, 249, *251*
Arlin, P. K., 196, *204*
Armington, D. C., 136, *178*
Arnold, P. M., 134, *168*
Ashby, W. R., 59, 61, *80*
Astin, H. S., 272, 277, 278, 280, *290*
Averill, J. R., 325, *332*
Axelrod, S., 89, 90, *105, 106*

B

Bachtold, L. M., 276, *290*
Bacon, L., 278, *290*

Baer, D. M., 7, 10, 20, *39, 40*, 192, *204*
Baffa, G., 91, *106*
Bailey, M. M., 270, 281, *295*
Bailyn, L., 284, *290*
Baltes, M. M., 3, 4, *39*, 193, *207*
Baltes, P. B., 2, 3, 4, 6, 7, 9, 10, 11, 12, 13, 14, 15, 16, 23, 24, 31, *39, 40, 42, 43, 44*, 52, 54, 57, 76, *80, 81*, 139, *166*, 182, 184, 186, 187, 190, 191, 193, 196, 197, 202, *204, 206, 207, 208, 209*, 215, 250, *251, 252, 253*, 259, 260, 262, *290, 293, 295*, 300, 311, 325, 327, 328, *332*
Ban, P. L., 21, 22, 27, *40, 42*
Bandura, A., 192, *204*
Bane, M. J., 213, *254*
Baratz, J. S., 200, *204*
Baratz, S. S., 200, *204*
Barbee, A. H., 277, 282, *295*
Barnaby, D., 317, *333*
Barnes, R. H., 120, *176*
Barnet, A. B., 139, *175*
Barnett, C. R., 25, *42*
Barrett, W., *204*
Barry, A. J., 190, *204*
Bartlett, F. C., 229, *252*
Baruch, G. K., 260, 261, 280, *290*
Bateen, R. J., 320, *332*
Battle, E. S., 276, 277, *291*
Bayer, A. E., 272, *290*
Bayley, N., 240, *256*
Beaglehole, E., 298, 300, 301, 302, 303, 304, 314, 316, 319, *332*
Bearison, D., 198, 199, *204*
Beaton, A. E., 213, *254*
Beatty, J., 136, 164, *166*
Beck, E. C., 138, 139, 140, 141, *166, 169, 176*
Becker, D., 134, *168*

337

Donders, F. C., 88, *106*
Dondey, M., 119, *176*
Douvan, E., 281, *291*
Doyle, J. D., 152, *169*
Drachman, D., 244, *252*
Dreyfus-Brisac, C., 117, 120, 121, 124, 127, *169*
Dustman, R. E., 138, 139, 140, 141, *166, 169, 176*
Dweck, C. S., 270, *291*

E

Ebert, P., 92, 99, 100, *106*
Eeg-Olofsson, O., 118, *169*
Ehrlich, A. H., 299, *333*
Ehrlich, R., 299, *333*
Eichorn, D. H., 127, *169*
Eifler, D., 269, *296*
Eimas, P. D., 153, *169*
Eisdorfer, C., 89, 90, 92, 104, *105, 106,* 137, *169,* 189, 197, *205, 208*
Eisengart, M. A., 138, *169*
Eisner, D. A., 89, *106*
Ekstrom, R. B., 224, *252*
Elder, G. H., Jr., 260, *291*
Elias, M. F., 163, *169*
Ellingson, R. J., 116, 117, 118, 120, 123, 124, 125, 139, 140, 142, *169, 170*
Ellis, R. R., 152, *170*
Ellwood, C., 303, *333*
Emerson, P. E., 25, 26, 27, 31, 33, *43*
Emery, F. E., 60, *79*
Emmerich, W., 29, 30, *41,* 260, *291*
Epstein, S., 321, *333*
Erickson, V. L., 283, *291*
Erikson, E. H., 4, 20, *41,* 321, *333*
Etaugh, C. F., 262, 280, *291*

F

Fagan, J. F., 126, *170*
Fagot, B. I., 283, *291*
Fantz, R. L., 126, *170*
Farguhar, M., 89, *106*

Featherman, D. L., 328, *335*
Fedio, P. M., 135, 151, *167, 170*
Fegy, M. J., 142, *172*
Feinberg, I., 117, *170*
Feiring, C., 34, *42*
Feld, S., 285, 286, *292, 296*
Feldman, H., 285, 286, *292*
Feldman, S. D., 279, *292*
Feldman, S. S., 24, 26, 29, *42*
Feldman-Summers, S., 270, *292*
Ferguson, G. A., 236, *252*
Fernandez, C. A., 309, *333*
Fichter, J. H., 263, *292*
Fidell, L. S., 268, *292*
Fifer, G., 238, *254*
Filbey, R. A., 151, *170*
Finesinger, J. E., 120, *167*
Finn, J. D., 237, *252*
Fiorentino, M. R., 125, *170*
Fischer, K. W., 233, *252*
Fiske, D., 27, *40*
Flaherty, D., 21, *44*
Flavell, J. H., 3, 4, *41,* 182, 184, 192, 198, 199, *206*
Fleener, D. E., 21, 33, *41*
Fletcher, R., 299, *333*
Fling, S., 282, *292*
Foner, A., 23, *43*
Forthomme, J., 120, *175*
Fox, C., 87, *106*
Fozard, J. L., 163, *166,* 195, 196, *206,* 249, *251*
Fraiberg, S., 24, *41*
Frank, L. K., 48, *81*
Freedman, N. L., 135, *170*
Freeman, R. B., Jr., 153, 154, 155, 156, *174*
French, J. W., 224, *252*
French, T. M., 321, *333*
Freud, S., 3, 4, 20, *41*
Friedlander, W. J., 120, *170*
Friedman, M., 299, *333*
Friedrich, L. K., 269, *296*
Frieze, I. H., 270, *292*
Froehling, S., 137, *170*
Froehling-Moss, S., 147, *171*
Fromkin, H. L., 317, *333*
Furby, L., 305, 311, 328, *333*
Furry, C. A., 197, *206*
Furstenburg, F. F., Jr., 264, *294*
Fuster, J. M., 135, *170*

Subject Index

Motivation, for possession, 315–320
Mueller-Lyer illusion, changes in magnitude of, 99–101
Multilinearity, in cognitive development, 200–203
Multisynchronicity, in cognitive development, 199–200

O

Organization, systems view and, 63–64
 performance as function of, 69

P

Peers, female role choices and, 282–284
Perceptual development
 in adulthood, Mueller-Lyer illusion, 99–101
 Delboeuf illusion and Usnadze effect, 101–103
 research and theory in, 92–99
 stimulus persistence model, 90–92
 visual, 86–87
  absolute threshold, 87–88
  critical flicker frequency, 88–89
  figural aftereffects, 89
  illusions, 89–90
  structural modifications, 87
  visual acuity, 88
Possession(s), 298–300
 among nonhumans, 300–302
 anthropological approaches to, 302–310
 future directions in, 324–330
 life-span approach to, 310–320
 nature of, 320–324

R

Resource input, performance as function of, 69
Role, female, *see* Female development

S

Satisfaction, female role choices and, 285–286

School proficiency, brain lateralization and, 156–159
Self-esteem, female role choices and, 285–286
Socialization
 female role choices and, 279–284
 of possession, 304–309
Stereotypes, female role choices and, 266–271
Stimulus persistence model, 90–92
Systems view
 analytic representations of extant systems and, 71–73
 applicability of, 73–75
 characteristics of, 63–68
 determinants of a systems performance, 68–70
 future directions for, 76–78
 historical aspects of, 58–59
 life-span development and, 75–76
 present status of, 61–62
 related developments, 59–61
 system transformation and, 70–71

T

Thought processes, 227–228

U

Usnadze effect, changes in magnitude of, 101–103

V

Vision, in aged, 86–87
 absolute threshold, 87–88
 critical flicker frequency, 88–89
 figural aftereffects, 89
 illusions, 89–90
 structural modifications, 87
 visual acuity, 88

W

Work, family patterns and, 263–266, 279–281

A
B
C 8
D 9
E 0
F 1
G 2
H 3
I 4
J 5